Get the eBooks FREE!

(PDF, ePub, Kindle, and liveBook all included)

We believe that once you buy a book from us, you should be able to read it in any format we have available. To get electronic versions of this book at no additional cost to you, purchase and then register this book at the Manning website.

Go to https://www.manning.com/freebook and follow the instructions to complete your pBook registration.

That's it!
Thanks from Manning!

Spring Microservices in Action

Spring Microservices
in Action

JOHN CARNELL

MANNING
SHELTER ISLAND

For online information and ordering of this and other Manning books, please visit
www.manning.com. The publisher offers discounts on this book when ordered in quantity.
For more information, please contact

Special Sales Department
Manning Publications Co.
20 Baldwin Road
PO Box 761
Shelter Island, NY 11964
Email: orders@manning.com

Manning Publications Co.
20 Baldwin Road
PO Box 761
Shelter Island, NY 11964

Acquisition editor: Greg Wild
Development editor: Marina Michaels
Technical development editor: Raphael Villela
Copyeditor: Katie Petito
Proofreader: Melody Dolab
Technical proofreader: Joshua White
Review editor: Aleksandar Dragosavljevic
Typesetter: Marija Tudor
Cover designer: Marija Tudor

ISBN 9781617293986
Printed in the United States of America
7 8 9 10 – SP – 24 23 22 21 20 19

*To my brother Jason, who even in his darkest moments
showed me the true meaning of strength and dignity.
You are a role model as a brother, husband, and father.*

brief contents

contents

preface

It's ironic that in writing a book, the last part of the book you write is often the beginning of the book. It's also often the most difficult part to put down on paper. Why? Because you have to explain to everyone why you're so passionate about a subject that you spent the last one and a half years of your life writing a book about it. It's hard to articulate why anyone would spend such a large amount of time on a technical book. One rarely writes software books for the money or the fame.

Here's the reason why I wrote this book: I love writing code. It's a calling for me and it's also a creative activity—akin to drawing, painting, or playing an instrument. Those outside the field of software development have a hard time understanding this. I especially like building distributed applications. For me, it's an amazing thing to see an application work across dozens (even hundreds) of servers. It's like watching an orchestra playing a piece of music. While the final product of an orchestra is beautiful, the making of it is often a lot of hard work and requires a significant amount of practice. The same goes for writing a massively distributed application.

Since I entered the software development field 25 years ago, I've watched the industry struggle with the "right" way to build distributed applications. I've seen distributed service standards such as CORBA rise and fall. Monstrously big companies have tried to push big and, often, proprietary protocols. Anyone remember Microsoft's Distributed Component Object Model (DCOM) or Oracle's J2EE's Enterprise Java Beans 2 (EJB)? I watched as technology companies and their followers rushed to build service-oriented architectures (SOA) using heavy XML-based schemas.

In each case, these approaches for building distributed systems often collapsed under their own weight. I'm not saying that these technologies weren't used to build some very powerful applications. The reality is that they couldn't keep up with the demand of the users. Ten years ago, smartphones were just being introduced to the market and cloud computing was in the earliest stage of infancy. Also, the standards and technology for distributed application development were too complicated for the average developer to understand and easily use in practice. Nothing speaks truth in the software development industry like written code. When the standards get in the way of this, the standards quickly get discarded.

When I first heard of the microservices approach to building applications I was more than a little skeptical. "Great, another silver-bullet approach to building distributed applications," I thought. However, as I started diving into the concepts, I realized the simplicity of microservices could be a game changer. A microservice architecture focuses on building small services that use simple protocols (HTTP and JSON) to communicate. That's it. You can write a microservice with nearly any programming language. There's beauty in this simplicity.

However, while building an individual microservice is easy, operationalizing and scaling it is difficult. Getting hundreds of small distributed components to work together and then building a resilient application from them can be incredibly difficult to do. In distributed computing, failure is a fact of life and how your application deals with it is incredibly difficult to get right. To paraphrase my colleagues Chris Miller and Shawn Hagwood: "If it's not breaking once in a while, you're not building."

It's these failures that inspired me to write this book. I hate to build things from scratch when I don't have to. The reality is that Java is the lingua franca for most application development efforts, especially in the enterprise. The Spring framework has for many organizations become the de facto framework for most application development. I'd already been doing application development in Java for almost 20 years (I remember the Dancing Duke applet) and Spring for almost 10 years. As I began my microservices journey, I was delighted and excited to watch the emergence of Spring Cloud.

The Spring Cloud framework provides out-of-the-box solutions for many of the common development and operational problems you'll run into as a microservice developer. Spring Cloud lets you use only the pieces you need and minimizes the amount of work you need to do to build and deploy production-ready Java microservices. It does this by using other battle-hardened technologies from companies and groups such as Netflix, HashiCorp, and the Apache foundation.

I've always considered myself an average developer who, at the end of the day, has deadlines to meet. That's why I undertook the project of writing this book. I wanted a book that I could use in my day-to-day work. I wanted something with direct (and hopefully) straightforward code examples. I always want to make sure that the material in this book can be consumed as individual chapters or in its entirety. I hope you find this book useful and I hope you enjoy reading it as much as I enjoyed writing it.

acknowledgments

As I sit down to write these acknowledgments, I can't help but think back to 2014 when I ran my first marathon. Writing a book is a lot like running a marathon. Writing the proposal and the outline for the book is much like the training process. It gets your thoughts in shape, it focuses you for what's ahead and, yes, near the end of the process, it can be more than a little tedious and brutal.

When you start writing the book, it's a lot like race day. You start the marathon excited and full of energy. You know you're trying to do something bigger than anything you might have done before and it's both exciting and nerve-wracking. This is what you've trained for, but at the same time, there's always that small voice of doubt in the back of your mind that says you won't finish what you started.

What I've learned from running is that races aren't completed one mile at a time. Instead, they're run one foot in front of the other. The miles run are the sum of the individual footsteps. When my children are struggling with something, I laugh and ask them, "How do you write a book? One word, one single step at a time." They usually roll their eyes, but in the end there's no other way around this indisputable and iron-clad law.

However, when you run a marathon, you might be the one running the race, but you're never running it alone. There's a whole team of people there to give you support, time, and advice along the way. It has been the same experience writing this book.

I'd like to start by thanking Manning for the support they gave me in writing this book. It started with Greg Wild, my acquisitions editor, who patiently worked with me as I refined the core concepts in this book and guided me through the proposal process. Along the way, Marina Michaels, my development editor, kept me honest and challenged me to become a better author. I'd also like to thank Raphael Villela and Joshua White, my technical editors, who constantly checked my work and ensured the overall quality of the examples and the code I produced. I'm extremely grateful for the time, talent, and commitment each of these individuals put into into the overall project. I'd also like to thank the reviewers who provided feedback on the manuscript throughout the writing and development process: Aditya Kumar, Adrian M. Rossi, Ashwin Raj, Christian Bach, Edgar Knapp, Jared Duncan, Jiri Pik, John Guthrie, Mirko Bernardoni, Paul Balogh, Pierluigi Riti, Raju Myadam, Rambabu Posa, Sergey Evsikov, and Vipul Gupta.

I want to close these acknowledgments with a deep sense of thanks for the love and time my family has given me in working on this project. To my wife Janet, you have been my best friend and the love of my life. When I'm tired and want to give up, I only have to listen for the sound of your footsteps next to me to know that you're always running beside me, never telling me no, and always pushing me forward.

To my son Christopher, you're growing up to be an incredible young man. I cannot wait for the day when you truly discover your passion, because there will be nothing in this world that can stop you from reaching your goals.

To my daughter Agatha, I'd give all the money I have to see the world through your eyes for just 10 minutes. The experience would make me a better author and more importantly a better person. Your intellect, your power of observation, and creativity humble me.

To my four-year-old son, Jack: Buddy, thank you being patient with me whenever I said, "I can't play right now because Daddy has to work on the book." You always make me laugh and you make this whole family complete. Nothing makes me happier than when I see you being the jokester and playing with everyone in the family.

My race with this book is done. Like my marathon, I've left nothing on the table in writing this book. I have nothing but gratitude for the Manning team and the MEAP readers who bought this book early and gave me so much valuable feedback. I hope in the end that you enjoy this book as much as I enjoyed writing it. Thank you.

about this book

Spring Microservices in Action was written for the practicing Java/Spring developer who needs hands-on advice and examples of how to build and operationalize microservice-based applications. When I wrote this book, I wanted it to be based around core microservice patterns that aligned with Spring Boot and Spring Cloud examples that demonstrated the patterns in action. As such, you'll find specific microservice design patterns discussed in almost every chapter, along with examples of the patterns implemented using Spring Boot and Spring Cloud.

You should read this book if

- You're a Java developer who has experience building distributed applications (1-3 years).
- You have a background in Spring (1+ years).
- You're interested in learning how to build microservice-based applications.
- You're interested in how you can use microservices for building cloud-based applications.
- You want to know if Java and Spring are relevant technologies for building microservice-based applications.
- You're interested in seeing what goes into deploying a microservice-based application to the cloud.

How this book is organized

Spring Microservices in Action consists of 10 chapters and two appendixes:

- Chapter 1 introduces you to why the microservices architecture is an important and relevant approach to building applications, especially cloud-based applications.

- Chapter 2 walks you through how to build your first REST-based microservice using Spring Boot. This chapter will guide you in how to look at your microservices through the eyes of an architect, an application engineer, and a DevOps engineer.

- Chapter 3 introduces you to how to manage the configuration of your microservices using Spring Cloud Config. Spring Cloud Config helps you guarantee that your service's configuration information is centralized in a single repository, versioned and repeatable across all instances of your services.

- Chapter 4 introduces you to one of the first microservice routing patterns: service discovery. In this chapter, you'll learn how to use Spring Cloud and Netflix's Eureka service to abstract away the location of your services from the clients consuming them.

- Chapter 5 is all about protecting the consumers of your microservices when one or more microservice instances is down or in a degraded state. This chapter will demonstrate how to use Spring Cloud and Netflix Hystrix (and Netflix Ribbon) to implement client-side load balancing of calls, the circuit breaker pattern, the fallback pattern, and the bulkhead pattern.

- Chapter 6 covers the microservice routing pattern: the service gateway. Using Spring Cloud with Netflix's Zuul server, you'll build a single entry point for all microservices to be called through. We'll discuss how to use Zuul's filter API to build policies that can be enforced against all services flowing through the service gateway.

- Chapter 7 covers how to implement service authentication and authorization using Spring Cloud security and OAuth2. We'll cover the basics of setting up an OAuth2 service to protect your services and also how to use JavaScript Web Tokens (JWT) in your OAuth2 implementation.

- Chapter 8 looks at how you can introduce asynchronous messaging into your microservices using Spring Cloud Stream and Apache Kafka.

- Chapter 9 shows how to implement common logging patterns such as log correlation, log aggregation, and tracing using Spring Cloud Sleuth and Open Zipkin.

- Chapter 10 is the cornerstone project for the book. You'll take the services you've built in the book and deploy them to Amazon Elastic Container Service (ECS). We'll also discuss how to automate the build and deployment of your microservices using tools such as Travis CI.

- Appendix A covers how to set up your desktop development environment so that you can run all the code examples in this book. This appendix covers how the local build process works and also how to start up Docker locally if you want to run the code examples locally.

- Appendix B is supplemental material on OAuth2. OAuth2 is an extremely flexible authentication model, and this chapter provides a brief overview of the different manners in which OAuth2 can be used to protect an application and its corresponding microservices.

About the code

Spring Microservices in Action includes code in every chapter. All code examples are available in my GitHub repository, and each chapter has its own repository. You can find an overview page with links to each chapter's code repository at https://github.com/carnellj/spmia_overview. A zip containing all source code is also available from the publisher's website at www.manning.com/books/spring-microservices-in-action.

All code in this book is built to run on Java 8 using Maven as the main build tool. Please refer to appendix A of this book for full details on the software tools you'll need to compile and run the code examples.

One of the core concepts I followed as I wrote this book was that the code examples in each chapter should run independently of those in the other chapters. As such, every service we create for a chapter builds to a corresponding Docker image. When code from previous chapters is used, it's included as both source and a built Docker image. We use Docker compose and the built Docker images to guarantee that you have a reproducible run-time environment for every chapter.

This book contains many examples of source code both in numbered listings and in line with normal text. In both cases, source code is formatted in a `fixed-width font like this` to separate it from ordinary text. Sometimes code is also **in bold** to highlight code that has changed from previous steps in the chapter, such as when a new feature adds to an existing line of code.

In many cases, the original source code has been reformatted; we've added line breaks and reworked indentation to accommodate the available page space in the book. In rare cases, even this wasn't enough, and listings include line-continuation markers (➥). Additionally, comments in the source code have often been removed from the listings when the code is described in the text. Code annotations accompany many of the listings, highlighting important concepts.

Author Online

Purchase of *Spring Microservices in Action* includes free access to a private web forum run by Manning Publications where you can make comments about the book, ask technical questions, and receive help from the author and from other users. To access the forum and subscribe to it, point your web browser to www.manning.com/books/spring-microservices-in-action. This page provides information on how to get on the forum once you're registered, what kind of help is available, and the rules of conduct on the forum.

Manning's commitment to our readers is to provide a venue where a meaningful dialog between individual readers and between readers and the author can take place. It is not a commitment to any specific amount of participation on the part of the author, whose contributions to the AO remain voluntary (and unpaid). We suggest you ask the author challenging questions, lest his interest stray!

about the author

JOHN CARNELL is a senior cloud engineer at Genesys, where he works in Genesys's PureCloud division. John spends the majority of his day hands-on building telephony-based microservices using the AWS platform. His day-to-day job centers on designing and building microservices across a number of technology platforms including Java, Clojure, and Go.

John is a prolific speaker and writer. He regularly speaks at local user groups and has been a regular speaker on "The No Fluff Just Stuff Software Symposium." Over the last 20 years, John has authored, co-authored, and been a technical reviewer for a number of Java-based technology books and industry publications.

John holds a Bachelor of the Arts (BA) from Marquette University and a Masters of Business Administration (MBA) from the University of Wisconsin Oshkosh.

John is a passionate technologist and is constantly exploring new technologies and programming languages. When John isn't speaking, writing, or coding, he lives with his wife Janet, his three children, Christopher, Agatha, and Jack, and yes, his dog Vader, in Cary, North Carolina.

During his free time (which there's very little of) John runs, chases after his children, and studies Filipino martial arts.

John can be reached at john_carnell@yahoo.com.

about the cover illustration

The figure on the cover of *Spring Microservices in Action* is captioned a "A Man from Croatia." This illustration is taken from a recent reprint of Balthasar Hacquet's *Images and Descriptions of Southwestern and Eastern Wenda, Illyrians, and Slavs*, published by the Ethnographic Museum in Split, Croatia, in 2008. Hacquet (1739–1815) was an Austrian physician and scientist who spent many years studying the botany, geology, and ethnography of many parts of the Austrian Empire, as well as the Veneto, the Julian Alps, and the western Balkans, inhabited in the past by peoples of the Illyrian tribes. Hand drawn illustrations accompany the many scientific papers and books that Hacquet published.

The rich diversity of the drawings in Hacquet's publications speaks vividly of the uniqueness and individuality of the eastern Alpine and northwestern Balkan regions just 200 years ago. This was a time when the dress codes of two villages separated by a few miles identified people uniquely as belonging to one or the other, and when members of a social class or trade could be easily distinguished by what they were wearing. Dress codes have changed since then and the diversity by region, so rich at the time, has faded away. It is now often hard to tell the inhabitant of one continent from another, and today the inhabitants of the picturesque towns and villages in the Slovenian Alps or Balkan coastal towns are not readily distinguishable from the residents of other parts of Europe.

We at Manning celebrate the inventiveness, the initiative, and the fun of the computer business with book covers based on costumes from two centuries ago, brought back to life by illustrations such as this one.

Welcome to the cloud, Spring

This chapter covers

- Understanding microservices and why companies use them
- Using Spring, Spring Boot, and Spring Cloud for building microservices
- Learning why the cloud and microservices are relevant to microservice-based applications
- Building microservices involves more than building service code
- Understanding the parts of cloud-based development
- Using Spring Boot and Spring Cloud in microservice development

The one constant in the field of software development is that we as software developers sit in the middle of a sea of chaos and change. We all feel the churn as new technologies and approaches appear suddenly on the scene, causing us to reevaluate how we build and deliver solutions for our customers. One example of this churn is the rapid adoption by many organizations of building applications using

1

microservices. Microservices are distributed, loosely coupled software services that carry out a small number of well-defined tasks.

This book introduces you to the microservice architecture and why you should consider building your applications with them. We're going to look at how to build microservices using Java and two Spring framework projects: Spring Boot and Spring Cloud. If you're a Java developer, Spring Boot and Spring Cloud will provide an easy migration path from building traditional, monolithic Spring applications to microservice applications that can be deployed to the cloud.

1.1   *What's a microservice?*

Before the concept of microservices evolved, most web-based applications were built using a monolithic architectural style. In a monolithic architecture, an application is delivered as a single deployable software artifact. All the UI (user interface), business, and database access logic are packaged together into a single application artifact and deployed to an application server.

While an application might be a deployed as a single unit of work, most of the time there will be multiple development teams working on the application. Each development team will have their own discrete pieces of the application they're responsible for and oftentimes specific customers they're serving with their functional piece. For example, when I worked at a large financial services company, we had an in-house, custom-built customer relations management (CRM) application that involved the coordination of multiple teams including the UI, the customer master, the data warehouse, and the mutual funds team. Figure 1.1 illustrates the basic architecture of this application.

The problem here is that as the size and complexity of the monolithic CRM application grew, the communication and coordination costs of the individual teams working on the application didn't scale. Every time an individual team needed to make a change, the entire application had to be rebuilt, retested and redeployed.

The concept of a microservice originally crept into the software development community's consciousness around 2014 and was a direct response to many of the challenges of trying to scale both technically and organizationally large, monolithic applications. Remember, a microservice is a small, loosely coupled, distributed service. Microservices allow you to take a large application and decompose it into easy-to-manage components with narrowly defined responsibilities. Microservices help combat the traditional problems of complexity in a large code base by decomposing the large code base down into small, well-defined pieces. The key concept you need to embrace as you think about microservices is decomposing and unbundling the functionality of

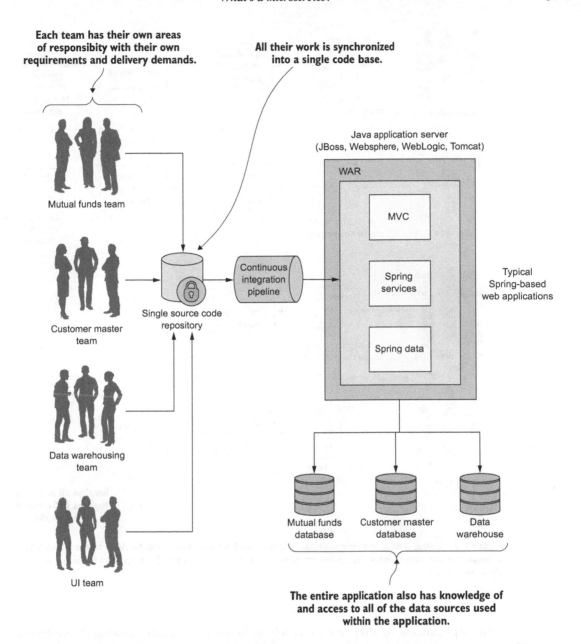

Figure 1.1 Monolithic applications force multiple development teams to artificially synchronize their delivery because their code needs to be built, tested, and deployed as an entire unit.

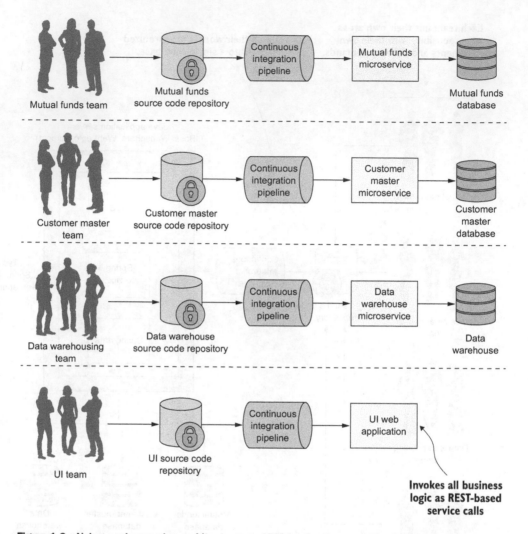

Figure 1.2   Using a microservice architecture our CRM application would be decomposed into a set of microservices completely independent of each other, allowing each development team to move at their own pace.

your applications so they're completely independent of one another. If we take the CRM application we saw in figure 1.1 and decompose it into microservices, it might look like what's shown in figure 1.2.

Looking at figure 1.2, you can see that each functional team completely owns their service code and service infrastructure. They can build, deploy, and test independently of each other because their code, source control repository, and the infrastructure (app server and database) are now completely independent of the other parts of the application.

A microservice architecture has the following characteristics:

- Application logic is broken down into small-grained components with well-defined boundaries of responsibility that coordinate to deliver a solution.
- Each component has a small domain of responsibility and is deployed completely independently of one another. Microservices should have responsibility for a single part of a business domain. Also, a microservice should be reusable across multiple applications.
- Microservices communicate based on a few basic principles (notice I said principles, not standards) and employ lightweight communication protocols such as HTTP and JSON (JavaScript Object Notation) for exchanging data between the service consumer and service provider.
- The underlying technical implementation of the service is irrelevant because the applications always communicate with a technology-neutral protocol (JSON is the most common). This means an application built using a microservice application could be built with multiple languages and technologies.
- Microservices—by their small, independent, and distributed nature—allow organizations to have small development teams with well-defined areas of responsibility. These teams might work toward a single goal such as delivering an application, but each team is responsible only for the services on which they're working.

I often joke with my colleagues that microservices are the gateway drug for building cloud applications. You start building microservices because they give you a high degree of flexibility and autonomy with your development teams, but you and your team quickly find that the small, independent nature of microservices makes them easily deployable to the cloud. Once the services are in the cloud, their small size makes it easy to start up large numbers of instances of the same service, and suddenly your applications become more scalable and, with forethought, more resilient.

1.2 What is Spring and why is it relevant to microservices?

Spring has become the de facto development framework for building Java-based applications. At its core, Spring is based on the concept of dependency injection. In a normal Java application, the application is decomposed into classes where each class often has explicit linkages to other classes in the application. The linkages are the invocation of a class constructor directly in the code. Once the code is compiled, these linkage points can't be changed.

This is problematic in a large project because these external linkages are brittle and making a change can result in multiple downstream impacts to other code. A dependency injection framework, such as Spring, allows you to more easily manage large Java projects by externalizing the relationship between objects within your application through convention (and annotations) rather than those objects having hard-coded knowledge about each other. Spring sits as an intermediary between the different Java classes of your application and manages their dependencies. Spring essentially lets you assemble your code together like a set of Lego bricks that snap together.

Spring's rapid inclusion of features drove its utility, and the framework quickly became a lighter weight alternative for enterprise application Java developers looking for a way to building applications using the J2EE stack. The J2EE stack, while powerful, was considered by many to be bloatware, with many features that were never used by application development teams. Further, a J2EE application forced you to use a full-blown (and heavy) Java application server to deploy your applications.

What's amazing about the Spring framework and a testament to its development community is its ability to stay relevant and reinvent itself. The Spring development team quickly saw that many development teams were moving away from monolithic applications where the application's presentation, business, and data access logic were packaged together and deployed as a single artifact. Instead, teams were moving to highly distributed models where services were being built as small, distributed services that could be easily deployed to the cloud. In response to this shift, the Spring development team launched two projects: Spring Boot and Spring Cloud.

Spring Boot is a re-envisioning of the Spring framework. While it embraces core features of Spring, Spring Boot strips away many of the "enterprise" features found in Spring and instead delivers a framework geared toward Java-based, REST-oriented (Representational State Transfer)[1] microservices. With a few simple annotations, a Java developer can quickly build a REST microservice that can be packaged and deployed without the need for an external application container.

> **NOTE** While we cover REST in more detail in chapter 2, the core concept behind REST is that your services should embrace the use of the HTTP verbs (GET, POST, PUT, and DELETE) to represent the core actions of the service and use a lightweight web-oriented data serialization protocol, such as JSON, for requesting and receiving data from the service.

Because microservices have become one of the more common architectural patterns for building cloud-based applications, the Spring development community has given us Spring Cloud. The Spring Cloud framework makes it simple to operationalize and deploy microservices to a private or public cloud. Spring Cloud wraps several popular cloud-management microservice frameworks under a common framework and makes the use and deployment of these technologies as easy to use as annotating your code. I cover the different components within Spring Cloud later in this chapter.

1.3 What you'll learn in this book

This book is about building microservice-based applications using Spring Boot and Spring Cloud that can be deployed to a private cloud run by your company or a public

---

[1] While we cover REST later in chapter 2, it's worthwhile to read Roy Fielding's PHD dissertation on building REST-based applications (http://www.ics.uci.edu/~fielding/pubs/dissertation/top.htm). It's still one of the best explanations of REST available.

cloud such as Amazon, Google, or Pivotal. With this book, we cover with hands-on examples

- What a microservice is and the design considerations that go into building a microservice-based application
- When you shouldn't build a microservice-based application
- How to build microservices using the Spring Boot framework
- The core operational patterns that need to be in place to support microservice applications, particularly a cloud-based application
- How you can use Spring Cloud to implement these operational patterns
- How to take what you've learned and build a deployment pipeline that can be used to deploy your services to a private, internally managed cloud or a public cloud provider

By the time you're done reading this book, you should have the knowledge needed to build and deploy a Spring Boot-based microservice. You'll also understand the key design decisions need to operationalize your microservices. You'll understand how service configuration management, service discovery, messaging, logging and tracing, and security all fit together to deliver a robust microservices environment. Finally, you'll see how your microservices can be deployed within a private or public cloud.

1.4 Why is this book relevant to you?

If you've gotten this far into reading chapter 1, I suspect that

- You're a Java developer.
- You have a background in Spring.
- You're interested in learning how to build microservice-based applications.
- You're interested in how to use microservices to build cloud-based applications.
- You want to know if Java and Spring are relevant technologies for building microservice-based applications.
- You're interested in seeing what goes into deploying a microservice-based application to the cloud.

I chose to write this book for two reasons. First, while I've seen many good books on the conceptual aspects of microservices, I couldn't a find a good Java-based book on implementing microservices. While I've always considered myself a programming language polyglot (someone who knows and speaks several languages), Java is my core development language and Spring has been the development framework I "reach" for whenever I build a new application. When I first came across Spring Boot and Spring Cloud, I was blown away. Spring Boot and Spring Cloud greatly simplified my development life when it came to building microservice-based applications running in the cloud.

Second, as I've worked throughout my career as both an architect and engineer, I've found that many times the technology books that I purchase have tended to go to one of two extremes. They are either conceptual without concrete code examples, or are mechanical overviews of a particular framework or programming language. I wanted a book that would be a good bridge and middle ground between the architecture and engineering disciplines. As you read this book, I want to give you a solid introduction to the microservice patterns development and how they're used in real-world application development, and then back these patterns up with practical and easy-to-understand code examples using Spring Boot and Spring Cloud.

Let's shift gears for a moment and walk through building a simple microservice using Spring Boot.

1.5   *Building a microservice with Spring Boot*

I've always had the opinion that a software development framework is well thought out and easy to use if it passes what I affectionately call the "Carnell Monkey Test." If a monkey like me (the author) can figure out a framework in 10 minutes or less, it has promise. That's how I felt the first time I wrote a sample Spring Boot service. I want you to have to the same experience and joy, so let's take a minute to see how to write a simple "Hello World" REST-service using Spring Boot.

In this section, we're not going to do a detailed walkthrough of much of the code presented. Our goal is to give you a taste of writing a Spring Boot service. We'll go into much more detail in chapter 2.

Figure 1.3 shows what your service is going to do and the general flow of how Spring Boot microservice will process a user's request.

This example is by no means exhaustive or even illustrative of how you should build a production-level microservice, but it should cause you to take a pause because of how little code it took to write it. We're not going to go through how to set up the project build files or the details of the code until chapter 2. If you'd like to see the Maven pom.xml file and the actual code, you can find it in the chapter 1 section of the downloadable code. All the source code for chapter 1 can be retrieved from the GitHub repository for the book at https://github.com/carnellj/spmia-chapter1.

> **NOTE**   Please make sure you read appendix A before you try to run the code examples for the chapters in this book. Appendix A covers the general project layout of all the projects in the book, how to run the build scripts, and how to fire up the Docker environment. The code examples in this chapter are simple and designed to be run natively right from your desktop without the information in additional chapters. However, in later chapters you'll quickly begin using Docker to run all the services and infrastructure used in this book. Don't go too far into the book without reading appendix A on setting up your desktop environment.

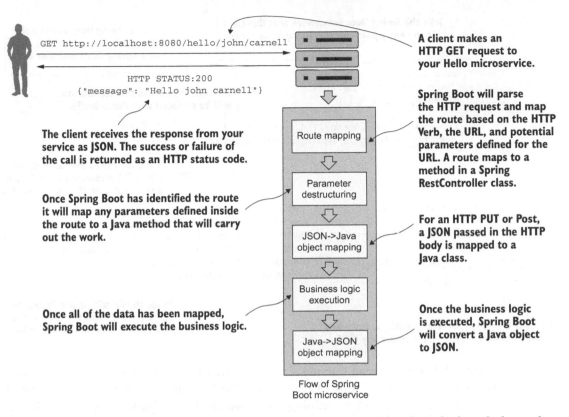

Figure 1.3   Spring Boot abstracts away the common REST microservice task (routing to business logic, parsing HTTP parameters from the URL, mapping JSON to/from Java Objects), and lets the developer focus on the business logic for the service.

For this example, you're going to have a single Java class called simpleservice/ src/com/thoughtmechanix/application/simpleservice/Application.java that will be used to expose a REST endpoint called /hello.

The following listing shows the code for Application.java.

Listing 1.1   Hello World with Spring Boot: a simple Spring microservice

```
package com.thoughtmechanix.simpleservice;

import org.springframework.boot.SpringApplication;
import org.springframework.boot.autoconfigure.SpringBootApplication;
import org.springframework.web.bind.annotation.RequestMapping;
import org.springframework.web.bind.annotation.RequestMethod;
import org.springframework.web.bind.annotation.RestController;
import org.springframework.web.bind.annotation.PathVariable;
```

Tells the Spring Boot framework that this class is the entry point for the Spring Boot service

Tells Spring Boot you're going to expose the code in this class as a Spring RestController class

```
@SpringBootApplication          ←
@RestController
@RequestMapping(value="hello")
public class Application {

    public static void main(String[] args) {
        SpringApplication.run(Application.class, args);
    }
```

All URLs exposed in this application will be prefaced with /hello prefix.

Spring Boot will expose an endpoint as a GET-based REST endpoint that will take two parameters: firstName and lastName.

```
    @RequestMapping(value="/{firstName}/{lastName}",
                    method = RequestMethod.GET)
    public String hello( @PathVariable("firstName") String firstName,   ←
                         @PathVariable("lastName") String lastName) {
        return String.format("{\"message\":\"Hello %s %s\"}",
                             firstName, lastName);
    }
}
```

Maps the firstName and lastName parameters passed in on the URL to two variables passed into the hello function

Returns a simple JSON string that you manually build. In chapter 2 you won't create any JSON.

In listing 1.1 you're basically exposing a single GET HTTP endpoint that will take two parameters (`firstName` and `lastName`) on the URL and then return a simple JSON string that has a payload containing the message "Hello *firstName lastName*". If you were to call the endpoint /hello/john/carnell on your service (which I'll show shortly) the return of the call would be

```
{"message":"Hello john carnell"}
```

Let's fire up your service. To do this, go to the command prompt and issue the following command:

```
mvn spring-boot:run
```

This command, `mvn`, will use a Spring Boot plug-in to start the application using an embedded Tomcat server.

Java vs. Groovy and Maven vs. Gradle

The Spring Boot framework has strong support for both Java and the Groovy programming languages. You can build microservices with Groovy and no project setup. Spring Boot also supports both Maven and the Gradle build tools. I've limited the examples in this book to Java and Maven. As a long-time Groovy and Gradle aficionado, I have a healthy respect for the language and the build tool, but to keep the book manageable and the material focused, I've chosen to go with Java and Maven to reach the largest audience possible.

Our /hello endpoint is mapped with two variables: firstName and lastName.

```
o.s.b.w.servlet.FilterRegistrationBean      Mapping filter: 'requestContextFilter' to: [/*]
s.w.s.m.m.a.RequestMappingHandlerAdapter    Looking for @ControllerAdvice: org.springframework.boot.contex
tartup date [Thu Mar 23 06:09:30 EDT 2017]  root of context hierarchy
s.w.s.m.m.a.RequestMappingHandlerMapping  : Mapped "{[/hello/{firstName}/{lastName}],methods=[GET]}" onto
on.hello(java.lang.String,java.lang.String)
s.w.s.m.m.a.RequestMappingHandlerMapping  : Mapped "{[/error]}" onto public org.springframework.http.Respo
ringframework.boot.autoconfigure.web.BasicErrorController.error(javax.servlet.http.HttpServletRequest)
s.w.s.m.m.a.RequestMappingHandlerMapping  : Mapped "{[/error],produces=[text/html]}" onto public org.sprin
ifigure.web.BasicErrorController.errorHtml(javax.servlet.http.HttpServletRequest,javax.servlet.http.HttpSe

o.s.w.s.handler.SimpleUrlHandlerMapping   : Mapped URL path [/webjars/**] onto handler of type [class org.

o.s.w.s.handler.SimpleUrlHandlerMapping   : Mapped URL path [/**] onto handler of type [class org.springfr

o.s.w.s.handler.SimpleUrlHandlerMapping   : Mapped URL path [/**/favicon.ico] onto handler of type [class

o.s.j.e.a.AnnotationMBeanExporter         : Registering beans for JMX exposure on startup
s.b.c.e.t.TomcatEmbeddedServletContainer  : Tomcat started on port(s): 8080 (http)
c.t.simpleservice.Application             : Started Application in 2.261 seconds (JVM running for 5.113)
```

The service will listen to port 8080 for incoming HTTP requests.

Figure 1.4 Your Spring Boot service will communicate the endpoints exposed and the port of the service via the console.

If everything starts correctly, you should see what's shown in figure 1.4 from your command-line window.

If you examine the screen in figure 1.4, you'll notice two things. First, a Tomcat server was started on port 8080. Second, a GET endpoint of /hello/{firstName}/ {lastName} is exposed on the server.

HTTP GET for the /hello/john/carnell endpoint

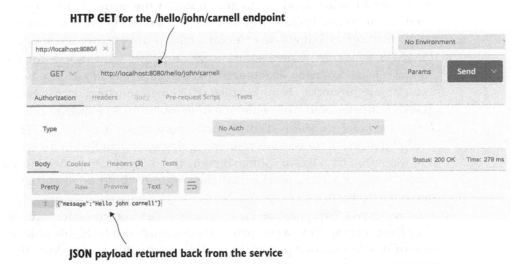

JSON payload returned back from the service

Figure 1.5 The response from the /hello endpoint shows the data you've requested represented as a JSON payload.

You're going to call your service using a browser-based REST tool called POSTMAN (https://www.getpostman.com/). Many tools, both graphical and command line, are available for invoking a REST-based service, but I'll use POSTMAN for all my examples in this book. Figure 1.5 shows the POSTMAN call to the `http://localhost:8080/hello/john/carnell` endpoint and the results returned from the service.

Obviously, this simple example doesn't demonstrate the full power of Spring Boot. But what it should show is that you can write a full HTTP JSON REST-based service with route-mapping of URL and parameters in Java with as few as 25 lines of code. As any experienced Java developer will tell you, writing anything meaningful in 25 lines of code in Java is extremely difficult. Java, while being a powerful language, has acquired a reputation of being wordy compared to other languages.

We're done with our brief tour of Spring Boot. We now have to ask this question: because we can write our applications using a microservice approach, does this mean we should? In the next section, we'll walk through why and when a microservice approach is justified for building your applications.

1.6   Why change the way we build applications?

We're at an inflection point in history. Almost all aspects of modern society are now wired together via the internet. Companies that used to serve local markets are suddenly finding that they can reach out to a global customer base. However, with a larger global customer base also comes global competition. These competitive pressures mean the following forces are impacting the way developers have to think about building applications:

- *Complexity has gone way up*—Customers expect that all parts of an organization know who they are. "Siloed" applications that talk to a single database and don't integrate with other applications are no longer the norm. Today's applications need to talk to multiple services and databases residing not only inside a company's data center, but also to external service providers over the internet.

- *Customers want faster delivery*—Customers no longer want to wait for the next annual release or version of a software package. Instead, they expect the features in a software product to be unbundled so that new functionality can be released quickly in weeks (even days) without having to wait for an entire product release.

- *Performance and scalability*—Global applications make it extremely difficult to predict how much transaction volume is going to be handled by an application and when that transaction volume is going to hit. Applications need to scale up across multiple servers quickly and then scale back down when the volume needs have passed.

- *Customers expect their applications to be available*—Because customers are one click away from a competitor, a company's applications must be highly resilient. Failures or problems in one part of the application shouldn't bring down the entire application.

To meet these expectations, we, as application developers, have to embrace the paradox that to build high-scalable and highly redundant applications we need to break our applications into small services that can be built and deployed independently of one another. If we "unbundle" our applications into small services and move them away from a single monolithic artifact, we can build systems that are

- *Flexible*—Decoupled services can be composed and rearranged to quickly deliver new functionality. The smaller the unit of code that one is working with, the less complicated it is to change the code and the less time it takes to test deploy the code.
- *Resilient*—Decoupled services mean an application is no longer a single "ball of mud" where a degradation in one part of the application causes the whole application to fail. Failures can be localized to a small part of the application and contained before the entire application experiences an outage. This also enables the applications to degrade gracefully in case of an unrecoverable error.
- *Scalable*—Decoupled services can easily be distributed horizontally across multiple servers, making it possible to scale the features/services appropriately. With a monolithic application where all the logic for the application is intertwined, the entire application needs to scale even if only a small part of the application is the bottleneck. Scaling on small services is localized and much more cost-effective.

To this end, as we begin our discussion of microservices keep the following in mind:

Small, Simple, and Decoupled Services = Scalable, Resilient, and Flexible Applications

1.7 What exactly is the cloud?

The term "cloud" has become overused. Every software vendor has a cloud and everyone's platform is cloud-enabled, but if you cut through the hype, three basic models exist in cloud-based computing. These are

- Infrastructure as a Service (IaaS)
- Platform as a Service (PaaS)
- Software as a Service (SaaS)

To better understand these concepts, let's map the everyday task of making a meal to the different models of cloud computing. When you want to eat a meal, you have four choices:

1 You can make the meal at home.
2 You can go to the grocery store and buy a meal pre-made that you heat up and serve.
3 You can get a meal delivered to your house.
4 You can get in the car and eat at restaurant.

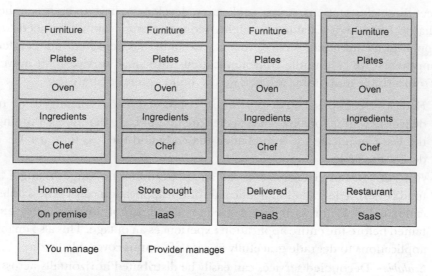

Figure 1.6   The different cloud computing models come down to who's responsible for what: the cloud vendor or you.

Figure 1.6 shows each model.

The difference between these options is about who's responsible for cooking these meals and where the meal is going to be cooked. In the on-premise model, eating a meal at home requires you to do all the work, using your own oven and ingredients already in the home. A store-bought meal is like using the Infrastructure as a Service (IaaS) model of computing. You're using the store's chef and oven to pre-bake the meal, but you're still responsible for heating the meal and eating it at the house (and cleaning up the dishes afterward).

In a Platform as a Service (PaaS) model you still have responsibility for the meal, but you further rely on a vendor to take care of the core tasks associated with making a meal. For example, in a PaaS model, you supply the plates and furniture, but the restaurant owner provides the oven, ingredients, and the chef to cook them. In the Software as a Service (SaaS) model, you go to a restaurant where all the food is prepared for you. You eat at the restaurant and then you pay for the meal when you're done. you also have no dishes to prepare or wash.

The key items at play in each of these models are ones of control: who's responsible for maintaining the infrastructure and what are the technology choices available for building the application? In a IaaS model, the cloud vendor provides the basic infrastructure, but you're accountable for selecting the technology and building the final solution. On the other end of the spectrum, with a SaaS model, you're a passive consumer of the service provided by the vendor and have no input on the technology selection or any accountability to maintain the infrastructure for the application.

Emerging cloud platforms

I've documented the three core cloud platform types (IaaS, PaaS, SaaS) that are in use today. However, new cloud platform types are emerging. These new platforms include Functions as a Service (FaaS) and Container as a Service (CaaS). FaaS-based (https://en.wikipedia.org/wiki/Function_as_a_Service) applications use technologies like Amazon's Lambda technologies and Google Cloud functions to build applications deployed as "serverless" chunks of code that run completely on the cloud provider's platform computing infrastructure. With a FaaS platform, you don't have to manage any server infrastructure and only pay for the computing cycles required to execute the function.

With the Container as a Service (CaaS) model, developers build and deploy their microservices as portable virtual containers (such as Docker) to a cloud provider. Unlike an IaaS model, where you the developer have to manage the virtual machine the service is deployed to, with CaaS you're deploying your services in a lightweight virtual container. The cloud provider runs the virtual server the container is running on as well as the provider's comprehensive tools for building, deploying, monitoring, and scaling containers. Amazon's Elastic Container Service (ECS) is an example of a CaaS-based platform. In chapter 10 of this book, we'll see how to deploy the microservices you've built to Amazon ECS.

It's important to note that with both the FaaS and CaaS models of cloud computing, you can still build a microservice-based architecture. Remember, the concept of microservices revolves around building small services, with limited responsibility, using an HTTP-based interface to communicate. The emerging cloud computing platforms, such as FaaS and CaaS, are really about alternative infrastructure mechanisms for deploying microservices.

1.8   *Why the cloud and microservices?*

One of the core concepts of a microservice-based architecture is that each service is packaged and deployed as its own discrete and independent artifact. Service instances should be brought up quickly and each instance of the service should be indistinguishable from another.

As a developer writing a microservice, sooner or later you're going to have to decide whether your service is going to be deployed to one of the following:

- *Physical server*—While you can build and deploy your microservices to a physical machine(s), few organizations do this because physical servers are constrained. You can't quickly ramp up the capacity of a physical server and it can become extremely costly to scale your microservice horizontally across multiple physical servers.
- *Virtual machine images*—One of the key benefits of microservices is their ability to quickly start up and shut down microservice instances in response to scalability and service failure events. Virtual machines are the heart and soul of the

major cloud providers. A microservice can be packaged up in a virtual machine image and multiple instances of the service can then be quickly deployed and started in either a IaaS private or public cloud.

- *Virtual container*—Virtual containers are a natural extension of deploying your microservices on a virtual machine image. Rather than deploying a service to a full virtual machine, many developers deploy their services as Docker containers (or equivalent container technology) to the cloud. Virtual containers run inside a virtual machine; using a virtual container, you can segregate a single virtual machine into a series of self-contained processes that share the same virtual machine image.

The advantage of cloud-based microservices centers around the concept of elasticity. Cloud service providers allow you to quickly spin up new virtual machines and containers in a matter of minutes. If your capacity needs for your services drop, you can spin down virtual servers without incurring any additional costs. Using a cloud provider to deploy your microservices gives you significantly more horizontal scalability (adding more servers and service instances) for your applications. Server elasticity also means that your applications can be more resilient. If one of your microservices is having problems and is falling over, spinning up new service instances can you keep your application alive long enough for your development team to gracefully resolve the issue.

For this book, all the microservices and corresponding service infrastructure will be deployed to an IaaS-based cloud provider using Docker containers. This is a common deployment topology used for microservices:

- *Simplified infrastructure management*—IaaS cloud providers give you the ability to have the most control over your services. New services can be started and stopped with simple API calls. With an IaaS cloud solution, you only pay for the infrastructure that you use.
- *Massive horizontal scalability*—IaaS cloud providers allow you to quickly and succinctly start one or more instances of a service. This capability means you can quickly scale services and route around misbehaving or failing servers.
- *High redundancy through geographic distribution*—By necessity, IaaS providers have multiple data centers. By deploying your microservices using an IaaS cloud provider, you can gain a higher level of redundancy beyond using clusters in a data center.

Why not PaaS-based microservices?

Earlier in the chapter we discussed three types of cloud platforms (Infrastructure as a Service, Platform as a Service, and Software as a Services). For this book, I've chosen to focus specifically on building microservices using an IaaS-based approach. While certain cloud providers will let you abstract away the deployment infrastructure for your microservice, I've chosen to remain vendor-independent and deploy all parts of my application (including the servers).

For instance, Amazon, Cloud Foundry, and Heroku give you the ability to deploy your services without having to know about the underlying application container. They provide a web interface and APIs to allow you to deploy your application as a WAR or JAR file. Setting up and tuning the application server and the corresponding Java container are abstracted away from you. While this is convenient, each cloud provider's platform has different idiosyncrasies related to its individual PaaS solution.

An IaaS approach, while more work, is portable across multiple cloud providers and allows us to reach a wider audience with our material. Personally, I've found that PaaS-based cloud solutions can allow you to quickly jump start your development effort, but once your application reaches enough microservices, you start to need the flexibility the IaaS style of cloud development provides.

Earlier in the chapter, I mentioned new cloud computing platforms such as Function as a Service (FaaS) and Container as a Service (CaaS). If you're not careful, FaaS-based platforms can lock your code into a cloud vendor platform because your code is deployed to a vendor-specific runtime engine. With a FaaS-based model, you might be writing your service using a general programming language (Java, Python, JavaScript, and so on), but you're still tying yourself heavily to the underlying vendor APIs and runtime engine that your function will be deployed to.

The services built in this book are packaged as Docker containers. One of the reasons why I chose Docker is that as a container technology, Docker is deployable to all the major cloud providers. Later in chapter 10, I demonstrate how to package microservices using Docker and then deploy these containers to Amazon's cloud platform.

1.9 *Microservices are more than writing the code*

While the concepts around building individual microservices are easy to understand, running and supporting a robust microservice application (especially when running

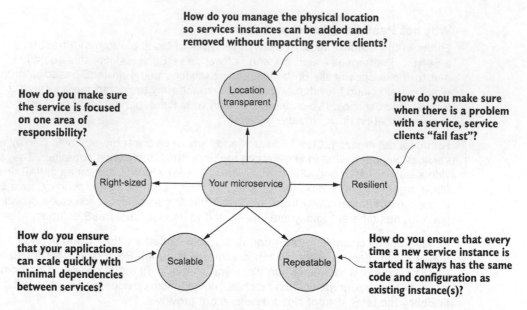

Figure 1.7   Microservices are more than the business logic. You need to think about the environment where the services are going to run and how the services will scale and be resilient.

in the cloud) involves more than writing the code for the service. Writing a robust service includes considering several topics. Figure 1.7 highlights these topics.

Let's walk through the items in figure 1.7 in more detail:

- *Right-sized*—How do you ensure that your microservices are properly sized so that you don't have a microservice take on too much responsibility? Remember, properly sized, a service allows you to quickly make changes to an application and reduces the overall risk of an outage to the entire application.

- *Location transparent*—How you we manage the physical details of service invocation when in a microservice application, multiple service instances can quickly start and shut down?

- *Resilient*—How do you protect your microservice consumers and the overall integrity of your application by routing around failing services and ensuring that you take a "fail-fast" approach?

- *Repeatable*—How do you ensure that every new instance of your service brought up is guaranteed to have the same configuration and code base as all the other service instances in production?

- *Scalable*—How do you use asynchronous processing and events to minimize the direct dependencies between your services and ensure that you can gracefully scale your microservices?

This book takes a patterns-based approach as we answer these questions. With a patterns-based approach, we lay out common designs that can be used across different technology implementations. While we've chosen to use Spring Boot and Spring Cloud to implement the patterns we're going to use in this book, nothing will keep you from taking the concepts presented here and using them with other technology platforms. Specifically, we cover the following six categories of microservice patterns:

- Core development patterns
- Routing patterns
- Client resiliency patterns
- Security patterns
- Logging and tracing patterns
- Build and deployment patterns

Let's walk through these patterns in more detail.

1.9.1 *Core microservice development pattern*

The core development microservice development pattern addresses the basics of building a microservice. Figure 1.8 highlights the topics we'll cover around basic service design.

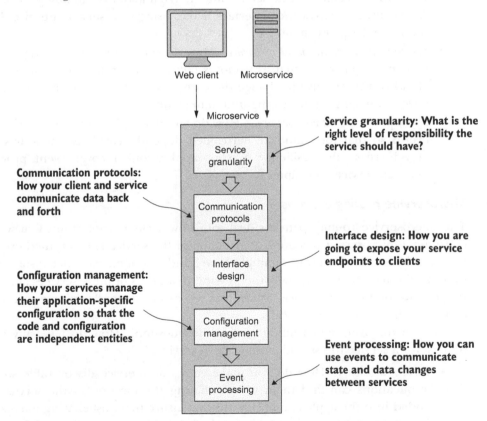

Figure 1.8   When designing your microservice, you have to think about how the service will be consumed and communicated with.

- *Service granularity*—How do you approach decomposing a business domain down into microservices so that each microservice has the right level of responsibility? Making a service too coarse-grained with responsibilities that overlap into different business problems domains makes the service difficult to maintain and change over time. Making the service too fine-grained increases the overall complexity of the application and turns the service into a "dumb" data abstraction layer with no logic except for that needed to access the data store. I cover service granularity in chapter 2.

- *Communication protocols*—How will developers communicate with your service? Do you use XML (Extensible Markup Language), JSON (JavaScript Object Notation), or a binary protocol such as Thrift to send data back and forth your microservices? We'll go into why JSON is the ideal choice for microservices and has become the most common choice for sending and receiving data to microservices. I cover communication protocols in chapter 2.

- *Interface design*—What's the best way to design the actual service interfaces that developers are going to use to call your service? How do you structure your service URLs to communicate service intent? What about versioning your services? A well-design microservice interface makes using your service intuitive. I cover interface design in chapter 2.

- *Configuration management of service*—How do you manage the configuration of your microservice so that as it moves between different environments in the cloud you never have to change the core application code or configuration? I cover managing service configuration in chapter 3.

- *Event processing between services*—How do you decouple your microservice using events so that you minimize hardcoded dependencies between your services and increase the resiliency of your application? I cover event processing between services in chapter 8.

1.9.2 Microservice routing patterns

The microservice routing patterns deal with how a client application that wants to consume a microservice discovers the location of the service and is routed over to it. In a cloud-based application, you might have hundreds of microservice instances running. You'll need to abstract away the physical IP address of these services and have a single point of entry for service calls so that you can consistently enforce security and content policies for all service calls.

Service discovery and routing answer the question, "How do I get my client's request for a service to a specific instance of a service?"

- *Service discovery*—How do you make your microservice discoverable so client applications can find them without having the location of the service hardcoded into the application? How do you ensure that misbehaving microservice instances are removed from the pool of available service instances? I cover service discovery in chapter 4.

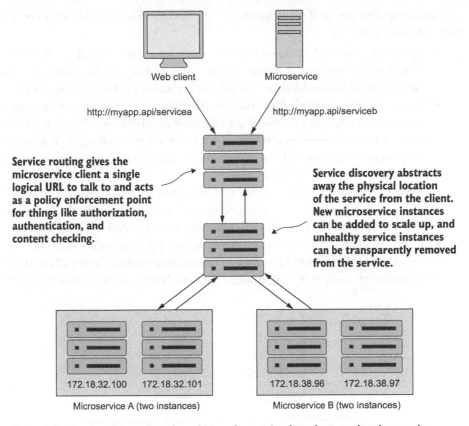

Web client   Microservice

http://myapp.api/servicea   http://myapp.api/serviceb

Service routing gives the microservice client a single logical URL to talk to and acts as a policy enforcement point for things like authorization, authentication, and content checking.

Service discovery abstracts away the physical location of the service from the client. New microservice instances can be added to scale up, and unhealthy service instances can be transparently removed from the service.

172.18.32.100   172.18.32.101   172.18.38.96   172.18.38.97

Microservice A (two instances)   Microservice B (two instances)

Figure 1.9 Service discovery and routing are key parts of any large-scale microservice application.

- *Service routing*—How do you provide a single entry point for all of your services so that security policies and routing rules are applied uniformly to multiple services and service instances in your microservice applications? How do you ensure that each developer in your team doesn't have to come up with their own solutions for providing routing to their services? I cover service routing in chapter 6.

In figure 1.9, service discovery and service routing appear to have a hard-coded sequence of events between them (first comes service routing and the service discovery). However, the two patterns aren't dependent on one another. For instance, we can implement service discovery without service routing. You can implement service routing without service discovery (even though its implementation is more difficult).

1.9.3 *Microservice client resiliency patterns*

Because microservice architectures are highly distributed, you have to be extremely sensitive in how you prevent a problem in a single service (or service instance) from cascading up and out to the consumers of the service. To this end, we'll cover four client resiliency patterns:

- *Client-side load balancing*—How do you cache the location of your service instances on the service client so that calls to multiple instances of a microservice are load balanced to all the health instances of that microservice?
- *Circuit breakers pattern*—How do you prevent a client from continuing to call a service that's failing or suffering performance problems? When a service is running slowly, it consumes resources on the client calling it. You want failing microservice calls to fail fast so that the calling client can quickly respond and take an appropriate action.
- *Fallback pattern*—When a service call fails, how do you provide a "plug-in" mechanism that will allow the service client to try to carry out its work through alternative means other than the microservice being called?
- *Bulkhead pattern*—Microservice applications use multiple distributed resources to carry out their work. How do you compartmentalize these calls so that the misbehavior of one service call doesn't negatively impact the rest of the application?

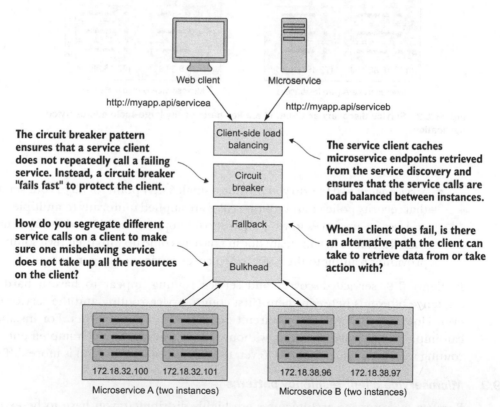

Figure 1.10   With microservices, you must protect the service caller from a poorly behaving service. Remember, a slow or down service can cause disruptions beyond the immediate service.

Figure 1.10 shows how these patterns protect the consumer of service from being impacted when a service is misbehaving. I cover these four topics in chapter 5.

1.9.4 *Microservice security patterns*

I can't write a book on microservices without talking about microservice security. In chapter 7 we'll cover three basic security patterns. These patterns are

- *Authentication*—How do you determine the service client calling the service is who they say they are?
- *Authorization*—How do you determine whether the service client calling a microservice is allowed to undertake the action they're trying to undertake?
- *Credential management and propagation*—How do you prevent a service client from constantly having to present their credentials for service calls involved in a transaction? Specifically, we'll look at how token-based security standards such as OAuth2 and JavaScript Web Tokens (JWT) can be used to obtain a token that can be passed from service call to service call to authenticate and authorize the user.

Figure 1.11 shows how you can implement the three patterns described previously to build an authentication service that can protect your microservices.

At this point I'm not going to go too deeply into the details of figure 1.10. There's a reason why security requires a whole chapter. (It could honestly be a book in itself.)

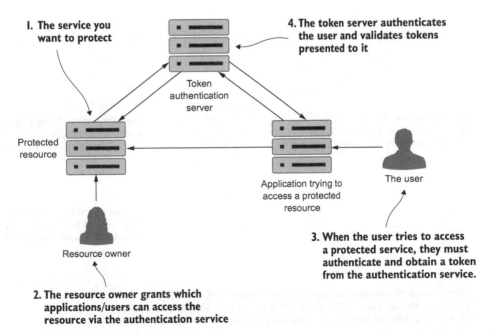

Figure 1.11 Using a token-based security scheme, you can implement service authentication and authorization without passing around client credentials.

1.9.5 *Microservice logging and tracing patterns*

The beauty of the microservice architecture is that a monolithic application is broken down into small pieces of functionality that can be deployed independently of one another. The downside of a microservice architecture is that it's much more difficult to debug and trace what the heck is going on within your application and services.

For this reason, we'll look at three core logging and tracing patterns:

- *Log correlation*—How do you tie together all the logs produced between services for a single user transaction? With this pattern, we'll look at how to implement a correlation ID, which is a unique identifier that will be carried across all service calls in a transaction and can be used to tie together log entries produced from each service.

- *Log aggregation*—With this pattern we'll look at how to pull together all of the logs produced by your microservices (and their individual instances) into a single queryable database. We'll also look at how to use correlation IDs to assist in searching your aggregated logs.

- *Microservice tracing*—Finally, we'll explore how to visualize the flow of a client transaction across all the services involved and understand the performance characteristics of services involved in the transaction.

Figure 1.12 shows how these patterns fit together. We'll cover the logging and tracing patterns in greater detail in chapter 9.

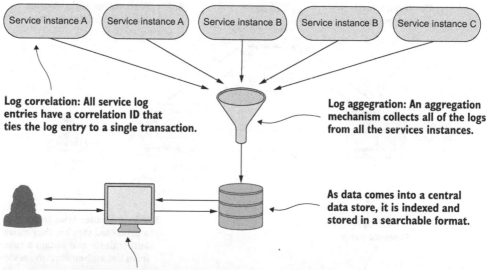

Log correlation: All service log entries have a correlation ID that ties the log entry to a single transaction.

Log aggregation: An aggregation mechanism collects all of the logs from all the services instances.

As data comes into a central data store, it is indexed and stored in a searchable format.

Microservice transaction tracing: The development and operations teams can query the log data to find individual transactions. They should also be able to visualize the flow of all the services involved in a transaction.

Figure 1.12   A well-thought-out logging and tracing strategy makes debugging transactions across multiple services manageable.

1.9.6 Microservice build/deployment patterns

One of the core parts of a microservice architecture is that each instance of a microservice should be identical to all its other instances. You can't allow "configuration drift" (something changes on a server after it's been deployed) to occur, because this can introduce instability in your applications.

A phrase too often said

"I made only one small change on the stage server, but I forgot to make the change in production." The resolution of many down systems when I've worked on critical situations teams over the years has often started with those words from a developer or system administrator. Engineers (and most people in general) operate with good intentions. They don't go to work to make mistakes or bring down systems. Instead they're doing the best they can, but they get busy or distracted. They tweak something on a server, fully intending to go back and do it in all the environments.

At a later point, an outage occurs and everyone is left scratching their heads wondering what's different between the lower environments in production. I've found that the small size and limited scope of a microservice makes it the perfect opportunity to introduce the concept of "immutable infrastructure" into an organization: once a service is deployed, the infrastructure it's running on is never touched again by human hands.

An immutable infrastructure is a critical piece of successfully using a microservice architecture, because you have to guarantee in production that every microservice instance you start for a particular microservice is identical to its brethren.

To this end, our goal is to integrate the configuration of your infrastructure right into your build-deployment process so that you no longer deploy software artifacts such as a Java WAR or EAR to an already-running piece of infrastructure. Instead, you want to build and compile your microservice and the virtual server image it's running on as part of the build process. Then, when your microservice gets deployed, the entire machine image with the server running on it gets deployed.

Figure 1.13 illustrates this process. At the end of the book we'll look at how to change your build and deployment pipeline so that your microservices and the servers they run on are deployed as a single unit of work. In chapter 10 we cover the following patterns and topics:

- *Build and deployment pipeline*—How do you create a repeatable build and deployment process that emphasizes one-button builds and deployment to any environment in your organization?
- *Infrastructure as code*—How do you treat the provisioning of your services as code that can be executed and managed under source control?
- *Immutable servers*—Once a microservice image is created, how do you ensure that it's never changed after it has been deployed?
- *Phoenix servers*—The longer a server is running, the more opportunity for configuration drift. How do you ensure that servers that run microservices get torn down on a regular basis and recreated off an immutable image?

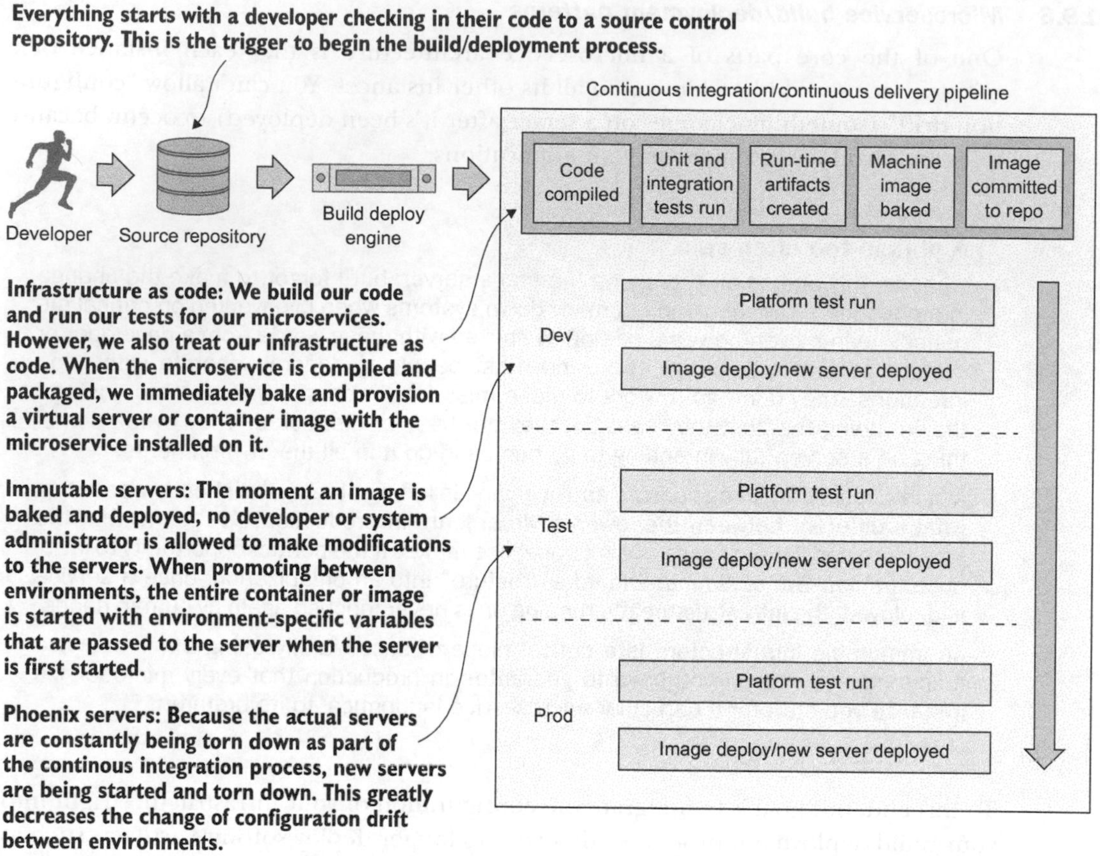

Everything starts with a developer checking in their code to a source control repository. This is the trigger to begin the build/deployment process.

Continuous integration/continuous delivery pipeline

Developer   Source repository   Build deploy engine

| Code compiled | Unit and integration tests run | Run-time artifacts created | Machine image baked | Image committed to repo |

Infrastructure as code: We build our code and run our tests for our microservices. However, we also treat our infrastructure as code. When the microservice is compiled and packaged, we immediately bake and provision a virtual server or container image with the microservice installed on it.

Dev

Platform test run

Image deploy/new server deployed

Immutable servers: The moment an image is baked and deployed, no developer or system administrator is allowed to make modifications to the servers. When promoting between environments, the entire container or image is started with environment-specific variables that are passed to the server when the server is first started.

Test

Platform test run

Image deploy/new server deployed

Phoenix servers: Because the actual servers are constantly being torn down as part of the continous integration process, new servers are being started and torn down. This greatly decreases the change of configuration drift between environments.

Prod

Platform test run

Image deploy/new server deployed

Figure 1.13   You want the deployment of the microservice and the server it's running on to be one atomic artifact that's deployed as a whole between environments.

Our goal with these patterns and topics is to ruthlessly expose and stamp out configuration drift as quickly as possible before it can hit your upper environments, such as stage or production.

NOTE   For the code examples in this book (except chapter 10), everything will run locally on your desktop machine. The first two chapters can be run natively directly from the command line. Starting in chapter 3, all the code will be compiled and run as Docker containers.

1.10   *Using Spring Cloud in building your microservices*

In this section, I briefly introduce the Spring Cloud technologies that you'll use as you build out your microservices. This is a high-level overview; when you use each technology in this book, I'll teach you the details on each as needed.

Implementing all these patterns from scratch would be a tremendous amount of work. Fortunately for us, the Spring team has integrated a wide number of battle-tested open source projects into a Spring subproject collectively known as Spring Cloud. (http://projects.spring.io/spring-cloud/).

Spring Cloud wraps the work of open source companies such as Pivotal, HashiCorp, and Netflix in delivering patterns. Spring Cloud simplifies setting up and configuring of these projects into your Spring application so that you can focus on writing code, not getting buried in the details of configuring all the infrastructure that can go with building and deploying a microservice application.

Figure 1.14 maps the patterns listed in the previous section to the Spring Cloud projects that implement them.

Let's walk through these technologies in greater detail.

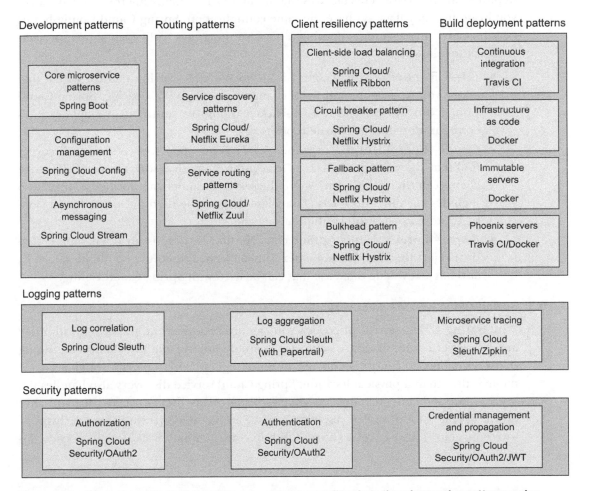

Figure 1.14   You can map the technologies you're going to use directly to the microservice patterns we've explored so far in this chapter.

1.10.1 Spring Boot

Spring Boot is the core technology used in our microservice implementation. Spring Boot greatly simplifies microservice development by simplifying the core tasks of building REST-based microservices. Spring Boot also greatly simplifies mapping HTTP-style verbs (GET, PUT, POST, and DELETE) to URLs and the serialization of the JSON protocol to and from Java objects, as well as the mapping of Java exceptions back to standard HTTP error codes.

1.10.2 Spring Cloud Config

Spring Cloud Config handles the management of application configuration data through a centralized service so your application configuration data (particularly your environment specific configuration data) is cleanly separated from your deployed microservice. This ensures that no matter how many microservice instances you bring up, they'll always have the same configuration. Spring Cloud Config has its own property management repository, but also integrates with open source projects such as the following:

- *Git*—Git (https://git-scm.com/) is an open source version control system that allows you to manage and track changes to any type of text file. Spring Cloud Config can integrate with a Git-backed repository and read the application's configuration data out of the repository.
- *Consul*—Consul (https://www.consul.io/) is an open source service discovery tool that allows service instances to register themselves with the service. Service clients can then ask Consul where the service instances are located. Consul also includes key-value store based database that can be used by Spring Cloud Config to store application configuration data.
- *Eureka*—Eureka (https://github.com/Netflix/eureka) is an open source Netflix project that, like Consul, offers similar service discovery capabilities. Eureka also has a key-value database that can be used with Spring Cloud Config.

1.10.3 Spring Cloud service discovery

With Spring Cloud service discovery, you can abstract away the physical location (IP and/or server name) of where your servers are deployed from the clients consuming the service. Service consumers invoke business logic for the servers through a logical name rather than a physical location. Spring Cloud service discovery also handles the registration and deregistration of services instances as they're started up and shut down. Spring Cloud service discovery can be implemented using Consul (https://www.consul.io/) and Eureka (https://github.com/Netflix/eureka) as its service discovery engine.

1.10.4 *Spring Cloud/Netflix Hystrix and Ribbon*

Spring Cloud heavily integrates with Netflix open source projects. For microservice client resiliency patterns, Spring Cloud wraps the Netflix Hystrix libraries (https://github .com/Netflix/Hystrix) and Ribbon project (https://github.com/Netflix/Ribbon) and makes using them from within your own microservices trivial to implement.

Using the Netflix Hystrix libraries, you can quickly implement service client resiliency patterns such as the circuit breaker and bulkhead patterns.

While the Netflix Ribbon project simplifies integrating with service discovery agents such as Eureka, it also provides client-side load-balancing of service calls from a service consumer. This makes it possible for a client to continue making service calls even if the service discovery agent is temporarily unavailable.

1.10.5 *Spring Cloud/Netflix Zuul*

Spring Cloud uses the Netflix Zuul project (https://github.com/Netflix/zuul) to provide service routing capabilities for your microservice application. Zuul is a service gateway that proxies service requests and makes sure that all calls to your microservices go through a single "front door" before the targeted service is invoked. With this centralization of service calls, you can enforce standard service policies such as a security authorization authentication, content filtering, and routing rules.

1.10.6 *Spring Cloud Stream*

Spring Cloud Stream (https://cloud.spring.io/spring-cloud-stream/) is an enabling technology that allows you to easily integrate lightweight message processing into your microservice. Using Spring Cloud Stream, you can build intelligent microservices that can use asynchronous events as they occur in your application. With Spring Cloud Stream, you can quickly integrate your microservices with message brokers such as RabbitMQ (https://www.rabbitmq.com/) and Kafka (http://kafka.apache.org/).

1.10.7 *Spring Cloud Sleuth*

Spring Cloud Sleuth (https://cloud.spring.io/spring-cloud-sleuth/) allows you to integrate unique tracking identifiers into the HTTP calls and message channels (RabbitMQ, Apache Kafka) being used within your application. These tracking numbers, sometimes referred to as correlation or trace ids, allow you to track a transaction as it flows across the different services in your application. With Spring Cloud Sleuth, these trace IDs are automatically added to any logging statements you make in your microservice.

The real beauty of Spring Cloud Sleuth is seen when it's combined with logging aggregation technology tools such as Papertrail (http://papertrailapp.com) and tracing tools such as Zipkin (http://zipkin.io). Papertail is a cloud-based logging platform used to aggregate logs in real time from different microservices into one queryable database. Open Zipkin takes data produced by Spring Cloud Sleuth and allows you to visualize the flow of your service calls involved for a single transaction.

1.10.8 Spring Cloud Security

Spring Cloud Security (https://cloud.spring.io/spring-cloud-security/) is an authentication and authorization framework that can control who can access your services and what they can do with your services. Spring Cloud Security is token-based and allows services to communicate with one another through a token issued by an authentication server. Each service receiving a call can check the provided token in the HTTP call to validate the user's identity and their access rights with the service.

In addition, Spring Cloud Security supports the JavaScript Web Token (https://jwt.io). The JavaScript Web Token (JWT) framework standardizes the format of how a OAuth2 token is created and provides standards for digitally signing a created token.

1.10.9 What about provisioning?

For the provisioning implementations, we're going to make a technology shift. The Spring framework(s) are geared toward application development. The Spring frameworks (including Spring Cloud) don't have tools for creating a "build and deployment" pipeline. To implement a "build and deployment" pipeline you're going to use the following tools: Travis CI (https://travis-ci.org) for your build tool and Docker (https://www.docker.com/) to build the final server image containing your microservice.

To deploy your built Docker containers, we end the book with an example of how to deploy the entire application stack built throughout this book to Amazon's cloud.

1.11 Spring Cloud by example

In the last section, we walked through all the different Spring Cloud technologies that you're going to use as you build out your microservices. Because each of these technologies are independent services, it's obviously going to take more than one chapter to explain all of them in detail. However, as I wrap up this chapter, I want to leave you with a small code example that again demonstrates how easy it is to integrate these technologies into your own microservice development effort.

Unlike the first code example in listing 1.1, you can't run this code example because a number of supporting services need to be set up and configured to be used. Don't worry, though; the setup costs for these Spring Cloud services (configuration service, service discovery) are a one-time cost in terms of setting up the service. Once they're set up, your individual microservices can use these capabilities over and over again. We couldn't fit all that goodness into a single code example at the beginning of the book.

The code shown in the following listing quickly demonstrates how the service discovery, circuit breaker, bulkhead, and client-side load balancing of remote services were integrated into our "Hello World" example.

Listing 1.2 Hello World Service using Spring Cloud

```
package com.thoughtmechanix.simpleservice;

//Removed other imports for conciseness
import com.netflix.hystrix.contrib.javanica.annotation.HystrixCommand;
import com.netflix.hystrix.contrib.javanica.annotation.HystrixProperty;
import org.springframework.cloud.netflix.eureka.EnableEurekaClient;
import  org.springframework.cloud.client.circuitbreaker.EnableCircuitBreaker;

@SpringBootApplication
@RestController
@RequestMapping(value="hello")
@EnableCircuitBreaker
@EnableEurekaClient
public class Application {

    public static void main(String[] args) {
        SpringApplication.run(Application.class, args);
    }

    @HystrixCommand(threadPoolKey = "helloThreadPool")
public String helloRemoteServiceCall(String firstName,
                                                String lastName){
    ResponseEntity<String> restExchange =
        restTemplate.exchange(
            "http://logical-service-id/name/
            [ca]{firstName}/{lastName}",
             HttpMethod.GET,
             null, String.class, firstName, lastName);

    return restExchange.getBody();

    }

@RequestMapping(value="/{firstName}/{lastName}",
    method = RequestMethod.GET)
    public String hello( @PathVariable("firstName") String firstName,
                        @PathVariable("lastName") String lastName) {
        return helloRemoteServiceCall(firstName, lastName)
}
}
```

Enables the service to use the Hystrix and Ribbon libraries

Tells the service that it should register itself with a Eureka service discovery agent and that service calls are to use service discovery to "lookup" the location of remote services

Wrappers calls to the helloRemoteServiceCall method with a Hystrix circuit breaker

Uses a decorated RestTemplate class to take a "logical" service ID and Eureka under the covers to look up the physical location of the service

This code has a lot packed into it, so let's walk through it. Keep in mind that this listing is only an example and isn't found in the chapter 1 GitHub repository source code. I've included it here to give you a taste of what's to come later in the book.

The first thing you should notice is the @EnableCircuitBreaker and @EnableEurekaClient annotations. The @EnableCircuitBreaker annotation tells your Spring microservice that you're going to use the Netflix Hystrix libraries in your application. The @EnableEurekaClient annotation tells your microservice to register itself with a Eureka Service Discovery agent and that you're going to use service discovery to look up remote REST services endpoints in your code. Note that configuration is happening in a property file that will tell the simple service the location and port number of a Eureka server to contact. You first see Hystrix being used when you declare your hello method:

```
@HystrixCommand(threadPoolKey = "helloThreadPool")
public String helloRemoteServiceCall(String firstName, String lastName)
```

The @HystrixCommand annotation is doing two things. First, any time the helloRemoteServiceCall method is called, it won't be directly invoked. Instead, the method will be delegated to a thread pool managed by Hystrix. If the call takes too long (default is one second), Hystrix steps in and interrupts the call. This is the implementation of the circuit breaker pattern. The second thing this annotation does is create a thread pool called helloThreadPool that's managed by Hystrix. All calls to helloRemoteServiceCall method will only occur on this thread pool and will be isolated from any other remote service calls being made.

The last thing to note is what's occurring inside the helloRemoteServiceCall method. The presence of the @EnableEurekaClient has told Spring Boot that you're going to use a modified RestTemplate class (this isn't how the Standard Spring RestTemplate would work out of the box) whenever you make a REST service call. This RestTemplate class will allow you to pass in a logical service ID for the service you're trying to invoke:

```
ResponseEntity<String> restExchange = restTemplate.exchange
    (http://logical-service-id/name/{firstName}/{lastName}
```

Under the covers, the RestTemplate class will contact the Eureka service and look up the physical location of one or more of the "name" service instances. As a consumer of the service, your code never has to know where that service is located.

Also, the RestTemplate class is using Netflix's Ribbon library. Ribbon will retrieve a list of all the physical endpoints associated with a service. Every time the service is called by the client, it "round-robins" the call to the different service instances on the client without having to go through a centralized load balancer. By eliminating a centralized load balancer and moving it to the client, you eliminate another failure point (load balancer going down) in your application infrastructure.

I hope that at this point you're impressed, because you've added a significant number of capabilities to your microservice with only a few annotations. That's the real beauty behind Spring Cloud. You as a developer get to take advantage of battle-hardened microservice capabilities from premier cloud companies like Netflix and Consul. These capabilities, if used outside of Spring Cloud, can be complex and obtuse to set up. Spring Cloud simplifies their use to literally nothing more than a few simple Spring Cloud annotations and configuration entries.

1.12   *Making sure our examples are relevant*

I want to make sure this book provides examples that you can relate to as you go about your day-to-day job. To this end, I've structured the chapters in this book and the corresponding code examples around the adventures (misadventures) of a fictitious company called ThoughtMechanix.

ThoughtMechanix is a software development company whose core product, Eagle-Eye, provides an enterprise-grade software asset management application. It provides coverage for all the critical elements: inventory, software delivery, license management, compliance, cost, and resource management. Its primary goal is to enable organizations to gain an accurate point-in-time picture of its software assets.

The company is approximately 10 years old. While they've experienced solid revenue growth, internally they're debating whether they should be re-platforming their core product from a monolithic on-premise-based application or move their application to the cloud. The re-platforming involved with EagleEye can be a "make or break" moment for a company.

The company is looking at rebuilding their core product EagleEye on a new architecture. While much of the business logic for the application will remain in place, the application itself will be broken down from a monolithic design to a much smaller microservice design whose pieces can be deployed independently to the cloud. The examples in this book won't build the entire ThoughtMechanix application. Instead you'll build specific microservices from the problem domain at hand and then build the infrastructure that will support these services using various Spring Cloud (and some non-Spring-Cloud) technologies.

The ability to successfully adopt cloud-based, microservice architecture will impact all parts of a technical organization. This includes the architecture, engineering, testing, and operations teams. Input will be needed from each group and, in the end, they're probably going to need reorganization as the team reevaluates their responsibilities in this new environment. Let's start our journey with ThoughtMechanix as you begin the fundamental work of identifying and building out several of the microservices used in EagleEye and then building these services using Spring Boot.

1.13   *Summary*

- Microservices are extremely small pieces of functionality that are responsible for one specific area of scope.
- No industry standards exist for microservices. Unlike other early web service protocols, microservices take a principle-based approach and align with the concepts of REST and JSON.
- Writing microservices is easy, but fully operationalizing them for production requires additional forethought. We introduced several categories of microservice development patterns, including core development, routing patterns, client resiliency, security, logging, and build/deployment patterns.

- While microservices are language-agnostic, we introduced two Spring frameworks that significantly help in building microservices: Spring Boot and Spring Cloud.
- Spring Boot is used to simplify the building of REST-based/JSON microservices. Its goal is to make it possible for you to build microservices quickly with nothing more than a few annotations.
- Spring Cloud is a collection of open source technologies from companies such as Netflix and HashiCorp that have been "wrapped" with Spring annotations to significantly simplify the setup and configuration of these services.

2

Building microservices with Spring Boot

This chapter covers

- Learning the key characteristics of a microservice
- Understanding how microservices fit into a cloud architecture
- Decomposing a business domain into a set of microservices
- Implementing a simple microservice using Spring Boot
- Understanding the perspectives for building microservice-based applications
- Learning when not to use microservices

The history of software development is littered with the tales of large development projects that after an investment of millions of dollars and hundreds of thousands of software developer hours, and with many of the best and brightest minds in the industry working on them, somehow never managed to deliver anything of value to their customers and literally collapsed under their own complexity and weight.

These mammoth projects tended to follow large, traditional waterfall development methodologies that insisted that all the application's requirements and design be defined at the beginning of the project. So much emphasis was placed on getting all the specifications for the software "correct" that there was little leeway to meet new business requirements, or refactor and learn from mistakes made in the early stages of development.

The reality, though, is that software development isn't a linear process of definition and execution, but rather an evolutionary one where it takes several iterations of *communicating with, learning from, and delivering to* the customer before the development team truly understands the problem at hand.

Compounding the challenges of using traditional waterfall methodologies is that many times the granularity of the software artifacts being delivered in these projects are

- *Tightly coupled*—The invocation of business logic happens at the programming-language level instead of through implementation-neutral protocols such as SOAP and REST. This greatly increases the chance that even a small change to an application component can break other pieces of the application and introduce new bugs.

- *Leaky*—Most large software applications manage different types of data. For instance, a customer relationship management (CRM) application might manage customer, sales, and product information. In a traditional model, this data is kept in the same data model and within the same data store. Even though there are obvious boundaries between the data, too often it's tempting for a team from one domain to directly access the data that belongs to another team.

  This easy access to data creates hidden dependencies and allows implementation details of one component's internal data structures to leak through the entire application. Even small changes to a single database table can require a significant number of code changes and regression-testing throughout the entire application.

- *Monolithic*—Because most of the application components for a traditional application reside in a single code base that's shared across multiple teams, any time a change to the code is made, the entire application has to be recompiled, rerun through an entire testing cycle, and redeployed. Even small changes to the application's code base, whether they're new customer requirements or bug fixes, become expensive and time-consuming, and large changes become nearly impossible to do in a timely fashion.

A microservice-based architecture takes a different approach to delivering functionality. Specifically, microservice-based architectures have these characteristics:

- *Constrained*—Microservices have a single set of responsibilities and are narrow in scope. Microservices embrace the UNIX philosophy that an application is nothing more than a collection of services where each service does one thing and does that one thing really well.

- *Loosely coupled*—A microservice-based application is a collection of small services that only interact with one another through a non–implementation specific interface using a non-proprietary invocation protocol (for example, HTTP and REST). As long as the interface for the service doesn't change, the owners of the microservice have more freedom to make modifications to the service than in a traditional application architecture.

- *Abstracted*—Microservices completely own their data structures and data sources. Data owned by a microservice can only be modified by that service. Access control to the database holding the microservice's data can be locked down to only allow the service access to it.
- *Independent*—Each microservice in a microservice application can be compiled and deployed independently of the other services used in the application. This means changes can be isolated and tested much more easily than with a more heavily interdependent, monolithic application.

Why are these microservice architecture attributes important to cloud-based development? Cloud-based applications in general have the following:

- *A large and diverse user base*—Different customers want different features, and they don't want to have to wait for a long application release cycle before they can start using these features. Microservices allow features to be delivered quickly, because each service is small in scope and accessed through a well-defined interface.
- *Extremely high uptime requirements*—Because of the decentralized nature of microservices, microservice-based applications can more easily isolate faults and problems to specific parts of an application without taking down the entire application. This reduces overall downtime for applications and makes them more resistent to problems.
- *Uneven volume requirements*—Traditional applications deployed within the four walls of a corporate data center usually have consistent usage patterns that emerge over time. This makes capacity planning for these types of applications simple. But in a cloud-based application, a simple tweet on Twitter or a post on Slashdot can drive demand for a cloud-based application through the roof.

  Because microservice applications are broken down into small components that can be deployed independently of one another, it's much easier to focus on the components that are under load and scale those components horizontally across multiple servers in a cloud.

This chapter provides you with the foundation you need to target and identify microservices in your business problem, build the skeleton of a microservice, and then understand the operational attributes that need to be in place for a microservice to be deployed and managed successfully in production.

To successfully design and build microservices, you need to approach microservices as if you're a police detective interviewing witnesses to a crime. Even though every witness saw the same events take place, their interpretation of the crime is shaped by their background, what was important to them (for example, what motivates them), and what environmental pressures were brought to bear at that moment they witnessed the event. Participants each have their own perspectives (and biases) of what they consider important.

Like a successful police detective trying to get to the truth, the journey to build a successful microservice architecture involves incorporating the perspectives of multiple individuals within your software development organization. Although it takes more than technical people to deliver an entire application, I believe that the foundation for successful microservice development starts with the perspectives of three critical roles:

- *The architect*—The architect's job is to see the big picture and understand how an application can be decomposed into individual microservices and how the microservices will interact to deliver a solution.

- *The software developer*—The software developer writes the code and understands in detail how the language and development frameworks for the language will be used to deliver a microservice.

- *The DevOps engineer*—The DevOps engineer brings intelligence to how the services are deployed and managed throughout not only production, but also all the nonproduction environments. The watchwords for the DevOps engineer are *consistency* and *repeatability* in every environment.

In this chapter, I'll demonstrate how to design and build a set of microservices from the perspective of each of these roles using Spring Boot and Java. By the time the chapter concludes, you'll have a service that can be packaged and deployed to the cloud.

2.1   The architect's story: designing the microservice architecture

An architect's role on a software project is to provide a working model of the problem that needs to be solved. The job of the architect is to provide the scaffolding against which developers will build their code so that all the pieces of the application fit together.

When building a microservices architecture, a project's architect focuses on three key tasks:

1 Decomposing the business problem
2 Establishing service granularity
3 Defining the service interfaces

2.1.1   Decomposing the business problem

In the face of complexity, most people try to break the problem on which they're working into manageable chunks. They do this so they don't have to try to fit all the details of the problem in their heads. Instead, they break the problem down abstractly into a few key parts and then look for the relationships that exist between these parts.

In a microservices architecture, the architect breaks the business problem into chunks that represent discrete domains of activity. These chunks encapsulate the business rules and the data logic associated with a particular part of the business domain.

Although you want microservices to encapsulate all the business rules for carrying out a single transaction, this isn't always feasible. You'll often have situations where you need to have groups of microservices working across different parts of the business domain to complete an entire transaction. An architect teases apart the service boundaries of a set of microservices by looking at where the data domain doesn't seem to fit together.

For example, an architect might look at a business flow that's to be carried out by code and realize that they need both customer and product information. The presence of two discrete data domains is a good indication that multiple microservices are at play. How the two different parts of the business transaction interact usually becomes the service interface for the microservices.

Breaking apart a business domain is an art form rather than a black-and-white science. Use the following guidelines for identifying and decomposing a business problem into microservice candidates:

1 *Describe the business problem, and listen to the nouns you're using to describe the problem.* Using the same nouns over and over in describing the problem is usually an indication of a core business domain and an opportunity for a microservice. Examples of target nouns for the EagleEye domain from chapter 1 might look something like *contracts, licenses,* and *assets.*

2 *Pay attention to the verbs.* Verbs highlight actions and often represent the natural contours of a problem domain. If you find yourself saying "transaction X needs to get data from thing A and thing B," that usually indicates that multiple services are at play. If you apply to EagleEye the approach of watching for verbs, you might look for statements such as, "When Mike from desktop services is setting up a new PC, he looks up the number of licenses available for software X and, if licenses are available, installs the software. He then updates the number of licenses used in his tracking spreadsheet." The key verbs here are *looks* and *updates.*

3 *Look for data cohesion.* As you break apart your business problem into discrete pieces, look for pieces of data that are highly related to one another. If suddenly, during the course of your conversation, you're reading or updating data that's radically different from what you've been discussing so far, you potentially have another service candidate. *Microservices should completely own their data.*

Let's take these guidelines and apply them to a real-world problem. Chapter 1 introduced an existing software product called EagleEye that's used for managing software assets such as software licenses and secure socket layer (SSL) certificates. These items are deployed to various servers throughout an organization.

EagleEye is a traditional monolithic web application that's deployed to a J2EE application server residing within a customer's data center. Your goal is to tease apart the existing monolithic application into a set of services.

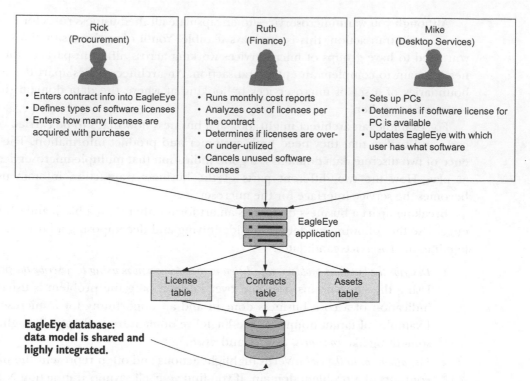

Figure 2.1   Interview the EagleEye users, and understand how they do their day-to-day work.

You're going to start by interviewing all the users of the EagleEye application and discussing with them how they interact and use EagleEye. Figure 2.1 captures a summary of the conversations you might have with the different business customers. By looking at how the users of EagleEye interact with the application and how the data model for the application is broken out, you can decompose the EagleEye problem domain into the following microservice candidates.

In the figure, I've highlighted a number of nouns and verbs that have come up during conversations with the business users. Because this is an existing application, you can look at the application and map the major nouns back to tables in the physical data model. An existing application may have hundreds of tables, but each table will usually map back to a single set of logical entities.

Figure 2.2 shows a simplified data model based on conversations with EagleEye customers. Based on the business interviews and the data model, the microservice candidates are organization, license, contract, and assets services.

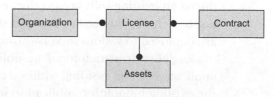

Figure 2.2   A simplified EagleEye data model

2.1.2 Establishing service granularity

Once you have a simplified data model, you can begin the process of defining what microservices you're going to need in the application. Based on the data model in figure 2.2, you can see the potential for four microservices based on the following elements:

- Assets
- License
- Contract
- Organization

The goal is to take these major pieces of functionality and extract them into completely self-contained units that can be built and deployed independently of each other. But extracting services from the data model involves more than repackaging code into separate projects. It's also about teasing out the actual database tables the services are accessing and only allowing each individual service to access the tables in its specific domain. Figure 2.3 shows how the application code and the data model become "chunked" into individual pieces.

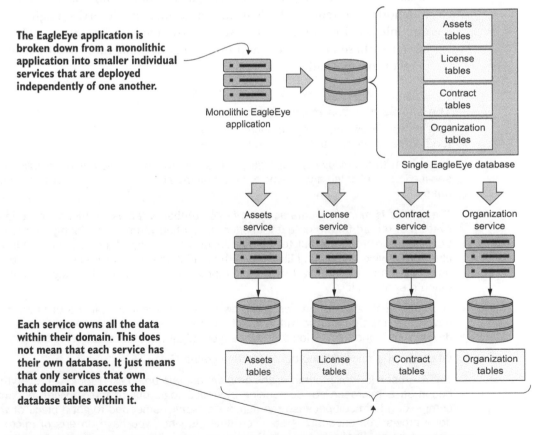

Figure 2.3 You use the data model as the basis for decomposing a monolithic application into microservices.

After you've broken a problem domain down into discrete pieces, you'll often find yourself struggling to determine whether you've achieved the right level of granularity for your services. A microservice that's too coarse- or fine-grained will have a number of telltale attributes that we'll discuss shortly.

When you're building a microservice architecture, the question of granularity is important, but you can use the following concepts to determine the correct solution:

1 *It's better to start broad with your microservice and refactor to smaller services*—It's easy to go overboard when you begin your microservice journey and make everything a microservice. But decomposing the problem domain into small services often leads to premature complexity because microservices devolve into nothing more than fine-grained data services.

2 *Focus first on how your services will interact with one another*—This will help establish the coarse-grained interfaces of your problem domain. It's easier to refactor from being too coarse-grained to being too fine-grained.

3 *Service responsibilities will change over time as your understanding of the problem domain grows*—Often, a microservice gains responsibilities as new application functionality is requested. What starts as a single microservice might grow into multiple services, with the original microservice acting as an orchestration layer for these new services and encapsulating their functionality from other parts of the application.

The smells of a bad microservice

How do you know whether your microservices are the right size? If a microservice is too coarse-grained, you'll likely see the following:

A service with too many responsibilities—The general flow of the business logic in the service is complicated and seems to be enforcing an overly diverse array of business rules.

The service is managing data across a large number of tables—A microservice is the system of record for the data it manages. If you find yourself persisting data to multiple tables or reaching out to tables outside of the immediate database, this is a clue the service is too big. I like to use the guideline that a microservice should own no more than three to five tables. Any more, and your service is likely to have too much responsibility.

Too many test cases—Services can grow in size and responsibility over time. If you have a service that started with a small number of test cases and ends up with hundreds of unit and integration test cases, you might need to refactor.

What about a microservice that's too fine-grained?

The microservices in one part of the problem domain breed like rabbits—If everything becomes a microservice, composing business logic out of the services becomes complex and difficult because the number of services needed to get a piece of work done grows tremendously. A common smell is when you have dozens of microservices in an application and each service interacts with only a single database table.

Your microservices are heavily interdependent on one another—You find that the microservices in one part of the problem domain keep calling back and forth between each other to complete a single user request.

Your microservices become a collection of simple CRUD (Create, Replace, Update, Delete) services—Microservices are an expression of business logic and not an abstraction layer over your data sources. If your microservices do nothing but CRUD-related logic, they're probably too fine-grained.

A microservices architecture should be developed with an evolutionary thought process where you know that you aren't going to get the design right the first time. That's why it's better to start with your first set of services being more coarse-grained than fine-grained. It's also important not to be dogmatic with your design. You may run into physical constraints on your services where you'll need to make an aggregation service that joins data together because two separate services will be too chatty, or where no clear boundaries exist between the domain lines of a service.

In the end, take a pragmatic approach and deliver, rather than waste time trying to get the design perfect and then have nothing to show for your effort.

2.1.3 *Talking to one another: service interfaces*

The last part of the of the architect's input is about defining how the microservices in your application are going to talk with one another. When building business logic with microservices, the interfaces for the services should be intuitive and developers should get a rhythm of how all the services work in the application by learning one or two of the services in the application.

In general, the following guidelines can be used for thinking about service interface design:

1 *Embrace the REST philosophy*—The REST approach to services is at heart the embracing of HTTP as the invocation protocol for the services and the use of standard HTTP verbs (GET, PUT, POST, and DELETE). Model your basic behaviors around these HTTP verbs.

2 *Use URI's to communicate intent*—The URI you use as endpoints for the service should describe the different resources in your problem domain and provide a basic mechanism for relationships of resources within your problem domain.

3 *Use JSON for your requests and responses*—JavaScript Object Notation (in other words, JSON) is an extremely lightweight data-serialization protocol and is much easier to consume then XML.

4 *Use HTTP status codes to communicate results*—The HTTP protocol has a rich body of standard response codes to indicate the success or failure of a service. Learn these status codes and most importantly use them consistently across all your services.

All the basic guidelines drive to one thing, making your service interfaces easy to understand and consumable. You want a developer to sit down and look at the service interfaces and start using them. If a microservice isn't easy to consume, developers will go out of their way to work around and subvert the intention of the architecture.

2.2 *When not to use microservices*

We've spent this chapter talking about why microservices are a powerful architectural pattern for building applications. But I haven't touched on when you shouldn't use microservices to build your applications. Let's walk through them:

1 Complexity building distributed systems
2 Virtual server/container sprawl
3 Application type
4 Data transactions and consistency

2.2.1 *Complexity of building distributed systems*

Because microservices are distributed and fine-grained (small), they introduce a level of complexity into your application that wouldn't be there in more monolithic applications. Microservice architectures require a high degree of operational maturity. Don't consider using microservices unless your organization is willing to invest in the automation and operational work (monitoring, scaling) that a highly distributed application needs to be successful.

2.2.2 *Server sprawl*

One of the most common deployment models for microservices is to have one microservice instance deployed on one server. In a large microservices-based application, you might end up with 50 to 100 servers or containers (usually virtual) that have to be built and maintained in production alone. Even with the lower cost of running these services in the cloud, the operational complexity of having to manage and monitor these servers can be tremendous.

> **NOTE** The flexibility of microservices has to be weighed against the cost of running all of these servers.

2.2.3 *Type of application*

Microservices are geared toward reusability and are extremely useful for building large applications that need to be highly resilient and scalable. This is one of the reasons why so many cloud-based companies have adopted microservices. If you're building small, departmental-level applications or applications with a small user base, the complexity associated with building on a distributed model such as microservices might be more expense than it's worth.

2.2.4   *Data transformations and consistency*

As you begin looking at microservices, you need to think through the data usage patterns of your services and how service consumers are going to use them. A microservice wraps around and abstracts away a small number of tables and works well as a mechanism for performing "operational" tasks such as creating, adding, and performing simple (non-complex) queries against a store.

If your applications need to do complex data aggregation or transformation across multiple sources of data, the distributed nature of microservices will make this work difficult. Your microservices will invariably take on too much responsibility and can also become vulnerable to performance problems.

Also keep in mind that no standard exists for performing transactions across microservices. If you need transaction management, you will need to build that logic yourself. In addition, as you'll see in chapter 7, microservices can communicate amongst themselves by using messages. Messaging introduces latency in data updates. Your applications need to handle eventual consistency where updates that are applied to your data might not immediately appear.

2.3   *The developer's tale: building a microservice with Spring Boot and Java*

When building a microservice, moving from the conceptual space to the implementation space requires a shift in perspective. Specifically, as a developer, you need to establish a basic pattern of how each of the microservices in your application is going to be implemented. While each service is going to be unique, you want to make sure that you're using a framework that removes boilerplate code and that each piece of your microservice is laid out in the same consistent fashion.

In this section, we'll explore the developer's priorities in building the licensing microservice from your EagleEye domain model. Your licensing service is going to be written using Spring Boot. Spring Boot is an abstraction layer over the standard Spring libraries that allows developers to quickly build Groovy- and Java-based web applications and microservices with significantly less ceremony and configuration than a full-blown Spring application.

For your licensing service example, you'll use Java as your core programming language and Apache Maven as your build tool.

Over the next several sections you're going to

1 Build the basic skeleton of the microservice and a Maven script to build the application

2 Implement a Spring bootstrap class that will start the Spring container for the microservice and initiate the kick-off of any initialization work for the class

3 Implement a Spring Boot controller class for mapping an endpoint to expose the endpoints of the service

2.3.1 *Getting started with the skeleton project*

To begin, you'll create a skeleton project for the licensing. You can either pull down the source code down from GitHub (https://github.com/carnellj/spmia-chapter2) or create a licensing-service project directory with the following directory structure:

- licensing-service
- src/main/java/com/thoughtmechanix/licenses
- controllers
- model
- services
- resources

Once you've pulled down or created this directory structure, begin by writing your Maven script for the project. This will be the pom.xml file located at the root of the project directory. The following listing shows the Maven POM file for your licensing service.

Listing 2.1   Maven pom file for the licensing service

```xml
<?xml version="1.0" encoding="UTF-8"?>
<project xmlns="http://maven.apache.org/POM/4.0.0"
    xmlns:xsi="http://www.w3.org/2001/XMLSchema-instance"
     xsi:schemaLocation="http://maven.apache.org/POM/4.0.0
    http://maven.apache.org/xsd/maven-4.0.0.xsd">
  <modelVersion>4.0.0</modelVersion>

  <groupId>com.thoughtmechanix</groupId>
  <artifactId>licensing-service</artifactId>
  <version>0.0.1-SNAPSHOT</version>
  <packaging>jar</packaging>

  <name>EagleEye Licensing Service</name>
  <description>Licensing Service</description>

  <parent>
     <groupId>org.springframework.boot</groupId>
     <artifactId>spring-boot-starter-parent</artifactId>
      <version>1.4.4.RELEASE</version>
      <relativePath/>
  </parent>
  <dependencies>
    <dependency>
       <groupId>org.springframework.boot</groupId>
       <artifactId>spring-boot-starter-web</artifactId>
    </dependency>
    <dependency>
       <groupId>org.springframework.boot</groupId>
       <artifactId>spring-boot-starter-actuator</artifactId>
    </dependency>
  </dependencies>
```

Tells Maven to include the Spring Boot Starter Kit dependencies

Tells Maven to include the Spring Boot web dependencies

Tells Maven to include the Spring Actuator dependencies

```
<!--Note: Some the build properties and Docker build plugins have been
    excluded from the pom.xml in this pom (not in the source code in the
    github repository) because they are not relevant to our discussion here.
    -->

<build>
        <plugins>
      <plugin>
        <groupId>org.springframework.boot</groupId>
        <artifactId>spring-boot-maven-plugin</artifactId>
      </plugin>
    </plugins>
  </build>
</project>
```

Tells Maven to include Spring specific maven plugins for building and deploying Spring Boot applications

We won't go through the entire script in detail, but note a few key areas as we begin. Spring Boot is broken into many individual projects. The philosophy is that you shouldn't have to "pull down the world" if you aren't going to use different pieces of Spring Boot in your application. This also allows the various Spring Boot projects to release new versions of code independently of one another. To help simplify the life of the developers, the Spring Boot team has gathered related dependent projects into various "starter" kits. In part 1 of the Maven POM you tell Maven that you need to pull down version 1.4.4 of the Spring Boot framework

In parts 2 and 3 of the Maven file, you identify that you're pulling down the Spring Web and Spring Actuator starter kits. These two projects are at the heart of almost any Spring Boot REST-based service. You'll find that as you build more functionality into your services, the list of these dependent projects becomes longer.

Also, Spring Source has provided Maven plugins that simplify the build and deployment of the Spring Boot applications. Step 4 tells your Maven build script to install the latest Spring Boot Maven plugin. This plugin contains a number of add-on tasks (such as `spring-boot:run`) that simplify your interaction between Maven and Spring Boot.

Finally, you'll see a comment that sections of the Maven file have been removed. For the sake of the trees, I didn't include the Spotify Docker plugins in listing 2.1.

> **NOTE** Every chapter in this book includes Docker files for building and deploying the application as Docker containers. You can find details of how to build these Docker images in the README.md file in the code sections of each chapter.

2.3.2 *Booting your Spring Boot application: writing the Bootstrap class*

Your goal is to get a simple microservice up and running in Spring Boot and then iterate on it to deliver functionality. To this end, you need to create two classes in your licensing service microservice:

- A Spring Bootstrap class that will be used by Spring Boot to start up and initialize the application
- A Spring Controller class that will expose the HTTP endpoints that can be invoked on the microservice

As you'll see shortly, Spring Boot uses annotations to simplify setting up and configuring the service. This becomes evident as you look at the bootstrap class in the following listing. This bootstrap class is in the `src/main/java/com/thoughtmechanix/licenses/Application.java` file.

Listing 2.2   Introducing the `@SpringBootApplication` annotation

```
package com.thoughtmechanix.licenses;

import org.springframework.boot.SpringApplication;
import org.springframework.boot.autoconfigure.SpringBootApplication;

@SpringBootApplication                                          ⟵————
public class Application {
  public static void main(String[] args) {
SpringApplication.run(Application.class, args);   ⟵——
  }
}
```

> **@SpringBootApplication tells the Spring Boot framework that this is the bootstrap class for the project**

> **Call to start the entire Spring Boot service**

The first thing to note in this code is the use of the `@SpringBootApplication` annotation. Spring Boot uses this annotation to tell the Spring container that this class is the source of bean definitions for use in Spring. In a Spring Boot application, you can define Spring Beans by

1 Annotating a Java class with a `@Component`, `@Service` or `@Repository` annotation tag
2 Annotating a class with a `@Configuration` tag and then defining a constructor method for each Spring Bean you want to build with a `@Bean` tag.

Under the covers, the `@SpringBootApplication` annotation marks the Application class in listing 2.2 as a configuration class, then begins auto-scanning all the classes on the Java class path for other Spring Beans.

The second thing to note is the Application class's `main()` method. In the `main()` method, the `SpringApplication.run(Application.class, args)`, the call starts the Spring container and returns a Spring `ApplicationContext` object. (You aren't doing anything with the `ApplicationContext`, so it isn't shown in the code.)

The easiest thing to remember about the `@SpringBootApplication` annotation and the corresponding `Application` class is that it's the bootstrap class for the entire microservice. Core initialization logic for the service should be placed in this class.

2.3.3   Building the doorway into the microservice: the Spring Boot controller

Now that you've gotten the build script out of the way and implemented a simple Spring Boot Bootstrap class, you can begin writing your first code that will do something. This code will be your `Controller` class. In a Spring boot application, a

`Controller` class exposes the services endpoints and maps the data from an incoming HTTP request to a Java method that will process the request.

Give it a REST

All the microservices in this book follow the REST approach to building your services. An in-depth discussion of REST is outside of the scope this book,[a] but for your purposes, all the services you build will have the following characteristics:

Use HTTP as the invocation protocol for the service—The service will be exposed via HTTP endpoint and will use the HTTP protocol to carry data to and from the services.

Map the behavior of the service to standard HTTP verbs—REST emphasizes having services map their behavior to the HTTP verbs of POST, GET, PUT, and DELETE verbs. These verbs map to the CRUD functions found in most services.

Use JSON as the serialization format for all data going to and from the service—This isn't a hard-and-fast principle for REST-based microservices, but JSON has become lingua franca for serializing data that's going to be submitted and returned by a microservice. XML can be used, but many REST-based applications make heavy use of JavaScript and JSON (JavaScript Object Notation). JSON is the native format for serializing and deserializing data being consumed by JavaScript-based web front-ends and services.

Use HTTP status codes to communicate the status of a service call—The HTTP protocol has developed a rich set of status codes to indicate the success or failure of a service. REST-based services take advantage of these HTTP status codes and other web-based infrastructure, such as reverse proxies and caches, which can be integrated with your microservices with relative ease.

HTTP is the language of the web and using HTTP as the philosophical framework for building your service is a key to building services in the cloud.

[a] Probably the most comprehensive coverage of the design of REST services is the book *REST in Practice* by Ian Robinson, et al (O'Reilly, 2010).

Your first controller class is located in `src/main/java/com/thoughtmechanix/licenses/controllers/LicenseServiceController.java`. This class will expose four HTTP endpoints that will map to the POST, GET, PUT, and DELETE verbs.

Let's walk through the controller class and look at how Spring Boot provides a set of annotations that keeps the effort needed to expose your service endpoints to a minimum and allows you to focus on building the business logic for the service. We'll start by looking at the basic controller class definition without any class methods in it yet. The following listing shows the controller class that you built for your licensing service.

Listing 2.3   Marking the `LicenseServiceController` as a Spring `RestController`

```
package com.thoughtmechanix.licenses.controllers;

import … // Removed for conciseness
```

```
@RestController
@RequestMapping(value="/v1/organizations/{organizationId}/licenses")
public class LicenseServiceController {
    //Body of the class removed for conciseness
}
```

@RestController tells Spring Boot this is a REST-based services and will automatically serialize/deserialize service request/response to JSON.

Exposes all the HTTP endpoints in this class with a prefix of /v1/organizations/{organizationID}/licenses

We'll begin our exploration by looking at the @RestController annotation. The @RestController is a class-level Java annotation and tells the Spring Container that this Java class is going to be used for a REST-based service. This annotation automatically handles the serialization of data passed into the services as JSON or XML (by default the @RestController class will serialize returned data into JSON). Unlike the traditional Spring @Controller annotation, the @RestController annotation doesn't require you as the developer to return a ResponseBody class from your controller class. This is all handled by the presence of the @RestController annotation, which includes the @ResponseBody annotation.

Why JSON for microservices?

Multiple protocols can be used to send data back and forth between HTTP-based microservices. JSON has emerged as the de facto standard for several reasons.

First, compared to other protocols such as the XML-based SOAP (Simple Object Access Protocol), it's extremely lightweight in that you can express your data without having much textual overhead.

Second, it's easily read and consumed by a human being. This is an underrated quality for choosing a serialization protocol. When a problem arises, it's critical for developers to look at a chunk of JSON and quickly, visually process what's in it. The simplicity of the protocol makes this incredibly easy to do.

Third, JSON is the default serialization protocol used in JavaScript. Since the dramatic rise of JavaScript as a programming language and the equally dramatic rise of Single Page Internet Applications (SPIA) that rely heavily on JavaScript, JSON has become a natural fit for building REST-based applications because it's what the front-end web clients use to call services.

Other mechanisms and protocols are more efficient than JSON for communicating between services. The Apache Thrift (http://thrift.apache.org) framework allows you to build multi-language services that can communicate with one another using a binary protocol. The Apache Avro protocol (http://avro.apache.org) is a data serialization protocol that converts data back and forth to a binary format between client and server calls.

If you need to minimize the size of the data you're sending across the wire, I recommend you look at these protocols. But it has been my experience that using straight-up JSON in your microservices works effectively and doesn't interpose another layer of communication to debug between your service consumers and service clients.

The second annotation shown in listing 2.3 is the @RequestMapping annotation. You can use the @RequestMapping annotation as a class-level and method-level annotation. The @RequestMapping annotation is used to tell the Spring container the HTTP endpoint that the service is going to expose to the world. When you use the class-level @RequestMapping annotation, you're establishing the root of the URL for all the other endpoints exposed by the controller.

In listing 2.3, the @RequestMapping(value="/v1/organizations/{organizationId}/licenses") uses the value attribute to establish the root of the URL for all endpoints exposed in the controller class. All service endpoints exposed in this controller will start with /v1/organizations/{organizationId}/licenses as the root of their endpoint. The {organizationId} is a placeholder that indicates how you expect the URL to be parameterized with an organizationId passed in every call. The use of organizationId in the URL allows you to differentiate between the different customers who might use your service.

Now you'll add the first method to your controller. This method will implement the GET verb used in a REST call and return a single License class instance, as shown in the following listing. (For purposes of this discussion you'll instantiate a Java class called License.)

Listing 2.4   Exposing an individual GET HTTP endpoint

> **Creates a GET endpoint with the value
> vl/organizations/{organizationId}/licenses{licenseId}**

```
@RequestMapping(value="/{licenseId}",method = RequestMethod.GET)      ⟵
public License getLicenses(
      @PathVariable("organizationId") String organizationId,
@PathVariable("licenseId")    String licenseId) {              ⟵
    return new License()
      .withId(licenseId)
      .withProductName("Teleco")           Maps two parameters from the
      .withLicenseType("Seat")             URL (organizationId and licenseId)
      .withOrganizationId("TestOrg");                to method parameters
}
```

The first thing you've done in this listing is annotate the getLicenses() method with a method level @RequestMapping annotation, passing in two parameters to the annotation: value and method. With a method-level @RequestMapping annotation, you're building on the root-level annotation specified at the top of the class to match all HTTP requests coming to the controller with the endpoint /v1/organizations/{organizationId}/licences/{licensedId}. The second parameter of the annotation, method, specifies the HTTP verb that the method will be matched on. In the previous example, you're matching on the GET method as represented by the RequestMethod.GET enumeration.

The second thing to note about listing 2.4 is that you use the @PathVariable annotation in the parameter body of the getLicenses() method. (2) The @PathVariable annotation is used to map the parameter values passed in the incoming URL (as denoted by the {parameterName} syntax) to the parameters of your method. In your code example from listing 2.4, you're mapping two parameters from the URL, organizationId and licenseId, to two parameter-level variables in the method:

```
@PathVariable("organizationId") String organizationId,
@PathVariable("licenseId")   String licenseId
```

Endpoint names matter

Before you get too far down the path of writing microservices, make sure that you (and potentially other teams in your organization) establish standards for the endpoints that will be exposed via your services. The URLs (Uniform Resource Locator) for the microservice should be used to clearly communicate the intent of the service, the resources the service manages, and the relationships that exist between the resources managed within the service. I've found the following guidelines useful for naming service endpoints:

1 *Use clear URL names that establish what resource the service represents*— Having a canonical format for defining URLs will help your API feel more intuitive and easier to use. Be consistent in your naming conventions.

2 *Use the URL to establish relationships between resources*—Oftentimes you'll have a parent-child relationship between resources within your microservices where the child doesn't exist outside the context of the parent (hence you might not have a separate microservice for the child). Use the URLs to express these relationships. But if you find that your URLs tend to be excessively long and nested, your microservice may be trying to do too much.

3 *Establish a versioning scheme for URLS early*—The URL and its corresponding endpoints represent a contract between the service owner and consumer of the service. One common pattern is to prepend all endpoints with a version number. Establish your versioning scheme early and stick to it. It's extremely difficult to retrofit versioning to URLS after you already have several consumers using them.

At this point you have something you can call as a service. From a command line window, go to your project directory where you've downloaded the sample code and execute the following Maven command:

```
mvn spring-boot:run
```

As soon as you hit the Return key, you should see Spring Boot launch an embedded Tomcat server and start listening on port 8080.

```
o.s.j.e.a.AnnotationMBeanExporter          : Registering beans for JMX exposure on startup
o.s.c.support.DefaultLifecycleProcessor    : Starting beans in phase 0
s.b.c.e.t.TomcatEmbeddedServletContainer   : Tomcat started on port(s): 8080 (http)
c.thoughtmechanix.licenses.Application     : Started Application in 3.465 seconds (JVM running for
```

The license server starting on port 8080

Figure 2.4   **The licensing service starting successfully**

Once the service is started, you can directly hit the exposed endpoint. Because your first method exposed is a GET call, you can use a number of methods for invoking the service. My preferred method is to use a chrome-based tool like POSTMAN or CURL for calling the service. Figure 2.5 shows a GET performed on the `http://local-host:8080/v1/organizations/e254f8c-c442-4ebe-a82a-e2fc1d1ff78a/licenses/f3831f8c-c338-4ebe-a82a-e2fc1d1ff78a` endpoint.

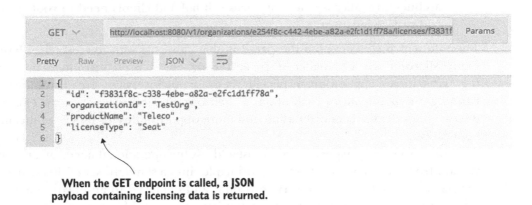

When the GET endpoint is called, a JSON
payload containing licensing data is returned.

Figure 2.5   Your licensing service being called with POSTMAN

At this point you have a running skeleton of a service. But from a development perspective, this service isn't complete. A good microservice design doesn't eschew segregating the service into well-defined business logic and data access layers. As you progress in later chapters, you'll continue to iterate on this service and delve further into how to structure it.

Let's switch to the final perspective: exploring how a DevOps engineer would operationalize the service and package it for deployment to the cloud.

2.4   *The DevOps story: building for the rigors of runtime*

For the DevOps engineer, the design of the microservice is all about managing the service after it goes into production. Writing the code is often the easy part. Keeping it running is the hard part.

While DevOps is a rich and emerging IT field, you'll start your microservice development effort with four principles and build on these principles later in the book. These principles are

1 A microservice should be *self-contained* and *independently deployable* with multiple instances of the service being started up and torn down with a single software artifact.

2 A microservice should be *configurable*. When a service instance starts up, it should read the data it needs to configure itself from a central location or have

its configuration information passed on as environment variables. No human intervention should be required to configure the service.

3   A microservice instance needs to be *transparent* to the client. The client should never know the exact location of a service. Instead, a microservice client should talk to a service discovery agent that will allow the application to locate an instance of a microservice without having to know its physical location.

4   A microservice should *communicate* its health. This is a critical part of your cloud architecture. Microservice instances will fail and clients need to route around bad service instances.

These four principles expose the paradox that can exist with microservice development. Microservices are smaller in size and scope, but their use introduces more moving parts in an application, especially because microservices are distributed and running independently of each other in their own distributed containers. This introduces a high degree of coordination and more opportunities for failure points in the application.

From a DevOps perspective, you must address the operational needs of a microservice up front and translate these four principles into a standard set of lifecycle events that occur every time a microservice is built and deployed to an environment. The four principles can be mapped to the following operational lifecycle steps:

- *Service assembly*—How do you package and deploy your service to guarantee repeatability and consistency so that the same service code and runtime is deployed exactly the same way?

- *Service bootstrapping*—How do you separate your application and environment-specific configuration code from the runtime code so you can start and deploy a microservice instance quickly in any environment without human intervention to configure the microservice?

- *Service registration/discovery*—When a new microservice instance is deployed, how do you make the new service instance discoverable by other application clients?

- *Service monitoring*—In a microservices environment it's extremely common for multiple instances of the same service to be running due to high availability needs. From a DevOps perspective, you need to monitor microservice instances and ensure that any faults in your microservice are routed around and that ailing service instances are taken down.

Figure 2.6 shows how these four steps fit together.

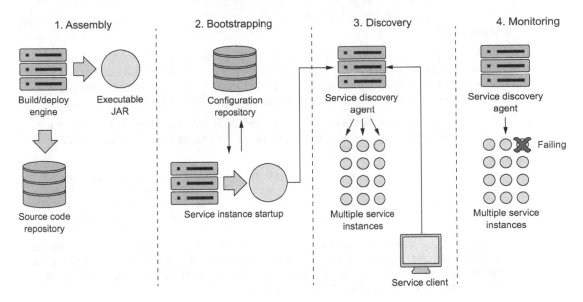

Figure 2.6   When a microservice starts up, it goes through multiple steps in its lifecycle.

Building the Twelve-Factor microservice service application

One of my biggest hopes with this book is that you realize that a successful microservice architecture requires strong application development and DevOps practices. One of the most succinct summaries of these practices can be found in Heroku's Twelve-Factor Application manifesto (https://12factor.net/). This document provides 12 best practices you should always keep in the back of your mind when building microservices. As you read this book, you'll see these practices intertwined into the examples. I've summarized them as follows:

Codebase—All application code and server provisioning information should be in version control. Each microservice should have its own independent code repository within the source control systems.

Dependencies—Explicitly declare the dependencies your application uses through build tools such as Maven (Java). Third-party JAR dependence should be declared using their specific version numbers. This allows your microservice to always be built using the same version of libraries.

Config—Store your application configuration (especially your environment-specific configuration) independently from your code. Your application configuration should never be in the same repository as your source code.

Backing services—Your microservice will often communicate over a network to a database or messaging system. When it does, you should ensure that at any time, you can swap out your implementation of the database from an in-house managed service to a third-party service. In chapter 10, we demonstrate this when you move your services away from a locally managed Postgres database to one managed by Amazon.

(continued)

Build, release, run—Keep your build, release, and run pieces of deploying your application completely separate. Once code is built, the developer should never make changes to the code at runtime. Any changes need to go back to the build process and be redeployed. A built service is immutable and cannot be changed.

Processes—Your microservices should always be stateless. They can be killed and replaced at any timeout without the fear that a loss-of-a-service instance will result in data loss.

Port binding—A microservice is completely self-contained with the runtime engine for the service packaged in the service executable. You should run the service without the need for a separated web or application server. The service should start by itself on the command line and be accessed immediately through an exposed HTTP port.

Concurrency—When you need to scale, don't rely on a threading model within a single service. Instead, launch more microservice instances and scale out horizontally. This doesn't preclude using threading within your microservice, but don't rely on it as your sole mechanism for scaling. Scale out, not up.

Disposability—Microservices are disposable and can be started and stopped on demand. Startup time should be minimized and processes should shut down gracefully when they receive a kill signal from the operating system.

Dev/prod parity—Minimize the gaps that exist between all of the environments in which the service runs (including the developer's desktop). A developer should use the same infrastructure locally for the service development in which the actual service will run. It also means that the amount of time that a service is deployed between environments should be hours, not weeks. As soon as code is committed, it should be tested and then promoted as quickly as possible from Dev all the way to Prod.

Logs—Logs are a stream of events. As logs are written out, they should be streamable to tools, such as Splunk (http://splunk.com) or Fluentd (http://fluentd.org), that will collate the logs and write them to a central location. The microservice should never be concerned about the mechanics of how this happens and the developer should visually look at the logs via STDOUT as they're being written out.

Admin processes—Developers will often have to do administrative tasks against their services (data migration or conversion). These tasks should never be ad hoc and instead should be done via scripts that are managed and maintained through the source code repository. These scripts should be repeatable and non-changing (the script code isn't modified for each environment) across each environment they're run against.

2.4.1   *Service assembly: packaging and deploying your microservices*

From a DevOps perspective, one of the key concepts behind a microservice architecture is that multiple instances of a microservice can be deployed quickly in response to a change application environment (for example, a sudden influx of user requests, problems within the infrastructure, and so on).

To accomplish this, a microservice needs to be packaged and installable as a single artifact with all of its dependencies defined within it. This artifact can then be deployed to any server with a Java JDK installed on it. These dependencies will also include the runtime engine (for example, an HTTP server or application container) that will host the microservice.

This process of consistently building, packaging, and deploying is the service assembly (step 1 in figure 2.6). Figure 2.7 shows additional details about the service assembly step.

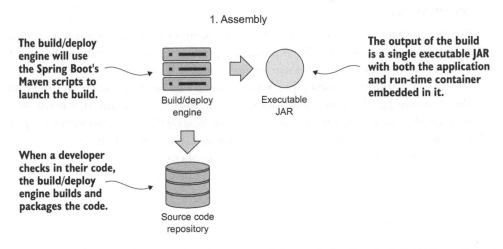

Figure 2.7 In the Service Assembly step, source code is compiled and packaged with its runtime engine.

Fortunately, almost all Java microservice frameworks will include a runtime engine that can be packaged and deployed with the code. For instance, in the Spring Boot example in figure 2.7, you can use Maven and Spring Boot to build an executable Java jar file that has an embedded Tomcat engine built right into the JAR. In the following command-line example, you're building the licensing service as an executable JAR and then starting the JAR file from the command-line:

```
mvn clean package && java –jar target/licensing-service-0.0.1-SNAPSHOT.jar
```

For certain operation teams, the concept of embedding a runtime environment right in the JAR file is a major shift in the way they think about deploying applications. In a traditional J2EE enterprise organization, an application is deployed to an application server. This model implies that the application server is an entity in and of itself and would often be managed by a team of system administrators who managed the configuration of the servers independently of the applications being deployed to them.

This separation of the application server configuration from the application introduces failure points in the deployment process, because in many organizations the configuration of the application servers isn't kept under source control and is managed through a combination of the user interface and home-grown management scripts. It's too easy for configuration drift to creep into the application server environment and suddenly cause what, on the surface, appear to be random outages.

The use of a single deployable artifact with the runtime engine embedded in the artifact eliminates many of these opportunities for configuration drift. It also allows you to put the whole artifact under source control and allows the application team to be able to better reason through how their application is built and deployed.

2.4.2   *Service bootstrapping: managing configuration of your microservices*

Service bootstrapping (step 2 in figure 2.6) occurs when the microservice is first starting up and needs to load its application configuration information. Figure 2.8 provides more context for the bootstrapping processing.

As any application developer knows, there will be times when you need to make the runtime behavior of the application configurable. Usually this involves reading your application configuration data from a property file deployed with the application or reading the data out of a data store such as a relational database.

Microservices often run into the same type of configuration requirements. The difference is that in microservice application running in the cloud, you might have

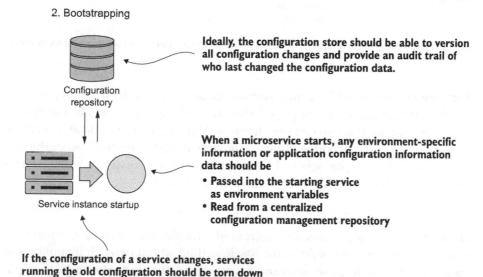

Figure 2.8   As a service starts (boot straps), its reads its configuration from a central repository.

hundreds or even thousands of microservice instances running. Further complicating this is that the services might be spread across the globe. With a high number of geographically dispersed services, it becomes unfeasible to redeploy your services to pick up new configuration data.

Storing the data in a data store external to the service solves this problem, but microservices in the cloud offer a set of unique challenges:

1 Configuration data tends to be simple in structure and is usually read frequently and written infrequently. Relational databases are overkill in this situation because they're designed to manage much more complicated data models than a simple set of key-value pairs.

2 Because the data is accessed on a regular basis but changes infrequently, the data must be readable with a low level of latency.

3 The data store has to be highly available and close to the services reading the data. A configuration data store can't go down completely, because it would become a single-point of failure for your application.

In chapter 3, I show how to manage your microservice application configuration data using things like a simple key-value data store.

2.4.3 Service registration and discovery: how clients communicate with your microservices

From a microservice consumer perspective, a microservice should be location-transparent, because in a cloud based environment, servers are ephemeral. Ephemeral means the servers that a service is hosted on usually have shorter lives than a service running in a corporate data center. Cloud-based services can be started and torn down quickly with an entirely new IP address assigned to the server on which the services are running.

By insisting that services are treated as short-lived disposable objects, microservice architectures can achieve a high-degree of scalability and availability by having multiple instances of a service running. Service demand and resiliency can be managed as quickly as the situation warrants. Each service has a unique and non-permanent IP address assigned to it. The downside to ephemeral services is that with services constantly coming up and down, managing a large pool of ephemeral services manually or by hand is an invitation to an outage.

A microservice instance needs to register itself with the third-party agent. This registration process is called service discovery (see step 3, service discovery, in figure 2.6; see figure 2.9 for details on this process). When a microservice instance registers with a service discovery agent, it will tell the discovery agent two things: the physical IP address or domain address of the service instance, and a logical name that an application can use to look up in a service. Certain service discovery agents will also require a

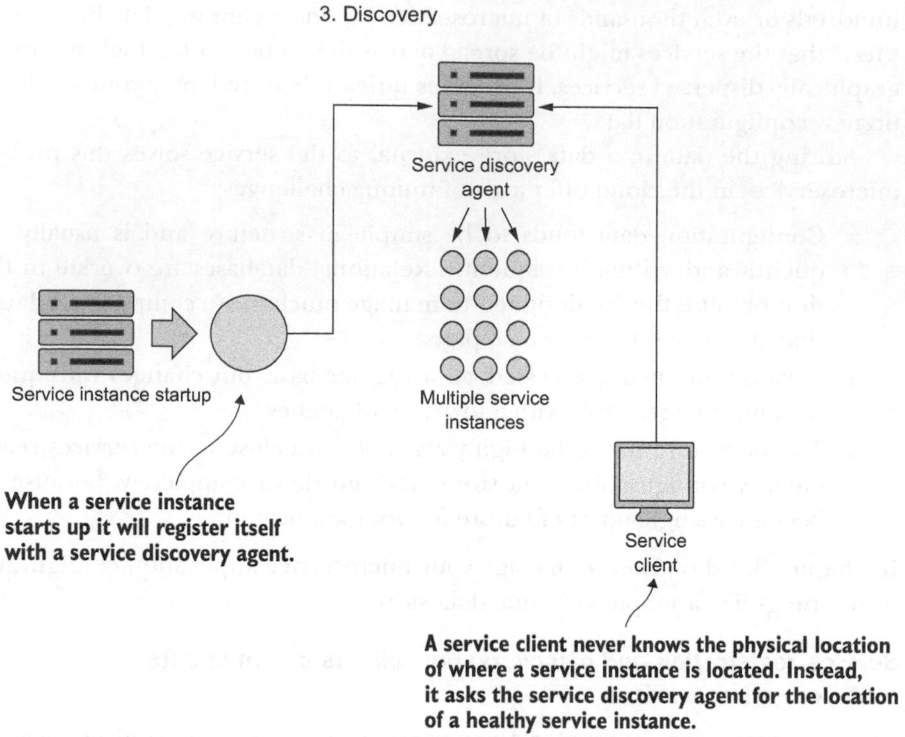

3. Discovery

Service discovery
agent

Service instance startup

Multiple service
instances

**When a service instance
starts up it will register itself
with a service discovery agent.**

Service
client

**A service client never knows the physical location
of where a service instance is located. Instead,
it asks the service discovery agent for the location
of a healthy service instance.**

Figure 2.9 A service discovery agent abstracts away the physical location of a service.

URL back to the registering service that can be used by the service discovery agent to perform health checks.

The service client then communicates with the discovery agent to look up the service's location.

2.4.4 Communicating a microservice's health

A service discovery agent doesn't act only as a traffic cop that guides the client to the location of the service. In a cloud-based microservice application, you'll often have multiple instances of a service running. Sooner or later, one of those service instances will fail. The service discovery agent monitors the health of each service instance registered with it and removes any service instances from its routing tables to ensure that clients aren't sent a service instance that has failed.

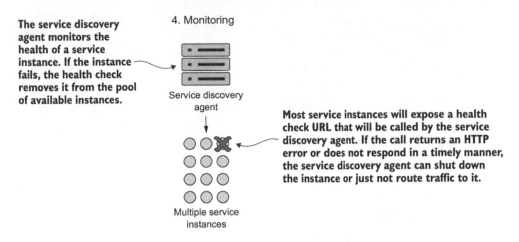

The service discovery agent monitors the health of a service instance. If the instance fails, the health check removes it from the pool of available instances.

4. Monitoring

Service discovery agent

Most service instances will expose a health check URL that will be called by the service discovery agent. If the call returns an HTTP error or does not respond in a timely manner, the service discovery agent can shut down the instance or just not route traffic to it.

Multiple service instances

Figure 2.10   The service discovery agent uses the exposes health URL to check microservice health.

After a microservice has come up, the service discovery agent will continue to monitor and ping the health check interface to ensure that that service is available. This is step 4 in figure 2.6. Figure 2.10 provides context for this step.

By building a consistent health check interface, you can use cloud-based monitoring tools to detect problems and respond to them appropriately.

If the service discovery agent discovers a problem with a service instance, it can take corrective action such as shutting down the ailing instance or bringing additional service instances up.

In a microservices environment that uses REST, the simplest way to build a health check interface is to expose an HTTP end-point that can return a JSON payload and HTTP status code. In a non-Spring-Boot-based microservice, it's often the developer's responsibility to write an endpoint that will return the health of the service.

In Spring Boot, exposing an endpoint is trivial and involves nothing more than modifying your Maven build file to include the Spring Actuator module. Spring Actuator provides out-of-the-box operational endpoints that will help you understand and manage the health of your service. To use Spring Actuator, you need to make sure you include the following dependencies in your Maven build file:

```
<dependency>
  <groupId>org.springframework.boot</groupId>
  <artifactId>spring-boot-starter-actuator</artifactId>
</dependency>
```

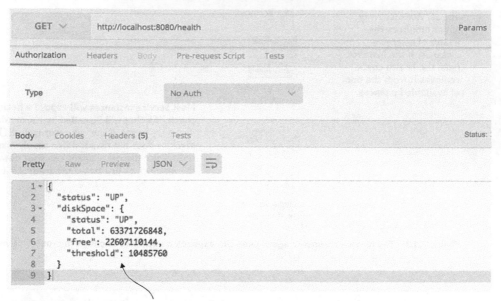

The "out of the box" Spring Boot health check will return whether the service is
up and some basic information like how much disk space is left on the server.

Figure 2.11   A health check on each service instance allows monitoring tools to determine if the
service instance is running.

If you hit the `http://localhost:8080/health` endpoint on the licensing service,
you should see health data returned. Figure 2.11 provides an example of the data
returned.

As you can see in figure 2.11, the health check can be more than an indicator of
what's up and down. It also can give information about the state of the server on
which the microservice instance is running. This allows for a much richer monitoring
experience.[1]

2.5   *Pulling the perspectives together*

Microservices in the cloud seem deceptively simple. But to be successful with them,
you need to have an integrated view that pulls the perspective of the architect, the
developer, and DevOps engineer together into a cohesive vision. The key takeaways
for each of these perspectives are

  1 *Architect*—Focus on the natural contours of your business problem. Describe
     your business problem domain and listen to the story you're telling. Target

---

[1]   Spring Boot offers a significant number of options for customizing your health check. For more details on
this, please check out the excellent book *Spring Boot in Action* (Manning Publications, 2015). Author Craig
Walls gives an exhaustive overview of all the different mechanisms for configuring Spring Boot Actuators.

microservice candidates will emerge. Remember, too, that it's better to start with a "coarse-grained" microservice and refactor back to smaller services than to start with a large group of small services. Microservice architectures, like most good architectures, are emergent and not preplanned to-the-minute.

2 *Software engineer*—The fact that the service is small doesn't mean good design principles get thrown out the window. Focus on building a layered service where each layer in the service has discrete responsibilities. Avoid the temptation to build frameworks in your code and try to make each microservice completely independent. Premature framework design and adoption can have massive maintenance costs later in the lifecycle of the application.

3 *DevOps engineer*—Services don't exist in a vacuum. Establish the lifecycle of your services early. The DevOps perspective needs to focus not only on how to automate the building and deployment of a service, but also on how to monitor the health of the service and react when something goes wrong. Operationalizing a service often takes more work and forethought than writing business logic.

2.6 Summary

- To be successful with microservices, you need to integrate in the architect's, software developer's, and DevOps' perspectives.
- Microservices, while a powerful architectural paradigm, have their benefits and tradeoffs. Not all applications should be microservice applications.
- From an architect's perspective, microservices are small, self-contained, and distributed. Microservices should have narrow boundaries and manage a small set of data.
- From a developer's perspective, microservices are typically built using a REST-style of design, with JSON as the payload for sending and receiving data from the service.
- Spring Boot is the ideal framework for building microservices because it lets you build a REST-based JSON service with a few simple annotations.
- From a DevOp's perspective, how a microservice is packaged, deployed, and monitored are of critical importance.
- Out of the box, Spring Boot allows you to deliver a service as a single executable JAR file. An embedded Tomcat server in the producer JAR file hosts the service.
- Spring Actuator, which is included with the Spring Boot framework, exposes information about the operational health of the service along with information about the services runtime.

Controlling your configuration with Spring Cloud configuration server

3

This chapter covers

- Separating service configuration from service code
- Configuring a Spring Cloud configuration server
- Integrating a Spring Boot microservice
- Encrypting sensitive properties

At one point or another, a developer will be forced to separate configuration information from their code. After all, it has been drilled into their heads since school that they shouldn't hard-code values into the application code. Many developers will use a constants class file in their application to help centralize all their configuration in one place. Application configuration data written directly into the code is often problematic because every time a change to the configuration has to be made the application has to be recompiled and/or redeployed. To avoid this, developers will separate the configuration information from the application code completely. This makes it easy to make changes to configuration without going through a recompile process, but also introduces complexity because you now have another artifact that needs to be managed and deployed with the application.

Many developers will turn to the lowly property file (or YAML, JSON, or XML) to store their configuration information. This property file will sit out on a server often containing database and middleware connection information and metadata about the application that will drive the application's behavior. Segregating your application into a property file is easy and most developers never do any more operationalization of their application configuration then placing their configuration file under source control (if that) and deploying it as part of their application.

This approach might work with a small number of applications, but it quickly falls apart when dealing with cloud-based applications that may contain hundreds of microservices, where each microservice in turn might have multiple service instances running.

Suddenly configuration management becomes a big deal as application and operations team in a cloud-based environment have to wrestle with a rat's nest of which configuration files go where. Cloud-based microservices development emphasizes

1 Completely separating the configuration of an application from the actual code being deployed
2 Building the server and the application and an immutable image that *never* changes as it's promoted through your environments
3 Injecting any application configuration information at startup time of the server through either environment variables or through a centralized repository the application's microservices read on startup

This chapter will introduce you to the core principles and patterns needed to manage application configuration data in a cloud-based microservice application.

3.1 On managing configuration (and complexity)

Managing application configuration is critical for microservices running in the cloud because microservice instances need to be launched quickly with minimal human intervention. Every time a human being needs to manually configure or touch a service to get it deployed is an opportunity for configuration drift, an unexpected outage and a lag-time in responding to scalability challenges with the application.

Let's begin our discussion about application configuration management by establishing four principles we want to follow:

1 *Segregate*—We want to completely separate the services configuration information from the actual physical deployment of a service. Application configuration shouldn't be deployed with the service instance. Instead, configuration information should either be passed to the starting service as environment variables or read from a centralized repository when the service starts.
2 *Abstract*—Abstract the access of the configuration data behind a service interface. Rather than writing code that directly accesses the service repository (that

is, read the data out of a file or a database using JDBC), have the application use a REST-based JSON service to retrieve the configuration data.

3   *Centralize*—Because a cloud-based application might literally have hundreds of services, it's critical to minimize the number of different repositories used to hold configuration information. Centralize your application configuration into as few repositories as possible.

4   *Harden*—Because your application configuration information is going to be completely segregated from your deployed service and centralized, it's critical that whatever solution you utilize can be implemented to be highly available and redundant.

One of the key things to remember is that when you separate your configuration information outside of your actual code, you're creating an external dependency that will need to be managed and version controlled. I can't emphasize enough that the application configuration data needs to be tracked and version-controlled because mismanaged application configuration is a fertile breeding ground for difficult-to-detect bugs and unplanned outages.

On accidental complexity

I've experienced firsthand the dangers of not having a strategy for managing your application configuration data. While working at a Fortune 500 financial services company, I was asked to help bring a large WebSphere upgrade project back on track. The company In question had more than 120 applications on WebSphere and needed to upgrade their infrastructure from WebSphere 6 to WebSphere 7 before the entire application environment went end-of-life in terms of maintenance by the vendor.

The project had already been going on for a year and had only one out of 120 applications deployed. The project had cost a million dollars of effort in people and hardware costs, and with its current trajectory was on track to take another two years to finish the upgrade.

When I started working with the application team, one (and just one) of the major problems I uncovered was that the application team managed all their configuration for their databases and the endpoints for their services inside of property files. These property files were managed by hand and weren't under source control. With 120 applications spread across four environments and multiple WebSphere nodes for each application, this rat's nest of configuration files led to the team trying to migrate 12,000 configuration files that were spread across hundreds of servers and applications running on the server. (You're reading that number right: 12,000.) These files were only for application configuration, not even application server configuration.

I convinced the project sponsor to take two months to consolidate all the application information down to a centralized, version-controlled configuration repository with 20 configuration files. When I asked the framework team how things got to the point where they had 12,000 configuration files, the lead engineer on the team said that originally they designed their configuration strategy around a small group of applications. However, the number of web applications built and deployed exploded over five years, and even though they begged for money and time to rework their configuration management approach, their business partners and IT leaders never considered it a priority.

Not spending the time up front to figure out how you're going to do configuration management can have real (and costly) downstream impacts.

3.1.1 Your configuration management architecture

As you'll remember from chapter 2, the loading of configuration management for a microservice occurs during the bootstrapping phase of the microservice. As a reminder, figure 3.1 shows the microservice lifecycle.

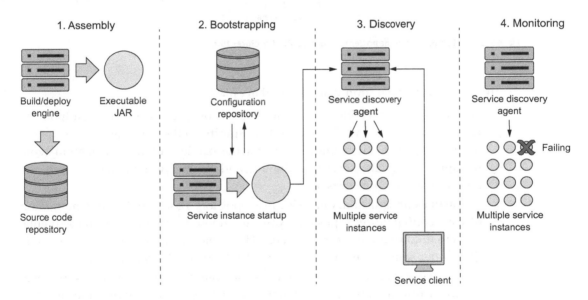

Figure 3.1 The application configuration data is read during the service bootstrapping phase.

Let's take the four principles we laid out earlier in section 3.1 (segregate, abstract, centralize, and harden) and see how these four principles apply when the service is bootstrapping. Figure 3.2 explores the bootstrapping process in more detail and shows how a configuration service plays a critical role in this step.

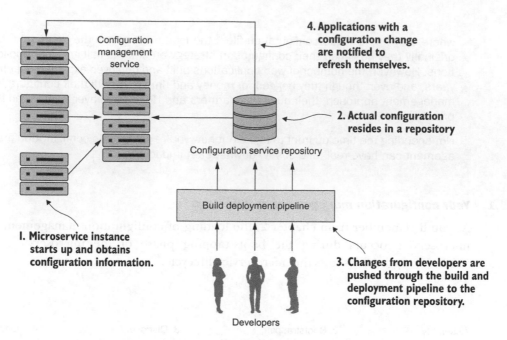

Figure 3.2   Configuration management conceptual architecture

In figure 3.2, you see several activities taking place:

1 When a microservice instance comes up, it's going to call a service endpoint to read its configuration information that's specific to the environment it's operating in. The connection information for the configuration management (connection credentials, service endpoint, and so on) will be passed into the microservice when it starts up.

2 The actual configuration will reside in a repository. Based on the implementation of your configuration repository, you can choose to use different implementations to hold your configuration data. The implementation choices can include files under source control, a relational database, or a key-value data store.

3 The actual management of the application configuration data occurs independently of how the application is deployed. Changes to configuration management are typically handled through the build and deployment pipeline where changes of the configuration can be tagged with version information and deployed through the different environments.

4 When a configuration management change is made, the services that use that application configuration data must be notified of the change and refresh their copy of the application data.

At this point we've worked through the conceptual architecture that illustrates the different pieces of a configuration management pattern and how these pieces fit together. We're now going to move on to look at the different solutions for the pattern and then see a concrete implementation.

3.1.2 Implementation choices

Fortunately, you can choose among a large number of battle-tested open source projects to implement a configuration management solution. Let's look at several of the different choices available and compare them. Table 3.1 lays out these choices.

Table 3.1   **Open source projects for implementing a configuration management system**

Project Name	Description	Characteristics
Etcd	Open source project written in Go. Used for service discovery and key-value management. Uses the raft (https://raft.github.io/) protocol for its distributed computing model.	Very fast and scalable Distributable Command-line driven Easy to use and setup
Eureka	Written by Netflix. Extremely battle-tested. Used for both service discovery and key-value management.	Distribute key-value store. Flexible; takes effort to set up Offers dynamic client refresh out of the box
Consul	Written by Hashicorp. Similar to Etcd and Eureka in features, but uses a different algorithm for its distributed computing model (SWIM protocol; https://www.cs.cornell.edu/~asdas/research/dsn02-swim.pdf).	Fast Offers native service discovery with the option to integrate directly with DNS Doesn't offer client dynamic refresh right out of the box
ZooKeeper	An Apache project that offers distributed locking capabilities. Often used as a configuration management solution for accessing key-value data.	Oldest, most battle-tested of the solutions The most complex to use Can be used for configuration management, but should be considered only if you're already using ZooKeeper in other pieces of your architecture
Spring Cloud configuration server	An open source project that offers a general configuration management solution with different back ends. It can integrate with Git, Eureka, and Consul as a back end.	Non-distributed key/value store Offers tight integration for Spring and non-Spring services Can use multiple back ends for storying configuration data including a shared filesystem, Eureka, Consul, and Git

All the solutions in table 3.1 can easily be used to build a configuration management solution. For the examples in this chapter and throughout the rest of the book, you'll use Spring Cloud configuration server. I chose this solution for several reasons, including the following:

1. Spring Cloud configuration server is easy to set up and use.
2. Spring Cloud configuration integrates tightly with Spring Boot. You can literally read all your application's configuration data with a few simple-to-use annotations.

3   Spring Cloud configuration server offers multiple back ends for storing configuration data. If you're already using tools such as Eureka and Consul, you can plug them right into Spring Cloud configuration server.

4   Of all the solutions in table 3.1, Spring Cloud configuration server can integrate directly with the Git source control platform. Spring Cloud configuration's integration with Git eliminates an extra dependency in your solutions and makes versioning your application configuration data a snap.

   The other tools (Etcd, Consul, Eureka) don't offer any kind of native versioning, and if you wanted that, you'd have to build it yourself. If your shop uses Git, the use of Spring Cloud configuration server is an attractive option.

For the rest of this chapter, you're going to

1   Set up a Spring Cloud configuration server and demonstrate two different mechanisms for serving application configuration data—one using the filesystem and another using a Git repository

2   Continue to build out the licensing service to retrieve data from a database

3   Hook the Spring Cloud configuration service into your licensing service to serve up application configuration data

3.2   *Building our Spring Cloud configuration server*

The Spring Cloud configuration server is a REST-based application that's built on top of Spring Boot. It doesn't come as a standalone server. Instead, you can choose to either embed it in an existing Spring Boot application or start a new Spring Boot project with the server embedded it.

The first thing you need to do is set up a new project directory called confsvr. Inside the consvr directory you'll create a new Maven file that will be used to pull down the JARs necessary to start up on your Spring Cloud configuration server. Rather than walk through the entire Maven file, I'll list the key parts in the following listing.

Listing 3.1   Setting up the pom.xml for the Spring Cloud configuration server

```
<?xml version="1.0" encoding="UTF-8"?>
<project xmlns="http://maven.apache.org/POM/4.0.0" xmlns:xsi="http://
    www.w3.org/2001/XMLSchema-instance"
        xsi:schemaLocation="http://maven.apache.org/POM/4.0.0 http://
    maven.apache.org/xsd/maven-4.0.0.xsd">
<modelVersion>4.0.0</modelVersion>

<groupId>com.thoughtmechanix</groupId>
<artifactId>configurationserver</artifactId>
<version>0.0.1-SNAPSHOT</version>
<packaging>jar</packaging>

<name>Config Server</name>
<description>Config Server demo project</description>
```

```
<parent>
    <groupId>org.springframework.boot</groupId>
    <artifactId>spring-boot-starter-parent</artifactId>
    <version>1.4.4.RELEASE</version>              ◄─── The Spring Boot
</parent>                                               version you'll use
<dependencyManagement>
    <dependencies>
      <dependency>
        <groupId>org.springframework.cloud</groupId>
        <artifactId>spring-cloud-dependencies</artifactId>
        <version>Camden.SR5</version>            ◄─── The Spring Cloud version
        <type>pom</type>                              that's going to be used
        <scope>import</scope>
      </dependency>
    </dependencies>                                    The bootstrap class
</dependencyManagement>                                 that will be used for
                                                       the configuration server
    <properties>
      <project.build.sourceEncoding>UTF-8</project.build.sourceEncoding>
      <start-class>com.thoughtmechanix.confsvr.
      ➡ConfigServerApplication </start-class>    ◄───
      <java.version>1.8</java.version>
      <docker.image.name>johncarnell/tmx-confsvr</docker.image.name>
      <docker.image.tag>chapter3</docker.image.tag>
    </properties>

    <dependencies>
      <dependency>
        <groupId>org.springframework.cloud</groupId>    ◄───
        <artifactId>spring-cloud-starter-config</artifactId>  The Spring Cloud
      </dependency>                                            projects you're
                                                               going to use in
      <dependency>                                             this specific service
        <groupId>org.springframework.cloud</groupId>    ◄───
        <artifactId>spring-cloud-config-server</artifactId>
      </dependency>
    </dependencies>

<!--Docker build Config  Not Displayed -->
</project>
```

In the Maven file in this previous listing, you start out by declaring the version of Spring Boot you're going to use for your microservice (version 1.4.4). The next important part of the Maven definition is the Spring Cloud Configuration parent BOM (Bill of Materials) that you're going to use. Spring Cloud is a massive collection of independent projects all moving with their own releases. This parent BOM contains all the third-party libraries and dependencies that are used in the cloud project and the version numbers of the individual projects that make up that version. In this example, you're using version Camden.SR5 of Spring Cloud. By using the BOM definition, you can guarantee that you're using compatible versions of the subprojects in Spring Cloud. It also means that you don't have to declare version numbers for your sub-dependencies. The rest of the example in listing 3.1 deals with declaring the specific Spring Cloud dependencies that you'll use in the service. The first dependency is the `spring-cloud-starter-config` dependency that's used by all Spring Cloud projects. The second dependency is the `spring-cloud-config-server` starter project. This contains the core libraries for the spring-cloud-config-server.

Come on, ride the train, the release train

Spring Cloud uses a non-traditional mechanism for labeling Maven projects. Spring Cloud is a collection of independent subprojects. The Spring Cloud team does their releases through what they call the "release train." All the subprojects that make up Spring Cloud are packaged under one Maven bill of materials (BOM) and released as a whole. The Spring Cloud team has been using the name of London subway stops as the name of their releases, with each incrementing major release giving a London subway stop that has the next highest letter. There have been three releases: Angel, Brixton, and Camden. Camden is by far the newest release, but still has multiple release candidate branches for the subprojects within it.

One thing to note is that Spring Boot is released independently of the Spring Cloud release train. Therefore, different versions of Spring Boot are incompatible with different releases of Spring Cloud. You can see the version dependences between Spring Boot and Spring Cloud, along with the different subproject versions contained within the release train, by referring to the Spring Cloud website (http://projects .spring.io/spring-cloud/).

You still need to set up one more file to get the core configuration server up and running. This file is your application.yml file and is in the confsvr/src/main/resources directory. The application.yml file will tell your Spring Cloud configuration service what port to listen to and where to locate the back end that will serve up the configuration data.

You're almost ready to bring up your Spring Cloud configuration service. You need to point the server to a back-end repository that will hold your configuration data. For this chapter, you'll use the licensing service that you began to build in chapter 2 as an example of how to use Spring Cloud Config. To keep things simple, you'll set up application configuration data for three environments: a default environment for when you run the service locally, a dev environment, and a production environment.

In Spring Cloud configuration, everything works off a hierarchy. Your application configuration is represented by the name of the application and then a property file for each environment you want to have configuration information for. In each of these environments, you'll set up two configuration properties:

- An example property that will be used directly by your licensing service
- The database configuration for the Postgres database you'll use to store licensing service data

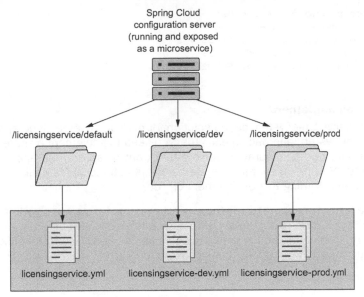

Spring Cloud
configuration server
(running and exposed
as a microservice)

/licensingservice/default   /licensingservice/dev   /licensingservice/prod

licensingservice.yml   licensingservice-dev.yml   licensingservice-prod.yml

Configuration repository (filesystem or git)

**Figure 3.3   Spring Cloud
configuration exposes
environment-specific
properties as HTTP-based
endpoints.**

Figure 3.3 illustrates how you'll set up and use the Spring Cloud configuration service. One thing to note is that as you build out your config service, it will be another microservice running in your environment. Once it's set up, the contents of the service can be access via a http-based REST endpoint.

The naming convention for the application configuration files are *appname-env*.yml. As you can see from the diagram in figure 3.3, the environment names translate directly into the URLs that will be accessed to browse configuration information. Later, when you start the licensing microservice example, the environment you want to run the service against is specified by the Spring Boot profile that you pass in on the command-line service startup. If a profile isn't passed in on the command line, Spring Boot will always default to the configuration data contained in the application.yml file packaged with the application.

Here's an example of some of the application configuration data you'll serve up for the licensing service. This is the data that will be contained within the confsvr/src/main/resources/config/licensingservice/licensingservice.yml file that was referred to in figure 3.3. Here's part of the contents of this file:

```
tracer.property: "I AM THE DEFAULT"
spring.jpa.database: "POSTGRESQL"
spring.datasource.platform:  "postgres"
spring.jpa.show-sql: "true"
spring.database.driverClassName: "org.postgresql.Driver"
spring.datasource.url: "jdbc:postgresql://database:5432/eagle_eye_local"
spring.datasource.username: "postgres"
```

```
spring.datasource.password: "p0stgr@s"
spring.datasource.testWhileIdle: "true"
spring.datasource.validationQuery: "SELECT 1"
spring.jpa.properties.hibernate.dialect:
    "org.hibernate.dialect.PostgreSQLDialect"
```

Think before you implement

I advise against using a filesystem-based solution for medium-to-large cloud applications. Using the filesystem approach means that you need to implement a shared file mount point for all cloud configuration servers that want to access the application configuration data. Setting up shared filesystem servers in the cloud is doable, but it puts the onus of maintaining this environment on you.

I'm showing the filesystem approach as the easiest example to use when getting your feet wet with Spring Cloud configuration server. In a later section, I'll show how to configure Spring Cloud configuration server to use a cloud-based Git provider like Bitbucket or GitHub to store your application configuration.

3.2.1   Setting up the Spring Cloud Config Bootstrap class

Every Spring Cloud service covered in this book always needs a bootstrap class that will be used to launch the service. This bootstrap class will contain two things: a Java `main()` method that acts as the entry point for the Service to start in, and a set of Spring Cloud annotations that tell the starting service what kind of Spring Cloud behaviors it's going to launch for the service.

The following listing shows the `confsvr/src/main/java/com/thought mechanix/confsvr/Application.java` class that's used as the bootstrap class for your configuration service.

Listing 3.2   The bootstrap class for your Spring Cloud Config server

Your Spring Cloud Config service is a Spring Boot Application, so you mark it with @SpringBootApplication.

```
package com.thoughtmechanix.confsvr;

import org.springframework.boot.SpringApplication;
import org.springframework.boot.autoconfigure.SpringBootApplication;
import org.springframework.cloud.config.server.EnableConfigServer;

@SpringBootApplication
@EnableConfigServer
public class ConfigServerApplication {
    public static void main(String[] args) {
            SpringApplication.run(ConfigServerApplication.class, args);
    }
}
```

The main method launches the service and starts the Spring container.

The @EnableConfigServer annotation enables the service as a Spring Cloud Config service.

Next you'll set up your Spring Cloud configuration server with our simplest example: the filesystem.

3.2.2 *Using Spring Cloud configuration server with the filesystem*

The Spring Cloud configuration server uses an entry in the confsvr/src/main/resources/application.yml file to point to the repository that will hold the application configuration data. Setting up a filesystem-based repository is the easiest way to accomplish this.

To do this, add the following information to the configuration server's application.yml file. The following listing shows the contents of your Spring Cloud configuration server's application.yml file.

Listing 3.3   Spring Cloud configuration's application.yml file

```
server:
   port: 8888                          <--- Port the Spring Cloud configuration
spring:                                     server will listen on
  profiles:
    active: native                        <--- The backend repository (filesystem) that
  cloud:                                       will be used to store the configuration
     config:
       server:
          native:
             searchLocations: file:///Users/johncarnell1/book/
             native_cloud_apps/ch4-config-managment/confsvr/src/main/
             resources/config/licensingservice
```

The path to where the configuration files are stored

In the configuration file in this listing, you started by telling the configuration server what port number it should listen to for all requests for configuration:

```
server:
   port: 8888
```

Because you're using the filesystem for storing application configuration information, you need to tell Spring Cloud configuration server to run with the "native" profile:

```
profiles:
   active: native
```

The last piece in the application.yml file provides Spring Cloud configuration with the directory where the application data resides:

```
server:
   native:
      searchLocations: file:///Users/johncarnell1/book/spmia_code/chapter3-
      code/confsvr/src/main/resources/config
```

The important parameter in the configuration entry is the searchLocations attribute. This attribute provides a comma separated list of the directories for each application that's going to have properties managed by the configuration server. In the previous example, you only have the licensing service configured.

NOTE   Be aware that if you use the local filesystem version of Spring Cloud Config, you'll need to modify the `spring.cloud.config.server` `.native.searchLocations` attribute to reflect your local file path when running your code locally.

You now have enough work done to start the configuration server. Go ahead and start the configuration server using the `mvn spring-boot:run` command. The server should now come up with the Spring Boot splash screen on the command line. If you point your browser over to http://localhost:8888/licensingservice/default, you'll see JSON payload being returned with all of properties contained within the licensingservice.yml file. Figure 3.4 shows the results of calling this endpoint.

```
{
  "name": "licensingservice",
  "profiles": [
    "default"
  ],
  "label": "master",
  "version": "8b20dd9432ef9ef08216a5775859afb24a5e7d43",
  "propertySources": [
    {
      "name": "https://github.com/carnellj/config-repo/licensingservice/licensingservice.yml",
      "source": {
        "example.property": "I AM IN THE DEFAULT",
        "spring.jpa.database": "POSTGRESQL",
        "spring.datasource.platform": "postgres",
        "spring.jpa.show-sql": "true",
        "spring.database.driverClassName": "org.postgresql.Driver",
        "spring.datasource.url": "jdbc:postgresql://database:5432/eagle_eye_local",
        "spring.datasource.username": "postgres",
        "spring.datasource.password": "{cipher}4788dfe1ccbe6485934aec2ffeddb06163ea3d616df5fd75be96aadd4df1da91",
        "spring.datasource.testWhileIdle": "true",
        "spring.datasource.validationQuery": "SELECT 1",
        "spring.jpa.properties.hibernate.dialect": "org.hibernate.dialect.PostgreSQLDialect",
        "redis.server": "redis",
        "redis.port": "6379",
        "signing.key": "345345fsdfsf5345"
      }
    }
  ]
}
```

The source file containing the properties in the config repository

Figure 3.4   Retrieving default configuration information for the licensing service

If you want to see the configuration information for the dev-based licensing service environment, hit the GET http://localhost:8888/licensingservice/dev endpoint. Figure 3.5 shows the result of calling this endpoint.

If you look closely, you'll see that when you hit the dev endpoint, you're returning back both the default configuration properties for the licensing service and the dev licensing service configuration. The reason why Spring Cloud configuration is returning both sets of configuration information is that the Spring framework implements a hierarchical mechanism for resolving properties. When the Spring Framework does

```
"propertySources": [
  {
    "name": "https://github.com/carnellj/config-repo/licensingservice/licensingservice-dev.yml",
    "source": {
      "spring.jpa.database": "POSTGRESQL",
      "spring.datasource.platform": "postgres",
      "spring.jpa.show-sql": "true",
      "spring.database.driverClassName": "org.postgresql.Driver",
      "spring.datasource.url": "jdbc:postgresql://database:5432/eagle_eye_dev",
      "spring.datasource.username": "postgres_dev",
      "spring.datasource.password": "{cipher}d495ce8603af958b2526967648aa9620b7e834c4eaff66014aa805450736e119",
      "spring.datasource.testWhileIdle": "true",
      "spring.datasource.validationQuery": "SELECT 1",
      "spring.jpa.properties.hibernate.dialect": "org.hibernate.dialect.PostgreSQLDialect",
      "redis.server": "redis",
      "redis.port": "6379",
      "signing.key": "345345fsdfsf5345"
    }
  },
  {
    "name": "https://github.com/carnellj/config-repo/licensingservice/licensingservice.yml",
    "source": {
      "example.property": "I AM IN THE DEFAULT",
      "spring.jpa.database": "POSTGRESQL",
      "spring.datasource.platform": "postgres",
      "spring.jpa.show-sql": "true",
```

When you request an environment-specific profile, both the requested profile and the default profile are returned.

Figure 3.5 Retrieving configuration information for the licensing service using the dev profile

property resolution, it will always look for the property in the default properties first and then override the default with an environment-specific value if one is present.

In concrete terms, if you define a property in the licensingservice.yml file and don't define it in any of the other environment configuration files (for example, the licensingservice-dev.yml), the Spring framework will use the default value.

NOTE This isn't the behavior you'll see by directly calling the Spring Cloud configuration REST endpoint. The REST endpoint will return all configuration values for both the default and environment specific value that was called.

Let's see how you can hook up the Spring Cloud configuration server to your licensing microservice.

3.3 *Integrating Spring Cloud Config with a Spring Boot client*

In the previous chapter, you built a simple skeleton of your licensing service that did nothing more than return a hardcoded Java object representing a single licensing record from your database. In the next example, you'll build out the licensing service and talk to a Postgres database holding your licensing data.

You're going to communicate with the database using Spring Data and map your data from the licensing table to a POJO holding the data. Your database connection

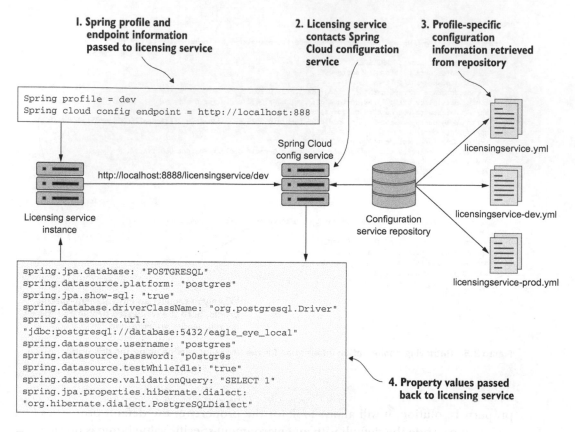

Figure 3.6   Retrieving configuration information using the dev profile

and a simple property are going to be read out of Spring Cloud configuration server. Figure 3.6 shows what's going to happen between the licensing service and the Spring Cloud configuration service.

When the licensing service is first started, you'll pass it via the command line two pieces of information: the Spring profile and the endpoint the licensing service should use to communicate with the Spring Cloud configuration service. The Spring profile value maps to the environment of the properties being retrieved for the Spring service. When the licensing service first boots up, it will contact the Spring Cloud Config service via an endpoint built from the Spring profile passed into it. The Spring Cloud Config service will then use the configured back end config repository (filesystem, Git, Consul, Eureka) to retrieve the configuration information specific to the Spring profile value passed in on the URI. The appropriate property values are then passed back to the licensing service. The Spring Boot framework will then inject these values into the appropriate parts of the application.

3.3.1 Setting up the licensing service Spring Cloud Config server dependencies

Let's change our focus from the configuration server to the licensing service. The first thing you need to do is add a couple of more entries to the Maven file in your licensing service. The entries that need to be added are shown in the following listing.

Listing 3.4 Additional Maven dependencies needed by the licensing service

```
<dependency>
  <groupId>org.springframework.boot</groupId>
  <artifactId>spring-boot-starter-data-jpa</artifactId>
</dependency>
```

Tells Spring Boot you're going to use Java Persistence API (JPA) in your service

```
<dependency>
  <groupId>postgresql</groupId>
  <artifactId>postgresql</artifactId>
  <version>9.1-901.jdbc4</version>
</dependency>
```

Tells Spring Boot to pull down the Postgres JDBC drivers

```
<dependency>
  <groupId>org.springframework.cloud</groupId>
  <artifactId>spring-cloud-config-client</artifactId>
</dependency>
```

Tells Spring Boot that you should pull down the dependencies need for the Spring Cloud Config client

The first and second dependencies, `spring-boot-starter-data-jpa` and Post-greSQL, import the Spring Data Java Persistence API (JPA) and the Postgres JDBC drivers. The last dependency, the `spring-cloud-config-client`, contains all the classes needed to interact with the Spring Cloud configuration server.

3.3.2 Configuring the licensing service to use Spring Cloud Config

After the Maven dependencies have been defined, you need to tell the licensing service where to contact the Spring Cloud configuration server. In a Spring Boot service that uses Spring Cloud Config, configuration information can be set in one of two configuration files: `bootstrap.yml` and `application.yml`.

The `bootstrap.yml` file reads the application properties before any other configuration information used. In general, the `bootstrap.yml` file contains the application name for the service, the application profile, and the URI to connect to a Spring Cloud Config server. Any other configuration information that you want to keep local to the service (and not stored in Spring Cloud Config) can be set locally in the services in the `application.yml` file. Usually, the information you store in the `application.yml` file is configuration data that you might want to have available to a service even if the Spring Cloud Config service is unavailable. Both the `bootstrap.yml` and `application.yml` files are stored in a projects `src/main/resources` directory.

To have the licensing service communicate with your Spring Cloud Config service, you need to add a licensing-service/src/main/resources/bootstrap.yml file and set three properties: `spring.application.name`, `spring.profiles.active`, and `spring.cloud.config.uri`.

The licensing services `bootstrap.yml` file is shown in the following listing.

Listing 3.5   Configuring the licensing services bootstrap.yml

```
spring:
 application:
   name: licensingservice        ◄─── Specify the name of the licensing service
 profiles:                            so that Spring Cloud Config client knows
   active:                            which service is being looked up.
     default            ◄─── Specify the default profile the service
 cloud:                        should run. Profile maps to environment.
   config:
     uri: http://localhost:8888    ◄─── Specify the location of the
                                        Spring Cloud Config server.
```

NOTE   The Spring Boot applications support two mechanisms to define a property: YAML (YAML Ain't Markup Language) and a "." separated property name. We chose YAML as the means for configuring our application. The hierarchical format of YAML property values map directly to the `spring.application.name`, `spring.profiles.active`, and `spring.cloud.config.uri` names.

The `spring.application.name` is the name of your application (for example, licensingservice) and *must* map directly to the name of the directory within your Spring Cloud configuration server. For the licensing service, you want a directory on the Spring Cloud configuration server called licensingservice.

The second property, the `spring.profiles.active`, is used to tell Spring Boot what profile the application should run as. A *profile* is a mechanism to differentiate the configuration data consumed by the Spring Boot application. For the licensing service's profile, you'll support the environment the service is going to map directly to in your cloud configuration environment. For instance, by passing in dev as our profile, the Spring Cloud config server will use the dev properties. If you don't set a profile, the licensing service will use the default profile.

The third and last property, the `spring.cloud.config.uri`, is the location where the licensing service should look for the Spring Cloud configuration server endpoint. By default, the licensing service will look for the configuration server at http://localhost:8888. Later in the chapter you'll see how to override the different properties defined in the bootstrap.yml and application.yml files on application startup. This will allow you to tell the licensing microservice which environment it should be running in.

Now, if you bring up the Spring Cloud configuration service, with the corresponding Postgres database running on your local machine, you can launch the licensing service using its default profile. This is done by changing to the licensing-services directory and issuing the following commands:

```
mvn spring-boot: run
```

By running this command without any properties set, the licensing server will automatically attempt to connect to the Spring Cloud configuration server using the endpoint (http://localhost:8888) and the active profile (default) defined in the bootstrap.yml file of the licensing service.

If you want to override these default values and point to another environment, you can do this by compiling the `licensingservice` project down to a JAR and then run the JAR with a `-D` system property override. The following command line call demonstrates how to launch the licensing service with a non-default profile:

```
java  -Dspring.cloud.config.uri=http://localhost:8888 \
      -Dspring.profiles.active=dev \
      -jar target/licensing-service-0.0.1-SNAPSHOT.jar
```

With the previous command line, you're overriding the two parameters: `spring.cloud.config.uri` and `spring.profiles.active`. With the `-Dspring.cloud.config.uri=http://localhost:8888` system property, you're pointing to a configuration server running away from your local box.

> **NOTE** If you try to run the licensing service downloaded from the GitHub repository (https://github.com/carnellj/spmia-chapter3) from your desktop using the previous Java command, it will fail because you don't have a desktop Postgres server running and the source code in the GitHub repository is using encryption on the config server. We'll cover using encryption later in the chapter. The previous example demonstrates how to override Spring properties via the command line.

With the `-Dspring.profiles.active=dev` system property, you're telling the licensing service to use the dev profile (read from the configuration server) to connect to a dev instance of a database.

Use environment variables to pass startup information

In the examples you're hard-coding the values to pass in to the –D parameter values. In the cloud, most of the application config data you need will be in your configuration server. However, for the information you need to start your service (such as the data for the configuration server), you'd start the VM instance or Docker container and pass in an environment variable.

All the code examples for each chapter can be completely run from within Docker containers. With Docker, you simulate different environments through environment-specific Docker-compose files that orchestrate the startup of all of your services. Environment-specific values needed by the containers are passed in as environment

(continued)

variables to the container. For example, to start your licensing service in a dev environment, the docker/dev/docker-compose.yml file contains the following entry for the licensing-service:

```
licensingservice:
    image: ch3-thoughtmechanix/licensing-service
    ports:
      - "8080:8080"
    environment:
      PROFILE: "dev"
      CONFIGSERVER_URI: http://configserver:8888
      CONFIGSERVER_PORT: "8888"
      DATABASESERVER_PORT: "5432"
```

Specifies the start of the environment variables for the licensing-service container

The PROFILE environment variable is passed to the Spring Boot service command-line and tells Spring Boot what profile should be run.

The endpoint of the config service

The environment entry in the file contains the values of two variables PROFILE, which is the Spring Boot profile the licensing service is going to run under. The CONFIGSERVER_URI is passed to your licensing service and defines the Spring Cloud configuration server instance the service is going to read its configuration data from.

In your startup scripts that are run by the container, you then pass these environment variables as –D parameters to our JVMS starting the application. In each project, you bake a Docker container, and that Docker container uses a startup script that starts the software in the container. For the licensing service, the startup script that gets baked into the container can be found at licensing-service/src/main/docker/run.sh. In the run.sh script, the following entry starts your licensing-service JVM:

```
echo "*********************************************************"
echo "Starting License Server with Configuration Service :
    $CONFIGSERVER_URI";
echo "*********************************************************"
java -Dspring.cloud.config.uri=$CONFIGSERVER_URI
-Dspring.profiles.active=$PROFILE -jar /usr/local/licensingservice/
    licensing-service-0.0.1-SNAPSHOT.jar
```

Because you enhance all your services with introspection capabilities via Spring Boot Actuator, you can confirm the environment you are running against by hitting http://localhost:8080/env. The /env endpoint will provide a complete list of the configuration information about the service, including the properties and endpoints the service has booted with, as shown in figure 3.7.

The key thing to note from figure 3.7 is that the active profile for the licensing service is dev. By inspecting the returned JSON, you can also see that the Postgres database being returned is a development URI of jdbc:postgresql://database:5432/eagle_eye_dev.

```
{
  "profiles": [
    "default"
  ],
  "server.ports": {
    "local.server.port": 8080
  },
  "decrypted": {
    "spring.datasource.password": "******"
  },
  "configService:configClient": {
    "config.client.version": "8907411ed638d7a66e2ae4142f83671425f4113f"
  },
  "configService:https://github.com/carnellj/config-repo/licensingservice/licensingservice.yml": {
    "example.property": "I AM IN THE DEFAULT",
    "spring.jpa.database": "POSTGRESQL",
    "spring.datasource.platform": "postgres",
    "spring.jpa.show-sql": "true",|
    "spring.database.driverClassName": "org.postgresql.Driver",
    "spring.datasource.url": "jdbc:postgresql://database:5432/eagle_eye_dev",
    "spring.datasource.username": "postgres",
    "spring.datasource.password": "******",
    "spring.datasource.testWhileIdle": "true",
    "spring.datasource.validationQuery": "SELECT 1",
    "spring.jpa.properties.hibernate.dialect": "org.hibernate.dialect.PostgreSQLDialect",
    "redis.server": "redis",
    "redis.port": "6379",
    "signing.key": "******"
  },
}
```

Figure 3.7 The configuration the licensing service loads can be checked by calling the
`/env` **endpoint.**

On exposing too much information

Every organization is going to have different rules about how to implement security around their services. Many organizations believe services shouldn't broadcast any information about themselves and won't allow things like a `/env` endpoint to be active on a service as they believe (rightfully so) that this will provide too much information for a potential hacker. Spring Boot provides a wealth of capabilities on how to configure what information is returned by the Spring Actuators endpoints that are the outside the scope of this book. Craig Walls' excellent book, *Spring Boot in Action*, covers this subject in detail, and I highly recommend that you review your corporate security policies and Walls' book to provide the right level of detail you want exposed through Spring Actuator.

3.3.3 *Wiring in a data source using Spring Cloud configuration server*

At this point, you have the database configuration information being directly injected into your microservice. With the database configuration set, configuring your licensing microservice becomes an exercise in using standard Spring components to build and retrieve the data from the Postgres database. The licensing service has been refactored into different classes with each class having separate responsibilities. These classes are shown in table 3.2.

Table 3.2   Licensing Service Classes and Locations

Class Name	Location
License	licensing-service/src/main/java/com/thoughtmechanix/licenses/model
LicenseRepository	licensing-service/src/main/java/com/thoughtmechanix/licenses/repository
LicenseService	licensing-service/src/main/java/com/thoughtmechanix/licenses/services

The License class is the model class that will hold the data retrieved from your licensing database. The following listing shows the code for the `License` class.

Listing 3.6   The JPA model code for a single license record

```
package com.thoughtmechanix.licenses.model;

import javax.persistence.Column;
import javax.persistence.Entity;
import javax.persistence.Id;
import javax.persistence.Table;

@Entity
@Table(name = "licenses")
public class License{
    @Id
    @Column(name = "license_id", nullable = false)
    private String licenseId;

    @Column(name = "organization_id", nullable = false)
    private String organizationId;

    @Column(name = "product_name", nullable = false)
    private String productName;

    /*The rest of the code has been removed for conciseness*/

}
```

@Entity tells Spring that this is a JPA class.

@Table maps to the database table.

@Id marks this field as a primary key.

@Column maps the field to a specific database table.

The class uses several Java Persistence Annotations (JPA) that help the Spring Data framework map the data from the licenses table in the Postgres database to the Java object. The `@Entity` annotation lets Spring know that this Java POJO is going to be mapping objects that will hold data. The `@Table` annotation tells Spring/JPA what database table should be mapped. The `@Id` annotation identifies the primary key for the database. Finally, each one of the columns from the database that is going to be mapped to individual properties is marked with a `@Column` attribute.

The Spring Data and JPA framework provides your basic CRUD methods for accessing a database. If you want to build methods beyond that, you can use a Spring Data Repository interface and basic naming conventions to build those methods. Spring will at startup parse the name of the methods from the Repository interface, convert them over to a SQL statement based on the names, and then generate a dynamic proxy class under the covers to do the work. The repository for the licensing service is shown in the following listing.

Listing 3.7   `LicenseRepository` interface defines the query methods

```
package com.thoughtmechanix.licenses.repository;

import com.thoughtmechanix.licenses.model.License;
import org.springframework.data.repository.CrudRepository;
import org.springframework.stereotype.Repository;

import java.util.List;                                    Tells Spring Boot that this
                                                          is a JPA repository class
@Repository
public interface LicenseRepository
   extends CrudRepository<License,String>                Defines that you're extending
{                                                         the Spring CrudRepository
    public List<License> findByOrganizationId
    ➥(String organizationId);                            Individual query methods
    public License findByOrganizationIdAndLicenseId       are parsed by Spring into
    ➥(String organizationId,String licenseId);           a SELECT...FROM query.
}
```

The repository interface, `LicenseRepository`, is marked with the `@Repository` annotation which tells Spring that it should treat this interface as a repository and generate a dynamic proxy for it. Spring offers different types of repositories for data access. You've chosen to use the Spring `CrudRepository` base class to extend your `LicenseRepository` class. The `CrudRepository` base class contains basic CRUD methods. In addition to the CRUD method extended from `CrudRepository`, you've added two custom query methods for retrieving data from the licensing table. The Spring Data framework will pull apart the name of the methods to build a query to access the underlying data.

NOTE   The Spring Data framework provides an abstraction layer over various database platforms and isn't limited to relational databases. NoSQL databases such as MongoDB and Cassandra are also supported.

Unlike the previous incarnation of the licensing service in chapter 2, you've now separated the business and data access logic for the licensing service out of the `LicenseController` and into a standalone Service class called `LicenseService`.

Listing 3.8   `LicenseService` class used to execute database commands

```
package com.thoughtmechanix.licenses.services;

import com.thoughtmechanix.licenses.config.ServiceConfig;
import com.thoughtmechanix.licenses.model.License;
import com.thoughtmechanix.licenses.repository.LicenseRepository;
import org.springframework.beans.factory.annotation.Autowired;
import org.springframework.stereotype.Service;
```

```
import java.util.List;
import java.util.UUID;

@Service
public class LicenseService {

    @Autowired
    private LicenseRepository licenseRepository;

    @Autowired
    ServiceConfig config;

    public License getLicense(String organizationId,String licenseId) {
        License license = licenseRepository.findByOrganizationIdAndLicenseId(
organizationId, licenseId);
        return license.withComment(config.getExampleProperty());
    }

    public List<License> getLicensesByOrg(String organizationId){
        return licenseRepository.findByOrganizationId( organizationId );
    }

    public void saveLicense(License license){
        license.withId( UUID.randomUUID().toString());
        licenseRepository.save(license);
    }
      /*Rest of the code removed for conciseness*/
}
```

The controller, service, and repository classes are wired together using the standard Spring @Autowired annotation.

3.3.4   *Directly Reading Properties using the @Value Annotation*

In the LicenseService class in the previous section, you might have noticed that you're setting the license.withComment() value in the getLicense() code with a value from the config.getExampleProperty() class. The code being referred to is shown here:

```
public License getLicense(String organizationId,String licenseId) {
        License license = licenseRepository.findByOrganizationIdAndLicenseId(
organizationId, licenseId);
return license.withComment(config.getExampleProperty());
    }
```

If you look at the licensing-service/src/main/java/com/thoughtmechanix/ licenses/config/ServiceConfig.java class, you'll see a property annotated with the @Value annotation. The following listing shows the @Value annotation being used.

Listing 3.9   ServiceConfig used to centralize application properties

```
package com.thoughtmechanix.licenses.config;

import org.springframework.beans.factory.annotation.Value;
import org.springframework.stereotype.Component;
```

```
@Component
public class ServiceConfig{

  @Value("${example.property}")
  private String exampleProperty;

  public String getExampleProperty(){
    return exampleProperty;
  }
}
```

While Spring Data "auto-magically" injects the configuration data for the database into a database connection object, all other properties must be injected using the `@Value` annotation. With the previous example, the `@Value` annotation pulls the `example.property` from the Spring Cloud configuration server and injects it into the `example.property` attribute on the `ServiceConfig` class.

> **TIP** While it's possible to directly inject configuration values into properties in individual classes, I've found it useful to centralize all of the configuration information into a single configuration class and then inject the configuration class into where it's needed.

3.3.5 *Using Spring Cloud configuration server with Git*

As mentioned earlier, using a filesystem as the backend repository for Spring Cloud configuration server can be impractical for a cloud-based application because the development team has to set up and manage a shared filesystem that's mounted on all instances of the Cloud configuration server.

Spring Cloud configuration server integrates with different backend repositories that can be used to host application configuration properties. One I've used successfully is to use Spring Cloud configuration server with a Git source control repository.

By using Git you can get all the benefits of putting your configuration management properties under source control and provide an easy mechanism to integrate the deployment of your property configuration files in your build and deployment pipeline.

To use Git, you'd swap out the filesystem back configuration in the configuration service's bootstrap.yml file with the following listing's configuration.

Listing 3.10   Spring Cloud config application.yml

```
server:
  port: 8888
spring:
  cloud:
    config:
      server:
        git:
          uri: https://github.com/carnellj/config-repo/
```

Tells Spring Cloud Config to use Git as a backend repository

Tells Spring Cloud Config the URL to the Git server and Git repo

```
        searchPaths: licensingservice,organizationservice
        username: native-cloud-apps                          ◄─────────┐
        password: 0ffended
```

Tells Spring Cloud Config what the path in Git is to look for config files

The three key pieces of configuration in the previous example are the `spring.cloud.config.server`, `spring.cloud.config.server.git.uri`, and the `spring.cloud.config.server.git.searchPaths` properties. The `spring.cloud.config.server` property tells the Spring Cloud configuration server to use a non-filesystem-based backend repository. In the previous example you're going to connect to the cloud-based Git repository, GitHub.

The `spring.cloud.config.server.git.uri` properties provide the URL of the repository you're connecting to. Finally, the `spring.cloud.config.server.git.searchPaths` property tells the Spring Cloud Config server the relative paths on the Git repository that should be searched when the Cloud configuration server comes up. Like the filesystem version of the configuration, the value in the `spring.cloud.config.server.git.seachPaths` attribute will be a comma-separated list for each service hosted by the configuration service.

3.3.6   *Refreshing your properties using Spring Cloud configuration server*

One of the first questions that comes up from development teams when they want to use the Spring Cloud configuration server is how can they dynamically refresh their applications when a property changes. The Spring Cloud configuration server will always serve the latest version of a property. Changes made to a property via its underlying repository will be up-to-date.

However, Spring Boot applications will only read their properties at startup time, so property changes made in the Spring Cloud configuration server won't be automatically picked up by the Spring Boot application. Spring Boot Actuator does offer a `@RefreshScope` annotation that will allow a development team to access a `/refresh` endpoint that will force the Spring Boot application to reread its application configuration. The following listing shows the `@RefreshScope` annotation in action.

Listing 3.11   The `@RefreshScope` annotation

```java
package com.thoughtmechanix.licenses;

import org.springframework.boot.SpringApplication;
import org.springframework.boot.autoconfigure.SpringBootApplication;
import org.springframework.cloud.context.config.annotation.RefreshScope;


@SpringBootApplication
@RefreshScope
public class Application {
    public static void main(String[] args) {
        SpringApplication.run(Application.class, args);
    }
}
```

Note a couple of things about the @RefreshScope annotation. First, the annotation will only reload the custom Spring properties you have in your application configuration. Items such as your database configuration that are used by Spring Data won't be reloaded by the @RefreshScope annotation. To perform the refresh, you can hit the http://<yourserver>:8080/refresh endpoint.

On refreshing microservices

When using Spring Cloud configuration service with microservices, one thing you need to consider before you dynamically change properties is that you might have multiple instances of the same service running, and you'll need to refresh all of those services with their new application configurations. There are several ways you can approach this problem:

Spring Cloud configuration service does offer a "push"-based mechanism called Spring Cloud Bus that will allow the Spring Cloud configuration server to publish to all the clients using the service that a change has occurred. Spring Cloud configuration requires an extra piece of middleware running (RabbitMQ). This is an extremely useful means of detecting changes, but not all Spring Cloud configuration backends support the "push" mechanism (that is, the Consul server).

In the next chapter you'll use Spring Service Discovery and Eureka to register all instances of a service. One technique I've used to handle application configuration refresh events is to refresh the application properties in Spring Cloud configuration and then write a simple script to query the service discovery engine to find all instances of a service and call the /refresh endpoint directly.

Finally, you can restart all the servers or containers to pick up the new property. This is a trivial exercise, especially if you're running your services in a container service such as Docker. Restarting Docker containers literally takes seconds and will force a reread of the application configuration.

Remember, cloud-based servers are ephemeral. Don't be afraid to start new instances of a service with their new configuration, direct traffic to the new services, and then tear down the old ones.

3.4 Protecting sensitive configuration information

By default, Spring Cloud configuration server stores all properties in plain text within the application's configuration files. This includes sensitive information such as database credentials.

It's an extremely poor practice to keep sensitive credentials stored as plain text in your source code repository. Unfortunately, it happens far more often than you think. Spring Cloud Config does give you the ability to encrypt your sensitive properties easily. Spring Cloud Config supports using both symmetric (shared secret) and asymmetric encryption (public/private key).

We're going to see how to set up your Spring Cloud configuration server to use encryption using with a symmetric key. To do this you'll need to

1 Download and install the Oracle JCE jars needed for encryption
2 Set up an encryption key.
3 Encrypt and decrypt a property.
4 Configure microservices to use encryption on the client side

3.4.1   *Download and install Oracle JCE jars needed for encryption*

To begin, you need to download and install Oracle's Unlimited Strength Java Cryptography Extension (JCE). This isn't available through Maven and must be downloaded from Oracle Corporation.[1] Once you've downloaded the zip files containing the JCE jars, you must do the following:

1 Locate your `$JAVA_HOME/jre/lib/security` directory.
2 Back up the `local_policy.jar` and `US_export_policy.jar` files in the `$JAVA_HOME/jre/lib/security` directory to a different location.
3 Unzip the JCE zip file you downloaded from Oracle.
4 Copy the `local_policy.jar` and `US_export_policy.jar` to your `$JAVA_HOME/jre/lib/security` directory.
5 Configure Spring Cloud Config to use encryption.

Automating the process of installing Oracle's JCE files

I've walked through the manual steps you need to install JCE on your laptop. Because we use Docker to build all our services as Docker containers, I've scripted the download and installation of these JAR files in the Spring Cloud Config Docker container. The following OS X shell script snippet shows how I automated this using the curl (https://curl.haxx.se/) command-line tool:

```
cd /tmp/
curl -k-LO "http://download.oracle.com/otn-pub/java/jce/8/jce_policy-
    8.zip"
    -H 'Cookie: oraclelicense=accept-securebackup-cookie' && unzip
    jce_policy-8.zip
rm jce_policy-8.zip
yes |cp -v /tmp/UnlimitedJCEPolicyJDK8/*.jar /usr/lib/jvm/java-1.8-
    openjdk/jre/lib/security/
```

I'm not going to walk through all of the details, but basically I use CURL to download the JCE zip files (note the `Cookie` header parameter passed via the `-H` attribute on the `curl` command) and then unzip the files and copy them to the /usr/lib/jvm/java-1.8-openjdk/jre/lib/security directory in my Docker container.

If you look at the src/main/docker/Dockerfile file in the source code for this chapter, you can see an example of this scripting in action.

[1] http://www.oracle.com/technetwork/java/javase/downloads/jce8-download-2133166.html. This URL might be subject to change. A quick search on Google for Java Cryptography Extensions should always return you the right values.

3.4.2   Setting up an encryption key

Once the JAR files are in place, you need to set a symmetric encryption key. The symmetric encryption key is nothing more than a shared secret that's used by the encrypter to encrypt a value and the decrypter to decrypt a value. With the Spring Cloud configuration server, the symmetric encryption key is a string of characters you select that's passed to the service via an operating system environment variable called `ENCRYPT_KEY`. For the purposes of this book you'll always set the `ENCRYPT_KEY` environment variable to be

```
export ENCRYPT_KEY=IMSYMMETRIC
```

Note two things regarding symmetric keys:

1   Your symmetric key should be 12 or more characters long and ideally be a random set of characters.
2   Don't lose your symmetric key. Once you've encrypted something with your encrypted key, you can't unencrypt it.

> **Managing encryption keys**
>
> For the purposes of this book, I did two things that I wouldn't normally recommend in a production deployment:
>
> - I set the encryption key to be a phrase. I wanted to keep the key simple so that I could remember it and it would fit nicely in reading the text. In a real-world deployment, I'd use a separate encryption key for each environment I was deploying to and I'd use random characters as my key.
> - I've hardcoded the `ENCRYPT_KEY` environment variable directly in the Docker files used within the book. I did this so that you as the reader could download the files and start them up without having to remember to set an environment variable. In a real runtime environment, I would reference the `ENCRYPT_KEY` as an operating system environment variable inside my Dockerfile. Be aware of this and don't hardcode your encryption key inside your Dockerfiles. Remember, your Dockerfiles are supposed to be kept under source control.

3.4.3   Encrypting and decrypting a property

You're now ready to begin encrypting properties for use in Spring Cloud Config. You'll encrypt the licensing services Postgres database password you've been using to access EagleEye data. This property, called `spring.datasource.password`, is currently set as plain text to be the value `p0stgr@s`.

When you fire up your Spring Cloud Config instance, Spring Cloud Config detects that the `ENCRYPT_KEY` environment variable is set and automatically adds two new endpoints (`/encrypt` and `/decrypt`) to the Spring Cloud Config service. You'll use the `/encrypt` endpoint to encrypt the `p0stgr@s` value.

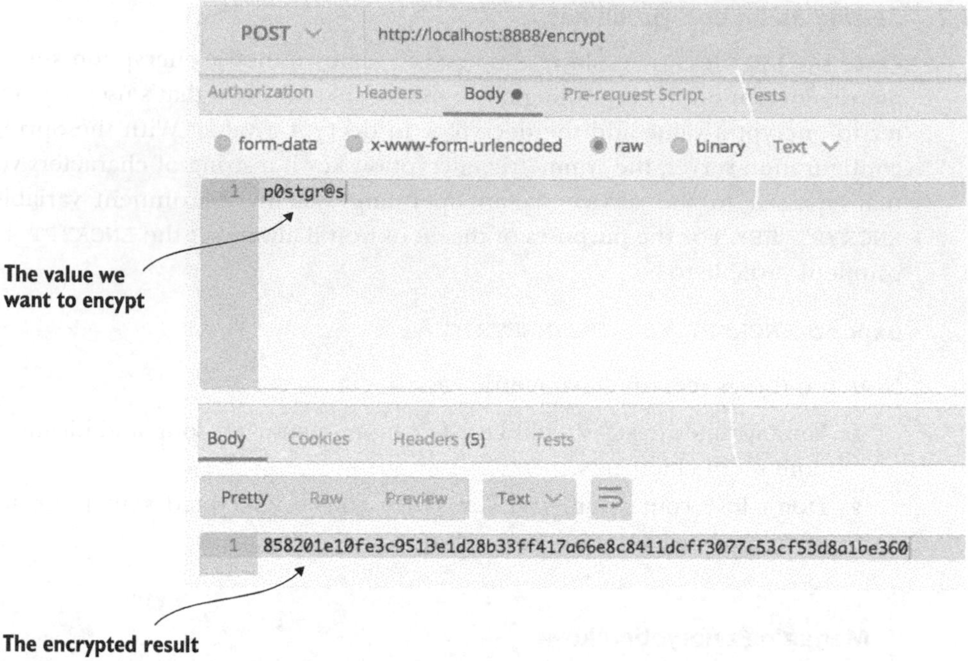

The value we
want to encypt

The encrypted result

Figure 3.8   Using the /encrypt endpoint you can encrypt values.

Figure 3.8 shows how to encrypt the p0stgr@s value using the /encrypt endpoint and POSTMAN. Please note that whenever you call the /encrypt or /decrypt endpoints, you need to make sure you do a POST to these endpoints.

If you wanted to decrypt the value, you'd use the /decrypt endpoint passing in the encrypted string in the call.

You can now add the encrypted property to your GitHub or filesystem-based configuration file for the licensing service using the following syntax:

```
spring.datasource.password:"{cipher}
    858201e10fe3c9513e1d28b33ff417a66e8c8411dcff3077c53cf53d8a1be360"
```

Spring Cloud configuration server requires all encrypted properties to be prepended with a value of {cipher}. The {cipher} value tells Spring Cloud configuration server it's dealing with an encrypted value. Fire up your Spring Cloud configuration server and hit the GET http://localhost:8888/licensingservice/default endpoint.

Figure 3.9 shows the results of this call.

You've made the spring.datasource.password more secure by encrypting the property, but you still have a problem. The database password is exposed as plain text when you hit the http://localhost:8888/licensingservice/default endpoint.

```
GET  ∨          http://localhost:8888/licensingservice/default

 Pretty    Raw    Preview    JSON ∨    ⇉

  1 ▾ {
  2      "name": "licensingservice",
  3 ▾    "profiles": [
  4          "default"
  5      ],
  6      "label": "master",
  7      "version": "8b20dd9432ef9ef08216a5775859afb24a5e7d43",
  8 ▾    "propertySources": [
  9 ▾        {
 10            "name": "https://github.com/carnellj/config-repo/licensingservice/licensingservice.yml",
 11 ▾          "source": {
 12              "example.property": "I AM IN THE DEFAULT",
 13              "spring.jpa.database": "POSTGRESQL",
 14              "spring.datasource.platform": "postgres",
 15              "spring.jpa.show-sql": "true",
 16              "spring.database.driverClassName": "org.postgresql.Driver",
 17              "spring.datasource.url": "jdbc:postgresql://database:5432/eagle_eye_local",
 18              "spring.datasource.username": "postgres",
 19              "spring.datasource.testWhileIdle": "true",
 20              "spring.datasource.validationQuery": "SELECT 1",
 21              "spring.jpa.properties.hibernate.dialect": "org.hibernate.dialect.PostgreSQLDialect",
 22              "redis.server": "redis",
 23              "redis.port": "6379",
 24              "signing.key": "345345fsdfsf5345",
 25              "spring.datasource.password": "p0stgr@s"
 26            }
 27        }
```

**spring.datasource.password property
stored as an encrypted value**

Figure 3.9   While the `spring.datasource.password` **is encrypted in the property file, it's decrypted when the configuration for the licensing service is retrieved. This is still problematic.**

By default, Spring Cloud Config will do all the property decryption on the server and pass the results back to the applications consuming the properties as plain, unencrypted text. However, you can tell Spring Cloud Config to not decrypt on the server and make it the responsibility of the application retrieving the configuration data to decrypt the encrypted properties.

3.4.4   *Configure microservices to use encryption on the client side*

To enable client side decryption of properties, you need to do three things:

1 Configure Spring Cloud Config to not decrypt properties on the server side.
2 Set the symmetric key on the licensing server.
3 Add the `spring-security-rsa` JARs to the licensing services pom.xml file.

The first thing you need to do is disable the server-side decryption of properties in Spring Cloud Config. This is done by setting the Spring Cloud Config's src/main/ resources/application.yml file to set the property `spring.cloud.config.server` `.encrypt.enabled: false`. That's all you have to do on the Spring Cloud Config server.

Because the licensing service is now responsible for decrypting the encrypted properties, you need to first set the symmetric key on the licensing service by making sure that the ENCRYPT_KEY environment variable is set with the same symmetric key (for example, IMSYMMETRIC) that you used with your Spring Cloud Config server.

Next you need to include the spring-security-rsa JAR dependencies in with licensing service:

```
<dependency>
    <groupId>org.springframework.security</groupId>
    <artifactId>spring-security-rsa</artifactId>
</dependency>
```

These JAR files contain the Spring code needed to decrypt the encrypted properties being retrieved from Spring Cloud Config. With these changes in place, you can start the Spring Cloud Config and licensing services. If you hit the http://local-host:8888/licensingservice/default endpoint you'll see the spring.data-source.password returned in it is encrypted form. Figure 3.10 shows the output from the call.

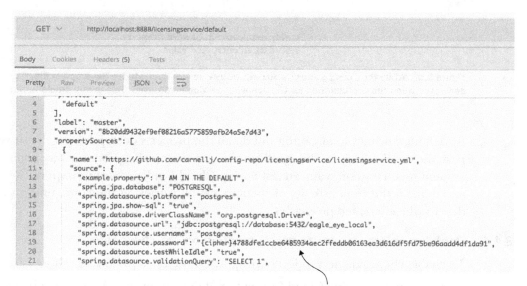

The spring.datasource.password property is encrypted.

Figure 3.10   With client-side decryption turned on, sensitive properties will no longer be returned in plain text from the Spring Cloud Config REST call. Instead, the property will be decrypted by the calling service when it loads its properties from Spring Cloud Config.

3.5 *Closing thoughts*

Application configuration management might seem like a mundane topic, but it's of critical importance in a cloud-based environment. As we'll discuss in more detail in later chapters, it's critical that your applications and the servers they run on be immutable and that the entire server being promoted is never manually configured between environments. This flies in the face of traditional deployment models where you deploy an application artifact (for example, a JAR or WAR file) along with its property files to a "fixed" environment.

With a cloud-based model, the application configuration data should be segregated completely from the application, with the appropriate configuration data needs injected at runtime so that the same server/application artifact are consistently promoted through all environments.

3.6 *Summary*

- Spring Cloud configuration server allows you to set up application properties with environment specific values.
- Spring uses Spring profiles to launch a service to determine what environment properties are to be retrieved from the Spring Cloud Config service.
- Spring Cloud configuration service can use a file-based or Git-based application configuration repository to store application properties.
- Spring Cloud configuration service allows you to encrypt sensitive property files using symmetric and asymmetric encryption.

On service discovery

This chapter covers

- Explaining why service discovery is important to any cloud-based application environment
- Understanding the pros and cons of service discovery vs. the more traditional load-balancer approach
- Setting up a Spring Netflix Eureka server
- Registering a Spring-Boot-based microservice with Eureka
- Using Spring Cloud and Netflix's Ribbon library to use client-side load balancing

In any distributed architecture, we need to find the physical address of where a machine is located. This concept has been around since the beginning of distributed computing and is known formally as service discovery. Service discovery can be something as simple as maintaining a property file with the addresses of all the remote services used by an application, or something as formalized (and complicated) as a UDDI (Universal Description, Discovery, and Integration) repository.[1]

---

[1] https://en.wikipedia.org/wiki/Web_Services_Discovery#Universal_Description_Discovery_and_Integration

Service discovery is critical to microservice, cloud-based applications for two key reasons. First, it offers the application team the ability to quickly horizontally scale up and down the number of service instances running in an environment. The service consumers are abstracted away from the physical location of the service via service discovery. Because the service consumers don't know the physical location of the actual service instances, new service instances can be added or removed from the pool of available services.

This ability to quickly scale services without disrupting the service consumers is an extremely powerful concept, because it moves a development team used to building monolithic, single-tenant (for example, one customer) applications away from thinking about scaling only in terms of adding bigger, better hardware (vertical scaling) to the more powerful approach to scaling by adding more servers (horizontal scaling).

A monolithic approach usually drives development teams down the path of over-buying their capacity needs. Capacity increases come in clumps and spikes and are rarely a smooth steady path. Microservices allow us to scale up/down new service instances. Service discovery helps abstract that these deployments are occurring away from the service consumer.

The second benefit of service discovery is that it helps increase application resiliency. When a microservice instance becomes unhealthy or unavailable, most service discovery engines will remove that instance from its internal list of available services. The damage caused by a down service will be minimized because the service discovery engine will route services around the unavailable service.

We've gone through the benefits of service discovery, but what's the big deal about it? After all, can't we use tried-and-true methods such as DNS (Domain Name Service) or a load balancer to help facilitate service discovery? Let's walk through why that won't work with a microservices-based application, particularly one that's running in the cloud.

4.1 Where's my service?

Whenever you have an application calling resources spread across multiple servers, it needs to locate the physical location of those resource. In the non-cloud world, this service location resolution was often solved through a combination of DNS and a network load balancer. Figure 4.1 illustrates this model.

An application needs to invoke a service located in another part of the organization. It attempts to invoke the service by using a generic DNS name along with a path that uniquely represents the service that the application was trying to invoke. The DNS name would resolve to a commercial load balancer, such as the popular F5 load balancer (http://f5.com) or an open source load balancer such as HAProxy (http://haproxy.org).

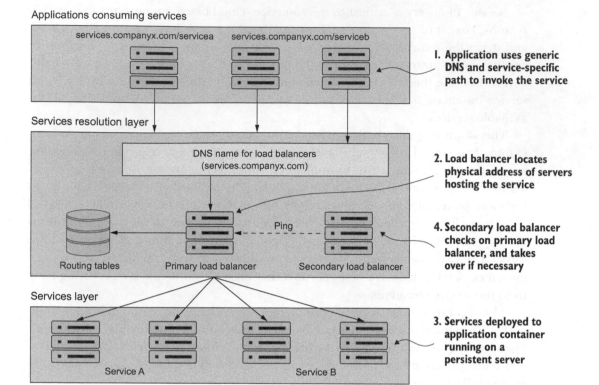

Figure 4.1 A traditional service location resolution model using DNS and a load balancer

The load balancer, upon receiving the request from the service consumer, locates the physical address entry in a routing table based on the path the user was trying to access. This routing table entry contains a list of one or more servers hosting the service. The load balancer then picks one of the servers in the list and forwards the request onto that server.

Each instance of a service is deployed to one or more application servers. The number of these application servers was often *static* (for example, the number of application servers hosting a service didn't go up and down) and *persistent* (for example, if a server running an application server crashed, it would be restored to the same state it was at the time of the crash, and would have the same IP and configuration that it had previously.)

To achieve a form of high availability, a secondary load balancer is sitting idle and pinging the primary load balancer to see if it's alive. If it isn't alive, the secondary load balancer becomes active, taking over the IP address of the primary load balancer and beginning serving requests.

While this type of model works well with applications running inside of the four walls of a corporate data center and with a relatively small number of services running on a group of static servers, it doesn't work well for cloud-based microservice applications. Reasons for this include

- *Single point of failure*—While the load balancer can be made highly available, it's a single point of failure for your entire infrastructure. If the load balancer goes down, every application relying on it goes down too. While you can make a load balancer highly available, load balancers tend to be centralized chokepoints within your application infrastructure.
- *Limited horizontal scalability*—By centralizing your services into a single cluster of load balancers, you have limited ability to horizontally scale your load-balancing infrastructure across multiple servers. Many commercial load balancers are constrained by two things: their redundancy model and licensing costs. Most commercial load balancers use a hot-swap model for redundancy so you only have a single server to handle the load, while the secondary load balancer is there only for fail-over in the case of an outage of the primary load balancer. You are, in essence, constrained by your hardware. Second, commercial load balancers also have restrictive licensing models geared toward a fixed capacity rather than a more variable model.
- *Statically managed*—Most traditional load balancers aren't designed for rapid registration and de-registration of services. They use a centralized database to store the routes for rules and the only way to add new routes is often through the vendor's proprietary API (Application Programming Interface).
- *Complex*—Because a load balancer acts as a proxy to the services, service consumer requests have to have their requests mapped to the physical services. This translation layer often added a layer of complexity to your service infrastructure because the mapping rules for the service have to be defined and deployed by hand. In a traditional load balancer scenario, this registration of new service instances was done by hand and not at startup time of a new service instance.

These four reasons aren't a general indictment of load balancers. They work well in a corporate environment where the size and scale of most applications can be handled through a centralized network infrastructure. In addition, load balancers still have a role to play in terms of centralizing SSL termination and managing service port security. A load balancer can lock down inbound (ingress) and outbound (egress) port access to all the servers sitting behind it. This concept of least network access is often a critical component when trying to meet industry-standard certification requirements such as PCI (Payment Card Industry) compliance.

However, in the cloud where you have to deal with massive amounts of transactions and redundancy, a centralized piece of network infrastructure doesn't ultimately work as well because it doesn't scale effectively and isn't cost-efficient. Let's now look at how you can implement a robust-service discovery mechanism for cloud-based applications.

4.2 On service discovery in the cloud

The solution for a cloud-based microservice environment is to use a service-discovery mechanism that's

- *Highly available*—Service discovery needs to be able to support a "hot" clustering environment where service lookups can be shared across multiple nodes in a service discovery cluster. If a node becomes unavailable, other nodes in the cluster should be able to take over.
- *Peer-to-peer*—Each node in the service discovery cluster shares the state of a service instance.
- *Load balanced*—Service discovery needs to dynamically load balance requests across all service instances to ensure that the service invocations are spread across all the service instances managed by it. In many ways, service discovery replaces the more static, manually managed load balancers used in many early web application implementations.
- *Resilient*—The service discovery's client should "cache" service information locally. Local caching allows for gradual degradation of the service discovery feature so that if service discovery service does become unavailable, applications can still function and locate the services based on the information maintained in its local cache.
- *Fault-tolerant*—Service discovery needs to detect when a service instance isn't healthy and remove the instance from the list of available services that can take client requests. It should detect these faults with services and take action without human intervention.

In the following section(s) we're going to

- Walk through the conceptual architecture of how a cloud-based service discovery agent will work
- Show how client-side caching and load-balancing allows a service to continue to function even when the service discovery agent is unavailable
- See how to implement service discovery using Spring Cloud and Netflix's Eureka service discovery agent

4.2.1 The architecture of service discovery

To begin our discussion around service discovery architecture, we need to understand four concepts. These general concepts are shared across all service discovery implementations:

- *Service registration*—How does a service register with the service discovery agent?
- *Client lookup of service address*—What's the means by which a service client looks up service information?
- *Information sharing*—How is service information shared across nodes?
- *Health monitoring*—How do services communicate their health back to the service discovery agent?

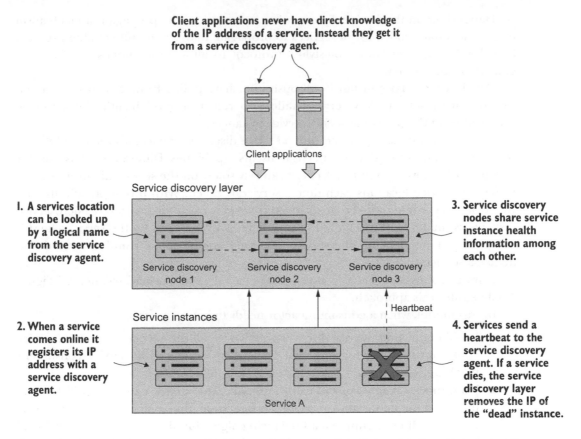

Figure 4.2 As service instances are added/removed, they will update the service discovery agent and become available to process user requests.

Figure 4.2 shows the flow of these four bullets and what typically occurs in a service discovery pattern implementation.

In figure 4.2, one or more service discovery nodes have been started. These service discovery instances are usually unique and don't have a load balancer that sits in front of them.

As service instances start up, they'll register their physical location, path, and port that they can be accessed by with one or more service discovery instances. While each instance of a service will have a unique IP address and port, each service instance that comes up will register under the same service ID. A service ID is nothing more than a key that uniquely identifies a group of the same service instances.

A service will usually only register with one service discovery service instance. Most service discovery implementations use a peer-to-peer model of data propagation where the data around each service instance is communicated to all the other nodes in the cluster.

Depending on the service discovery implementation, the propagation mechanism might use a hard-coded list of services to propagate to or use a multi-casting protocol like the "gossip"[2] or "infection-style"[3] protocol to allow other nodes to "discover" changes in the cluster.

Finally, each service instance will push to or have pulled from its status by the service discovery service. Any services failing to return a good health check will be removed from the pool of available service instances.

Once a service has registered with a service discovery service, it's ready to be used by an application or service that needs to use its capabilities. Different models exist for a client to "discover" a service. A client can rely solely on the service discovery engine to resolve service locations each time a service is called. With this approach, the service discovery engine will be invoked every time a call to a registered microservice instance is made. Unfortunately, this approach is brittle because the service client is completely dependent on the service discovery engine to be running to find and invoke a service.

A more robust approach is to use what's called *client-side* load balancing.[4] Figure 4.3 illustrates this approach.

In this model, when a consuming actor needs to invoke a service

1 It will contact the service discovery service for all the service instances a service consumer is asking for and then cache data locally on the service consumer's machine.

2 Each time a client wants to call the service, the service consumer will look up the location information for the service from the cache. Usually client-side caching will use a simple load balancing algorithm like the "round-robin" load balancing algorithm to ensure that service calls are spread across multiple service instances.

3 The client will then periodically contact the service discovery service and refresh its cache of service instances. The client cache is eventually consistent, but there's always a risk that between when the client contacts the service discovery instance for a refresh and calls are made, calls might be directed to a service instance that isn't healthy.

   If, during the course of calling a service, the service call fails, the local service discovery cache is invalidated and the service discovery client will attempt to refresh its entries from the service discovery agent.

Let's now take the generic service discovery pattern and apply it to your EagleEye problem domain.

---

[2]   https://en.wikipedia.org/wiki/Gossip_protocol

[3]   https://www.cs.cornell.edu/~asdas/research/dsn02-swim.pdf

[4]   https://en.wikipedia.org/wiki/Load_balancing_(computing)#Client-Side_Random_Load_Balancing

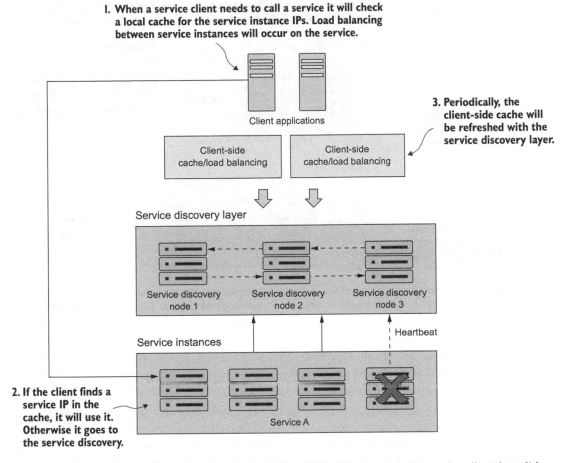

Figure 4.3   Client-side load balancing caches the location of the services so that the service client doesn't have to contact service discovery on every call.

4.2.2 Service discovery in action using Spring and Netflix Eureka

Now you're going to implement service discovery by setting up a service discovery agent and then registering two services with the agent. You'll then have one service call another service by using the information retrieved by service discovery. Spring Cloud offers multiple methods for looking up information from a service discovery agent. We'll also walk through the strengths and weakness of each approach.

Once again, the Spring Cloud project makes this type of setup trivial to undertake. You'll use Spring Cloud and Netflix's Eureka service discovery engine to implement your service discovery pattern. For the client-side load balancing you'll use Spring Cloud and Netflix's Ribbon libraries.

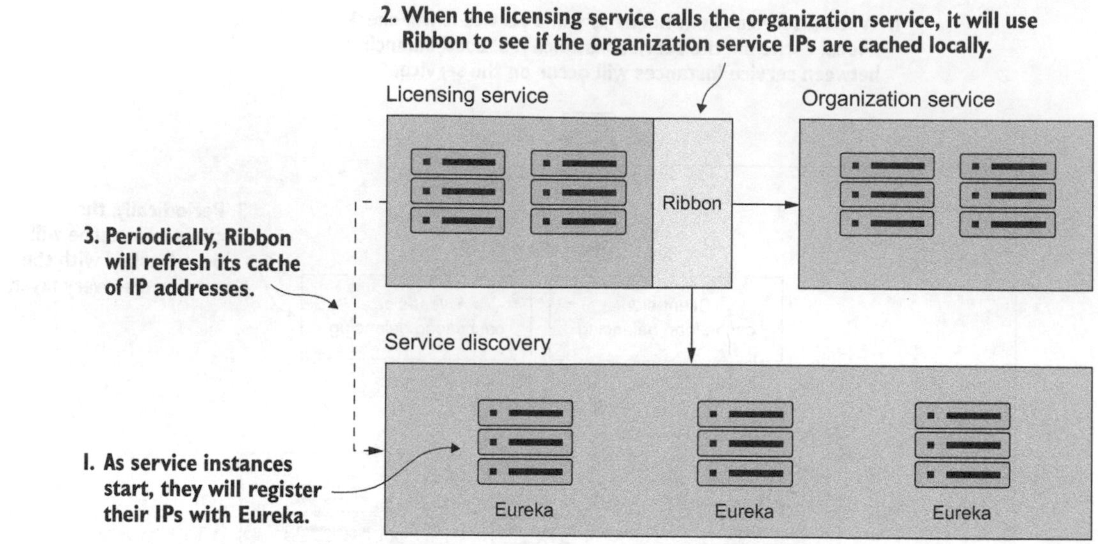

Figure 4.4 By implementing client-side caching and Eureka with the licensing and organization services, you can lessen the load on the Eureka servers and improve client stability if Eureka becomes unavailable.

In the previous two chapters, you kept your licensing service simple and included the organization name for the licenses with the license data. In this chapter, you'll break the organization information into its own service.

When the licensing service is invoked, it will call the organization service to retrieve the organization information associated with the designated organization ID. The actual resolution of the organization service's location will be held in a service discovery registry. For this example, you'll register two instances of the organization service with a service discovery registry and then use client-side load balancing to look up and cache the registry in each service instance. Figure 4.4 shows this arrangement:

1 As the services are bootstrapping, the licensing and organization services will also register themselves with the Eureka Service. This registration process will tell Eureka the physical location and port number of each service instance along with a service ID for the service being started.

2 When the licensing service calls to the organization service, it will use the Netflix Ribbon library to provide client-side load balancing. Ribbon will contact the Eureka service to retrieve service location information and then cache it locally.

3 Periodically, the Netflix Ribbon library will ping the Eureka service and refresh its local cache of service locations.

Any new organization services instance will now be visible to the licensing service locally, while any non-healthy instances will be removed from the local cache.

Next, you'll implement this design by setting up your Spring Cloud Eureka service.

4.3 *Building your Spring Eureka Service*

In this section, you'll set up our Eureka service using Spring Boot. Like the Spring Cloud configuration service, setting up a Spring Cloud Eureka Service starts with building a new Spring Boot project and applying annotations and configurations. Let's begin with your maven pom.xml.[5] The following listing shows the Eureka service dependencies you'll need for the Spring Boot project you're setting up.

Listing 4.1 Adding dependencies to your pom.xml

```
<?xml version="1.0" encoding="UTF-8"?>
<project xmlns="http://maven.apache.org/POM/4.0.0" xmlns:xsi="http://
    www.w3.org/2001/XMLSchema-instance"
    xsi:schemaLocation="http://maven.apache.org/POM/4.0.0 http://
    maven.apache.org/xsd/maven-4.0.0.xsd">

  <modelVersion>4.0.0</modelVersion>

  <groupId>com.thoughtmechanix</groupId>
  <artifactId>eurekasvr</artifactId>
  <version>0.0.1-SNAPSHOT</version>
  <packaging>jar</packaging>

  <name>Eureka Server</name>
  <description>Eureka Server demo project</description>

<!--Not showing the maven definitions for using Spring Cloud Parent-->
  <dependencies>
    <dependency>
      <groupId>org.springframework.cloud</groupId>
      <artifactId>spring-cloud-starter-eureka-server</artifactId>       ◄──┐
    </dependency>
  </dependencies>

Rest of pom.xml removed for conciseness
....
</project>
```

Tells your maven build to include the Eureka libraries (which will include Ribbon)

You'll then need to set up the src/main/resources/application.yml file with the configuration needed to set up the Eureka service running in standalone mode (for example, no other nodes in the cluster), as shown in the next listing.

Listing 4.2 Setting up your Eureka configuration in the application.yml file

```
server:
  port: 8761               ◄──┐ Port Eureka Server
                                is going to listen on
eureka:
  client:                                              Don't register with
    registerWithEureka: false      ◄──────────────────  Eureka service.
```

---

[5] All source code in this chapter can be downloaded from GitHub (https://github.com/carnellj/spmia-chapter4). The Eureka service is in the chapter 4/eurekasvr example. All services in this chapter were built using Docker and Docker Compose so they can be brought up in a single instance.

```
fetchRegistry: false          ←──┐ Don't cache registry
server:                              information locally.
   waitTimeInMsWhenSyncEmpty: 5   ←──┐ Initial time to wait before
                                        server takes requests
```

The key properties being set are the `server.port` attribute that sets the default port used for the Eureka service. The `eureka.client.registerWithEureka` attribute tells the service not to register with a Eureka service when the Spring Boot Eureka application starts because this is the Eureka service. The `eureka.client` `.fetchRegistry` attribute is set to false so that when the Eureka service starts, it doesn't try to cache its registry information locally. When running a Eureka client, you'll want to change this value for the Spring Boot services that are going to register with Eureka.

You'll notice that the last attribute, `eureka.server.waitTimeInMsWhenSync Empty`, is commented out. When you're testing your service locally you should uncomment this line because Eureka won't immediately advertise any services that register with it. It will wait five minutes by default to give all of the services a chance to register with it before advertising them. Uncommenting this line for local testing will help speed up the amount of time it will take for the Eureka service to start and show services registered with it.

Individual services registering will take up to 30 seconds to show up in the Eureka service because Eureka requires three consecutive heartbeat pings from the service spaced 10 seconds apart before it will say the service is ready for use. Keep this in mind as you're deploying and testing your own services.

The last piece of setup work you're going to do in setting up your Eureka service is adding an annotation to the application bootstrap class you're using to start your Eureka service. For the Eureka service, the application bootstrap class can be found in the `src/main/java/com/thoughtmechanix/eurekasvr/EurekaServer-Application.java` class. The following listing shows where to add your annotations.

Listing 4.3   Annotating the bootstrap class to enable the Eureka server

```
package com.thoughtmechanix.eurekasvr;

import org.springframework.boot.SpringApplication;
import org.springframework.boot.autoconfigure.SpringBootApplication;
import org.springframework.cloud.netflix.eureka.server.EnableEurekaServer;

@SpringBootApplication
@EnableEurekaServer                        ←──┐ Enable Eureka server
public class EurekaServerApplication {           in the Spring service
  public static void main(String[] args) {
    SpringApplication.run(EurekaServerApplication.class, args);
  }
}
```

You use only one new annotation to tell your service to be a Eureka service; that's @EnableEurekaServer. At this point you can start up the Eureka service by running the mvn spring-boot:run or run docker-compose (see appendix A) to start the service. Once this command is run, you should have a running Eureka service with no services registered in it. Next you'll build out the organization service and register it with your Eureka service.

4.4 *Registering services with Spring Eureka*

At this point you have a Spring-based Eureka server up and running. In this section, you'll configure your organization and licensing services to register themselves with your Eureka server. This work is done in preparation for having a service client look up a service from your Eureka registry. By the time you're done with this section, you should have a firm understanding of how to register a Spring Boot microservice with Eureka.

Registering a Spring Boot-based microservice with Eureka is an extremely simple exercise. For the purposes of this chapter, we're not going to walk through all of the Java code involved with writing the service (we purposely kept that amount of code small), but instead focus on registering the service with the Eureka service registry you created in the previous section.

The first thing you need to do is add the Spring Eureka dependency to your organization service's pom.xml file:

```
<dependency>
    <groupId>org.springframework.cloud</groupId>
    <artifactId>spring-cloud-starter-eureka</artifactId>    ⟵┐  Includes the Eureka libraries
</dependency>                                                       so that the service can
                                                                    register with Eureka
```

The only new library that's being used is the spring-cloud-starter-eureka library. The spring-cloud-starter-eureka artifact holds the jar files that Spring Cloud will use to interact with your Eureka service.

After you've set up your pom.xml file, you need to tell Spring Boot to register the organization service with Eureka. This registration is done via additional configuration in the organization service's src/main/java/resources/application.yml file, as shown in the following listing.

Listing 4.4 Modifying your organization service's application.yml to talk to Eureka

```
spring:
 application:
  name: organizationservice    ⟵┐  Logical name of the service that
 profiles:                          will be registered with Eureka
  active:
   default
 cloud:
  config:
   enabled: true
```

```
eureka:
  instance:
    preferIpAddress: true
  client:
    registerWithEureka: true
    fetchRegistry: true
    serviceUrl:
      defaultZone: http://localhost:8761/eureka/
```

Register the IP of the service rather than the server name.

Register the service with Eureka.

Pull down a local copy of the registry.

Location of the Eureka Service

Every service registered with Eureka will have two components associated with it: the application ID and the instance ID. The application ID is used to represent a group service instance. In a Spring-Boot-based microservice, the application ID will always be the value set by the `spring.application.name` property. For your organization service, your `spring.application.name` is creatively named organizationservice. The instance ID will be a random number meant to represent a single service instance.

> **NOTE**   Remember that normally the `spring.application.name` property goes in the bootstrap.yml file. I've included it in the application.yml for illustrative purposes. The code will work with the `spring.application.name` but the proper place long-term for this attribute is the bootstrap.yml file.

The second part of your configuration provides how and where the service should register with the Eureka service. The `eureka.instance.preferIpAddress` property tells Eureka that you want to register the service's IP address to Eureka rather than its hostname.

Why prefer IP address?

By default, Eureka will try to register the services that contact it by hostname. This works well in a server-based environment where a service is assigned a DNS-backed host name. However, in a container-based deployment (for example, Docker), containers will be started with randomly generated hostnames and *no* DNS entries for the containers.

If you don't set the `eureka.instance.preferIpAddress` to true, your client applications won't properly resolve the location of the hostnames because there will be no DNS entry for that container. Setting the `preferIpAddress` attribute will inform the Eureka service that client wants to be advertised by IP address.

Personally, we always set this attribute to true. Cloud-based microservices are supposed to be ephemeral and stateless. They can be started up and shut down at will. IP addresses are more appropriate for these types of services.

The `eureka.client.registerWithEureka` attribute is the trigger to tell the organization service to register itself with Eureka. The `eureka.client.fetchRegistry` attribute is used to tell the Spring Eureka Client to fetch a local copy of the registry. Setting this attribute to true will cache the registry locally instead of calling the Eureka service with every lookup. Every 30 seconds, the client software will re-contact the Eureka service for any changes to the registry.

The last attribute, the `eureka.serviceUrl.defaultZone` attribute, holds a comma-separated list of Eureka services the client will use to resolve to service locations. For our purposes, you're only going to have one Eureka service.

Eureka high availability

Setting up multiple URL services isn't enough for high availability. The `eureka.serviceUrl.defaultZone` attribute only provides a list of Eureka services for the client to communicate with. You also need to set up the Eureka services to replicate the contents of their registry with each other.

A group of Eureka registries communicate with each other using a peer-to-peer communication model where each Eureka service has to be configured to know about the other nodes in the cluster. Setting up a Eureka cluster is outside of the scope of this book. If you're interested in setting up a Eureka cluster, please visit the Spring Cloud project's website for further information.[a]

---

[a] http://projects.spring.io/spring-cloud/spring-cloud.html

At this point you'll have a single service registered with your Eureka service.

You can use Eureka's REST API to see the contents of the registry. To see all the instances of a service, hit the following GET endpoint:

```
http://<eureka service>:8761/eureka/apps/<APPID>
```

For instance, to see the organization service in the registry you can call `http://localhost:8761/eureka/apps/organizationservice`.

Figure 4.5   **Calling the Eureka REST API to see the organization will show the IP address of the service instances registered in Eureka, along with the service status.**

The default format returned by the Eureka service is XML. Eureka can also return the data in figure 4.5 as a JSON payload, but you have to set the `Accept` HTTP header to be `application/json`. An example of the JSON payload is shown in figure 4.6.

The Accept HTTP header set to application/json will return the service information in JSON.

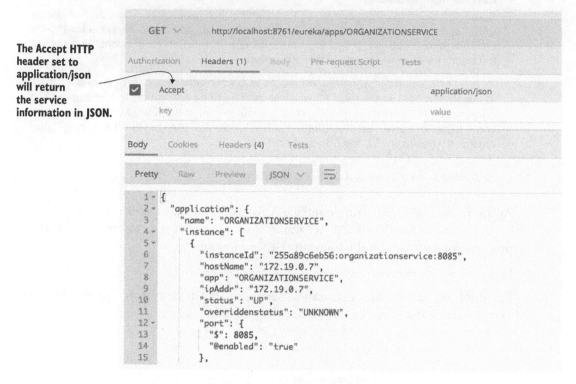

Figure 4.6   Calling the Eureka REST API with the results being JSON

On Eureka and service startups: don't be impatient

When a service registers with Eureka, Eureka will wait for three successive health checks over the course of 30 seconds before the service becomes available via a Eureka. This warm-up period throws developers off because they think that Eureka hasn't registered their services if they try to call their service immediately after the service has been launched. This is evident in our code examples running in the Docker environment, because the Eureka service and the application services (licensing and organization services) all start up at the same time. Be aware that after starting the application, you may receive 404 errors about services not being found, even though the service itself has started. Wait 30 seconds before trying to call your services.

In a production environment, your Eureka services will already be running and if you're deploying an existing service, the old services will still be in place to take requests.

4.5   *Using service discovery to look up a service*

You now have the organization service registered with Eureka. You can also have the licensing service call the organization service without having direct knowledge of the location of any of the organization services. The licensing service will look up the physical location of the organization by using Eureka.

For our purposes, we're going to look at three different Spring/Netflix client libraries in which a service consumer can interact with Ribbon. These libraries will move from the lowest level of abstraction for interacting with Ribbon to the highest. The libraries we'll explore include

- Spring Discovery client
- Spring Discovery client enabled RestTemplate
- Netflix Feign client

Let's walk through each of these clients and see their use in the context of the licensing service. Before we start into the specifics of the client, I wrote a few convenience classes and methods in the code so you can play with the different client types using the same service endpoint.

First, I've modified the `src/main/java/com/thoughtmechanix/licenses/controllers/LicenseServiceController.java` to include a new route for the license services. This new route will allow you to specify the type of client you want to invoke the service with. This is a helper route so that as we explore each of the different methods for invoking the organization service via Ribbon, you can try each mechanism through a single route. The following listing shows the code for the new route in the `LicenseServiceController` class.

Listing 4.5   Calling the licensing service with different REST Clients

```
@RequestMapping(value="/{licenseId}/{clientType}",
    method = RequestMethod.GET)              ◁──────────────
public License getLicensesWithClient(
    @PathVariable("organizationId") String organizationId,
    @PathVariable("licenseId")      String licenseId,
    @PathVariable("clientType")     String clientType) {

    return licenseService.getLicense(organizationId,
    licenseId, clientType);
}
```

> The clientType determines the type of Spring REST client to use.

In this code, the `clientType` parameter passed on the route will drive the type of client we're going to use in the code examples. The specific types you can pass in on this route include

- *Discovery*—Uses the discovery client and a standard Spring RestTemplate class to invoke the organization service
- *Rest*—Uses an enhanced Spring RestTemplate to invoke the Ribbon-based service
- *Feign*—Uses Netflix's Feign client library to invoke a service via Ribbon

NOTE Because I'm using the same code for all three types of client, you might see situations where you'll see annotations for certain clients even when they don't seem to be needed. For example, you'll see both the `@EnableDiscoveryClient` and `@EnableFeignClients` annotations in the code, even when the text is only explaining one of the client types. This is so I can use one code base for my examples. I'll call out these redundancies and code whenever they are encountered.

In the `src/main/java/com/thoughtmechanix/licenses/services/License Service.java` class, I've added a simple method called `retrieveOrgInfo()` that will resolve based on the `clientType` passed into the route the type of client that will be used to look up an organization service instance. The `getLicense()` method on the `LicenseService` class will use `retrieveOrgInfo()` to retrieve the organization data from the Postgres database.

Listing 4.6   `getLicense()` function will use multiple methods to perform a REST call

```
public License getLicense(String organizationId, String licenseId, String
    clientType) {
    License license = licenseRepository.findByOrganizationIdAndLicenseId(
            organizationId, licenseId);

    Organization org = retrieveOrgInfo(organizationId, clientType);

    return license
        .withOrganizationName( org.getName())
        .withContactName( org.getContactName())
        .withContactEmail( org.getContactEmail() )
        .withContactPhone( org.getContactPhone() )
        .withComment(config.getExampleProperty());
}
```

You can find each of the clients we built using the Spring DiscoveryClient, the Spring RestTemplate, or the Feign libraries in the src/main/java/com/thoughtmechanix/licenses/clients package of the licensing-service source code.

4.5.1   *Looking up service instances with Spring DiscoveryClient*

The Spring DiscoveryClient offers the lowest level of access to Ribbon and the services registered within it. Using the DiscoveryClient, you can query for all the services registered with the ribbon client and their corresponding URLs.

Next, you'll build a simple example of using the DiscoveryClient to retrieve one of the organization service URLs from Ribbon and then call the service using a standard RestTemplate class. To begin using the DiscoveryClient, you first need to annotate the `src/main/java/com/thoughtmechanix/licenses/Application.java` class with the `@EnableDiscoveryClient` annotation, as shown in the next listing.

Listing 4.7 Setting up the bootstrap class to use the Eureka Discovery Client

```
@SpringBootApplication
@EnableDiscoveryClient        ⟵  Activates the Spring
@EnableFeignClients                DiscoveryClient for use
public class Application {                     ⟵  Ignore this for now as we'll
  public static void main(String[] args) {         cover this later in the chapter.
    SpringApplication.run(Application.class, args);
  }
}
```

The @EnableDiscoveryClient annotation is the trigger for Spring Cloud to enable
the application to use the DiscoveryClient and Ribbon libraries. The @EnableFeign-
Clients annotation can be ignored for now as we'll be covering it shortly.

Now, let's look at your implementation of the code that calls the organization service
via the Spring DiscoveryClient, as shown in the following listing. You can find this in
src/main/java/com/thoughtmechanix/licenses/OrganizationDiscovery
Client.java.

Listing 4.8 Using the DiscoveryClient to look up information

```
/*Packages and imports removed for conciseness*/

@Component
public class OrganizationDiscoveryClient {

  @Autowired                                        DiscoveryClient is
  private DiscoveryClient discoveryClient;      ⟵  auto-injected into the class.

  public Organization getOrganization(String organizationId) {
    RestTemplate restTemplate = new RestTemplate();
    List<ServiceInstance> instances =                    Gets a list of all
                                                          the instances of
      discoveryClient.getInstances("organizationservice"); ⟵ organization services

    if (instances.size()==0) return null;
    String serviceUri = String.format("%s/v1/organizations/%s",

      instances.get(0).getUri().toString(),

      organizationId);
Retrieves
the service
endpoint we    ResponseEntity< Organization > restExchange =   ⟵
are going          restTemplate.exchange(                      Uses a standard Spring
to call              serviceUri,                                REST Template class to
                     HttpMethod.GET,                           call the service
                     null, Organization.class, organizationId);

    return restExchange.getBody();
  }
}
```

The first item of interest in the code is the `DiscoveryClient`. This is the class you'll use to interact with Ribbon. To retrieve all instances of the organization services registered with Eureka, you can use the `getInstances()` method, passing in the key of service you're looking for, to retrieve a list of `ServiceInstance` objects.

The `ServiceInstance` class is used to hold information about a specific instance of a service including its hostname, port and URI.

In listing 4.8, you take the first `ServiceInstance` class in your list to build a target URL that can then be used to call your service. Once you have a target URL, you can use a standard Spring RestTemplate to call your organization service and retrieve data.

The DiscoveryClient and real life

I'm walking through the DiscoveryClient to be completed in our discussion of building service consumers with Ribbon. The reality is that you should only use the Discovery-Client directly when your service needs to query Ribbon to understand what services and service instances are registered with it. There are several problems with this code including the following:

You aren't taking advantage of Ribbon's client side load-balancing—By calling the DiscoveryClient directly, you get back a list of services, but it becomes your responsibility to choose which service instances returned you're going to invoke.

You're doing too much work—Right now, you have to build the URL that's going to be used to call your service. It's a small thing, but every piece of code that you can avoid writing is one less piece of code that you have to debug.

Observant Spring developers might have noticed that you're directly instantiating the RestTemplate class in the code. This is antithetical to normal Spring REST invocations, as normally you'd have the Spring Framework inject the RestTemplate the class using it via the `@Autowired` annotation.

You instantiated the RestTemplate class in listing 4.8 because once you've enabled the Spring DiscoveryClient in the application class via the `@EnableDiscovery-Client` annotation, all RestTemplates managed by the Spring framework will have a Ribbon-enabled interceptor injected into them that will change how URLs are created with the RestTemplate class. Directly instantiating the RestTemplate class allows you to avoid this behavior.

In summary, there are better mechanisms for calling a Ribbon-backed service.

4.5.2 *Invoking services with Ribbon-aware Spring RestTemplate*

Next, we're going to see an example of how to use a `RestTemplate` that's Ribbon-aware. This is one of the more common mechanisms for interacting with Ribbon via Spring. To use a Ribbon-aware `RestTemplate` class, you need to define a Rest-Template bean construction method with a Spring Cloud annotation called `@Load-Balanced`. For the licensing service, the method that will be used to create the RestTemplate bean can be found in `src/main/java/com/thoughtmechanix/licenses/Application.java`.

The following listing shows the `getRestTemplate()` method that will create the Ribbon-backed Spring `RestTemplate` bean.

Listing 4.9   Annotating and defining a `RestTemplate` construction method

```
package com.thoughtmechanix.licenses;

//...Most of import statements have been removed for consiceness
import org.springframework.cloud.client.loadbalancer.LoadBalanced;
import org.springframework.context.annotation.Bean;
import org.springframework.web.client.RestTemplate;

@SpringBootApplication
@EnableDiscoveryClient
@EnableFeignClients
public class Application {

    @LoadBalanced
    @Bean
    public RestTemplate getRestTemplate(){
        return new RestTemplate();
    }

    public static void main(String[] args) {
        SpringApplication.run(Application.class, args);
    }
}
```

Because we're using multiple client types in the examples, I'm including them in the code. However, the @EnableDiscoveryClient and @EnableFeignClients application aren't needed when using the Ribbon backed RestTemplate and can be removed.

The @LoadBalanced annotation tells Spring Cloud to create a Ribbon backed RestTemplate class.

NOTE   In early releases of Spring Cloud, the RestTemplate class was automatically backed by Ribbon. It was the default behavior. However, since Spring Cloud Release Angel, the RestTemplate in Spring Cloud is no longer backed by Ribbon. If you want to use Ribbon with the RestTemplate, you must explicitly annotate it using the @LoadBalanced annotation.

Now that the bean definition for the Ribbon-backed `RestTemplate` class is defined, any time you want to use the `RestTemplate` bean to call a service, you only need to auto-wire it into the class using it.

Using the Ribbon-backed `RestTemplate` class pretty much behaves like a standard Spring `RestTemplate` class, except for one small difference in how the URL for target service is defined. Rather than using the physical location of the service in the `RestTemplate` call, you're going to build the target URL using the Eureka service ID of the service you want to call.

Let's see this difference by looking at the following listing. The code for this listing can be found in the `src/main/java/com/thoughtmechanix/licenses/clients/OrganizationRestTemplate.java` class.

Listing 4.10   Using a Ribbon-backed `RestTemplate` to call a service

```
/*Package and import definitions left off for conciseness*/
@Component
```

```
public class OrganizationRestTemplateClient {
  @Autowired
  RestTemplate restTemplate;

  public Organization getOrganization(String organizationId){
    ResponseEntity<Organization> restExchange =
        restTemplate.exchange(
            "http://organizationservice/v1/organizations/{organizationId}", ◁┐
            HttpMethod.GET,
            null, Organization.class, organizationId);

    return restExchange.getBody();
  }
}
```

When using a Ribbon-back RestTemplate, you build the target URL with the Eureka service ID.

This code should look somewhat similar to the previous example, except for two key differences. First, the Spring Cloud `DiscoveryClient` is nowhere in sight. Second, the URL being used in the `restTemplate.exchange()` call should look odd to you:

```
restTemplate.exchange(

  "http://organizationservice/v1/organizations/{organizationId}",
    HttpMethod.GET,
null, Organization.class, organizationId);
```

The server name in the URL matches the application ID of the organizationservice key that you registered the organization service with in Eureka:

```
http://{applicationid}/v1/organizations/{organizationId}
```

The Ribbon-enabled `RestTemplate` will parse the URL passed into it and use whatever is passed in as the server name as the key to query Ribbon for an instance of a service. The actual service location and port are completely abstracted from the developer.

In addition, by using the `RestTemplate` class, Ribbon will round-robin load balance all requests among all the service instances.

4.5.3 *Invoking services with Netflix Feign client*

An alternative to the Spring Ribbon-enabled `RestTemplate` class is Netflix's Feign client library. The Feign library takes a different approach to calling a REST service by having the developer first define a Java interface and then annotating that interface with Spring Cloud annotations to map what Eureka-based service Ribbon will invoke. The Spring Cloud framework will dynamically generate a proxy class that will be used to invoke the targeted REST service. There's no code being written for calling the service other than an interface definition.

To enable the Feign client for use in your licensing service, you need to add a new annotation, `@EnableFeignClients`, to the licensing service's `src/main/java/com/thoughtmechanix/licenses/Application.java` class. The following listing shows this code.

Listing 4.11   Enabling the Spring Cloud/Netflix Feign client in the licensing service

Because we're only using the FeignClient,
in your own code you can remove the
@EnableDiscoveryClient annotation.

```java
@SpringBootApplication
@EnableDiscoveryClient
@EnableFeignClients
public class Application {
  public static void main(String[] args) {
    SpringApplication.run(Application.class, args);
  }
}
```

The @EnableFeignClients
annotation is needed to use
the FeignClient in your code.

Now that you've enabled the Feign client for use in your licensing service, let's look at a Feign client interface definition that can be used to call an endpoint on the organization service. The following listing shows an example. The code in this listing can be found in the `src/main/java/com/thoughtmechanix/licenses/clients/OrganizationFeignClient.java` class.

Listing 4.12   Defining a Feign interface for calling the organization service

```java
/*Package and import left off for conciseness*/
@FeignClient("organizationservice")
public interface OrganizationFeignClient {
@RequestMapping(
     method= RequestMethod.GET,
     value="/v1/organizations/{organizationId}",
     consumes="application/json")
 Organization getOrganization(
  @PathVariable("organizationId") String organizationId);
}
```

Identify your service to Feign using
the FeignClient Annotation.

The path and action to your
endpoint is defined using the
@RequestMapping annotation.

The parameters passed into the endpoint are
defined using the @PathVariable endpoint.

You start the Feign example by using the `@FeignClient` annotation and passing it the name of the application id of the service you want the interface to represent. Next you'll define a method, `getOrganization()`, in your interface that can be called by the client to invoke the organization service.

How you define the `getOrganization()` method looks exactly like how you would expose an endpoint in a Spring Controller class. First, you're going to define a `@RequestMapping` annotation for the `getOrganization()` method that will map the HTTP verb and endpoint that will be exposed on the organization service invocation. Second, you'll map the organization ID passed in on the URL to an `organizationId` parameter on the method call, using the `@PathVariable` annotation. The return value from the call to the organization service will be automatically mapped to the `Organization` class that's defined as the return value for the `getOrganization()` method.

To use the `OrganizationFeignClient` class, all you need to do is autowire and use it. The Feign Client code will take care of all the coding work for you.

On error handling

When you use the standard Spring `RestTemplate` class, all service calls' HTTP status codes will be returned via the `ResponseEntity` class's `getStatusCode()` method. With the Feign Client, any HTTP 4xx – 5xx status codes returned by the service being called will be mapped to a `FeignException`. The `FeignException` will contain a JSON body that can be parsed for the specific error message.

Feign does provide you the ability to write an error decoder class that will map the error back to a custom Exception class. Writing this decoder is outside the scope of this book, but you can find examples of this in the Feign GitHub repository at (https://github.com/Netflix/feign/wiki/Custom-error-handling).

4.6   Summary

- The service discovery pattern is used to abstract away the physical location of services.
- A service discovery engine such as Eureka can seamlessly add and remove service instances from an environment without the service clients being impacted.
- Client-side load balancing can provide an extra level of performance and resiliency by caching the physical location of a service on the client making the service call.
- Eureka is a Netflix project that when used with Spring Cloud, is easy to set up and configure.
- You used three different mechanisms in Spring Cloud, Netflix Eureka, and Netflix Ribbon to invoke a service. These mechanisms included

  - Using a Spring Cloud service DiscoveryClient
  - Using Spring Cloud and Ribbon-backed RestTemplate
  - Using Spring Cloud and Netflix's Feign client

When bad things happen: client resiliency patterns with Spring Cloud and Netflix Hystrix

This chapter covers

- Implementing circuit breakers, fallbacks, and bulkheads
- Using the circuit breaker pattern to conserve microservice client resources
- Using Hystrix when a remote service is failing
- Implementing Hystrix's bulkhead pattern to segregate remote resource calls
- Tuning Hystrix's circuit breaker and bulkhead implementations
- Customizing Hystrix's concurrency strategy

All systems, especially distributed systems, will experience failure. How we build our applications to respond to that failure is a critical part of every software developer's job. However, when it comes to building resilient systems, most software engineers only take into account the complete failure of a piece of infrastructure or a key service. They focus on building redundancy into each layer of their application using techniques such as clustering key servers, load balancing between services, and segregation of infrastructure into multiple locations.

While these approaches take into account the complete (and often spectacular) loss of a system component, they address only one small part of building resilient systems. When a service crashes, it's easy to detect that it's no longer there, and the application can route around it. However, when a service is running slow, detecting that poor performance and routing around it is extremely difficult because

1   *Degradation of a service can start out as intermittent and build momentum*—The degradation might occur only in small bursts. The first signs of failure might be a small group of users complaining about a problem, until suddenly the application container exhausts its thread pool and collapses completely.

2   *Calls to remote services are usually synchronous and don't cut short a long-running call*—The caller of a service has no concept of a timeout to keep the service call from hanging out forever. The application developer calls the service to perform an action and waits for the service to return.

3   *Applications are often designed to deal with complete failures of remote resources, not partial degradations.* Often, as long as the service has not completely failed, an application will continue to call the service and won't fail fast. The application will continue to call the poorly behaving service. The calling application or service may degrade gracefully or, more likely, crash because of resource exhaustion. *Resource exhaustion* is when a limited resource such as a thread pool or database connection maxes out and the calling client must wait for that resource to become available.

What's insidious about problems caused by poorly performing remote services is that they're not only difficult to detect, but can trigger a cascading effect that can ripple throughout an entire application ecosystem. Without safeguards in place, a single poorly performing service can quickly take down multiple applications. Cloud-based, microservice-based applications are particularly vulnerable to these types of outages because these applications are composed of a large number of fine-grained, distributed services with different pieces of infrastructure involved in completing a user's transaction.

5.1   What are client-side resiliency patterns?

Client resiliency software patterns are focused on protecting a remote resource's (another microservice call or database lookup) client from crashing when the remote resource is failing because that remote service is throwing errors or performing poorly. The goal of these patterns is to allow the client to "fail fast," not consume valuable resources such as database connections and thread pools, and prevent the problem of the remote service from spreading "upstream" to consumers of the client.

There are four client resiliency patterns:

1   Client-side load balancing
2   Circuit breakers
3   Fallbacks
4   Bulkheads

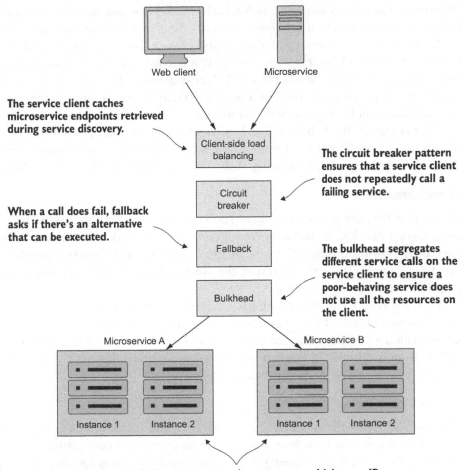

Figure 5.1   **The four client resiliency patterns act as a protective buffer between a service consumer and the service.**

Figure 5.1 demonstrates how these patterns sit between the microservice service consumer and the microservice.

These patterns are implemented in the client calling the remote resource. The implementation of these patterns logically sit between the client consuming the remote resources and the resource itself.

5.1.1   Client-side load balancing

We introduced the client-side load balancing pattern in the last chapter (chapter 4) when talking about service discovery. Client-side load balancing involves having the client look up all of a service's individual instances from a service discovery agent (like Netflix Eureka) and then caching the physical location of said service instances.

Whenever a service consumer needs to call that service instance, the client-side load balancer will return a location from the pool of service locations it's maintaining.

Because the client-side load balancer sits between the service client and the service consumer, the load balancer can detect if a service instance is throwing errors or behaving poorly. If the client-side load balancer detects a problem, it can remove that service instance from the pool of available service locations and prevent any future service calls from hitting that service instance.

This is exactly the behavior that Netflix's Ribbon libraries provide out of the box with no extra configuration. Because we covered client-side load balancing with Netflix Ribbon in chapter 4, we won't go into any more detail on that in this chapter.

5.1.2   Circuit breaker

The circuit breaker pattern is a client resiliency pattern that's modeled after an electrical circuit breaker. In an electrical system, a circuit breaker will detect if too much current is flowing through the wire. If the circuit breaker detects a problem, it will break the connection with the rest of the electrical system and keep the downstream components from the being fried.

With a software circuit breaker, when a remote service is called, the circuit breaker will monitor the call. If the calls take too long, the circuit breaker will intercede and kill the call. In addition, the circuit breaker will monitor all calls to a remote resource and if enough calls fail, the circuit break implementation will pop, failing fast and preventing future calls to the failing remote resource.

5.1.3   Fallback processing

With the fallback pattern, when a remote service call fails, rather than generating an exception, the service consumer will execute an alternative code path and try to carry out an action through another means. This usually involves looking for data from another data source or queueing the user's request for future processing. The user's call will not be shown an exception indicating a problem, but they may be notified that their request will have to be fulfilled at a later date.

For instance, suppose you have an e-commerce site that monitors your user's behavior and tries to give them recommendations of other items they could buy. Typically, you might call a microservice to run an analysis of the user's past behavior and return a list of recommendations tailored to that specific user. However, if the preference service fails, your fallback might be to retrieve a more general list of preferences that's based off all user purchases and is much more generalized. This data might come from a completely different service and data source.

5.1.4   Bulkheads

The bulkhead pattern is based on a concept from building ships. With a bulkhead design, a ship is divided into completely segregated and watertight compartments called bulkheads. Even if the ship's hull is punctured, because the ship is divided into watertight compartments (bulkheads), the bulkhead will keep the water confined to the area of the ship where the puncture occurred and prevent the entire ship from filling with water and sinking.

The same concept can be applied to a service that must interact with multiple remote resources. By using the bulkhead pattern, you can break the calls to remote resources into their own thread pools and reduce the risk that a problem with one slow remote resource call will take down the entire application. The thread pools act as the bulkheads for your service. Each remote resource is segregated and assigned to the thread pool. If one service is responding slowly, the thread pool for that one type of service call will become saturated and stop processing requests. Service calls to other services won't become saturated because they're assigned to other thread pools.

5.2   *Why client resiliency matters*

We've talked about these different patterns in the abstract; however, let's drill down to a more specific example of where these patterns can be applied. Let's walk through a common scenario I've run into and see why client resiliency patterns such as the circuit breaker pattern are critical for implementing a service-based architecture, particularly a microservice architecture running in the cloud.

In figure 5.2, I show a typical scenario involving the use of remote resource like a database and remote service.

In the scenario in figure 5.2, three applications are communicating in one fashion or another with three different services. Applications A and B communicate directly with Service A. Service A retrieves data from a database and calls Service B to do work for it. Service B retrieves data from a completely different database platform and calls out to another service, Service C, from a third-party cloud provider whose service relies heavily on an internal Network Area Storage (NAS) device to write data to a shared file system. In addition, Application C directly calls Service C.

Over the weekend, a network administrator made what they thought was a small tweak to the configuration on the NAS, as shown in bold in figure 5.2. This change appears to work fine, but on Monday morning, any reads to a particular disk subsystem start performing extremely slowly.

The developer who wrote Service B never anticipated slowdowns occurring with calls to Service C. They wrote their code so that the writes to their database and the reads from the service occur within the same transaction. When Service C starts running slowly, not only does the thread pool for requests to Service C start backing up, the number of database connections in the service container's connection pools become exhausted because these connections are being held open because the calls out to Service C never complete.

Finally, Service A starts running out of resources because it's calling Service B, which is running slow because of Service C. Eventually, all three applications stop responding because they run out of resources while waiting for requests to complete.

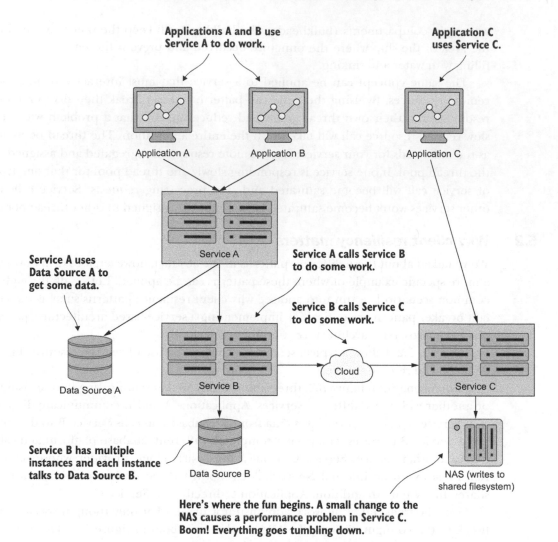

Applications A and B use Service A to do work.

Application C uses Service C.

Application A

Application B

Application C

Service A

Service A uses Data Source A to get some data.

Service A calls Service B to do some work.

Service B calls Service C to do some work.

Data Source A

Service B

Cloud

Service C

Service B has multiple instances and each instance talks to Data Source B.

Data Source B

NAS (writes to shared filesystem)

Here's where the fun begins. A small change to the NAS causes a performance problem in Service C. Boom! Everything goes tumbling down.

Figure 5.2 An application is a graph of interconnected dependencies. If you don't manage the remote calls between these, one poorly behaving remote resource can bring down all the services in the graph.

This whole scenario could be avoided if a circuit-breaker pattern had been implemented at each point where a distributed resource had been called (either a call to the database or a call to the service). In figure 5.2, if the call to Service C had been implemented with a circuit breaker, then when service C started performing poorly, the circuit breaker for that specific call to Service C would have been tripped and failed fast without eating up a thread. If Service B had multiple endpoints, only the endpoints that interacted with that specific call to Service C would be impacted. The rest of Service B's functionality would still be intact and could fulfill user requests.

A circuit breaker acts as a middle man between the application and the remote service. In the previous scenario, a circuit breaker implementation could have protected Applications A, B, and C from completely crashing.

In figure 5.3, the Service B (the client) is never going to directly invoke Service C. Instead, when the call is made, Service B is going to delegate the actual invocation of the service to the circuit breaker, which will take the call and wrap it in a thread (usually managed by a thread pool) that's independent of the originating caller. By wrapping the call in a thread, the client is no longer directly waiting for the call to complete. Instead, the circuit breaker is monitoring the thread and can kill the call if the thread runs too long.

Three scenarios are shown in figure 5.3. In the first scenario, the happy path, the circuit breaker will maintain a timer and if the call to the remote service completes before the timer runs out, everything is good and Service B can continue its work. In the partial degradation scenario, Service B will call Service C through the circuit breaker. This time, though, Service C is running slow and the circuit breaker will kill the connection out to the remote service if it doesn't complete before the timer on the thread maintained by the circuit breaker times out.

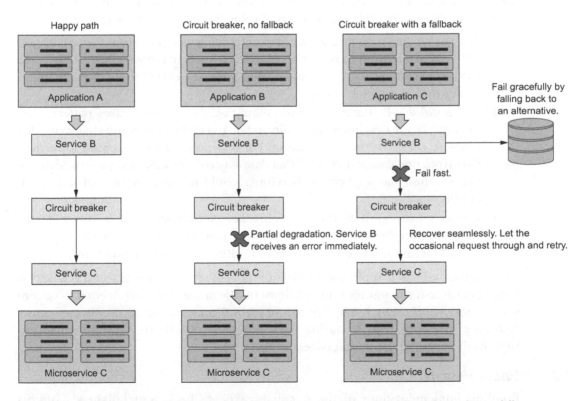

Figure 5.3   The circuit breaker trips and allows a misbehaving service call to fail quickly and gracefully.

Service B will then get an error from making the call, but Service B won't have resources (that is, its own thread or connection pools) tied up waiting for Service C to complete. If the call to Service C is timed-out by the circuit breaker, the circuit breaker will start tracking the number of failures that have occurred.

If enough errors on the service have occurred within a certain time period, the circuit breaker will now "trip" the circuit and all calls to Service C will fail without calling Service C.

This tripping of the circuit allows three things to occur:

1   Service B now immediately knows there's a problem without having to wait for a timeout from the circuit breaker.
2   Service B can now choose to either completely fail or take action using an alternative set of code (a fallback).
3   Service C will be given an opportunity to recover because Service B isn't calling it while the circuit breaker has been tripped. This allows Service C to have breathing room and helps prevent the cascading death that occurs when a service degradation occurs.

Finally, the circuit breaker will occasionally let calls through to a degraded service, and if those calls succeed enough times in a row, the circuit breaker will reset itself.

The key thing a circuit break patterns offers is the ability for remote calls to

1   *Fail fast*—When a remote service is experiencing a degradation, the application will fail fast and prevent resource exhaustion issues that normally shut down the entire application. In most outage situations, it's better to be partially down rather than completely down.
2   *Fail gracefully*—By timing out and failing fast, the circuit breaker pattern gives the application developer the ability to fail gracefully or seek alternative mechanisms to carry out the user's intent. For instance, if a user is trying to retrieve data from one data source, and that data source is experiencing a service degradation, then the application developer could try to retrieve that data from another location.
3   *Recover seamlessly*—With the circuit-breaker pattern acting as an intermediary, the circuit breaker can periodically check to see if the resource being requested is back on line and re-enable access to it without human intervention.

In a large cloud-based application with hundreds of services, this graceful recovery is critical because it can significantly cut down on the amount of time needed to restore service and significantly lessen the risk of a tired operator or application engineer causing greater problems by having them intervene directly (restarting a failed service) in the restoration of the service.

5.3   *Enter Hystrix*

Building implementations of the circuit breaker, fallback, and bulkhead patterns requires intimate knowledge of threads and thread management. Let's face it, writing robust threading code is an art (which I've never mastered) and doing it correctly is difficult. To implement a high-quality set of implementations for the circuit-breaker, fallback, and bulkhead patterns would require a tremendous amount of work. Fortunately, you can use Spring Cloud and Netflix's Hystrix library to provide you a battle-tested library that's used daily in Netflix's microservice architecture.

In the next several sections of this chapter we're going to cover how to

- Configure the licensing service's maven build file (pom.xml) to include the Spring Cloud/Hystrix wrappers.
- Use the Spring Cloud/Hystrix annotations to wrapper remote calls with a circuit breaker pattern.
- Customize the individual circuit breakers on a remote resource to use custom timeouts for each call made. I'll also demonstrate how to configure the circuit breakers so that you control how many failures occur before a circuit breaker "trips."
- Implement a fallback strategy in the event a circuit breaker has to interrupt a call or the call fails.
- Use individual thread pools in your service to isolate service calls and build bulkheads between different remote resources being called.

5.4   *Setting up the licensing server to use Spring Cloud and Hystrix*

To begin our exploration of Hystrix, you need to set up your project pom.xml to import the Spring Hystrix dependencies. You'll take your licensing service that we've been building and modify its pom.xml by adding the maven dependencies for Hystrix:

```
<dependency>
 <groupId>org.springframework.cloud</groupId>
 <artifactId>spring-cloud-starter-hystrix</artifactId>
</dependency>
<dependency>
  <groupId>com.netflix.hystrix</groupId>
  <artifactId>hystrix-javanica</artifactId>
  <version>1.5.9</version>
</dependency>
```

The first <dependency> tag (spring-cloud-starter-hystrix) tells Maven to pull down the Spring Cloud Hystrix dependencies. This second <dependency> tag (hystrix-javanica) will pull down the core Netflix Hystrix libraries. With the Maven dependencies set up, you can go ahead and begin your Hystrix implementation using the licensing and organization services you built in previous chapters.

> **NOTE** You don't have to include the hystrix-javanica dependencies directly in the pom.xml. By default, the spring-cloud-starter-hystrix includes a version of the hystrix-javanica dependencies. The Camden.SR5 release of the book used hystrix-javanica-1.5.6. The version of

hystrix-javanica had an inconsistency introduced into it that caused the Hystrix code without a fallback to throw a java.lang.reflect. UndeclaredThrowableException instead of a com.netflix. hystrix.exception.HystrixRuntimeException. This was a breaking change for many developers who used older versions of Hystrix. The hystrix-javanica libraries fixed this in later releases, so I've purposely used a later version of hystrix-javanica instead of using the default version pulled in by Spring Cloud.

The last thing that needs to be done before you can begin using Hystrix circuit breakers within your application code is to annotate your service's bootstrap class with the @EnableCircuitBreaker annotation. For example, for the licensing service, you'd add the @EnableCircuitBreaker annotation to the licensing-service/src/main/java/com/thoughtmechanix/licenses/Application.java class. The following listing shows this code.

> **Listing 5.1   The @EnableCircuitBreaker annotation used to activate Hystrix in a service**

```
package com.thoughtmechanix.licenses

import org.springframework.cloud.client.circuitbreaker.EnableCircuitBreaker;
//Rest of imports removed for conciseness

@SpringBootApplication
@EnableEurekaClient
@EnableCircuitBreaker          ◄——————   Tells Spring Cloud you're going
public class Application {                to use Hystrix for your service
    @LoadBalanced
    @Bean
    public RestTemplate restTemplate() {
        return new RestTemplate();
    }

    public static void main(String[] args) {
        SpringApplication.run(Application.class, args);
    }
}
```

NOTE   If you forget to add the @EnableCircuitBreaker annotation to your bootstrap class, none of your Hystrix circuit breakers will be active. You won't get any warning or error messages when the service starts up.

5.5   *Implementing a circuit breaker using Hystrix*

We're going to look at implementing Hystrix in two broad categories. In the first category, you're going to wrap all calls to your database in the licensing and organization service with a Hystrix circuit breaker. You're then going to wrap the inter-service calls between the licensing service and the organization service using Hystrix. While these

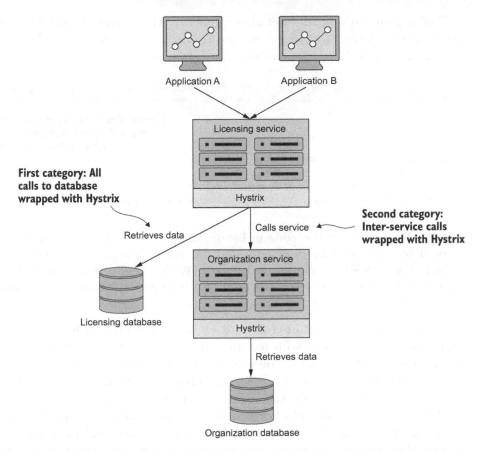

First category: All calls to database wrapped with Hystrix

Second category: Inter-service calls wrapped with Hystrix

Figure 5.4 **Hystrix sits between each remote resource call and protects the client. It doesn't matter if the remote resource call is a database call or a REST-based service call.**

are two different categories calls, you'll see that the use of Hystrix will be exactly the same. Figure 5.4 shows what remote resources you're going to wrap with a Hystrix circuit breaker.

Let's start our Hystrix discussion by showing how to wrap the retrieval of licensing service data from the licensing database using a synchronous Hystrix circuit breaker. With a synchronous call, the licensing service will retrieve its data but will wait for the SQL statement to complete or for a circuit-breaker time-out before continuing processing.

Hystrix and Spring Cloud use the `@HystrixCommand` annotation to mark Java class methods as being managed by a Hystrix circuit breaker. When the Spring framework sees the `@HystrixCommand`, it will dynamically generate a proxy that will wrapper the method and manage all calls to that method through a thread pool of threads specifically set aside to handle remote calls.

You're going to wrap the `getLicensesByOrg()` method in your `licensing-service/src/main/java/com/thoughtmechanix/licenses/services/LicenseService.java` class, as shown in the following listing.

Listing 5.2   Wrappering a remote resource call with a circuit breaker

> **@HystrixCommand annotation is used to wrapper the getLicenseByOrg() method with a Hystrix circuit breaker.**

```
//Imports removed for conciseness
@HystrixCommand                                                          ◄──────
public List<License> getLicensesByOrg(String organizationId){
    return licenseRepository.findByOrganizationId(organizationId);
}
```

NOTE   If you look at the code in listing 5.2 in the source code repository, you'll see several more parameters on the `@HystrixCommand` annotation than what's shown in the previous listing. We'll get into those parameters later in the chapter. The code in listing 5.2 is using the `@HystrixCommand` annotation with all its default values.

This doesn't look like a lot of code, and it's not, but there is a lot of functionality inside this one annotation. With the use of the `@HystrixCommand` annotation, any time the `getLicensesByOrg()` method is called, the call will be wrapped with a Hystrix circuit breaker. The circuit breaker will interrupt any call to the `getLicenses-ByOrg()` method any time the call takes longer than 1,000 milliseconds.

This code example would be boring if the database is working properly. Let's simulate the `getLicensesByOrg()` method running into a slow database query by having the call take a little over a second on approximately every one in three calls. The following listing demonstrates this.

Listing 5.3   Randomly timing out a call to the licensing service database

```
private void randomlyRunLong(){                          ◄──────  The randomlyRunLong() method
    Random rand = new Random();                                   gives you a one in three chance
                                                                  of a database call running long.
    int randomNum = rand.nextInt((3 - 1) + 1) + 1;

    if (randomNum==3) sleep();
}

private void sleep(){
    try {
        Thread.sleep(11000);                            ◄──────  You sleep for 11,000 milliseconds
    } catch (InterruptedException e) {                            (11 seconds). Default Hystrix behavior
        e.printStackTrace();                                      is to time a call out after 1 second.
    }
}

@HystrixCommand
```

```
public List<License> getLicensesByOrg(String organizationId){
    randomlyRunLong();

    return licenseRepository.findByOrganizationId(organizationId);
}
```

If you hit the `http://localhost:8080/v1/organizations/e254f8c-c442-4ebe -a82a-e2fc1d1ff78a/licenses/` endpoint enough times, you should see a time-out error message returned from the licensing service. Figure 5.5 shows this error.

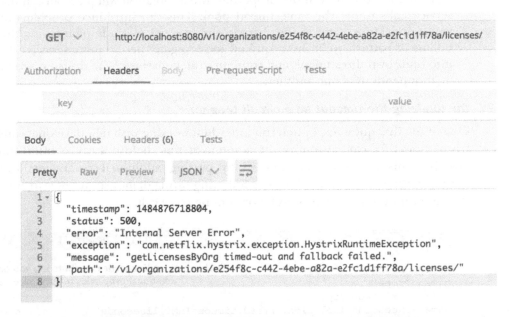

Figure 5.5 A HystrixRuntimeException is thrown when a remote call takes too long.

Now, with `@HystrixCommand` annotation in place, the licensing service will interrupt a call out to its database if the query takes too long. If the database calls take longer than 1,000 milliseconds to execute the Hystrix code wrapping, your service call will throw a `com.nextflix.hystrix.exception.HystrixRuntimeException` exception.

5.5.1 *Timing out a call to the organization microservice*

The beauty of using method-level annotations for tagging calls with circuit-breaker behavior is that it's the same annotation whether you're accessing a database or calling a microservice.

For instance, in your licensing service you need to look up the name of the organization associated with the license. If you want to wrap your call to the organization service with a circuit breaker, it's as simple as breaking the `RestTemplate` call into its own method and annotating it with the `@HystrixCommand` annotation:

```
@HystrixCommand
private Organization getOrganization(String organizationId) {
 return organizationRestClient.getOrganization(organizationId);
}
```

> **NOTE** While using the `@HystrixCommand` is easy to implement, you do need to be careful about using the default `@HystrixCommand` annotation with no configuration on the annotation. By default, when you specify a `@Hystrix-Command` annotation without properties, the annotation will place all remote service calls under the same thread pool. This can introduce problems in your application. Later in the chapter when we talk about implementing the bulkhead pattern, we'll show you how to segregate these remote service calls into their own thread pools and configure the behavior of the thread pools to be independent of one another.

5.5.2   Customizing the timeout on a circuit breaker

One of the first questions I often run into when working with new developers and Hystrix is how they can customize the amount of time before a call is interrupted by Hystrix. This is easily accomplished by passing additional parameters into the `@HystrixCommand` annotation. The following listing demonstrates how to customize the amount of time Hystrix waits before timing out a call.

Listing 5.4   Customizing the time out on a circuit breaker call

```
@HystrixCommand(
  commandProperties=
    {@HystrixProperty(
    name="execution.isolation.thread.timeoutInMilliseconds",
    value="12000")})
public List<License> getLicensesByOrg(String organizationId){
  randomlyRunLong();

  return licenseRepository.findByOrganizationId(organizationId);
}
```

The commandProperties attribute lets you provide additional properties to customize Hystrix.

The execution.isolation.thread.timeoutInMilliseconds is used to set the length of the timeout (in milliseconds) of the circuit breaker.

Hystrix allows you to customize the behavior of the circuit breaker through the `commandProperties` attribute. The `commandProperties` attribute accepts an array of `HystrixProperty` objects that can pass in custom properties to configure the Hystrix circuit breaker. In listing 5.4, you use the `execution.isolation.thread` `.timeoutInMilliseconds` property to set the maximum timeout a Hystrix call will wait before failing to be 12 seconds.

Now if you rebuild and rerun the code example, you'll never get a timeout error because your artificial timeout on the call is 11 seconds while your @HystrixCommand annotation is now configured to only time out after 12 seconds.

On service timeouts

It should be obvious that I'm using a circuit breaker timeout of 12 seconds as a teaching example. In a distributed environment, I often get nervous if I start hearing comments from development teams that a 1 second timeout on remote service calls is too low because their service X takes on average 5-6 seconds.

This usually tells me that unresolved performance problems exist with the service being called. Avoid the temptation to increase the default timeout on Hystrix calls unless you absolutely cannot resolve a slow running service call.

If you do have a situation where part of your service calls are going to take longer than other service calls, definitely look at segregating these service calls into separate thread pools.

5.6   *Fallback processing*

Part of the beauty of the circuit breaker pattern is that because a "middle man" is between the consumer of a remote resource and the resource itself, you have an opportunity for the developer to intercept a service failure and choose an alternative course of action to take.

In Hystrix, this is known as a fallback strategy and is easily implemented. Let's see how to build a simple fallback strategy for your licensing database that simply returns a licensing object that says no licensing information is currently available. The following listing demonstrates this.

Listing 5.5   Implementing a fallback in Hystrix

The fallbackMethod attribute defines a single function in your class that will be called if the call from Hystrix fails.

```
@HystrixCommand(fallbackMethod = "buildFallbackLicenseList")     ⟵
  public List<License> getLicensesByOrg(String organizationId){
    randomlyRunLong();

    return licenseRepository.findByOrganizationId(organizationId);
  }

private List<License> buildFallbackLicenseList(String organizationId){    ⟵
  List<License> fallbackList = new ArrayList<>();
  License license = new License()
    .withId("0000000-00-00000")
    .withOrganizationId( organizationId )
    .withProductName(
    "Sorry no licensing information currently available");
```

In the fallback method you return a hard-coded value.

```
        fallbackList.add(license);
        return fallbackList;
}
```

> **NOTE**   In the source code from the GitHub repository, I comment out the
> `fallbackMethod` line so that you can see the service call randomly fail. To
> see the fallback code in listing 5.5 in action you'll need to uncomment out
> the `fallbackMethod` attribute. Otherwise, you will never see the fallback
> actually being invoked.

To implement a fallback strategy with Hystrix you have to do two things. First, you
need to add an attribute called `fallbackMethod` to the `@HystrixCommand` annotation. This attribute will contain the name of a method that will be called when Hystrix
has to interrupt a call because it's taking too long.

The second thing you need to do is define a fallback method to be executed. This
fallback method must reside in the same class as the original method that was protected by the `@HystrixCommand`. The fallback method must have the exact same
method signature as the originating function as all of the parameters passed into the
original method protected by the `@HystrixCommand` will be passed to the fallback.

In the example in listing 5.5, the fallback method `buildFallbackLicense-`
`List()` is simply constructing a single `License` object containing dummy information. You could have your fallback method read this data from an alternative data
source, but for demonstration purposes you're going to construct a list that would
have been returned by your original function call.

On fallbacks

The fallback strategy works extremely well in situations where your microservice is
retrieving data and the call fails. In one organization I worked at, we had customer
information stored in an operational data store (ODS) and also summarized in a data
warehouse.

Our happy path was to always retrieve the most recent data and calculate summary
information for it on the fly. However, after a particularly nasty outage where a slow
database connection took down multiple services, we decided to protect the service
call that retrieved and summarized the customer's information with a Hystrix fallback
implementation. If the call to the ODS failed due to a performance problem or an error,
we used a fallback to retrieve the summarized data from our data warehouse tables.

Our business team decided that giving the customer's older data was preferable to
having the customer see an error or have the entire application crash. The key when
choosing whether to use a fallback strategy is the level of tolerance your customers
have to the age of their data and how important it is to never let them see the application having problems.

Here are a few things to keep in mind as you determine whether you want to implement a fallback strategy:

1 Fallbacks are a mechanism to provide a course of action when a resource
   has timed out or failed. If you find yourself using fallbacks to catch a timeout

exception and then doing nothing more than logging the error, then you should probably use a standard `try..catch` block around your service invocation, catch the `HystrixRuntimeException`, and put the logging logic in the `try..catch` block.

2 Be aware of the actions you're taking with your fallback functions. If you call out to another distributed service in your fallback service you may need to wrap the fallback with a `@HystrixCommand` annotation. Remember, the same failure that you're experiencing with your primary course of action might also impact your secondary fallback option. Code defensively. I have been bitten hard when I failed to take this into account when using fallbacks.

Now that you have your fallback in place, go ahead and call your endpoint again. This time when you hit it and encounter a timeout error (remember you have a one in 3 chance) you shouldn't get an exception back from the service call, but instead have the dummy license values returned.

Results of fallback code

Figure 5.6 Your service invocation using a Hystrix fallback

5.7   *Implementing the bulkhead pattern*

In a microservice-based application you'll often need to call multiple microservices to complete a particular task. Without using a bulkhead pattern, the default behavior for these calls is that the calls are executed using the same threads that are reserved for handling requests for the entire Java container. In high volumes, performance problems with one service out of many can result in all of the threads for the Java container being maxed out and waiting to process work, while new requests for work back up. The Java container will eventually crash. The bulkhead pattern segregates remote resource calls in their own thread pools so that a single misbehaving service can be contained and not crash the container.

Hystrix uses a thread pool to delegate all requests for remote services. By default, all Hystrix commands will share the same thread pool to process requests. This thread pool will have 10 threads in it to process remote service calls and those remote services calls could be anything, including REST-service invocations, database calls, and so on. Figure 5.7 illustrates this.

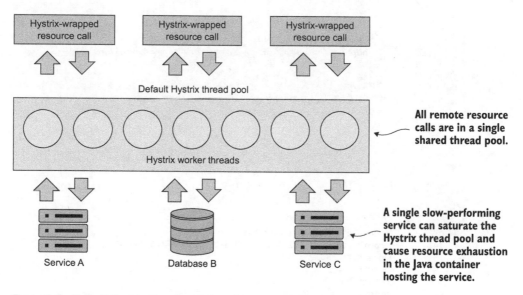

Figure 5.7   Default Hystrix thread pool shared across multiple resource types

This model works fine when you have a small number of remote resources being accessed within an application and the call volumes for the individual services are relatively evenly distributed. The problem is if you have services that have far higher volumes or longer completion times than other services, you can end up introducing thread exhaustion into your Hystrix thread pools because one service ends up dominating all of the threads in the default thread pool.

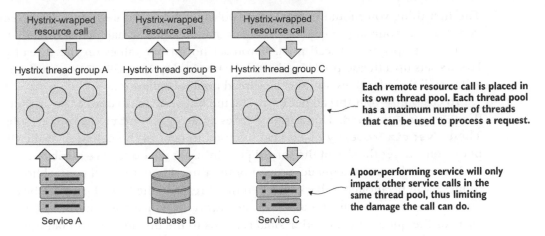

Each remote resource call is placed in its own thread pool. Each thread pool has a maximum number of threads that can be used to process a request.

A poor-performing service will only impact other service calls in the same thread pool, thus limiting the damage the call can do.

Figure 5.8   Hystrix command tied to segregated thread pools

Fortunately, Hystrix provides an easy-to-use mechanism for creating bulkheads between different remote resource calls. Figure 5.8 shows what Hystrix managed resources look like when they're segregated into their own "bulkheads."

To implement segregated thread pools, you need to use additional attributes exposed through the @HystrixCommand annotation. Let's look at some code that will

1 Set up a separate thread pool for the getLicensesByOrg() call
2 Set the number of threads in the thread pool
3 Set the queue size for the number of requests that can queue if the individual threads are busy

The following listing demonstrates how to set up a bulkhead around all calls surrounding the look-up of licensing data from our licensing service.

Listing 5.6   Creating a bulkhead around the `getLicensesByOrg()` **method**

The threadPoolProperties attribute lets you define and customize the behavior of the threadPool.

The threadPoolKey attribute defines the unique name of thread pool.

```
@HystrixCommand(fallbackMethod = "buildFallbackLicenseList",
        threadPoolKey = "licenseByOrgThreadPool",
        threadPoolProperties =
            {@HystrixProperty(name = "coreSize",value="30"),
            @HystrixProperty(name="maxQueueSize", value="10")}
    )

    public List<License> getLicensesByOrg(String organizationId){
        return licenseRepository.findByOrganizationId(organizationId);
    )
```

The coreSize attribute lets you define the maximum number of threads in the thread pool.

The maxQueueSize lets you define a queue that sits in front of your thread pool and that can queue incoming requests.

The first thing you should notice is that we've introduced a new attribute, thread-Poolkey, to your @HystrixCommand annotation. This signals to Hystrix that you want to set up a new thread pool. If you set no further values on the thread pool, Hystrix sets up a thread pool keyed off the name in the threadPoolKey attribute, but will use all default values for how the thread pool is configured.

To customize your thread pool, you use the threadPoolProperties attribute on the @HystrixCommand. This attribute takes an array of HystrixProperty objects. These HystrixProperty objects can be used to control the behavior of the thread pool. You can set the size of the thread pool by using the coreSize attribute.

You can also set up a queue in front of the thread pool that will control how many requests will be allowed to back up when the threads in the thread pool are busy. This queue size is set by the maxQueueSize attribute. Once the number of requests exceeds the queue size, any additional requests to the thread pool will fail until there is room in the queue.

Note two things about the maxQueueSize attribute. First, if you set the value to -1, a Java SynchronousQueue will be used to hold all incoming requests. A synchronous queue will essentially enforce that you can never have more requests in process than the number of threads available in the thread pool. Setting the maxQueueSize to a value greater than one will cause Hystrix to use a Java LinkedBlockingQueue. The use of a LinkedBlockingQueue allows the developer to queue up requests even if all threads are busy processing requests.

The second thing to note is that the maxQueueSize attribute can only be set when the thread pool is first initialized (for example, at startup of the application). Hystrix does allow you to dynamically change the size of the queue by using the queue-SizeRejectionThreshold attribute, but this attribute can only be set when the maxQueueSize attribute is a value greater than 0.

What's the proper sizing for a custom thread pool? Netflix recommends the following formula:

(requests per second at peak when the service is healthy * 99th percentile latency in seconds) + small amount of extra threads for overhead

You often don't know the performance characteristics of a service until it has been under load. A key indicator that the thread pool properties need to be adjusted is when a service call is timing out even if the targeted remote resource is healthy.

5.8   *Getting beyond the basics; fine-tuning Hystrix*

At this point we've looked at the basic concepts of setting up a circuit breaker and bulkhead pattern using Hystrix. We're now going to go through and see how to really customize the behavior of the Hystrix's circuit breaker. Remember, Hystrix does more than time out long-running calls. Hystrix will also monitor the number of times a call fails and if enough calls fail, Hystrix will automatically prevent future calls from reaching the service by failing the call before the requests ever hit the remote resource.

There are two reasons for this. First, if a remote resource is having performance problems, failing fast will prevent the calling application from having to wait for a call to time out. This significantly reduces the risk that the calling application or service will experience its own resource exhaustion problems and crashes. Second, failing fast and preventing calls from service clients will help a struggling service keep up with its load and not crash completely under the load. Failing fast gives the system experiencing performance degradation time to recover.

To understand how to configure the circuit breaker in Hystrix, you need to first understand the flow of how Hystrix determines when to trip the circuit breaker. Figure 5.9 shows the decision process used by Hystrix when a remote resource call fails.

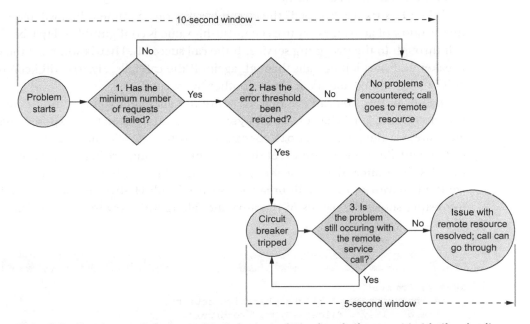

Figure 5.9   Hystrix goes through a series of checks to determine whether or not to trip the circuit breaker.

Whenever a Hystrix command encounters an error with a service, it will begin a 10-second timer that will be used to examine how often the service call is failing. This 10-second window is configurable. The first thing Hystrix does is look at the number of calls that have happened within the 10-second window. If the number of calls is less than a minimum number of calls that need to occur within the window, then Hystrix will not take action even if several of the calls failed. For example, the default number of calls that need to occur before Hystrix will even consider action within the 10-second window is 20. If 15 of those calls fail within a 10-second period, not enough of the calls have occurred for them to "trip" the circuit breaker even if all 15 calls failed. Hystrix will continue letting calls go through to the remote service.

When the minimum number of remote resource calls has occurred within the 10-second window, Hystrix will begin looking at the percentage of overall failures that have occurred. If the overall percentage of failures is over the threshold, Hystrix will trigger the circuit breaker and fail almost all future calls. As we'll discuss shortly, Hystrix will let part of the calls through to "test" and see if the service is backing up. The default value for the error threshold is 50%.

If that percentage has been exceeded, Hystrix will "trip" the circuit breaker and prevent further calls from hitting the remote resource. If that percentage of remote calls hasn't been triggered and the 10-second window has been passed, Hystrix will reset the circuit breaker statistics.

When Hystrix has "tripped" the circuit breaker on a remote call, it will try to start a new window of activity. Every five seconds (this value is configurable), Hystrix will let a call through to the struggling service. If the call succeeds, Hystrix will reset the circuit breaker and start letting calls through again. If the call fails, Hystrix will keep the circuit breaker closed and try again in another five seconds.

Based on this, you can see that there are five attributes you can use to customize the circuit breaker behavior. The `@HystrixCommand` annotation exposes these five attributes via the `commandPoolProperties` attribute. While the `threadPoolProperties` attribute allows you to set the behavior of the underlying thread pool used in the Hystrix command, the `commandPoolProperties` attribute allows you to customize the behavior of the circuit breaker associated with Hystrix command. The following listing shows the names of the attributes along with how to set values in each of them.

Listing 5.7 Configuring the behavior of a circuit breaker

```
@HystrixCommand(
    fallbackMethod = "buildFallbackLicenseList",
    threadPoolKey = "licenseByOrgThreadPool",
    threadPoolProperties ={
            @HystrixProperty(name = "coreSize",value="30"),
        @HystrixProperty(name="maxQueueSize"value="10"),
    },
    commandPoolProperties ={
      @HystrixProperty(
      name="circuitBreaker.requestVolumeThreshold",
      value="10"),
        @HystrixProperty(
      name="circuitBreaker.errorThresholdPercentage",
      value="75"),

        @HystrixProperty(
          name="circuitBreaker.sleepWindowInMilliseconds",
          value="7000"),
          @HystrixProperty(
```

```
            name="metrics.rollingStats.timeInMilliseconds",
                value="15000")
        @HystrixProperty(
            name="metrics.rollingStats.numBuckets",
                value="5")}
    )
public List<License> getLicensesByOrg(String organizationId){
    logger.debug("getLicensesByOrg Correlation id: {}",
    UserContextHolder
                .getContext()
                .getCorrelationId());
    randomlyRunLong();

    return licenseRepository.findByOrganizationId(organizationId);
}
```

The first property, `circuitBreaker.requestVolumeTheshold`, controls the amount of consecutive calls that must occur within a 10-second window before Hystrix will consider tripping the circuit breaker for the call. The second property, `circuit-Breaker.errorThresholdPercentage`, is the percentage of calls that must fail (due to timeouts, an exception being thrown, or a HTTP 500 being returned) after the `circuitBreaker.requestVolumeThreshold` value has been passed before the circuit breaker it tripped. The last property in the previous code example, `circuit-Breaker.sleepWindowInMilliseconds`, is the amount of time Hystrix will sleep once the circuit breaker is tripped before Hystrix will allow another call through to see if the service is healthy again.

The last two Hystrix properties (`metrics.rollingStats.timeInMilliseconds` and `metrics.rollingStats.numBuckets`) are named a bit differently than the previous properties, but they still control the behavior of the circuit breaker. The first property, `metrics.rollingStats.timeInMilliseconds`, is used to control the size of the window that will be used by Hystrix to monitor for problems with a service call. The default value for this is 10,000 milliseconds (that is, 10 seconds).

The second property, `metrics.rollingStats.numBuckets`, controls the number of times statistics are collected in the window you've defined. Hystrix collects metrics in buckets during this window and checks the stats in those buckets to determine if the remote resource call is failing. The number of buckets defined must evenly divide into the overall number of milliseconds set for `rollingStatus.inMilliseconds` stats. For example, in your custom settings in the previous listing, Hystrix will use a 15-second window and collect statistics data into five buckets of three seconds in length.

NOTE The smaller the statistics window you check in and the greater the number of buckets you keep within the window will drive up CPU and memory utilization on a high-volume service. Be aware of this and fight the temptation to set the metrics collection windows and buckets to be fine-grained until you need that level of visibility.

5.8.1   *Hystrix configuration revisited*

The Hystrix library is extremely configurable and lets you tightly control the behavior of the circuit breaker and bulkhead patterns you define with it. By modifying the configuration of a Hystrix circuit breaker, you can control the amount of time Hystrix will wait before timing out a remote call. You can also control the behavior of when a Hystrix circuit breaker will trip and when Hystrix tries to reset the circuit breaker.

With Hystrix you can also fine-tune your bulkhead implementations by defining individual thread groups for each remote service call and then configure the number of threads associated with each thread group. This allows you to fine-tune your remote service calls because certain calls will have higher volumes then others, while other remote resource calls will have higher volumes.

The key thing to remember as you look at configuring your Hystrix environment is that you have three levels of configuration with Hystrix:

1 Default for the entire application
2 Default for the class
3 Thread-pool level defined within the class

Every Hystrix property has values set by default that will be used by every @Hystrix-Command annotation in the application unless they're set at the Java class level or overridden for individual Hystrix thread pools within a class.

Hystrix does let you set default parameters at the class level so that all Hystrix commands within a specific class share the same configurations. The class-level properties are set via a class-level annotation called @DefaultProperties. For example, if you wanted all the resources within a specific class to have a timeout of 10 seconds, you could set the @DefaultProperties in the following manner:

```
@DefaultProperties(
  commandProperties = {
  @HystrixProperty(
    name = "execution.isolation.thread.timeoutInMilliseconds",
    value = "10000")}
class MyService { ... }
```

Unless explicitly overridden at a thread-pool level, all thread pools will inherit either the default properties at the application level or the default properties defined in the class. The Hystrix threadPoolProperties and commandProperties are also tied to the defined command key.

> **NOTE**   For the coding examples, I've hard-coded all the Hystrix values in the application code. In a production system, the Hystrix data that's most likely to need to be tweaked (timeout parameters, thread pool counts) would be externalized to Spring Cloud Config. This way if you need to change the parameter values, you could change the values and then restart the service instances without having to recompile and redeploy the application.

For individual Hystrix pools, I will keep the configuration as close to the code as possible and place the thread-pool configuration right in the @HystrixCommand annotation. Table 5.1 summarizes all of the configuration values used to set up and configure our @HystrixCommand annotations.

Table 5.1 Configuration Values for @HystrixCommand Annotations

Property Name	Default Value	Description
fallbackMethod	None	Identifies the method within the class that will be called if the remote call times out. The callback method must be in the same class as the @HystrixCommand annotation and must have the same method signature as the calling class. If no value, an exception will be thrown by Hystrix.
threadPoolKey	None	Gives the @HystrixCommand a unique name and creates a thread pool that is independent of the default thread pool. If no value is defined, the default Hystrix thread pool will be used.
threadPoolProperties	None	Core Hystrix annotation attribute that's used to configure the behavior of a thread pool.
coreSize	10	Sets the size of the thread pool.
maxQueueSize	-1	Maximum queue size that will set in front of the thread pool. If set to -1, no queue is used and instead Hystrix will block until a thread becomes available for processing.
circuitBreaker.request-VolumeThreshold	20	Sets the minimum number of requests that must be processed within the rolling window before Hystrix will even begin examining whether the circuit breaker will be tripped. Note: This value can only be set with the commandPoolProperties attribute.
circuitBreaker.error-ThresholdPercentage	50	The percentage of failures that must occur within the rolling window before the circuit breaker is tripped. Note: This value can only be set with the commandPoolProperties attribute.
circuitBreaker.sleep-WindowInMilliseconds	5,000	The number of milliseconds Hystrix will wait before trying a service call after the circuit breaker has been tripped. Note: This value can only be set with the commandPoolProperties attribute.
metricsRollingStats.timeInMilliseconds	10,000	The number of milliseconds Hystrix will collect and monitor statistics about service calls within a window.
metricsRollingStats.numBuckets	10	The number of metrics buckets Hystrix will maintain within its monitoring window. The more buckets within the monitoring window, the lower the level of time Hystrix will monitor for faults within the window.

5.9   *Thread context and Hystrix*

When an `@HystrixCommand` is executed, it can be run with two different isolation strategies: `THREAD` and `SEMAPHORE`. By default, Hystrix runs with a `THREAD` isolation. Each Hystrix command used to protect a call runs in an isolated thread pool that doesn't share its context with the parent thread making the call. This means Hystrix can interrupt the execution of a thread under its control without worrying about interrupting any other activity associated with the parent thread doing the original invocation.

With `SEMAPHORE`-based isolation, Hystrix manages the distributed call protected by the `@HystrixCommand` annotation without starting a new thread and will interrupt the parent thread if the call times out. In a synchronous container server environment (Tomcat), interrupting the parent thread will cause an exception to be thrown that cannot be caught by the developer. This can lead to unexpected consequences for the developer writing the code because they can't catch the thrown exception or do any resource cleanup or error handling.

To control the isolation setting for a command pool, you can set a `command-Properties` attribute on your `@HystrixCommand` annotation. For instance, if you wanted to set the isolation level on a Hystrix command to use a `SEMAPHORE` isolation, you'd use

```
@HystrixCommand(
commandProperties = {
 @HystrixProperty(
        name="execution.isolation.strategy", value="SEMAPHORE") })
```

NOTE   By default, the Hystrix team recommends you use the default isolation strategy of `THREAD` for most commands. This keeps a higher level of isolation between you and the parent thread. `THREAD` isolation is heavier than using the `SEMAPHORE` isolation. The `SEMAPHORE` isolation model is lighter-weight and should be used when you have a high-volume on your services and are running in an asynchronous I/O programming model (you are using an asynchronous I/O container such as Netty).

5.9.1   *ThreadLocal and Hystrix*

Hystrix, by default, will not propagate the parent thread's context to threads managed by a Hystrix command. For example, any values set as `ThreadLocal` values in the parent thread will not be available by default to a method called by the parent thread and protected by the `@HystrixCommand` object. (Again, this is assuming you are using a `THREAD` isolation level.)

This can be a little obtuse, so let's see a concrete example. Often in a REST-based environment you are going to want to pass contextual information to a service call that will help you operationally manage the service. For example, you might pass a correlation ID or authentication token in the HTTP header of the REST call that can then be propagated to any downstream service calls. The correlation ID allows you to have a unique identifier that can be traced across multiple service calls in a single transaction.

To make this value available anywhere in your service call, you might use a Spring Filter class to intercept every call into your REST service and retrieve this information from the incoming HTTP request and store this contextual information in a custom `User-Context` object. Then, anytime your code needs to access this value in your REST service call, your code can retrieve the `UserContext` from the `ThreadLocal` storage variable and read the value. The following listing shows an example Spring Filter that you can use in your licensing service. You can find the code at `licensingservice/src/main/java/com/thoughtmechanix/licenses/utils/UserContextFilter.java`.

Listing 5.8 The `UserContextFilter` parsing the HTTP header and retrieving data

```java
package com.thoughtmechanix.licenses.utils;

//Some code removed for conciseness
@Component
public class UserContextFilter implements Filter {
  private static final
    Logger logger =
    LoggerFactory.getLogger(UserContextFilter.class);
 @Override
 public void doFilter(
ServletRequest servletRequest,
 ServletResponse servletResponse,
 FilterChain filterChain)
     throws IOException, ServletException {
    HttpServletRequest httpServletRequest =
(HttpServletRequest) servletRequest;

    UserContextHolder
  .getContext()
  .setCorrelationId(
    httpServletRequest.getHeader(UserContext.CORRELATION_ID) );

UserContextHolder
  .getContext()
  .setUserId(
        httpServletRequest.getHeader(UserContext.USER_ID));
   UserContextHolder
      .getContext()
  .setAuthToken(
        httpServletRequest.getHeader(UserContext.AUTH_TOKEN));
   UserContextHolder
      .getContext()
      .setOrgId(
        httpServletRequest.getHeader(UserContext.ORG_ID));

    filterChain.doFilter(httpServletRequest, servletResponse);
  }
}
```

Retrieving values set in the HTTP header of the call into a UserContext, which is stored in UserContextHolder

The `UserContextHolder` class is used to store the `UserContext` in a `ThreadLocal` class. Once it's stored in the `ThreadLocal` storage, any code that's executed for a request will use the `UserContext` object stored in the `UserContextHolder`. The `UserContextHolder` class is shown in the following listing. This class is found at `licensing-service/src/main/java/com/thoughtmechanix/licenses/utils /UserContextHolder.java`.

Listing 5.9   All UserContext data is managed by UserContextHolder

```java
public class UserContextHolder {
    private static final ThreadLocal<UserContext> userContext
        = new ThreadLocal<UserContext>();                                    ⬅  The UserContext is
                                                                                stored in a static
    public static final UserContext getContext(){         ⬅                    ThreadLocal variable.
        UserContext context = userContext.get();

        if (context == null) {
            context = createEmptyContext();
            userContext.set(context);                             The getContext() method will
                                                                  retrieve the UserContext
        }                                                         object for consumption.
        return userContext.get();
    }

    public static final void setContext(UserContext context) {
        Assert.notNull(context,
                "Only non-null UserContext instances are permitted");
        userContext.set(context);
    }

    public static final UserContext createEmptyContext(){
        return new UserContext();
    }
}
```

At this point you can add a couple of log statements to your licensing service. You'll add logging to the following licensing service classes and methods:

- `com/thoughtmechanix/licenses/utils/UserContextFilter.java` `doFilter()` method
- `com/thoughtmechanix/licenses/controllers/LicenseService- Controller.java getLicenses()` method
- `com/thoughtmechanix/licenses/services/LicenseService.java getLicensesByOrg()` method. This method is annotated with a `@Hystrix- Command`.

Next you'll call your service passing in a correlation ID using an HTTP header called `tmx-correlation-id` and a value of `TEST-CORRELATION-ID`. Figure 5.10 shows a HTTP GET call to http://localhost:8080/v1/organizations/e254f8c-c442-4ebe-a82a-e2fc1d1ff78a/licenses/ in Postman.

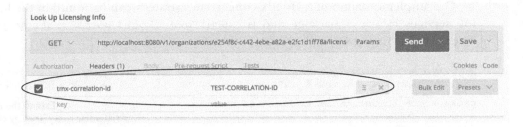

Figure 5.10   Adding a correlation ID to the licensing service call's HTTP header

Once this call is submitted, you should see three log messages writing out the passed-in correlation ID as it flows through the `UserContext`, `LicenseServiceController`, and `LicenseServer` classes:

```
UserContext Correlation id: TEST-CORRELATION-ID
LicenseServiceController Correlation id: TEST-CORRELATION-ID
LicenseService.getLicenseByOrg Correlation:
```

As expected, once the call hits the Hystrix protected method on `LicenseService.getLicensesByOrder()`, you'll get no value written out for the correlation ID. Fortunately, Hystrix and Spring Cloud offer a mechanism to propagate the parent thread's context to threads managed by the Hystrix Thread pool. This mechanism is called a `HystrixConcurrencyStrategy`.

5.9.2   The HystrixConcurrencyStrategy in action

Hystrix allows you to define a custom concurrency strategy that will wrap your Hystrix calls and allows you to inject any additional parent thread context into the threads managed by the Hystrix command. To implement a custom `HystrixConcurrencyStrategy` you need to carry out three actions:

1 Define your custom Hystrix Concurrency Strategy class
2 Define a Java `Callable` class to inject the `UserContext` into the Hystrix Command
3 Configure Spring Cloud to use your custom Hystrix Concurrency Strategy

All the examples for the `HystrixConcurrencyStrategy` can be found in the licensing-service/src/main/java/com/thoughtmechanix/licenses/hystrix package.

DEFINE YOUR CUSTOM HYSTRIX CONCURRENCY STRATEGY CLASS

The first thing you need to do is define your `HystrixConcurrencyStrategy`. By default, Hystrix only allows you to define one `HystrixConcurrencyStrategy` for an application. Spring Cloud already defines a concurrency strategy used to handle propagating Spring security information. Fortunately, Spring Cloud allows you to chain together Hystrix concurrency strategies so you can define and use your own concurrency strategy by "plugging" it into the Hystrix concurrency strategy.

Our implementation of a Hystrix concurrency strategy can be found in the licensing services `hystrix` package and is called `ThreadLocalAwareStrategy.java`. The following listing shows the code for this class.

Listing 5.10   Defining your own Hystrix concurrency strategy

```
package com.thoughtmechanix.licenses.hystrix;                        Extend the base
                                                          HystrixConcurrencyStrategy class.
//imports removed for conciseness
public class ThreadLocalAwareStrategy extends HystrixConcurrencyStrategy{  ⬅
    private HystrixConcurrencyStrategy existingConcurrencyStrategy;

    public ThreadLocalAwareStrategy(
             HystrixConcurrencyStrategy existingConcurrencyStrategy) {  ⬅
        this.existingConcurrencyStrategy = existingConcurrencyStrategy;
    }
                                    Spring Cloud already has a concurrency class defined.
                                    Pass the existing concurrency strategy into the class
                                       constructor of your HystrixConcurrencyStrategy.
    @Override
    public BlockingQueue<Runnable> getBlockingQueue(int maxQueueSize){    ⬅
        return existingConcurrencyStrategy != null
                ? existingConcurrencyStrategy.getBlockingQueue(maxQueueSize)
                : super.getBlockingQueue(maxQueueSize);
    }

    @Override
    public <T> HystrixRequestVariable<T> getRequestVariable(
            HystrixRequestVariableLifecycle<T> rv)
    {//Code removed for conciseness }


    //Code removed for conciseness              Several methods need to be
    @Override                                        overridden. Either call the
    public ThreadPoolExecutor getThreadPool(   existingConcurrencyStrategy method
    ⇒ HystrixThreadPoolKey threadPoolKey,       implementation or call the base
        HystrixProperty<Integer> corePoolSize,       HystrixConcurrencyStrategy.
        HystrixProperty<Integer> maximumPoolSize,
        HystrixProperty<Integer> keepAliveTime,
        TimeUnit unit,
        BlockingQueue<Runnable> workQueue)
    {//code removed for conciness}

@Override
public <T> Callable<T> wrapCallable(Callable<T> callable) {
return existingConcurrencyStrategy != null
  ? existingConcurrencyStrategy.wrapCallable(
  ⇒ new DelegatingUserContextCallable<T>(
        callable,
        ⇒ UserContextHolder.getContext())))         Inject your Callable
  : super.wrapCallable(                              implementation that will
    new DelegatingUserContextCallable<T>(           set the UserContext.
        callable,
        UserContextHolder.getContext()));
    }
}
```

Note a couple of things in the class implementation in listing 5.10. First, because Spring Cloud already defines a `HystrixConcurrencyStrategy`, every method that could be overridden needs to check whether an existing concurrency strategy is present and then either call the existing concurrency strategy's method or the base Hystrix concurrency strategy method. You have to do this as a convention to ensure that you properly invoke the already-existing Spring Cloud's `HystrixConcurrency-Strategy` that deals with security. Otherwise, you can have nasty behavior when trying to use Spring security context in your Hystrix protected code.

The second thing to note is the `wrapCallable()` method in listing 5.11. In this method, you pass in `Callable` implementation, `DelegatingUserContext-Callable`, that will be used to set the `UserContext` from the parent thread executing the user's REST service call to the Hystrix command thread protecting the method that's doing the work within.

DEFINE A JAVA CALLABLE CLASS TO INJECT THE USERCONTEXT INTO THE HYSTRIX COMMAND
The next step in propagating the thread context of the parent thread to your Hystrix command is to implement the `Callable` class that will do the propagation. For this example, this call is in the `hystrix` package and is called `DelegatingUser-ContextCallable.java`. The following listing shows the code from this class.

> **Listing 5.11 Propagating the UserContext with `DelegatingUserContextCallable.java`**

```
package com.thoughtmechanix.licenses.hystrix;

//import remove concisesness
public final class DelegatingUserContextCallable<V>
    implements Callable<V> {
    private final Callable<V> delegate;
    private UserContext originalUserContext;

    public DelegatingUserContextCallable(
        Callable<V> delegate,
                    UserContext userContext) {
        this.delegate = delegate;
        this.originalUserContext = userContext;
    }

    public V call() throws Exception {
        UserContextHolder.setContext( originalUserContext );

        try {
            return delegate.call();
        }
        finally {
            this.originalUserContext = null;
        }
    }

    public static <V> Callable<V> create(Callable<V> delegate,
                                    UserContext userContext) {
        return new DelegatingUserContextCallable<V>(delegate, userContext);
    }
}
```

Custom Callable class will be passed the original Callable class that will invoke your Hystrix protected code and UserContext coming in from the parent thread

The UserContext is set. The ThreadLocal variable that stores the UserContext is associated with the thread running the Hystrix protected method.

The call() function is invoked before the method protected by the @HystrixCommand annotation.

Once the UserContext is set invoke the call() method on the Hystrix protected method; for instance, your LicenseServer.getLicenseByOrg() method.

When a call is made to a Hystrix protected method, Hystrix and Spring Cloud will instantiate an instance of the `DelegatingUserContextCallable` class, passing in the `Callable` class that would normally be invoked by a thread managed by a Hystrix command pool. In the previous listing, this `Callable` class is stored in a Java property called `delegate`. Conceptually, you can think of the delegate property as being the handle to the method protected by a `@HystrixCommand` annotation.

In addition to the delegated `Callable` class, Spring Cloud is also passing along the `UserContext` object off the parent thread that initiated the call. With these two values set at the time the `DelegatingUserContextCallable` instance is created, the real action will occur in the `call()` method of your class.

The first thing to do in the `call()` method is set the `UserContext` via the `UserContextHolder.setContext()` method. Remember, the `setContext()` method stores a `UserContext` object in a `ThreadLocal` variable specific to the thread being run. Once the `UserContext` is set, you then invoke the `call()` method of the delegated `Callable` class. This call to `delegate.call()` invokes the method protected by the `@HystrixCommand` annotation.

CONFIGURE SPRING CLOUD TO USE YOUR CUSTOM HYSTRIX CONCURRENCY STRATEGY

Now that you have your `HystrixConcurrencyStrategy` via the `ThreadLocalAwareStrategy` class and your `Callable` class defined via the `DelegatingUserContextCallable` class, you need to hook them in Spring Cloud and Hystrix. To do this, you're going to define a new configuration class. This configuration, called `ThreadLocalConfiguration`, is shown in the following listing.

Listing 5.12   Hooking custom `HystrixConcurrencyStrategy` class into Spring Cloud

```
package com.thoughtmechanix.licenses.hystrix;

//Imports removed for conciseness
@Configuration
public class ThreadLocalConfiguration {
  @Autowired(required = false)
  private HystrixConcurrencyStrategy existingConcurrencyStrategy;

  @PostConstruct
  public void init() {
    // Keeps references of existing Hystrix plugins.
    HystrixEventNotifier eventNotifier =
    ➥ HystrixPlugins
        .getInstance()
        .getEventNotifier();
    HystrixMetricsPublisher metricsPublisher =
    ➥ HystrixPlugins
        .getInstance()
        .getMetricsPublisher();
    HystrixPropertiesStrategy propertiesStrategy =
    ➥ HystrixPlugins
        .getInstance()
        .getPropertiesStrategy();
```

> When the configuration object is constructed it will autowire in the existing **HystrixConcurrencyStrategy**.

> Because you're registering a new concurrency strategy, you're going to grab all the other Hystrix components and then reset the Hystrix plugin.

```
    HystrixCommandExecutionHook commandExecutionHook =
 ➥ HystrixPlugins
        .getInstance()
        .getCommandExecutionHook();
    HystrixPlugins.reset();

    HystrixPlugins.getInstance()
      .registerConcurrencyStrategy(
        new ThreadLocalAwareStrategy(existingConcurrencyStrategy));
    HystrixPlugins.getInstance()
      .registerEventNotifier(eventNotifier);
    HystrixPlugins.getInstance()
      .registerMetricsPublisher(metricsPublisher);
      HystrixPlugins.getInstance()
        .registerPropertiesStrategy(propertiesStrategy);
      HystrixPlugins.getInstance()
        .registerCommandExecutionHook(commandExecutionHook);
  }
}
```

> **You now register your HystrixConcurrencyStrategy (ThreadLocalAwareStrategy) with the Hystrix plugin.**

> **Then reregister all the Hystrix components used by the Hystrix plugin**

This Spring configuration class basically rebuilds the Hystrix plugin that manages all the different components running within your service. In the init() method, you're grabbing references to all the Hystrix components used by the plugin. You then register your custom HystrixConcurrencyStrategy (ThreadLocalAwareStrategy).

```
HystrixPlugins.getInstance().registerConcurrencyStrategy(
  new ThreadLocalAwareStrategy(existingConcurrencyStrategy));
```

Remember, Hystrix allows only one HystrixConcurrencyStrategy. Spring will attempt to autowire in any existing HystrixConcurrencyStrategy (if it exists). Finally, when you're all done, you re-register the original Hystrix components that you grabbed at the beginning of the init() method back with the Hystrix plugin.

With these pieces in place, you can now rebuild and restart your licensing service and call it via the GET (http://localhost:8080/v1/organizations/e254f8c-c442-4ebe-a82a-e2fc1d1ff78a/licenses/) shown earlier in figure 5.10. Now, when this call is completed, you should see the following output in your console window:

```
UserContext Correlation id: TEST-CORRELATION-ID
LicenseServiceController Correlation id: TEST-CORRELATION-ID
LicenseService.getLicenseByOrg Correlation: TEST-CORRELATION-ID
```

It's a lot of work to produce one little result, but it's unfortunately necessary when you use Hystrix with THREAD-level isolation.

5.10 *Summary*

- When designing highly distributed applications such as a microservice-based application, client resiliency must be taken into account.
- Outright failures of a service (for example, the server crashes) are easy to detect and deal with.

- A single poorly performing service can trigger a cascading effect of resource exhaustion as threads in the calling client are blocked waiting for a service to complete.
- Three core client resiliency patterns are the circuit-breaker pattern, the fallback pattern, and the bulkhead pattern.
- The circuit breaker pattern seeks to kill slow-running and degraded system calls so that the calls fail fast and prevent resource exhaustion.
- The fallback pattern allows you as the developer to define alternative code paths in the event that a remote service call fails or the circuit breaker for the call fails.
- The bulkhead pattern segregates remote resource calls away from each other, isolating calls to a remote service into their own thread pool. If one set of service calls is failing, its failures shouldn't be allowed to eat up all the resources in the application container.
- Spring Cloud and the Netflix Hystrix libraries provide implementations for the circuit breaker, fallback, and bulkhead patterns.
- The Hystrix libraries are highly configurable and can be set at global, class, and thread pool levels.
- Hystrix supports two isolation models: THREAD and SEMAPHORE.
- Hystrix's default isolation model, THREAD, completely isolates a Hystrix protected call, but doesn't propagate the parent thread's context to the Hystrix managed thread.
- Hystrix's other isolation model, SEMAPHORE, doesn't use a separate thread to make a Hystrix call. While this is more efficient, it also exposes the service to unpredictable behavior if Hystrix interrupts the call.
- Hystrix does allow you to inject the parent thread context into a Hystrix managed Thread through a custom `HystrixConcurrencyStrategy` implementation.

Service routing with Spring Cloud and Zuul

6

This chapter covers

- Using a services gateway with your microservices
- Implementing a service gateway using Spring Cloud and Netflix Zuul
- Mapping microservice routes in Zuul
- Building filters to use correlation ID and tracking
- Dynamic routing with Zuul

In a distributed architecture like a microservices one, there will come a point where you'll need to ensure that key behaviors such as security, logging, and tracking of users across multiple service calls occur. To implement this functionality, you'll want these attributes to be consistently enforced across all of your services without the need for each individual development team to build their own solutions. While it's possible to use a common library or framework to assist with building these capabilities directly in an individual service, doing so has three implications.

First, it's difficult to consistently implement these capabilities in each service being built. Developers are focused on delivering functionality, and in the whirlwind of day-to-day activity they can easily forget to implement service logging or tracking. (I personally am guilty of this.) Unfortunately, for those of us working in a heavily regulated industry, such as financial services or healthcare, showing consistent and documented behavior in your systems is often a key requirement for complying with government regulations.

Second, properly implementing these capabilities is a challenge. Things like microservice security can be a pain to set up and configure with each service being implemented. Pushing the responsibilities to implement a cross-cutting concern like security down to the individual development teams greatly increases the odds that someone will not implement it properly or will forget to do it.

Third, you've now created a hard dependency across all your services. The more capabilities you build into a common framework shared across all your services, the more difficult it is to change or add behavior in your common code without having to recompile and redeploy all your services. This might not seem like a big deal when you have six microservices in your application, but it's a big deal when you have a larger number of services, perhaps 30 or more. Suddenly an upgrade of core capabilities built into a shared library becomes a months-long migration process.

To solve this problem, you need to abstract these cross-cutting concerns into a service that can sit independently and act as a filter and router for all the microservice calls in your application. This cross-cutting concern is called a *services gateway.* Your service clients no longer directly call a service. Instead, all calls are routed through the service gateway, which acts as a single Policy Enforcement Point (PEP), and are then routed to a final destination.

In this chapter, we're going to see how to use Spring Cloud and Netflix's Zuul to implement a services gateway. Zuul is Netflix's open source services gateway implementation. Specifically, we're going to look at how to use Spring Cloud and Zuul to

- Put all service calls behind a single URL and map those calls using service discovery to their actual service instances
- Inject correlation IDs into every service call flowing through the service gateway
- Inject the correlation ID back from the HTTP response sent back from the client
- Build a dynamic routing mechanism that will route specific individual organizations to a service instance endpoint that's different than what everyone else is using

Let's dive into more detail on how a services gateway fits into the overall microservices being built in this book.

6.1 *What is a services gateway?*

Until now, with the microservices you've built in earlier chapters, you've either directly called the individual services through a web client or called them programmatically via a service discovery engine such as Eureka.

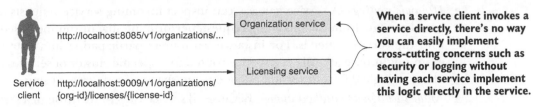

Figure 6.1 Without a services gateway, the service client will call distinct endpoints for each service.

A service gateway acts as an intermediary between the service client and a service being invoked. The service client talks only to a single URL managed by the service gateway. The service gateway pulls apart the path coming in from the service client call and determines what service the service client is trying to invoke. Figure 6.2 illustrates how like a "traffic" cop directing traffic, the service gateway directs the user to a target microservice and corresponding instance. The service gateway sits as the gatekeeper for all inbound traffic to microservice calls within your application. With a service gateway in place, your service clients never directly call the URL of an individual service, but instead place all calls to the service gateway.

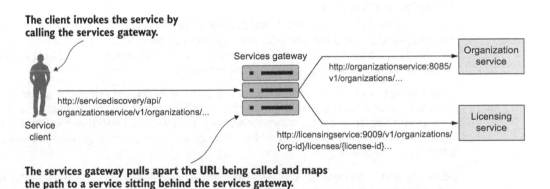

Figure 6.2 The service gateway sits between the service client and the corresponding service instances. All service calls (both internal-facing and external) should flow through the service gateway.

Because a service gateway sits between all calls from the client to the individual services, it also acts as a central Policy Enforcement Point (PEP) for service calls. The use of a centralized PEP means that cross-cutting service concerns can be implemented in a single place without the *individual* development teams having to implement these concerns. Examples of cross-cutting concerns that can be implemented in a service gateway include

- *Static routing*—A service gateway places all service calls behind a single URL and API route. This simplifies development as developers only have to know about one service endpoint for all of their services.

- *Dynamic routing*—A service gateway can inspect incoming service requests and, based on data from the incoming request, perform intelligent routing based on who the service caller is. For instance, customers participating in a beta program might have all calls to a service routed to a specific cluster of services that are running a different version of code from what everyone else is using.
- *Authentication and authorization*—Because all service calls route through a service gateway, the service gateway is a natural place to check whether the caller of a service has authenticated themselves and is authorized to make the service call.
- *Metric collection and logging*—A service gateway can be used to collect metrics and log information as a service call passes through the service gateway. You can also use the service gateway to ensure that key pieces of information are in place on the user request to ensure logging is uniform. This doesn't mean that shouldn't you still collect metrics from within your individual services, but rather a services gateway allows you to centralize collection of many of your basic metrics, like the number of times the service is invoked and service response time.

Wait—isn't a service gateway a single point of failure and potential bottleneck?

Earlier in chapter 4 when I introduced Eureka, I talked about how centralized load balancers can be single point of failure and a bottleneck for your services. A service gateway, if not implemented correctly, can carry the same risk. Keep the following in mind as you build your service gateway implementation.

Load balancers are still useful when out in front of individual groups of services. In this case, a load balancer sitting in front of multiple service gateway instances is an appropriate design and ensures your service gateway implementation can scale. Having a load balancer sit in front of all your service instances isn't a good idea because it becomes a bottleneck.

Keep any code you write for your service gateway stateless. Don't store any information in memory for the service gateway. If you aren't careful, you can limit the scalability of the gateway and have to ensure that the data gets replicated across all service gateway instances.

Keep the code you write for your service gateway light. The service gateway is the "chokepoint" for your service invocation. Complex code with multiple database calls can be the source of difficult-to-track-down performance problems in the service gateway.

Let's now look at how to implement a service gateway using Spring Cloud and Netflix Zuul.

6.2   *Introducing Spring Cloud and Netflix Zuul*

Spring Cloud integrates with the Netflix open source project Zuul. Zuul is a services gateway that's extremely easy to set up and use via Spring Cloud annotations. Zuul offers a number of capabilities, including

- *Mapping the routes for all the services in your application to a single URL*—Zuul isn't limited to a single URL. In Zuul, you can define multiple route entries, making the route mapping extremely fine-grained (each service endpoint gets its own route mapping). However, the first and most common use case for Zuul is to build a single entry point through which all service client calls will flow.
- *Building filters that can inspect and act on the requests coming through the gateway*— These filters allow you to inject policy enforcement points in your code and perform a wide number of actions on all of your service calls in a consistent fashion.

To get started with Zuul, you're going to do three things:

1 Set up a Zuul Spring Boot project and configure the appropriate Maven dependencies.
2 Modify your Spring Boot project with Spring Cloud annotations to tell it that it will be a Zuul service.
3 Configure Zuul to communicate with Eureka (optional).

6.2.1   *Setting up the Zuul Spring Boot project*

If you've been following the chapters sequentially in this book, the work you're about to do should be familiar. To build a Zuul server, you need to set up a new Spring Boot service and define the corresponding Maven dependencies. You can find the project source code for this chapter in the GitHub repository for this book (https://github.com/carnellj/spmia-chapter6). Fortunately, little is needed to set up Zuul in Maven. You only need to define one dependency in your zuulsvr/pom.xml file:

```
<dependency>
   <groupId>org.springframework.cloud</groupId>
   <artifactId>spring-cloud-starter-zuul</artifactId>
</dependency>
```

This dependency tells the Spring Cloud framework that this service will be running Zuul and initialize Zuul appropriately.

6.2.2   *Using Spring Cloud annotation for the Zuul service*

After you've defined the maven dependencies, you need to annotate the bootstrap class for the Zuul services. The bootstrap class for the Zuul service implementation can be found in the zuulsvr/src/main/java/com/thoughtmechanix/zuulsvr/Application.java class.

Listing 6.1   Setting up the Zuul Server bootstrap class

```
package com.thoughtmechanix.zuulsvr;

import org.springframework.boot.SpringApplication;
import org.springframework.boot.autoconfigure.SpringBootApplication;
import org.springframework.cloud.netflix.zuul.EnableZuulProxy;
import org.springframework.context.annotation.Bean;


@SpringBootApplication
@EnableZuulProxy                                        Enables the service
public class ZuulServerApplication {                    to be a Zuul server
    public static void main(String[] args) {
        SpringApplication.run(
        ZuulServerApplication.class,
        args);
    }
}
```

That's it. There's only one annotation that needs to be in place: @EnableZuulProxy.

> **NOTE**   If you look through the documentation or have auto-complete turned on, you might notice an annotation called @EnableZuulServer. Using this annotation will create a Zuul Server that doesn't load any of the Zuul reverse proxy filters or use Netflix Eureka for service discovery. (We'll get into the topic of Zuul and Eureka integration shortly.) @EnableZuulServer is used when you want to build your own routing service and not use any Zuul pre-built capabilities. An example of this would be if you wanted to use Zuul to integrate with a service discovery engine other than Eureka (for example, Consul). We'll only use the @EnableZuulProxy annotation in this book.

6.2.3   Configuring Zuul to communicate with Eureka

The Zuul proxy server is designed by default to work on the Spring products. As such, Zuul will automatically use Eureka to look up services by their service IDs and then use Netflix Ribbon to do client-side load balancing of requests from within Zuul.

> **NOTE**   I often read chapters out of order in a book, jumping to the specific topics I'm most interested in. If you do the same and don't know what Netflix Eureka and Ribbon are, I suggest you read chapter 4 before proceeding much further. Zuul uses those technologies heavily to carry out work, so understanding the service discovery capabilities that Eureka and Ribbon bring to the table will make understanding Zuul that much easier.

The last step in the configuration process is to modify your Zuul server's zuulsvr/src/ main/resources/application.yml file to point to your Eureka server. The following listing shows the Zuul configuration needed for Zuul to communicate with Eureka. The configuration in the listing should look familiar because it's the same configuration we walked through in chapter 4.

Listing 6.2   Configuring the Zuul server to talk to Eureka

```
eureka:
 instance:
  preferIpAddress: true
 client:
  registerWithEureka: true
  fetchRegistry: true
  serviceUrl:
    defaultZone: http://localhost:8761/eureka/
```

6.3   Configuring routes in Zuul

Zuul at its heart is a reverse proxy. A reverse proxy is an intermediate server that sits between the client trying to reach a resource and the resource itself. The client has no idea it's even communicating to a server other than a proxy. The reverse proxy takes care of capturing the client's request and then calls the remote resource on the client's behalf.

In the case of a microservices architecture, Zuul (your reverse proxy) takes a microservice call from a client and forwards it onto the downstream service. The service client thinks it's only communicating with Zuul. For Zuul to communicate with the downstream clients, Zuul has to know how to *map* the incoming call to a downstream route. Zuul has several mechanisms to do this, including

- Automated mapping of routes via service discovery
- Manual mapping of routes using service discovery
- Manual mapping of routes using static URLs

6.3.1   Automated mapping routes via service discovery

All route mappings for Zuul are done by defining the routes in the zuulsvr/src/main/resources/application.yml file. However, Zuul can automatically route requests based on their service IDs with zero configuration. If you don't specify any routes, Zuul will automatically use the Eureka service ID of the service being called and map it to a downstream service instance. For instance, if you wanted to call your `organization-service` and used automated routing via Zuul, you would have your client call the Zuul service instance, using the following URL as the endpoint:

```
http://localhost:5555/organizationservice/v1/organizations/e254f8c-c442-4ebe-
    a82a-e2fc1d1ff78a
```

Your Zuul server is accessed via `http://localhost:5555`. The service you're trying (`organizationservice`) to invoke is represented by the first part of the endpoint path in the service.

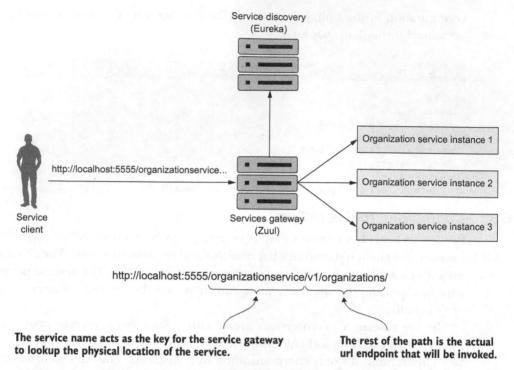

Figure 6.3   Zuul will use the `organizationservice` application name to map requests to organization service instances.

Figure 6.3 illustrates this mapping in action.

The beauty of using Zuul with Eureka is that not only do you now have a single endpoint that you can make calls through, but with Eureka, you can also add and remove instances of a service without ever having to modify Zuul. For instance, you can add a new service to Eureka, and Zuul will automatically route to it because it's communicating with Eureka about where the actual physical services endpoints are located.

If you want to see the routes being managed by the Zuul server, you can access the routes via the `/routes` endpoint on the Zuul server. This will return a listing of all the mappings on your service. Figure 6.4 shows the output from hitting `http://local-host:5555/routes`.

In figure 6.4 the mappings for the services registered with Zuul are shown on the left-hand side of the JSON body returned from the `/routes` calls. The actual Eureka service IDs the routes map to are shown on the right.

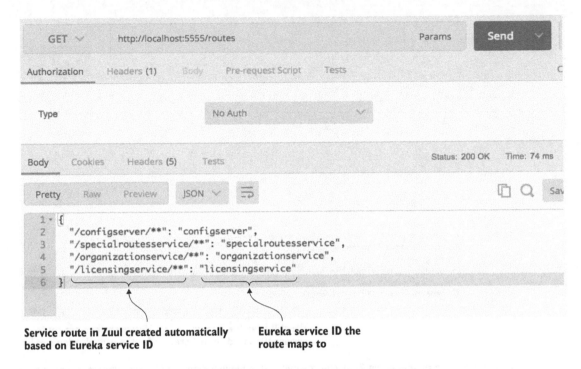

Service route in Zuul created automatically based on Eureka service ID

Eureka service ID the route maps to

Figure 6.4   Each service that's mapped in Eureka will now be mapped as a Zuul route.

6.3.2   *Mapping routes manually using service discovery*

Zuul allows you to be more fine-grained by allowing you to explicitly define route mappings rather than relying solely on the automated routes created with the service's Eureka service ID. Suppose you wanted to simplify the route by shortening the organization name rather than having your organization service accessed in Zuul via the default route of `/organizationservice/v1/organizations/{organization-id}`. You can do this by manually defining the route mapping in zuulsvr/src/main/resources/application.yml:

```
zuul:
  routes:
    organizationservice: /organization/**
```

By adding this configuration, you can now access the organization service by hitting the `/organization/v1/organizations/{organization-id}` route. If you check the Zuul server's endpoint again, you should see the results shown in figure 6.5.

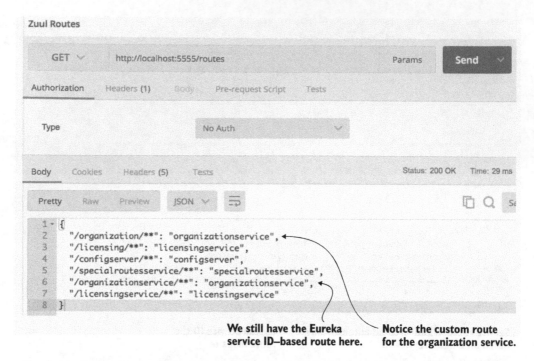

Figure 6.5   **The results of the Zuul /routes call with a manual mapping of the organization service**

If you look carefully at figure 6.5 you'll notice that two entries are present for the organization service. The first service entry is the mapping you defined in the application.yml file: "organization/**": "organizationservice". The second service entry is the automatic mapping created by Zuul based on the organization service's Eureka ID: "/organizationservice/**": "organizationservice".

> **NOTE**   When you use automated route mapping where Zuul exposes the service based solely on the Eureka service ID, if no instances of the service are running, Zuul will not expose the route for the service. However, if you manually map a route to a service discovery ID and there are no instances registered with Eureka, Zuul will still show the route. If you try to call the route for the non-existent service, Zuul will return a 500 error.

If you want to exclude the automated mapping of the Eureka service ID route and only have available the organization service route that you've defined, you can add an additional Zuul parameter to your application.yml file, called ignored-services.

The following code snippet shows how the `ignored-services` attribute can be used to exclude the Eureka service ID organizationservice from the automated mappings done by Zuul:

```
zuul:
 ignored-services: 'organizationservice'
 routes:
  organizationservice: /organization/**
```

The `ignored-services` attribute allows you to define a comma-separated list of Eureka service-IDs that you want to exclude from registration. Now, when your call the `/routes` endpoint on Zuul, you should only see the organization service mapping you've defined. Figure 6.6 shows the outcome of this mapping.

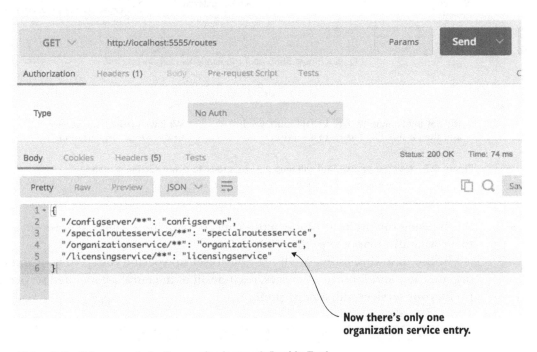

Now there's only one
organization service entry.

Figure 6.6   Only one organization service is now defined in Zuul.

If you want to exclude all Eureka-based routes, you can set the `ignored-services` attribute to "*".

A common pattern with a service gateway is to differentiate API routes vs. content routes by prefixing all your service calls with a type of label such as `/api`. Zuul supports

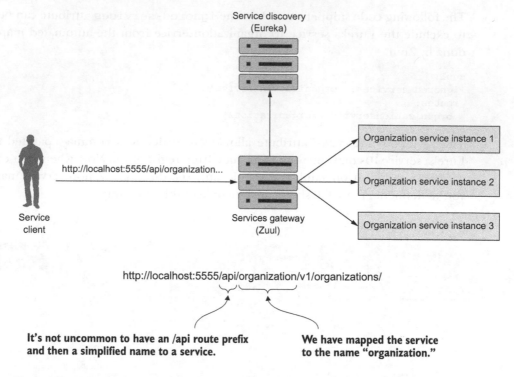

Service discovery
(Eureka)

Organization service instance 1

http://localhost:5555/api/organization...

Organization service instance 2

Service
client

Services gateway
(Zuul)

Organization service instance 3

http://localhost:5555/api/organization/v1/organizations/

**It's not uncommon to have an /api route prefix
and then a simplified name to a service.**

**We have mapped the service
to the name "organization."**

Figure 6.7   Using a prefix, Zuul will map a `/api` prefix to every service it manages.

this by using the prefix attribute in the Zuul configuration. Figure 6.7 lays out conceptually what this mapping prefix will look like.

In the following listing, we'll see how to set up specific routes to your individual
organization and Licensing services, exclude all of the eureka-generated services, and
prefix your services with a `/api` prefix.

Listing 6.3   Setting up custom routes with a prefix

**The ignored-services attribute is set
to * to exclude the registration of all
eureka service ID based routes.**

```
zuul:
  ignored-services: '*'
  prefix: /api
  routes:
    organizationservice: /organization/**
    licensingservice: /licensing/**
```

**All defined
services will
be prefixed
with /api.**

**Your organizationservice and licensingservice
are mapped to the organization and licensing
endpoints respectively.**

Figure 6.8   Your routes in Zuul now have an /api prefix.

Once this configuration is done and the Zuul service has been reloaded, you should see the following two entries when hitting the /route endpoint: /api/organization and /api/licensing. Figure 6.8 shows these entries.

Let's now look at how you can use Zuul to map to static URLs. Static URLs are URLs that point to services that aren't registered with a Eureka service discovery engine.

6.3.3   Manual mapping of routes using static URLs

Zuul can be used to route services that aren't managed by Eureka. In these cases, Zuul can be set up to directly route to a statically defined URL. For example, let's imagine that your license service is written in Python and you want to still proxy it through Zuul. You'd use the Zuul configuration in the following listing to achieve this.

Listing 6.4   Mapping the licensing service to a static route

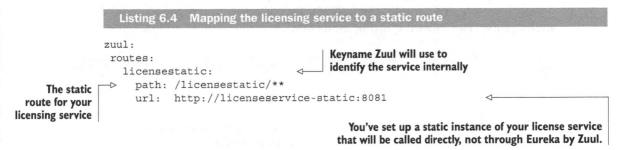

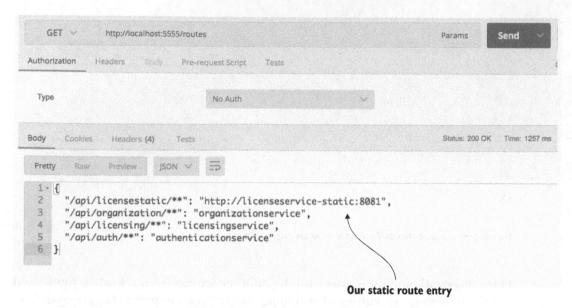

Figure 6.9   You've now mapped a static route to your licensing service.

Once this configuration change has been made, you can hit the /routes endpoint and see the static route added to Zuul. Figure 6.10 shows the results from the /routes listing.

At this point, the licensestatic endpoint won't use Eureka and will instead directly route the request to the http://licenseservice-static:8081 endpoint. The problem is that by bypassing Eureka, you only have a single route to point requests at. Fortunately, you can manually configure Zuul to disable Ribbon integration with Eureka and then list the individual service instances that ribbon will load balance against. The following listing shows this.

Listing 6.5   Mapping licensing service statically to multiple routes

```
zuul:
 routes:
   licensestatic:
     path: /licensestatic/**          Defines a service ID that will be used
     serviceId: licensestatic      ◁── to look up the service in Ribbon
ribbon:
 eureka:                              Disables Eureka
  enabled: false               ◁──  support in Ribbon
licensestatic:
  ribbon:
    listOfServers: http://licenseservice-static1:8081,      List of servers used to
      http://licenseservice-static2:8082          ◁──  route the request to
```

Once this configuration is in place, a call to the /routes endpoint now shows that the /api/licensestatic route has been mapped to a service ID called licensestatic. Figure 6.10 shows this.

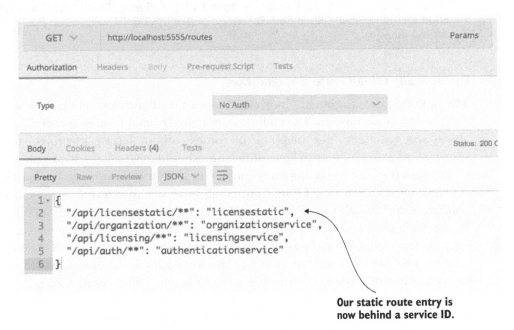

Our static route entry is now behind a service ID.

Figure 6.10   You now see that the /api/licensestatic **now maps to a service ID called** licensestatic

---

Dealing with non-JVM services

The problem with statically mapping routes and disabling Eureka support in Ribbon is that you've disabled Ribbon support for all your services running through your Zuul service gateway. This means that more load will be placed on your Eureka servers because Zuul can't use Ribbon to cache the look-up of services. Remember, Ribbon doesn't call Eureka every time it makes a call. Instead, it caches the location of the service instances locally and then checks with Eureka periodically for changes. With Ribbon out of the picture, Zuul will call Eureka every time it needs to resolve the location of a service.

Earlier in the chapter, I talked about how you might end up with multiple service gateways where different routing rules and policies would be enforced based on the type of services being called. For non-JVM applications, you could set up a separate Zuul server to handle these routes. However, I've found that with non-JVM-based languages, you're better off setting up a Spring Cloud "Sidecar" instance. The Spring Cloud sidecar allows you to register non-JVM services with a Eureka instance and then

6.3.4   *Dynamically reload route configuration*

The next thing we're going to look at in terms of configuring routes in Zuul is how to dynamically reload routes. The ability to dynamically reload routes is useful because it allows you to change the mapping of routes without having to recycle the Zuul server(s). Existing routes can be modified quickly and new routes added within have to go through the act of recycling each Zuul server in your environment. In chapter 3, we covered how to use Spring Cloud Configuration service to externalize a microservices configuration data. You can use Spring Cloud configuration to externalize Zuul routes. In the EagleEye examples you can set up a new application folder in your `config-repo` (http://github.com/carnellj/config-repo) called `zuulservice`. Like your organization and licensing services, you'll create three files—zuulservice.yml, zuulservice-dev.yml, and zuulservice-prod.yml—that will hold your route configuration.

To be consistent with the examples in the chapter 3 configuration, I've changed the route formats to move from a hierarchical format to the "." format. The initial route configuration will have a single entry in it:

```
zuul.prefix=/api
```

If you hit the `/routes` endpoint, you should see all your Eureka-based services currently shown in Zuul with the prefix of `/api`. Now, if you wanted to add new route mappings on the fly, all you have to do is make the changes to the config file and then commit them back to the Git repository where Spring Cloud Config is pulling its configuration data from. For instance, if you wanted to disable all Eureka-based service registration and only expose two routes (one for the organization and one for the licensing service), you could modify the zuulservice-*.yml files to look like this:

```
zuul.ignored-services: '*'
zuul.prefix: /api
zuul.routes.organizationservice: /organization/**
zuul.routes.organizationservice: /licensing/**
```

Then you can commit the changes to GitHub. Zuul exposes a POST-based endpoint route `/refresh` that will cause it to reload its route configuration. Once this `/refresh` is hit, if you then hit the `/routes` endpoint, you'll see that the two new routes are exposed and all the Eureka-based routes are gone.

6.3.5   *Zuul and service timeouts*

Zuul uses Netflix's Hystrix and Ribbon libraries to help prevent long-running service calls from impacting the performance of the services gateway. By default, Zuul will terminate and return an HTTP 500 error for any call that takes longer than one second to process a request. (This is the Hystrix default.) Fortunately, you can configure this behavior by setting the Hystrix timeout properties in your Zuul server's configuration.

   To set the Hystrix timeout for all of the services running through Zuul, you can use the `hystrix.command.default.execution.isolation.thread.timeoutInMilliseconds` property. For instance, if you wanted to set the default Hystrix time out to be 2.5 seconds, you could use the following configuration in your Zuul's Spring Cloud config file:

```
zuul.prefix:  /api
zuul.routes.organizationservice: /organization/**
zuul.routes.licensingservice: /licensing/**
zuul.debug.request: true
hystrix.command.default.execution.isolation.thread.timeoutInMilliseconds: 2500
```

If you need to set the Hystrix timeout for specific service, you can replace the `default` part of the property with the Eureka service ID name of the service whose timeout you want to override. For instance, if you wanted to change only the `licensingservice`'s timeout to three seconds and leave the rest of the services to use the default Hystrix timeout, you could use something like this in your configuration:

```
hystrix.command.licensingservice.execution.isolation.thread.timeoutInMillisec
     onds: 3000
```

Finally, you need to be aware of one other timeout property. While you've overridden the Hystrix timeout, the Netflix Ribbon also times out any calls that take longer than five seconds. While I highly recommend you revisit the design of any call that takes longer than five seconds, you can override the Ribbon timeout by setting the following property: `servicename.ribbon.ReadTimeout`. For example, if you wanted to override the `licensingservice` to have a seven-second timeout, you'd use the following configuration:

```
hystrix.command.licensingservice.execution.
  isolation.thread.timeoutInMilliseconds: 7000
licensingservice.ribbon.ReadTimeout: 7000
```

> **NOTE**   For configurations longer than five seconds you have to set both the Hystrix and the Ribbon timeouts.

6.4   *The real power of Zuul: filters*

While being able to proxy all requests through the Zuul gateway does allow you to simplify your service invocations, the real power of Zuul comes into play when you want to write custom logic that will be applied against all the service calls flowing through the gateway. Most often this custom logic is used to enforce a consistent set of application policies like security, logging, and tracking against all the services.

These application policies are considered *cross-cutting concerns* because you want them to be applied to all the services in your application without having to modify each service to implement them. In this fashion, Zuul filters can be used in a similar way as a J2EE servlet filter or a Spring Aspect that can intercept a wide body of behaviors and decorate or change the behavior of the call without the original coder being aware of the change. While a servlet filter or Spring Aspect is localized to a specific service, using Zuul and Zuul filters allows you implement cross-cutting concerns across all the services being routed through Zuul.

Zuul allows you to build custom logic using a filter within the Zuul gateway. A filter allows you to implement a chain of business logic that each service request passes through as it's being implemented.

Zuul supports three types of filters:

- *Pre-filters*—A pre-filter is invoked before the actual request to the target destination occurs with Zuul. A pre-filter usually carries out the task of making sure that the service has a consistent message format (key HTTP headers are in place, for example) or acts as a gatekeeper to ensure that the user calling the service is authenticated (they are who they say they are) and authorized (they can do what they're requesting to do).

- *Post filters*—A post filter is invoked after the target service has been invoked and a response is being sent back to the client. Usually a post filter will be implemented to log the response back from the target service, handle errors, or audit the response for sensitive information.

- *Route filters*—The route filter is used to intercept the call before the target service is invoked. Usually a route filter is used to determine if some level of dynamic routing needs to take place. For instance, later in the chapter you'll use a route-level filter that will route between two different versions of the same service so that a small percentage of calls to a service are routed to a new version of a service rather than the existing service. This will allow you to expose a small number of users to new functionality without having everyone use the new service.

Figure 6.11 shows how the pre-, post, and route filters fit together in terms of processing a service client's request.

If you follow the flow laid out in figure 6.11, you'll see everything start with a service client making a call to a service exposed through the service gateway. From there the following activities take place:

1 Any pre-filters defined in the Zuul gateway will be invoked by Zuul as a request enters the Zuul gateway. The pre-filters can inspect and modify a HTTP request before it gets to the actual service. A pre-filter cannot redirect the user to a different endpoint or service.

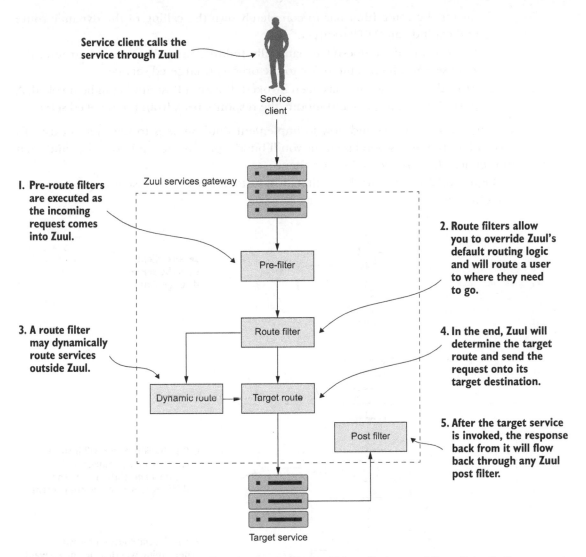

Service client calls the service through Zuul

Service client

Zuul services gateway

I. Pre-route filters are executed as the incoming request comes into Zuul.

Pre-filter

2. Route filters allow you to override Zuul's default routing logic and will route a user to where they need to go.

Route filter

3. A route filter may dynamically route services outside Zuul.

Dynamic route   Target route

4. In the end, Zuul will determine the target route and send the request onto its target destination.

Post filter

5. After the target service is invoked, the response back from it will flow back through any Zuul post filter.

Target service

Figure 6.11 The pre-, route, and post filters form a pipeline in which a client request flows through. As a request comes into Zuul, these filters can manipulate the incoming request.

2 After the pre-filters are executed against the incoming request by Zuul, Zuul will execute any defined route filters. Route filters can change the destination of where the service is heading.

3 If a route filter wants to redirect the service call to a place other than where the Zuul server is configured to send the route, it can do so. However, a Zuul route filter doesn't do an HTTP redirect, but will instead terminate the incoming HTTP request and then call the route on behalf of the original caller. This

means the route filter has to completely own the calling of the dynamic route and can't do an HTTP redirect.

4 If the route filter doesn't dynamically redirect the caller to a new route, the Zuul server will send the route to the originally targeted service.

5 After the target service has been invoked, the Zuul Post filters will be invoked. A post filter can inspect and modify the response back from the invoked service.

The best way to understand how to implement Zuul filters is to see them in use. To this end, in the next several sections you'll build a pre-, route, and post filter and then run service client requests through them.

Figure 6.12 shows how these filters will fit together in processing requests to your EagleEye services.

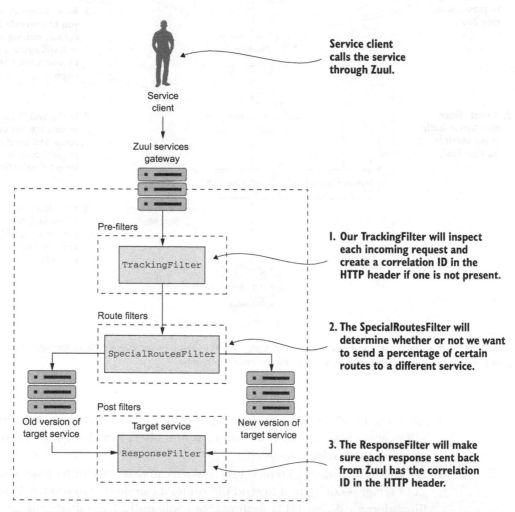

Figure 6.12   Zuul filters provide centralized tracking of service calls, logging, and dynamic routing. Zuul filters allows you to enforce custom rules and policies against microservice calls.

Following the flow of figure 6.12, you'll see the following filters being used:

1 `TrackingFilter`—The `TrackingFilter` will be a pre-filter that will ensure that every request flowing from Zuul has a correlation ID associated with it. A correlation ID is a unique ID that gets carried across all the microservices that are executed when carrying out a customer request. A correlation ID allows you to trace the chain of events that occur as a call goes through a series of microservice calls.

2 `SpecialRoutesFilter`—The `SpecialRoutesFilter` is a Zuul routes filter that will check the incoming route and determine if you want to do A/B testing on the route. A/B testing is a technique in which a user (in this case a service) is randomly presented with two different versions of services using the same service. The idea behind A/B testing is that new features can be tested before they're rolled out to the entire user base. In our example, you're going to have two different versions of the same organization service. A small number of users will be routed to the newer version of the service, while the majority of users will be routed to the older version of the service.

3 `ResponseFilter`—The `ResponseFilter` is a post filter that will inject the correlation ID associated with the service call into the HTTP response header being sent back to the client. This way, the client will have access to the correlation ID associated with the request they made.

6.5 *Building your first Zuul pre-filter generating correlation IDs*

Building filters in Zuul is an extremely simple activity. To begin, you'll build a Zuul pre-filter, called the `TrackingFilter`, that will inspect all incoming requests to the gateway and determine whether there's an HTTP header called `tmx-correlation-id` present in the request. The `tmx-correlation-id` header will contain a unique GUID (Globally Universal Id) that can be used to track a user's request across multiple microservices.

> **NOTE** We discussed the concept of a correlation ID in chapter 5. Here we're going to walk through in more detail how to use Zuul to generate a correlation ID. If you skipped around in the book, I highly recommend you look at chapter 5 and read the section on Hystrix and Thread context. Your implementation of correlation IDs will be implemented using `ThreadLocal` variables and there's extra work to do to have `ThreadLocal` variables work with Hystrix.

If the `tmx-correlation-id` isn't present on the HTTP header, your Zuul `TrackingFilter` will generate and set the correlation ID. If there's already a correlation ID present, Zuul won't do anything with the correlation ID. The presence of a correlation ID means that this particular service call is part of a chain of service calls carrying out the user's request. In this case, your `TrackingFilter` class will do nothing.

Let's go ahead and look at the implementation of the `TrackingFilter` in the following listing. This code can also be found in the book samples in `zuulsvr/src/main/java/com/thoughtmechanix/zuulsvr/filters/TrackingFilter.java`.

> **Listing 6.6   Zuul pre-filter for generating correlation IDs**

```java
package com.thoughtmechanix.zuulsvr.filters;

import com.netflix.zuul.ZuulFilter;
import org.springframework.beans.factory.annotation.Autowired;

//Removed other imports for conciseness

@Component
public class TrackingFilter extends ZuulFilter{
  private static final int    FILTER_ORDER = 1;
  private static final boolean SHOULD_FILTER=true;
  private static final Logger logger =
    LoggerFactory.getLogger(TrackingFilter.class);

  @Autowired
  FilterUtils filterUtils;

  @Override
  public String filterType() {
    return FilterUtils.PRE_FILTER_TYPE;
  }

  @Override
  public int filterOrder() {
    return FILTER_ORDER;
  }

  @Override
  public boolean shouldFilter() {
    return SHOULD_FILTER;
  }

  private boolean isCorrelationIdPresent(){
   if (filterUtils.getCorrelationId() !=null){
     return true;
   }

   return false;
  }

  private String generateCorrelationId(){
    return java.util.UUID.randomUUID().toString();
  }

  @Override
  public Object run() {
    if (isCorrelationIdPresent()) {
      logger.debug("tmx-correlation-id found in tracking filter: {}.
",
```

All Zuul filters must extend the ZuulFilter class and override four methods: filterType(), filterOrder(), shouldFilter(), and run().

Commonly used functions that are used across all your filters have been encapsulated in the FilterUtils class.

The filterType() method is used to tell Zuul whether the filter is a pre-, route, or post filter.

The filterOrder() method returns an integer value indicating what order Zuul should send requests through the different filter types.

The shouldFilter() method returns a Boolean indicating whether or not the filter should be active.

The helper methods that actually check if the tmx-correlation-id is present and can also generate a correlation ID GUIID value

The run() method is the code that is executed every time a service passes through the filter. In your run() function, you check to see if the tmx-correlation-id is present and if it isn't, you generate a correlation value and set the tmx-correlation-id HTTP

```
                    filterUtils.getCorrelationId());
   }
   else{
     filterUtils
        .setCorrelationId(generateCorrelationId());

  logger.debug("tmx-correlation-id generated
➡ in tracking filter: {}.",
➡ filterUtils.getCorrelationId());
}

 RequestContext ctx =
   RequestContext.getCurrentContext();
 logger.debug("Processing incoming request for {}.",
         ctx.getRequest().getRequestURI());
 return null;
}
}
```

To implement a filter in Zuul, you have to extend the `ZuulFilter` class and then override four methods: `filterType()`, `filterOrder()`, `shouldFilter()`, and `run()`. The first three methods in this list describe to Zuul what type of filter you're building, what order it should be run in compared to the other filters of its type, and whether it should be active. The last method, `run()`, contains the business logic the filter is going to implement.

You've implemented a class called `FilterUtils`. This class is used to encapsulate common functionality used by all your filters. The `FilterUtils` class is located in the zuulsvr/src/main/java/com/thoughtmechanix/zuulsvr/FilterUtils.java. We're not going to walk through the entire `FilterUtils` class, but the key methods we'll discuss here are the `getCorrelationId()` and `setCorrelationId()` functions. The following listing shows the code for the FilterUtils `getCorrelationId()` method.

Listing 6.7 Retrieving the `tmx-correlation-id` from the HTTP headers

```
public String getCorrelationId(){
  RequestContext ctx = RequestContext.getCurrentContext();

  if (ctx.getRequest()
        .getHeader(CORRELATION_ID) !=null) {
 return ctx.getRequest()
          .getHeader(CORRELATION_ID);
  }
  else{
 return ctx.getZuulRequestHeaders()
          .get(CORRELATION_ID);
  }
}
```

The key thing to notice in listing 6.7 is that you first check to see if the `tmx-correlation-ID` is already set on the HTTP Headers for the incoming request. You do this using the `ctx.getRequest().getHeader(CORRELATION_ID)` call.

> **NOTE** In a normal Spring MVC or Spring Boot service, the RequestContext would be of type `org.springframework.web.servletsupport.Request-Context`. However, Zuul gives a specialized `RequestContext` that has several additional methods for accessing Zuul-specific values. This request context is part of the `com.netflix.zuul.context` package.

If it isn't there, you then check the `ZuulRequestHeaders`. Zuul doesn't allow you to directly add or modify the HTTP request headers on an incoming request. If we add the `tmx-correlation-id` and then try to access it again later in the filter, it won't be available as part of the `ctx.getRequestHeader()` call. To work around this, you use the `FilterUtils getCorrelationId()` method. You may remember that earlier in the `run()` method on your `TrackingFilter` class, you did exactly this with the following code snippet:

```
else{
  filterUtils.setCorrelationId(generateCorrelationId());
  logger.debug("tmx-correlation-id generated
➥ in tracking filter: {}.",
  filterUtils.getCorrelationId());
}
```

The setting of the `tmx-correlation-id` occurs with the FilterUtils `set-CorrelationId()` method:

```
public void setCorrelationId(String correlationId){
  RequestContext ctx =
    RequestContext.getCurrentContext();
  ctx.addZuulRequestHeader(CORRELATION_ID, correlationId);
}
```

In the FilterUtils `setCorrelationId()` method, when you want to add a value to the HTTP request headers, you use the RequestContext's `addZuulRequestHeader()` method. This method will maintain a separate map of HTTP headers that were added while a request was flowing through the filters with your Zuul server. The data contained within the `ZuulRequestHeader` map will be merged when the target service is invoked by your Zuul server.

6.5.1 *Using the correlation ID in your service calls*

Now that you've guaranteed that a correlation ID has been added to every microservice call flowing through Zuul, how do you ensure that

- The correlation-ID is readily accessible to the microservice that's being invoked
- Any downstream service calls the microservice might make also propagate the correlation-ID on to the downstream call

To implement this, you're going to build a set of three classes into each of your microservices. These classes will work together to read the correlation ID (along with other information you'll add later) off the incoming HTTP request, map it to a class that's easily accessible and useable by the business logic in the application, and then ensure that the correlation ID is propagated to any downstream service calls.

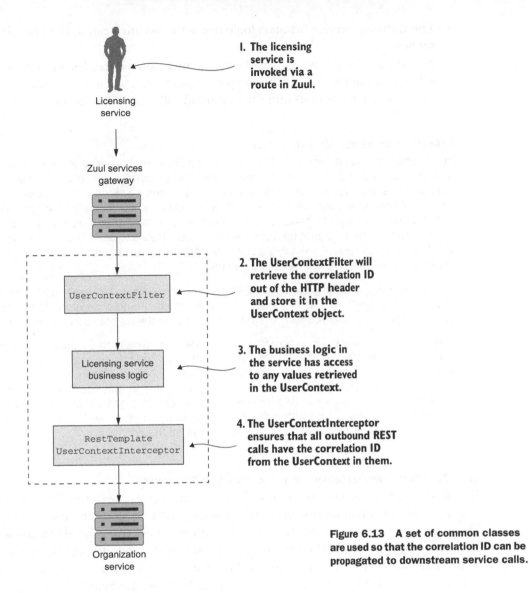

I. **The licensing service is invoked via a route in Zuul.**

2. **The UserContextFilter will retrieve the correlation ID out of the HTTP header and store it in the UserContext object.**

3. **The business logic in the service has access to any values retrieved in the UserContext.**

4. **The UserContextInterceptor ensures that all outbound REST calls have the correlation ID from the UserContext in them.**

Figure 6.13   A set of common classes are used so that the correlation ID can be propagated to downstream service calls.

Figure 6.13 demonstrates how these different pieces are going to be built out using your licensing service.

Let's walk through what's happening in figure 6.13:

1 When a call is made to the licensing service through the Zuul gateway, the `TrackingFilter` will inject a correlation ID into the incoming HTTP header for any calls coming into Zuul.

2 The `UserContextFilter` class is a custom HTTP ServletFilter. It maps a correlation ID to the `UserContext` class. The `UserContext` class is stored values in thread-local storage for use later in the call.

3   The licensing service business logic needs to execute a call to the organization service.

4   A `RestTemplate` is used to invoke the organization service. The `RestTemplate` will use a custom Spring Interceptor class (`UserContextInterceptor`) to inject the correlation ID into the outbound call as an HTTP header.

Repeated code vs. shared libraries

The subject of whether you should use common libraries across your microservices is a gray area in microservice design. Microservice purists will tell you that you shouldn't use a custom framework across your services because it introduces artificial dependencies in your services. Changes in business logic or a bug can introduce wide scale refactoring of all your services. On the other side, other microservice practitioners will say that a purist approach is impractical because certain situations exist (like the previous `UserContextFilter` example) where it makes sense to build a common library and share it across services.

I think there's a middle ground here. Common libraries are fine when dealing with infrastructure-style tasks. If you start sharing business-oriented classes, you're asking for trouble because you're breaking down the boundaries between the services.

I seem to be breaking my own advice with the code examples in this chapter, because if you look at all the services in the chapter, they all have their own copies of the `UserContextFilter`, `UserContext`, and `UserContextInterceptor` classes. The reason I took a share-nothing approach here is that I don't want to complicate the code examples in this book by having to create a shared library that would have to be published to a third-party Maven repository. Hence, all the classes in the `utils` package of the service are shared across all the services.

USERCONTEXTFILTER: INTERCEPTING THE INCOMING HTTP REQUEST

The first class you're going to build is the `UserContextFilter` class. This class is an HTTP servlet filter that will intercept all incoming HTTP requests coming into the service and map the correlation ID (and a few other values) from the HTTP request to the `UserContext` class. The following listing shows the code for the `UserContext` class. The source for this class can be found in `licensing-service/src/main/java/com/thoughtmechanix/licenses/utils/UserContextFilter.java`.

Listing 6.8   Mapping the correlation ID to the `UserContext` class

```
package com.thoughtmechanix.licenses.utils;

//Remove the imports for conciseness
@Component
public class UserContextFilter implements Filter {
  private static final Logger logger =
    LoggerFactory.getLogger(
      UserContextFilter.class);
  @Override
```

The filter is registered and picked up by Spring through the use of the Spring @Component annotation and by implementing a javax.servler.Filter interface.

```
public void doFilter(ServletRequest servletRequest,
                     ServletResponse servletResponse,
                     FilterChain filterChain)
    throws IOException, ServletException {
  HttpServletRequest httpServletRequest = (HttpServletRequest)
    servletRequest;

  UserContextHolder
    .getContext()
    .setCorrelationId(
      httpServletRequest
        .getHeader(
          UserContext.CORRELATION_ID));
UserContextHolder.getContext().setUserId(
  httpServletRequest
      .getHeader(UserContext.USER_ID));
UserContextHolder
  .getContext()
  .setAuthToken(
      httpServletRequest
        .getHeader(UserContext.AUTH_TOKEN) );
UserContextHolder
  .getContext()
  .setOrgId(
      httpServletRequest
        .getHeader(UserContext.ORG_ID) );

  filterChain
    .doFilter(httpServletRequest, servletResponse);
}

// Not showing the empty init and destroy methods}
```

> Your filter retrieves the correlation ID from the header and sets the value on the UserContext class.

> The other values being scraped from the HTTP Headers will come into play if you use the authentication service example defined in the code's README file.

Ultimately, the `UserContextFilter` is used to map the HTTP header values you're interested in into a Java class, `UserContext`.

USERCONTEXT: MAKING THE HTTP HEADERS EASILY ACCESSIBLE TO THE SERVICE

The `UserContext` class is used to hold the HTTP header values for an individual service client request being processed by your microservice. It consists of a getter/setter method that retrieves and stores values from `java.lang.ThreadLocal`. The following listing shows the code from the `UserContext` class. The source for this class can be found in `licensing-service/src/main/java/com/thoughtmechanix/licenses/utils/UserContext.java`.

> **Listing 6.9 Storing the HTTP header values inside the `UserContext` class**

```
@Component
public class UserContext {
    public static final String CORRELATION_ID = "tmx-correlation-id";
    public static final String AUTH_TOKEN     = "tmx-auth-token";
    public static final String USER_ID        = "tmx-user-id";
    public static final String ORG_ID         = "tmx-org-id";
```

```
    private String correlationId= new String();
    private String authToken= new String();
    private String userId = new String();
    private String orgId = new String();

    public String getCorrelationId() { return correlationId;}
    public void setCorrelationId(String correlationId) {
      this.correlationId = correlationId;}

    public String getAuthToken() { return authToken;}
    public void setAuthToken(String authToken) {
      this.authToken = authToken;}

    public String getUserId() { return userId;}
    public void setUserId(String userId) { this.userId = userId;}

    public String getOrgId() { return orgId;}
    public void setOrgId(String orgId) {this.orgId = orgId;
  }
}
```

Now the UserContext class is nothing more than a POJO holding the values scraped from the incoming HTTP request. You use a class called zuulsvr/src/main/java/com/thoughtmechanix/zuulsvr/filters/UserContextHolder.java to store the UserContext in a ThreadLocal variable that is accessible in any method being invoked by the thread processing the user's request. The code for UserContext-Holder is shown in the following listing.

Listing 6.10   The UserContextHolder stores the UserContext in a ThreadLocal

```
public class UserContextHolder {
  private static final ThreadLocal<UserContext> userContext
      = new ThreadLocal<UserContext>();

  public static final UserContext getContext(){
      UserContext context = userContext.get();

      if (context == null) {
          context = createEmptyContext();
          userContext.set(context);
      }

      return userContext.get();
  }

  public static final void setContext(UserContext context) {
    Assert.notNull(context,
    ➥ "Only non-null UserContext instances are permitted");
      userContext.set(context);
  }

  public static final UserContext createEmptyContext(){
      return new UserContext();
  }
}
```

CUSTOM RESTTEMPLATE AND USERCONTEXTINTECEPTOR: ENSURING THAT THE CORRELATION ID GETS PROPAGATED FORWARD

The last piece of code that we're going to look at is the `UserContextInterceptor` class. This class is used to inject the correlation ID into any outgoing HTTP-based service requests being executed from a `RestTemplate` instance. This is done to ensure that you can establish a linkage between service calls.

To do this you're going to use a Spring Interceptor that's being injected into the `RestTemplate` class. Let's look at the `UserContextInterceptor` in the following listing.

Listing 6.11 All outgoing microservice calls have the correlation ID injected into them

```
package com.thoughtmechanix.licenses.utils;

//Removed imports for conciseness
public class UserContextInterceptor
  implements ClientHttpRequestInterceptor {

  @Override
  public ClientHttpResponse intercept(
      HttpRequest request, byte[] body,
      ClientHttpRequestExecution execution)
    throws IOException {

    HttpHeaders headers = request.getHeaders();
    headers.add(
      UserContext.CORRELATION_ID,
      UserContextHolder
        .getContext()
        .getCorrelationId());
    headers.add(UserContext.AUTH_TOKEN,
      UserContextHolder
        .getContext()
        .getAuthToken());

    return execution.execute(request, body);
  }
}
```

The UserContextIntercept implements the Spring frameworks ClientHttpRequestInterceptor.

The intercept() method is invoked before the actual HTTP service call occurs by the RestTemplate.

You take the HTTP request header that's being prepared for the outgoing service call and add the correlation ID stored in the UserContext.

To use the `UserContextInterceptor` you need to define a `RestTemplate` bean and then add the `UserContextInterceptor` to it. To do this, you're going to add your own `RestTemplate` bean definition to the `licensing-service/src/main/java/com/thoughtmechanix/licenses/Application.java` class. The following listing shows the method that's added to this class.

Listing 6.12 Adding the `UserContextInterceptor` to the `RestTemplate` class

```
@LoadBalanced
@Bean
public RestTemplate getRestTemplate(){
```

The @LoadBalanced annotation indicates that this RestTemplate object is going to use Ribbon.

```
        RestTemplate template = new RestTemplate();
        List interceptors = template.getInterceptors();
          if (interceptors==null){
            template.setInterceptors(
              Collections.singletonList(
                new UserContextInterceptor()));
          }
          else{
              interceptors.add(new UserContextInterceptor());
              template.setInterceptors(interceptors);
          }

          return template; }
```

Adding the UserContextInterceptor to the RestTemplate instance that has been created

With this bean definition in place, any time you use the `@Autowired` annotation and inject a `RestTemplate` into a class, you'll use the `RestTemplate` created in listing 6.11 with the `UserContextInterceptor` attached to it.

Log aggregation and authentication and more

Now that you have correlation ID's being passed to each service, it's possible to trace a transaction as it flows through all the services involved in the call. To do this you need to ensure that each service logs to a central log aggregation point that captures log entries from all of your services into a single point. Each log entry captured in the log aggregation service will have a correlation ID associated to each entry. Implementing a log aggregation solution is outside the scope of this chapter, but in chapter 9, we'll see how to use Spring Cloud Sleuth. Spring Cloud Sleuth won't use the `TrackingFilter` that you built here, but it will use the same concepts of tracking the correlation ID and ensuring that it's injected in every call.

6.6   *Building a post filter receiving correlation IDs*

Remember, Zuul executes the actual HTTP call on behalf of the service client. Zuul has the opportunity to inspect the response back from the target service call and then alter the response or decorate it with additional information. When coupled with capturing data with the pre-filter, a Zuul post filter is an ideal location to collect metrics and complete any logging associated with the user's transaction. You'll want to take advantage of this by injecting the correlation ID that you've been passing around to your microservices back to the user.

You're going to do this by using a Zuul post filter to inject the correlation ID back into the HTTP response headers being passed back to the caller of the service. This way, you can pass the correlation ID back to the caller without ever having to touch the message body. The following listing shows the code for building a post filter. This code can be found in `zuulsvr/src/main/java/com/thoughtmechanix/zuulsvr/filters/ResponseFilter.java`.

Listing 6.13   Injecting the correlation ID into the HTTP response

```java
package com.thoughtmechanix.zuulsvr.filters;

//Remove imports for conciseness

@Component
public class ResponseFilter extends ZuulFilter{
  private static final int FILTER_ORDER=1;
  private static final boolean SHOULD_FILTER=true;
  private static final Logger logger =
    LoggerFactory
      .getLogger(ResponseFilter.class);

  @Autowired
  FilterUtils filterUtils;

  @Override
  public String filterType() {
    return FilterUtils.POST_FILTER_TYPE;
  }

  @Override
  public int filterOrder() {
    return FILTER_ORDER;
  }

  @Override
  public boolean shouldFilter() {
    return SHOULD_FILTER;
  }

  @Override
  public Object run() {
    RequestContext ctx =
        RequestContext.getCurrentContext();

    logger.debug("Adding the correlation id to
      the outbound headers. {}",
      filterUtils.getCorrelationId());

    ctx.getResponse()
      .addHeader(
        FilterUtils.CORRELATION_ID,
        filterUtils.getCorrelationId());

    logger.debug("Completing outgoing request for {}.",
      ctx.getRequest().getRequestURI());

    return null;
  }
}
```

To build a post filter you need to set the filter type to be **POST_FILTER_TYPE**.

Grab the correlation ID that was passed in on the original HTTP request and inject it into the response.

Log the outgoing request URI so that you have "bookends" that will show the incoming and outgoing entry of the user's request into Zuul.

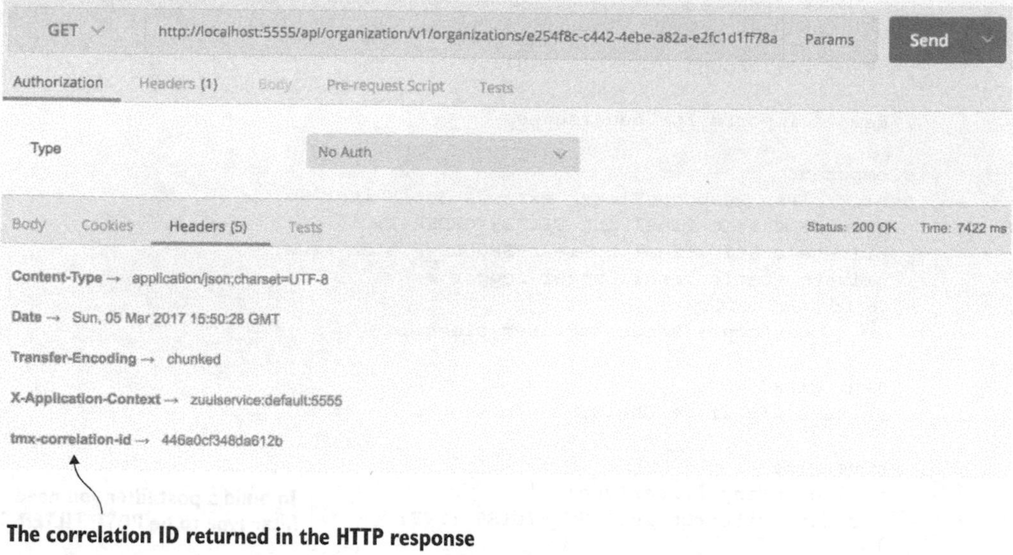

The correlation ID returned in the HTTP response

Figure 6.14   The tmx-correlation-id has been added to the response headers sent back to the service client.

Once the `ResponseFilter` has been implemented, you can fire up your Zuul service and call the EagleEye licensing service through it. Once the service has completed, you'll see a `tmx-correlation-id` on the HTTP response header from the call. Figure 6.14 shows the `tmx-correlation-id` being sent back from the call.

Up until this point, all our filter examples have dealt with manipulating the service client calls before and after it has been routed to its target destination. For our last filter example, let's look at how you can dynamically change the target route you want to send the user to.

6.7   *Building a dynamic route filter*

The last Zuul filter we'll look at is the Zuul route filter. Without a custom route filter in place, Zuul will do all its routing based on the mapping definitions you saw earlier in the chapter. However, by building a Zuul route filter, you can add intelligence to how a service client's invocation will be routed.

In this section, you'll learn about Zuul's route filter by building a route filter that will allow you to do A/B testing of a new version of a service. A/B testing is where you roll out a new feature and then have a percentage of the total user population use that feature. The rest of the user population still uses the old service. In this example, you're going to simulate rolling out a new version of the organization service where you want 50% of the users go to the old service and 50% of the users to go to the new service.

To do this you're going to build a Zuul route filter, called `SpecialRoutes-Filter`, that will take the Eureka service ID of the service being called by Zuul and call out to another microservice called `SpecialRoutes`. The `SpecialRoutes` service will check an internal database to see if the service name exists. If the targeted service name exists, it will return a weight and target destination of an alternative location for the service. The `SpecialRoutesFilter` will then take the weight returned and, based on the weight, randomly generate a number that will be used to determine whether the user's call will be routed to the alternative organization service or to the organization service defined in the Zuul route mappings. Figure 6.15 shows the flow of what happens when the `SpecialRoutesFilter` is used.

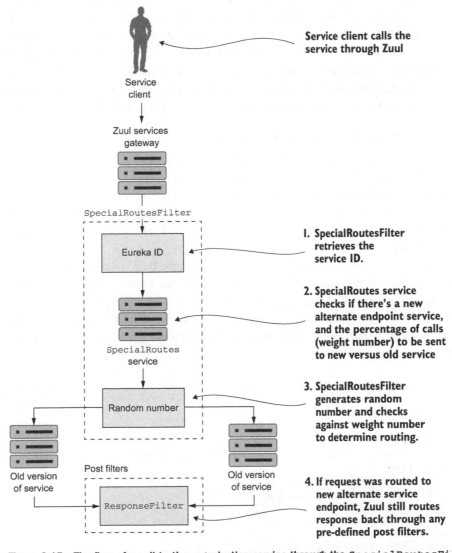

Figure 6.15   The flow of a call to the organization service through the `SpecialRoutesFilter`

In figure 6.15, after the service client has called a service "fronted" by Zuul, the `SpecialRoutesFilter` takes the following actions:

1 The `SpecialRoutesFilter` retrieves the service ID for the service being called.

2 The `SpecialRoutesFilter` calls the `SpecialRoutes` service. The `SpecialRoutes` service checks to see if there's an alternative endpoint defined for the targeted endpoint. If a record is found, it will contain a weight that will tell Zuul the percentage of service calls that should be sent to the old service and the new service.

3 The `SpecialRoutesFilter` then generates a random number and compares that against the weight returned by the `SpecialRoutes` service. If the randomly generated number is under the value of the alternative endpoint weight, `SpecialRoutesFilter` sends the request to the new version of the service.

4 If the `SpecialRoutesFilter` sends the request to new version of the service, Zuul maintains the original predefined pipelines and sends the response back from the alternative service endpoint through any defined post filters.

6.7.1 *Building the skeleton of the routing filter*

We're going to start walking through the code you used to build the `SpecialRoutesFilter`. Of all the filters we've looked at so far, implementing a Zuul route filter requires the most coding effort, because with a route filter you're taking over a core piece of Zuul functionality, routing, and replacing it with your own functionality. We're not going to go through the entire class in detail here, but rather work through the pertinent details.

The `SpecialRoutesFilter` follows the same basic pattern as the other Zuul filters. It extends the `ZuulFilter` class and sets the `filterType()` method to return the value of "route". I'm not going to go into any more explanation of the `filterOrder()` and `shouldFilter()` methods as they're no different from the previous filters discussed earlier in the chapter. The following listing shows the route filter skeleton.

Listing 6.14 The skeleton of your route filter

```
package com.thoughtmechanix.zuulsvr.filters;

@Component
public class SpecialRoutesFilter extends ZuulFilter {
  @Override
  public String filterType() {
    return filterUtils.ROUTE_FILTER_TYPE;
  }

  @Override
  public int filterOrder() {}
```

```
    @Override
    public boolean shouldFilter() {}

    @Override
    public Object run() {}
}
```

6.7.2 Implementing the run() method

The real work for the `SpecialRoutesFilter` begins in the `run()` method of the code. The following listing shows the code for this method.

Listing 6.15 The `run()` method for the `SpecialRoutesFilter` is where the work begins

```
public Object run() {                                              Executes call to
  RequestContext ctx = RequestContext.getCurrentContext();     SpecialRoutes service
                                                               to determine if there is a
  AbTestingRoute abTestRoute =                                 routing record for this org
    getAbRoutingInfo( filterUtils.getServiceId() );

  if (abTestRoute!=null &&
      useSpecialRoute(abTestRoute)) {                          The useSpecialRoute() method
    String route =                                             will take the weight of the route,
        buildRouteString(                                      generate a random number,
          ctx.getRequest().getRequestURI(),                    and determine if you're going
          abTestRoute.getEndpoint(),                           to forward the request onto
          ctx.get("serviceId").toString());                    the alternative service.
    forwardToSpecialRoute(route);
  }                          The forwardToSpecialRoute()
                             method does the work of         If there's a routing record, build the full
  return null;               forwarding onto the             URL (with path) to the service location
}                            alternative service.            specified by the specialroutes service.
```

The general flow of code in listing 6.15 is that when a route request hits the `run()` method in the `SpecialRoutesFilter`, it will execute a REST call to the `Special-Routes` service. This service will execute a lookup and determine if a routing record exists for the Eureka service ID of the target service being called. The call out to `SpecialRoutes` service is done in the `getAbRoutingInfo()` method. The `get-AbRoutingInfo()` method is shown in the following listing.

Listing 6.16 Invoking the `SpecialRouteservice` to see if a routing record exists

```
private AbTestingRoute getAbRoutingInfo(String serviceName){
  ResponseEntity<AbTestingRoute> restExchange = null;
  try {
    restExchange = restTemplate.exchange(                    Calls the SpecialRoutesService
      "http://specialroutesservice/v1                        endpoint
      /route/abtesting/{serviceName}",
      HttpMethod.GET,null, AbTestingRoute.class, serviceName);
}
```

```
catch(HttpClientErrorException ex){
  if (ex.getStatusCode()== HttpStatus.NOT_FOUND){
    return null;
    throw ex;
}
return restExchange.getBody();
}
```

> If the routes services doesn't find a record (it will return a 404 HTTP Status Code), the method will return null.

Once you've determined that there's a routing record present for the target service, you need to determine whether you should route the target service request to the alternative service location or to the default service location statically managed by the Zuul route maps. To make this determination, you call the useSpecialRoute() method. The following listing shows this method.

Listing 6.17   Determining whether to use the alternative service route

```
public boolean useSpecialRoute(AbTestingRoute testRoute){
  Random random = new Random();

  if (testRoute.getActive().equals("N"))
    return false;

  int value =
      random.nextInt((10 - 1) + 1) + 1;

  if (testRoute.getWeight()<value)
    return true;

  return false;
}
```

> Checks to see if the route is even active

> Determines whether you should use the alternative service route

This method does two things. First, the method checks the active field on the AbTestingRoute record returned from the SpecialRoutes service. If the record is set to "N," useSpecialRoute() method shouldn't do anything because you don't want to do any routing at this moment. Second, the method generates a random number between 1 and 10. The method will then check to see if the weight of the return route is less than the randomly generated number. If the condition is true, the use-SpecialRoute method returns true indicating you do want to use the route.

Once you've determined that you do want to route the service request coming into the SpecialRoutesFilter, you're going to forward the request onto the target service.

6.7.3   Forwarding the route

The actual forwarding of the route to the downstream service is where the majority of the work occurs in the SpecialRoutesFilter. While Zuul does provide helper functions to make this task easier, the majority of the work still lies with the developer. The forwardToSpecialRoute() method does the forwarding work for you. The code in this method borrows heavily from the source code for the Spring Cloud

SimpleHostRoutingFilter class. While we're not going to go through all of the helper functions called in the forwardToSpecialRoute() method, we'll walk through the code in this method, as shown in the following listing.

Listing 6.18 The forwardToSpecialRoute invokes the alternative service

```
private ProxyRequestHelper helper                        ◁——  The helper variable is an
   = new ProxyRequestHelper ();                                instance variable of type
                                                               ProxyRequestHelper class.
private void forwardToSpecialRoute(String route) {           This is a Spring Cloud class
 RequestContext context                                       with helper functions for
     = RequestContext.getCurrentContext();                    proxying service requests.
 HttpServletRequest request = context.getRequest();

 MultiValueMap<String, String>headers =
   helper.buildZuulRequestHeaders(request);      ◁———  Creates a copy of all the HTTP request
                                                        headers that will be sent to the service
 MultiValueMap<String, String> params =
   helper.buildZuulRequestQueryParams(request);     ◁———  Creates copy of all the
                                                           HTTP request parameters
 String verb = getVerb(request);
 InputStream requestEntity = getRequestBody(request);   ◁——  Makes a copy of the
 if (request.getContentLength() < 0)                         HTTP Body that will be
    context.setChunkedRequestBody();                         forwarded onto the
                                                             alternative service
 this.helper.addIgnoredHeaders();
 CloseableHttpClient httpClient = null;
 HttpResponse response = null;

 try {
  httpClient = HttpClients.createDefault();
   response = forward(                            ◁——  Invokes the alternative service
             httpClient,                                using the forward helper
             verb,                                      method (not shown)
           route,
           request,
           headers,
           params,
           requestEntity);
   setResponse(response);                    ◁———  The result of service call is
  }                                                saved back to the Zuul server
  catch (Exception ex ) {//Removed for conciseness}   through the setResponse()
                                                       helper method.
}
```

The key takeaway from the code in listing 6.18 is that you're copying all of the values from the incoming HTTP request (the header parameters, HTTP verb, and the body) into a new request that will be invoked on the target service. The forwardToSpecial-Route() method then takes the response back from the target service and sets it on the HTTP request context used by Zuul. This is done via the setResponse() helper method (not shown). Zuul uses the HTTP request context to return the response back from the calling service client.

6.7.4   *Pulling it all together*

Now that you've implemented the `SpecialRoutesFilter` you can see it an action by calling the licensing service. As you may remember from earlier chapters, the licensing service calls the organization service to retrieve the contact data for the organization.

In the code example, the `specialroutesservice` has a database record for the organization service that will route the requests for calls to the organization service 50% of the time to the existing organization service (the one mapped in Zuul) and 50% of the time to an alternative organization service. The alternative organization service route returned from the `SpecialRoutes` service will be `http://orgservice-new` and will not be accessible directly from Zuul. To differentiate between the two services, I've modified the organization service(s) to pre-pend the text "`OLD::`" and "`NEW::`" to contact names returned by the organization service.

If you now hit the licensing service endpoint through Zuul

```
http://localhost:5555/api/licensing/v1/organizations/e254f8c-c442-4ebe-a82a-
    e2fc1d1ff78a/licenses/f3831f8c-c338-4ebe-a82a-e2fc1d1ff78a
```

you should see the `contactName` returned from the licensing service call flip between the `OLD::` and `NEW::` values. Figure 6.16 shows this.

A Zuul routes filter does take more effort to implement then a pre- or post filter, but it's also one of the most powerful parts of Zuul because you're able to easily add intelligence to the way your services are routed.

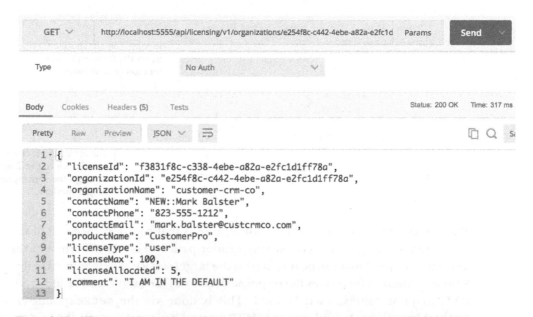

Figure 6.16   When you hit the alternative organization service, you see NEW prepended to the `contactName`.

6.8   *Summary*

- Spring Cloud makes it trivial to build a services gateway.
- The Zuul services gateway integrates with Netflix's Eureka server and can automatically map services registered with Eureka to a Zuul route.
- Zuul can prefix all routes being managed, so you can easily prefix your routes with something like /api.
- Using Zuul, you can manually define route mappings. These route mappings are manually defined in the applications configuration files.
- By using Spring Cloud Config server, you can dynamically reload the route mappings without having to restart the Zuul server.
- You can customize Zuul's Hystrix and Ribbon timeouts at global and individual service levels.
- Zuul allows you to implement custom business logic through Zuul filters. Zuul has three types of filters: pre-, post, and routing Zuul filters.
- Zuul pre-filters can be used to generate a correlation ID that can be injected into every service flowing through Zuul.
- A Zuul post filter can inject a correlation ID into every HTTP service response back to a service client.
- A custom Zuul route filter can perform dynamic routing based on a Eureka service ID to do A/B testing between different versions of the same service.

Securing your microservices

7

Security. The mention of the word will often cause an involuntary groan from the developer who hears it. You'll hear them mutter and curse under their breath, "It's obtuse, hard to understand, and even harder to debug." Yet you won't find any developer (except maybe for inexperienced developers) say that that they don't worry about security.

A secure application involves multiple layers of protection, including

- Ensuring that the proper user controls are in place so that you can validate that a user is who they say they are and that they have permission to do what they're trying to do
- Keeping the infrastructure the service is running on patched and up-to-date to minimize the risk of vulnerabilities.

192

- Implementing network access controls so that a service is only accessible through well-defined ports and accessible to a small number of authorized servers

This chapter is only going to deal with the first bullet point in this list: how to *authenticate* that the user calling your microservice is who they say they are and determine whether they're *authorized* to carry out the action they're requesting from your microservice. The other two topics are extremely broad security topics that are outside the scope of this book.

To implement authorization and authentication controls, you're going to use Spring Cloud security and the OAuth2 (Open Authentication) standard to secure your Spring-based services. OAuth2 is a token-based security framework that allows a user to authenticate themselves with a third-party authentication service. If the user successfully authenticates, they will be presented a token that must be sent with every request. The token can then be validated back to the authentication service. The main goal behind OAuth2 is that when multiple services are called to fulfill a user's request, the user can be authenticated by each service without having to present their credentials to each service processing their request. Spring Boot and Spring Cloud each provide an out-of-the-box implementation of an OAuth2 service and make it extremely easy to integrate OAuth2 security into your service.

> **NOTE** In this chapter, we'll show you how to protect your microservices using OAuth2; however, a full-blown OAuth2 implementation also requires a front-web application to enter your user credentials. We won't be going through how to set up the front-end application because that's out of scope for a book on microservices. Instead, we'll use a REST client, like POSTMAN, to simulate the presentation of credentials. For a good tutorial on how to configure your front-end application, I recommend you look at the following Spring tutorial: https://spring.io/blog/2015/02/03/sso-with-oauth2-angular-js-and-spring-security-part-v.

The real power behind OAuth2 is that it allows application developers to easily integrate with third-party cloud providers and do user authentication and authorization with those services without having to constantly pass the user's credentials to the third-party service. Cloud providers such as Facebook, GitHub, and Salesforce all support OAuth2 as a standard.

Before we get into the technical details of protecting our services with OAuth2, let's walk through the OAuth2 architecture.

7.1 Introduction to OAuth2

OAuth2 is a token-based security authentication and authorization framework that breaks security down into four components. These four components are

1 *A protected resource*—This is the resource (in our case, a microservice) you want to protect and ensure that only authenticated users who have the proper authorization can access.

2   *A resource owner*—A resource owner defines what applications can call their service, which users are allowed to access the service, and what they can do with the service. Each application registered by the resource owner will be given an application name that identifies the application along with an application secret key. The combination of the application name and the secret key are part of the credentials that are passed when authenticating an OAuth2 token.

3   *An application*—This is the application that's going to call the service on a behalf of a user. After all, users rarely invoke a service directly. Instead, they rely on an application to do the work for them.

4   *OAuth2 authentication server*—The OAuth2 authentication server is the intermediary between the application and the services being consumed. The OAuth2 server allows the user to authenticate themselves without having to pass their user credentials down to every service the application is going to call on behalf of the user.

The four components interact together to authenticate the user. The user only has to present their credentials. If they successfully authenticate, they're issued an authentication token that can be passed from service to service. This is shown in figure 7.1. OAuth2 is a token-based security framework. A user authenticates against the OAuth2 server by providing their credentials along with the application that they're using to access the resource. If the user's credentials are valid, the OAuth2 server provides a

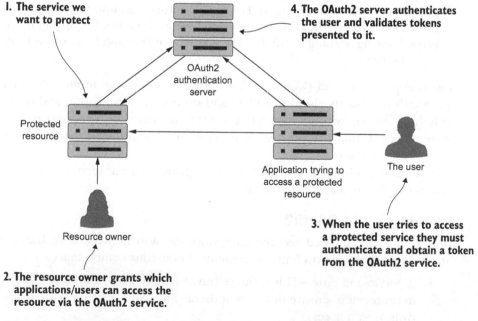

1. The service we want to protect

4. The OAuth2 server authenticates the user and validates tokens presented to it.

OAuth2 authentication server

Protected resource

Application trying to access a protected resource

The user

Resource owner

2. The resource owner grants which applications/users can access the resource via the OAuth2 service.

3. When the user tries to access a protected service they must authenticate and obtain a token from the OAuth2 service.

Figure 7.1   OAuth2 allows a user to authenticate without constantly having to present credentials.

token that can be presented every time a service being used by the user's application tries to access a protected resource (the microservice).

The protected resource can then contact the OAuth2 server to determine the validity of the token and retrieve what roles a user has assigned to them. Roles are used to group related users together and to define what resources that *group of users* can access. For the purposes of this chapter, you're going to use OAuth2 and roles to define what service endpoints and what HTTP verbs a user can call on an endpoint.

Web service security is an extremely complicated subject. You have to understand who's going to call your services (internal users to your corporate network, external users), how they're going to call your service (internal web-based client, mobile device, web application outside your corporate network), and what actions they're going to take with your code. OAuth2 allows you to protect your REST-based services across these different scenarios through different authentication schemes called grants. The OAuth2 specification has four types of grants:

- Password
- Client credential
- Authorization code
- Implicit

We aren't going to walk through each of these grant types or provide code examples for each grant type. That's simply too much material to cover in one chapter. Instead, I'll do the following:

- Discuss how your microservices service can use OAuth2 through one of the simpler OAuth2 grant types (the password grant type).
- Use JavaScript web tokens to provide a more robust OAuth2 solution and establish a standard for encoding information in a OAuth2 token.
- Walk through other security considerations that need to be taken into account when building microservices.

I do provide overview material on the other OAuth2 grant types in appendix B, "OAuth2 grant types." If you're interested in diving into more detail on the OAuth2 spec and how to implement all the grant types, I highly recommend Justin Richer and Antonio Sanso's book, *OAuth2 in Action* (Manning, 2017), which is a comprehensive explanation of OAuth2.

7.2 *Starting small: using Spring and OAuth2 to protect a single endpoint*

To understand how to set up the authentication and authorization pieces of OAuth2, you're going to implement the OAuth2 password grant type. To implement this grant, you'll do the following:

- Set up a Spring-Cloud-based OAuth2 authentication service.
- Register a faux EagleEye UI application as an authorized application that can authenticate and authorize user identities with your OAuth2 service.

- Use OAuth2 password grant to protect your EagleEye services. You're not going to build a UI for EagleEye, so instead you'll simulate a user logging in to use POSTMAN to authenticate against your EagleEye OAuth2 service.
- Protect the licensing and organization service so that they can only be called by an authenticated user.

7.2.1 Setting up the EagleEye OAuth2 authentication service

Like all the examples in this book's chapters, your OAuth2 authentication service is going to be another Spring Boot service. The authentication service will authenticate the user credentials and issue a token. Every time the user tries to access a service protected by the authentication service, the authentication service will validate that the OAuth2 token was issued by it and that it hasn't expired. The authentication service will be the equivalent of the authentication service in figure 7.1.

To get started, you're going to set up two things:

1 The appropriate Maven build dependencies needed for your bootstrap class
2 A bootstrap class that will act as an entry point to the service

You can find all code examples for the authentication service in the authentication-service directory. To set up an OAuth2 authentication server, you need the following Spring Cloud dependencies in the authentication-service/pom.xml file:

```
<dependency>
  <groupId>org.springframework.cloud</groupId>
  <artifactId>spring-cloud-security</artifactId>
</dependency>

<dependency>
  <groupId>org.springframework.security.oauth</groupId>
  <artifactId>spring-security-oauth2</artifactId>
</dependency>
```

The first dependency, `spring-cloud-security`, brings in the general Spring and Spring Cloud security libraries. The second dependency, `spring-security-oauth2`, pulls in the Spring OAuth2 libraries.

Now that the Maven dependencies are defined, you can work on the bootstrap class. This class can be found in the `authentication-service/src/main/java/com/thoughtmechanix/authentication/Application.java` class. The following listing shows the code for the `Application.java` class.

> **Listing 7.1 The `authentication-service` bootstrap class**

```
//Imports removed for conciseness

@SpringBootApplication
@RestController
@EnableResourceServer
@EnableAuthorizationServer          ⟵── Used to tell Spring Cloud that this service
public class Application {              is going to act as an OAuth2 service
```

```
@RequestMapping(value = { "/user" }, produces = "application/json")
public Map<String, Object> user(OAuth2Authentication user) {
  Map<String, Object> userInfo = new HashMap<>();
  userInfo.put(
          "user",
          user.getUserAuthentication()
          .getPrincipal());
  userInfo.put(
      "authorities",
      AuthorityUtils.authorityListToSet(
      user.getUserAuthentication()
        . getAuthorities()));
  return userInfo;
}

public static void main(String[] args) {
  SpringApplication.run(Application.class, args);
}
}
```

Used later in the chapter
to retrieve information
about the user

The first thing to note in this listing is the @EnableAuthorizationServer annotation. This annotation tells Spring Cloud that this service will be used as an OAuth2 service and to add several REST-based endpoints that will be used in the OAuth2 authentication and authorization processes.

The second thing you'll see in listing 7.1 is the addition of an endpoint called /user (which maps to /auth/user). You'll use this endpoint later in the chapter when you're trying to access a service protected by OAuth2. This endpoint is called by the protected service to validate the OAuth2 access token and retrieve the assigned roles of the user accessing the protected service. I'll discuss this endpoint in greater detail later in the chapter.

7.2.2   *Registering client applications with the OAuth2 service*

At this point you have an authentication service, but haven't defined any applications, users, or roles within the authentication server. You can begin by registering the Eagle-Eye application with your authentication service. To do this you're going to set up an additional class in your authentication service called `authentication-service/ src/main/java/com/thoughtmechanix/authentication/security/OAuth2 Config.java`.

This class will define what applications are registered with your OAuth2 authentication service. It's important to note that just because an application is registered with your OAuth2 service, it doesn't mean that the service will have access to any protected resources.

> **On authentication vs. authorization**
>
> I've often found that developers "mix and match" the meaning of the terms authentication and authorization. Authentication is the act of a user proving who they are by providing credentials. Authorization determines whether a user is allowed to do what

(continued)

they're trying to do. For instance, the user Jim could prove his identity by providing a user ID and password, but he may not be authorized to look at sensitive data such as payroll data. For the purposes of our discussion, a user must be authenticated before authorization takes place.

The `OAuth2Config` class defines what applications and the user credentials the OAuth2 service knows about. In the following listing you can see the `OAuth2Config.java` code.

Listing 7.2   `OAuth2Config` service defines what applications can use your service

```
                                       Extends the AuthorizationServerConfigurerAdapter class
                                       and marks the class with @Configuration annotation
//Imports removed for conciseness
@Configuration
public class OAuth2Config extends AuthorizationServerConfigurerAdapter {

  @Autowired
  private AuthenticationManager authenticationManager;
  @Autowired
  private UserDetailsService userDetailsService;

  @Override
  public void configure(ClientDetailsServiceConfigurer clients) throws
    Exception {
    clients.inMemory()                        Overrides the configure() method.
        .withClient("eagleeye")             This defines which clients are going
        .secret("thisissecret")                 to registered your service.
        .authorizedGrantTypes(
            "refresh_token",
            "password",
            "client_credentials")
        .scopes("webclient","mobileclient");
  }

  @Override
  public void configure(
      AuthorizationServerEndpointsConfigurer endpoints)
      throws Exception {                        This method defines the
    endpoints                              different components used
        .authenticationManager(authenticationManager)   within the Authentication-
        .userDetailsService(userDetailsService);      ServerConfigurer. This code
  }                                       is telling Spring to use the
}                                       default authentication manager
                                        and user details service that
                                          comes up with Spring.
```

The first thing to notice in the code is that you're extending Spring's `AuthorizationServerConfigurerAdapter` class and then marking the class with a

@Configuration annotation. The AuthorizationServerConfigurerAdapter class is a core piece of Spring Security. It provides the basic mechanisms for carrying out key authentication and authorization functions. For the OAuth2Config class you're going to override two methods. The first method, configure(), is used to define what client applications are registered with your authentication service. The configure() method takes a single parameter called clients of type ClientDetails-ServiceConfigurer. Let's start walking through the code in the configure() method in a little more detail. The first thing you do in this method is register which client applications are allowed to access services protected by the OAuth2 service. I'm using "access" here in the broadest terms, because you control what the users of the client applications can do later by checking whether the user that the service is being invoked for is authorized to take the actions they're trying to take:

```
clients.inMemory()
    .withClient("eagleeye")
    .secret("thisissecret")
    .authorizedGrantTypes("password",
                    ➥ "client_credentials")
    .scopes("webclient","mobileclient");
```

The ClientDetailsServiceConfigurer class supports two different types of stores for application information: an in-memory store and a JDBC store. For the purposes of this example, you're going to use the clients.inMemory() store.

The two method calls withClient() and secret() provide the name of the application (eagleeye) that you're registering along with a secret (a password, thisissecret) that will be presented when the EagleEye application calls your OAuth2 server to receive an OAuth2 access token.

The next method, authorizedGrantTypes(), is passed a comma-separated list of the authorization grant types that will be supported by your OAuth2 service. In your service, you'll support the password and client credential grants.

The scopes() method is used to define the boundaries that the calling application can operate in when they're asking your OAuth2 server for an access token. For instance, Thoughtmechanix might offer two different versions of the same application, a web-based application and a mobile phone based application. Each of these apps can use the same client name and secret key to ask for access to resources protected by the OAuth2 server. However, when the apps ask for a key, they need to define the specific scope they are operating in. By defining the scope, you can write authorization rules specific to the scope the client application is working in.

For instance, you might have a user who can access the EagleEye application with both the web-based client and the mobile-phone of the application. Each version of the application does the following:

1 Offers the same functionality
2 Is a "trusted application" where ThoughtMechanix owns both the EagleEye front-end applications and the end user services

Thus you're going to register the EagleEye application with the same application name and secret key, but the web application will only use the "webclient" scope while the mobile phone version of the application will use the "mobileclient" scope. By using scope, you can then define authorization rules in your protected services that can limit what actions a client application can take based on the application they are logging in with. This will be regardless of what permissions the user has. For example, you might want to restrict what data a user can see based on whether they're using a browser inside the corporate network versus browsing using an application on a mobile device. The practice of restricting data based on the access mechanism of the data is common when dealing with sensitive customer information (such as health records or tax information).

At this point you've registered a single application, EagleEye, with your OAuth2 server. However, because you're using a password grant, you need to set up user accounts and passwords for those users before you start.

7.2.3   *Configuring EagleEye users*

You've defined and stored application-level key names and secrets. You're now going to set up individual user credentials and the roles that they belong to. User roles will be used to define the actions a group of users can do with a service.

Spring can store and retrieve user information (the individual user's credentials and the roles assigned to the user) from an in-memory data store, a JDBC-backed relational database, or an LDAP server.

> **NOTE**   I want to be careful here in terms of definition. The OAuth2 application information for Spring can store its data in an in-memory or relational database. The Spring user credentials and security roles can be stored in an in-memory database, relational database, or LDAP (Active Directory) server. To keep things simple because our primary purpose is to walk through OAuth2, you're going to use an in-memory data store.

For the code examples in this chapter, you're going to define user roles using an in-memory data store. You're going to define two user accounts: john.carnell and william.woodward. The john.carnell account will have the role of USER and the william.woodward account will have the role of ADMIN.

To configure your OAuth2 server to authenticate user IDs, you have to set up a new class: authentication-service/src/main/com/thoughtmechanix/authentication/security/WebSecurityConfigurer.java. The following listing shows the code for this class.

Listing 7.3   Defining the User ID, password and roles for your application

```
package com.thoughtmechanix.authentication.security;

//Imports removed for conciseness

@Configuration
```

```
public class WebSecurityConfigurer
  extends
    WebSecurityConfigurerAdapter {        ◁——   Extends the core Spring Security
                                                  WebSecurityConfigurerAdapter
    @Override
    @Bean                                     ◁——   The Authentication-
    public AuthenticationManager authenticationManagerBean()   ManagerBean is used
        throws Exception{                            by Spring Security to
      return super.authenticationManagerBean();      handle authentication.
    }

    @Override
    @Bean                                                                     ◁——
    public UserDetailsService userDetailsServiceBean() throws Exception {
      return super.userDetailsServiceBean();
    }
                                              The UserDetailsService is used to
    @Override                                 hold user information that will be
    protected void configure(                  returned from Spring Security.
        AuthenticationManagerBuilder auth)
      throws Exception {
      auth.inMemoryAuthentication()          ◁——   The configure() method is
        .withUser("john.carnell")                  where you'll define users, their
        .password("password1")                     passwords, and their roles.
        .roles("USER")
        .and()
        .withUser("william.woodward")
        .password("password2")
        .roles("USER", "ADMIN");
    }
}
```

Like other pieces of the Spring Security framework, to set up users (and their roles), start by extending the `WebSecurityConfigurerAdapter` class and mark it with the `@Configuration` annotation. Spring Security is implemented in a fashion similar to how you snap Lego blocks together to build a toy car or model. As such, you need to provide the OAuth2 server a mechanism to authenticate users and return the user information about the authenticating user. This is done by defining two beans in your Spring `WebSecurityConfigurerAdapter` implementation: `authentication-ManagerBean()` and `userDetailsServiceBean()`. These two beans are exposed by using the default authentication `authenticationManagerBean()` and `user-DetailsServiceBean()` methods from the parent `WebSecurityConfigurer-Adapter` class.

As you'll remember from listing 7.2, these beans are injected into the `configure-(AuthorizationServerEndpointsConfigurer endpoints)` method shown in the `OAuth2Config` class:

```
public void configure(
  AuthorizationServerEndpointsConfigurer endpoints)
    throws Exception {
  endpoints
```

```
                .authenticationManager(authenticationManager)
                .userDetailsService(userDetailsService);
    }
```

These two beans are used to configure the `/auth/oauth/token` and `/auth/user` endpoints that we'll see in action shortly.

7.2.4   *Authenticating the user*

At this point you have enough of your base OAuth2 server functionality in place to perform application and user authentication for the password grant flow. Now you'll simulate a user acquiring an OAuth2 token by using POSTMAN to POST to the `http://localhost:8901/auth/oauth/token` endpoint and provide the application, secret key, user ID, and password.

First, you need to set up POSTMAN with the application name and secret key. You're going to pass these elements to your OAuth2 server endpoint using basic authentication. Figure 7.2 shows how POSTMAN is set up to execute a basic authentication call.

Figure 7.2   Setting up basic authentication using the application key and secret

However, you're not ready to make the call to get the token yet. Once the application name and secret key are configured, you need to pass in the following information in the service as HTTP form parameters:

- grant_type—The OAuth2 grant type you're executing. In this example, you'll use a `password` grant.
- Scope—The applications scope. Because you only defined two legitimate scopes when you registered the application (`webclient` and `mobileclient`) the value passed in must be one of these two scopes.
- Username—Name of the user logging in.
- Password—Password of the user logging in.

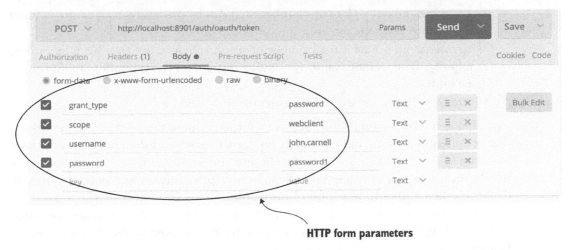

HTTP form parameters

Figure 7.3   When requesting a OAuth2 token, the user's credentials are passed in as HTTP form Parameters to the `/auth/oauth/token` **endpoint.**

Unlike other REST calls in this book, the parameters in this list will not be passed in as a JavaScript body. The OAuth2 standard expects all parameters passed to the token generation endpoint to be HTTP form parameters. Figure 7.3 shows how HTTP form parameters are configured for your OAuth2 call.

Figure 7.4 shows the JavaScript payload that's returned from the `/auth/oauth/` `token` call.

The payload returned contains five attributes:

- `access_token`—The OAuth2 token that will be presented with each service call the user makes to a protected resource.
- `token_type`—The type of token. The OAuth2 specification allows you to define multiple token types. The most common token type used is the bearer token. We won't cover any of the other token types in this chapter.

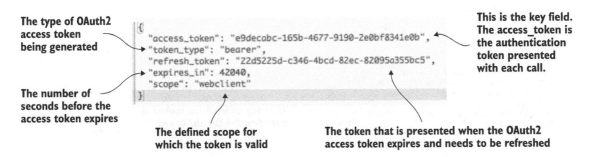

Figure 7.4   Payload returned after a successful client credential validation

- `refresh_token`—Contains a token that can be presented back to the OAuth2 server to reissue a token after it has been expired.
- `expires_in`—This is the number of seconds before the OAuth2 access token expires. The default value for authorization token expiration in Spring is 12 hours.
- `Scope`—The scope that this OAuth2 token is valid for.

Now that you have a valid OAuth2 access token, we can use the /auth/user endpoint that you created in your authentication service to retrieve information about the user associated with the token. Later in the chapter, any services that are going to be protected resources will call the authentication service's /auth/user endpoint to validate the token and retrieve the user information.

Figure 7.5 shows what the results would be if you called the /auth/user endpoint. As you look at figure 7.5, notice how the OAuth2 access token is passed in as an HTTP header.

In figure 7.5 you're issuing a HTTP GET against the /auth/user endpoint. However, any time you call an OAuth2 protected endpoint (including the OAuth2 /auth/user endpoint) you need to pass along the OAuth2 access token. To do this, always

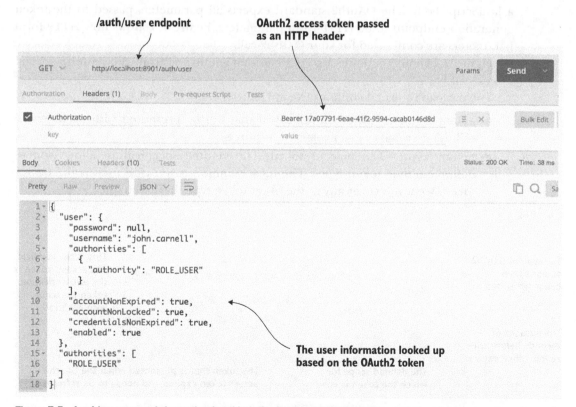

Figure 7.5   Looking up user information based on the issued OAuth2 token

create an HTTP header called `Authorization` and with a value of `Bearer XXXXX`. In the case of your call in figure 7.5, the HTTP header will be of the value `Bearer e9decabc-165b-4677-9190-2e0bf8341e0b`. The access token passed in is the access token returned when you called the `/auth/oauth/token` endpoint in figure 7.4.

If the OAuth2 access token is valid, the `/auth/user` endpoint will return information about the user, including what roles are assigned to them. For instance, from figure 7.10, you can see that the user `john.carnell` has the role of `USER`.

> **NOTE** Spring assigns the prefix of `ROLE_` to user's roles, so `ROLE_USER` means that `john.carnell` has the `USER` role.

7.3 *Protecting the organization service using OAuth2*

Once you've registered an application with your OAuth2 authentication service and set up individual user accounts with roles, you can begin exploring how to protect a resource using OAuth2. While the creation and management of OAuth2 access tokens is the responsibility of the OAuth2 server, in Spring, the definition of what user roles have permissions to do what actions occurs at the individual service level.

To set up a protected resource, you need to take the following actions:

- Add the appropriate Spring Security and OAuth2 jars to the service you're protecting
- Configure the service to point to your OAuth2 authentication service
- Define what and who can access the service

Let's start with one of the simplest examples of setting up a protected resource by taking your organization service and ensuring that it can only be called by an authenticated user.

7.3.1 *Adding the Spring Security and OAuth2 jars to the individual services*

As usual with Spring microservices, you have to add a couple of dependencies to the organization service's Maven organization-service/pom.xml file. Two dependencies are being added: Spring Cloud Security and Spring Security OAuth2. The Spring Cloud Security jars are the core security jars. They contain framework code, annotation definitions, and interfaces for implementing security within Spring Cloud. The Spring Security OAuth2 dependency contains all the classes needed to implement an OAuth2 authentication service. The maven entries for these two dependencies are

```
<dependency>
  <groupId>org.springframework.cloud</groupId>
  <artifactId>spring-cloud-security</artifactId>
</dependency>
<dependency>
  <groupId>org.springframework.security.oauth</groupId>
  <artifactId>spring-security-oauth2</artifactId>
</dependency>
```

7.3.2　Configuring the service to point to your OAuth2 authentication service

Remember that once you set up the organization service as a protected resource, every time a call is made to the service, the caller has to include the `Authentication` HTTP header containing an OAuth2 access token to the service. Your protected resource then has to call back to the OAuth2 service to see if the token is valid.

You define the callback URL in your organization service's application.yml file as the property `security.oauth2.resource.userInfoUri`. Here's the callback configuration used in the organization service's application.yml file.

```
security:
 oauth2:
  resource:
   userInfoUri: http://localhost:8901/auth/user
```

As you can see from the `security.oauth2.resource.userInfoUri` property, the callback URL is to the `/auth/user` endpoint. This endpoint was discussed earlier in the chapter in section 7.2.4, "Authenticating the user."

Finally, you also need to tell the organization service that it's a protected resource. Again, you do this by adding a Spring Cloud annotation to the organization service's bootstrap class. The organization service's bootstrap code is shown in the next listing and can be found in the `organization-service/src/main/java/com/thoughtmechanix/organization/Application.java` class.

Listing 7.4　Configuring the bootstrap class to be a protected resource

```
package com.thoughtmechanix.organization;

//Most Imports removed for conciseness
import org.springframework.security.oauth2.
    config.annotation.web.configuration.EnableResourceServer;

@SpringBootApplication
@EnableEurekaClient
@EnableCircuitBreaker
@EnableResourceServer          ⊲——————  The @EnableResourceServer annotation
public class Application {                 is used to tell your microservice it's a
 @Bean                                     protected resource.
public Filter userContextFilter() {
 UserContextFilter userContextFilter = new UserContextFilter();
 return userContextFilter;
}

public static void main(String[] args) {
 SpringApplication.run(Application.class, args);
}
}
```

The `@EnableResourceServer` annotation tells Spring Cloud and Spring Security that the service is a protected resource. The `@EnableResourceServer` enforces a filter that intercepts all incoming calls to the service, checks to see if there's an OAuth2 access token present in the incoming call's HTTP header, and then calls back to the callback URL defined in the `security.oauth2.resource.userInfoUri` to see if the token is valid. Once it knows the token is valid, the `@EnableResourceServer` annotation also applies any access control rules over who and what can access a service.

7.3.3 Defining who and what can access the service

You're now ready to begin defining the access control rules around the service. To define access control rules, you need to extend a Spring `ResourceServerConfigurerAdapter` class and override the classes `configure()` method. In the organization service, your `ResourceServerConfiguration` class is located in `organization-service/src/main/java/com/thoughtmechanix/organization/security/ResourceServerConfiguration.java`. Access rules can range from extremely coarse-grained (any authenticated user can access the entire service) to fine-grained (only the application with this role, accessing this URL through a DELETE is allowed).

We discuss every permutation of Spring Security's access control rules, but we can look at several of the more common examples. These examples include protecting a resource so that

- Only authenticated users can access a service URL
- Only users with a specific role can access a service URL

PROTECTING A SERVICE BY AN AUTHENTICATED USER

The first thing you're going to do is protect the organization service so that it can only be accessed by an authenticated user. The following listing shows how you can build this rule into the `ResourceServerConfiguration.java` class.

Listing 7.5   Restricting access to only authenticated users

```
package com.thoughtmechanix.organization.security;

    //Imports removed for conciseness
@Configuration                                          The class must be marked with
public class ResourceServerConfiguration extends        the @Configuration annotation.
        ResourceServerConfigurerAdapter {               The ResourceServiceConfiguration
                                                        class needs to extend
                                                        ResourceServerConfigurerAdapter.
        @Override
        public void configure(HttpSecurity http) throws Exception{
            http.authorizeRequests().anyRequest().authenticated();
        }
    }
```

All the access rules are defined inside the overridden configure() method

All access rules are configured off the HttpSecurity object passed into the method.

All access rules are going to be defined inside the `configure()` method. You'll use the `HttpSecurity` class passed in by Spring to define your rules. In this example, you're going to restrict all access to any URL in the organization service to authenticated users only.

If you were to access the organization service without an OAuth2 access token present in the HTTP header, you'd get a 401 HTTP response code along with a message indicating that a full authentication to the service is required.

Figure 7.6 shows the output of a call to the organization service without the OAuth2 HTTP header.

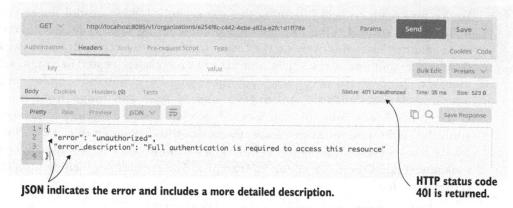

JSON indicates the error and includes a more detailed description.

HTTP status code 401 is returned.

Figure 7.6   Trying to call the organization service will result in a failed call.

Next, you'll call the organization service with an OAuth2 access token. To get an access token, see section 7.2.4, "Authenticating the user," on how to generate the OAuth2 token. You want to cut and paste the value of the access_token field from the returned JavaScript call out to the /auth/oauth/token endpoint and use it in your call to the organization service. Remember, when you call the organization service, you need to add an HTTP header called Authorization with the value Bearer access_token value.

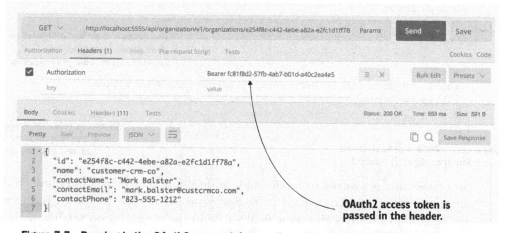

OAuth2 access token is passed in the header.

Figure 7.7   Passing in the OAuth2 access token on the call to the organization service

Figure 7.7 shows the callout to the organization service, but this time with an OAuth2 access token passed to it.

This is probably one of the simplest use cases for protecting an endpoint using OAuth2. Next, you'll build on this and restrict access to a specific endpoint to a specific role.

PROTECTING A SERVICE VIA A SPECIFIC ROLE

In the next example, you're going to lock down the DELETE call on your organization service to only those users with ADMIN access. As you'll remember from section 7.2.3, "Configuring some EagleEye Users," you created two user accounts that could access EagleEye services: john.carnell and william.woodward. The john.carnell account had the role of USER assigned to it. The william.woodward account had the USER role and the ADMIN role.

The following listing shows how to set up the configure() method to restrict access to the DELETE endpoint to only those authenticated users who have the ADMIN role.

Listing 7.6 Restricting deletes to the ADMIN role only

```
package com.thoughtmechanix.organization.security;

//Imports removed for conciseness
@Configuration
public class ResourceServerConfiguration extends
    ResourceServerConfigurerAdapter {
  @Override
  public void configure(HttpSecurity http) throws Exception{
    http
    .authorizeRequests()
     .antMatchers(HttpMethod.DELETE, "/v1/organizations/**")
     .hasRole("ADMIN")
     .anyRequest()
     .authenticated();
  }
}
```

The antMatchers() method allows you to restrict the URL and HTTP method that's protected.

The hasRole() method is a comma-separated list of roles that can be accessed.

In listing 7.6 you're restricting the DELETE call on any endpoint starting with /v1/organizations in your service to the ADMIN role.:

```
.authorizeRequests()
  .antMatchers(HttpMethod.DELETE, "/v1/organizations/**")
  .hasRole("ADMIN")
```

The antMatcher() method can take a comma-separated list of endpoints. These endpoints can use a wildcard style notation for defining the endpoints you want to access. For instance, if you want to restrict any of the DELETE calls regardless of the version in the URL name, you could use a * in place of the version number in your URL definitions:

```
.authorizeRequests()
  .antMatchers(HttpMethod.DELETE, "/*/organizations/**")
.hasRole("ADMIN")
```

The last part of the authorization rule definition still defines that any other endpoint in your service needs to be access by an authenticated user:

```
.anyRequest()
.authenticated();
```

Now, if you were to get an OAuth2 token for the user `john.carnell` (password: `password1`) and try to call the `DELETE` endpoint for the organization service (`http://localhost:8085/v1/organizations/e254f8c-c442-4ebe-a82a-e2fc1d1ff78a`), you'd get a 401 HTTP status code on the call and an error message indicating that the access was denied. The JavaScript text returned by your call would be

```
{
 "error": "access_denied",
 "error_description": "Access is denied"
}
```

If you tried the exact same call using the `william.woodward` user account (password: `password2`) and its OAuth2 token, you'd see a successful call would returned (a HTTP Status Code 204 – Not Content), and that organization would be deleted by the organization service.

At this point we've looked at two simple examples of calling and protecting a single service (the organization service) with OAuth2. However, often in a microservices environment, you're going to have multiple service calls used to carry out a single transaction. In these types of situations, you need to ensure that that the OAuth2 access token is propagated from service call to service call.

7.3.4   *Propagating the OAuth2 access token*

To demonstrate propagating an OAuth2 token between services, we're now going to see how to protect your licensing service with OAuth2. Remember, the licensing service calls the organization service to lookup information. The question becomes, how do you propagate the OAuth2 token from one service to another?

You're going to set up a simple example where you're going to have the licensing service call the organization service. Building on the examples from chapter 6, both services are running behind a Zuul gateway.

Figure 7.8 shows the basic flow of how an authenticated user's OAuth2 token is going to flow through the Zuul gateway, to the licensing service, and then down to the organization service.

The following activity occurs in figure 7.8:

1   The user has already authenticated against the OAuth2 server and places a call to the EagleEye web application. The user's OAuth2 access token is stored in the user's session. The EagleEye web application needs to retrieve some licensing data and will make a call to the licensing service REST endpoint. As part of the call to the licensing REST endpoint, the EagleEye web application will add the OAuth2 access token via the HTTP Header "Authorization". The licensing service is only accessible behind a Zuul services gateway.

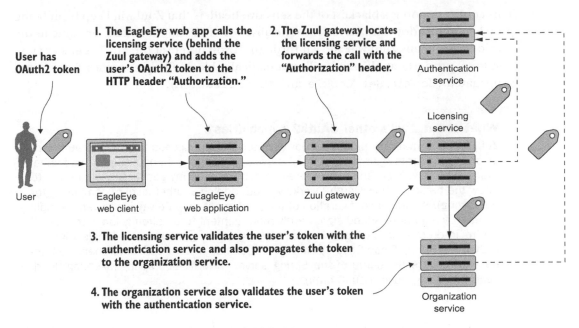

Figure 7.8   The OAuth2 token has to be carried throughout the entire call chain.

2   Zuul will look up the licensing service endpoint and then forward the call onto one of the licensing services servers. The services gateway will need to copy the "Authorization" HTTP header from the incoming call and ensure that the "Authorization" HTTP header is forwarded onto the new endpoint.

3   The licensing service will receive the incoming call. Because the licensing service is a protected resource, the licensing service will validate the token with EagleEye's OAuth2 service and then check the user's roles for the appropriate permissions.

    As part of its work, the licensing service invokes the organization service. In doing this call, the licensing service needs to propagate the user's OAuth2 access token to the organization service.

4   When the organization service receives the call, it will again take the "Authorization" HTTP header token and validate the token with the EagleEye OAuth2 server.

To implement these flows, you need to do two things. First, you need to modify your Zuul services gateway to propagate the OAuth2 token to the licensing service. By default, Zuul won't forward sensitive HTTP headers such as `Cookie`, `Set-Cookie`, and `Authorization` to downstream services. To allow Zuul to propagate the "Authorization" HTTP header, you need to set the following configuration in your Zuul services gateway's application.yml or Spring Cloud Config data store:

```
zuul.sensitiveHeaders: Cookie,Set-Cookie
```

This configuration is a blacklist of the sensitive headers that Zuul will keep from being propagated to a downstream service. The absence of the `Authorization` value in the previous list means Zuul will allow it through. If you don't set the `zuul.sensitive-Headers` property at all, Zuul will automatically block all three values from being propagated (`Cookie`, `Set-Cookie`, and `Authorization`).

> ### What about Zuul's other OAuth2 capabilities?
>
> Zuul can automatically propagate downstream OAuth2 access tokens and authorize incoming requests against the OAuth2 service by using the @EnableOAuth2Sso annotation. I purposely haven't used this approach because my goal in this chapter is to show the basics of how OAuth2 works without adding another level of complexity (or debugging). While the configuration of the Zuul service's gateway isn't overly complicated, it would have added significantly more content to an already large chapter. If you're interested in having a Zuul services gateway participate in Single Sign On (SSO), the Spring Cloud Security documentation has a short but comprehensive tutorial that covers the setup of the Spring server (http://cloud.spring.io/spring-cloud-security/spring-cloud-security.html).

The next thing you need to do is configure your licensing service to be an OAuth2 resource service and set up any authorization rules you want for the service. We're not going to discuss in detail the licensing service configuration because we already discussed authorization rules in section 7.3.3, "Defining who and what can access the service."

Finally, all you need to do is modify how the code in the licensing service calls the organization service. You need to ensure that the "Authorization" HTTP header is injected into the application call out to the Organization service. Without Spring Security, you'd have to write a servlet filter to grab the HTTP header off the incoming licensing service call and then manually add it to every outbound service call in the licensing service. Spring OAuth2 provides a new Rest Template class that supports OAuth2 calls. The class is called `OAuth2RestTemplate`. To use the `OAuth2RestTemplate` class you first need to expose it as a bean that can be auto-wired into a service calling another OAuth2 protected services. You do this in the `licensing-service/src/main/java/com/thoughtmechanix/licenses/Application.java` class:

```
@Bean
 public OAuth2RestTemplate oauth2RestTemplate(
        OAuth2ClientContext oauth2ClientContext,
        OAuth2ProtectedResourceDetails details) {
        return new OAuth2RestTemplate(details, oauth2ClientContext);
    }
```

To see the `OAuth2RestTemplate` class in action you can look in the `licensing-service/src/main/java/com/thoughtmechanix/licenses/clients/OrganizationRestTemplate.java` class. The following listing shows how `OAuth2RestTemplate` is auto-wired into this class.

Listing 7.7   Using the `OAuth2RestTemplate` **to propagate the OAuth2 access token**

```
package com.thoughtmechanix.licenses.clients;

//Removed for conciseness

@Component
public class OrganizationRestTemplateClient {
@Autowired
OAuth2RestTemplate restTemplate;

private static final Logger logger =
    LoggerFactory.getLogger(
        OrganizationRestTemplateClient.class);


public Organization getOrganization(String organizationId){
    logger.debug("In Licensing Service
        .getOrganization: {}",
    UserContext.getCorrelationId());

  ResponseEntity<Organization> restExchange =
    restTemplate.exchange(

"http://zuulserver:5555/api/organization
        /v1/organizations/{organizationId}",
    HttpMethod.GET,
    null, Organization.class, organizationId);

    /*Save the record from cache*/
    return restExchange.getBody();
  }
}
```

> The OAuth2RestTemplate is a drop-in replacement for the standard RestTemplate and handles the propagation of the OAuth2 access token.

> The invocation of the organization service is done in the exact same manner as a standard RestTemplate.

7.4   *JavaScript Web Tokens and OAuth2*

OAuth2 is a token-based authentication framework, but ironically it doesn't provide any standards for how the tokens in its specification are to be defined. To rectify the lack of standards around OAuth2 tokens, a new standard is emerging called JavaScript Web Tokens (JWT). JWT is an open standard (RFC-7519) proposed by the Internet Engineering Task Force (IETF) that attempts to provide a standard structure for OAuth2 tokens. JWT tokens are

- *Small*—JWT tokens are encoded to Base64 and can be easily passed via a URL, HTTP header, or an HTTP POST parameter.
- *Cryptographically signed*—A JWT token is signed by the authenticating server that issues it. This means you can be guaranteed that the token hasn't been tampered with.
- *Self-contained*—Because a JWT token is cryptographically signed, the microservice receiving the service can be guaranteed that the contents of the token are valid. There's no need to call back to the authenticating service to validate the contents of the token because the signature of the token can be validated and

the contents (such as the expiration time of the token and the user information) can be inspected by the receiving microservice.

- *Extensible*—When an authenticating service generates a token, it can place additional information in the token, before the token is sealed. A receiving service can decrypt the token payload and retrieve that additional context out of it.

Spring Cloud Security supports JWT out of the box. However, to use and consume JWT tokens, your OAuth2 authentication service and the services being protected by the authentication service must be configured in a different fashion. The configuration isn't difficult, so let's walk through the change.

> **NOTE** I've chosen to keep the JWT configuration on a separate branch (called `JWT_Example`) in the GitHub repository for this chapter (https:// github.com/carnellj/spmia-chapter7) because the standard Spring Cloud Security OAuth2 configuration and JWT-based OAuth2 configuration require different configuration classes.

7.4.1 *Modifying the authentication service to issue JavaScript Web Tokens*

For both the authentication service and the two microservices (licensing and organization service) that are going to be protected by OAuth2, you'll need to add a new Spring Security dependency to their Maven pom.xml files to include the JWT OAuth2 libraries. This new dependency is

```
<dependency>
    <groupId>org.springframework.security</groupId>
    <artifactId>spring-security-jwt</artifactId>
</dependency>
```

After the Maven dependency is added, you need to first tell your authentication service how it's going to generate and translate JWT tokens. To do this, you're going to set up in the authentication service a new configuration class called `authentication-service/src/java/com/thoughtmechanix/authentication/security/JWT TokenStoreConfig.java`. The following listing shows the code for the class.

Listing 7.8   Setting up the JWT token store

```
@Configuration
public class JWTTokenStoreConfig {

    @Autowired
    private ServiceConfig serviceConfig;

    @Bean
    public TokenStore tokenStore() {
        return new JwtTokenStore(jwtAccessTokenConverter());
    }

    @Bean
    @Primary
```

The @Primary annotation is used to tell Spring that if there is more than one bean of specific type (in this case DefaultTokenService), use the bean type marked as @Primary for auto-injection.

```
public DefaultTokenServices tokenServices() {
    DefaultTokenServices defaultTokenServices
        = new DefaultTokenServices();
    defaultTokenServices.setTokenStore(tokenStore());
    defaultTokenServices.setSupportRefreshToken(true);
    return defaultTokenServices;
}
```

**Used to read data
to and from a
token presented
to the service**

**Acts as the translator
between JWT and OAuth2 server**

```
@Bean
public JwtAccessTokenConverter jwtAccessTokenConverter() {
    JwtAccessTokenConverter converter =
        new JwtAccessTokenConverter();
    converter
        .setSigningKey(serviceConfig.getJwtSigningKey());
    return converter;
}
```

**Defines the signing
key that will be used
to sign a token**

```
@Bean
public TokenEnhancer jwtTokenEnhancer() {
    return new JWTTokenEnhancer();
}
}
```

The JWTTokenStoreConfig class is used to define how Spring will manage the creation, signing, and translation of a JWT token. The tokenServices() method is going to use Spring security's default token services implementation, so the work here is rote. The jwtAccessTokenConverter() method is the one we want to focus on. It defines how the token is going to be translated. The most important thing to note about this method is that you're setting the signing key that will be used to sign your token.

For this example, you're going to use a symmetrical key, which means both the authentication service and the services protected by the authentication service must share the same key between all of the services. The key is nothing more than a random string of values that's store in the authentication services Spring Cloud Config entry (https://github.com/carnellj/config-repo/blob/master/authenticationservice /authenticationservice.yml). The actual value for the signing key is

```
signing.key: "345345fsdgsf5345"
```

NOTE Spring Cloud Security supports symmetrical key encryption and asymmetrical encryption using public/private keys. We're not going to walk through setting up JWT using public/private keys. Unfortunately, little official documentation exists on the JWT, Spring Security, and public/private keys. If you're interested in how to do this, I highly recommend you look at Baeldung.com (http://www.baeldung.com/spring-security-oauth-jwt). They do an excellent job of explaining JWT and public/private key setup.

In the JWTTokenStoreConfig from listing 7.8, you defined how JWT tokens were going to be signed and created. You now need to hook this into your overall OAuth2 service. In listing 7.2 you used the OAuth2Config class to define the configuration of your OAuth2 service. You set up the authentication manager that was going to be used by your service along with the application name and secrets. You're going to replace the `OAuth2Config` class with a new class called `authentication-service/src/main/java/com/thoughtmechanix/authentication/security/JWTOAuth2Config.java`.

The following listing shows code for the JWTOAuth2Config class.

Listing 7.9   Hooking JWT into your authentication service via the `JWTOAuth2Config` class

```
package com.thoughtmechanix.authentication.security;

//Imports removed for conciseness
@Configuration
public class JWTOAuth2Config extends
➥ AuthorizationServerConfigurerAdapter {

    @Autowired
    private AuthenticationManager authenticationManager;

    @Autowired
    private UserDetailsService userDetailsService;

    @Autowired
    private TokenStore tokenStore;

    @Autowired
    private DefaultTokenServices tokenServices;

    @Autowired
    private JwtAccessTokenConverter jwtAccessTokenConverter;

    @Override
    public void configure(
    ➥ AuthorizationServerEndpointsConfigurer endpoints)

    ➥ throws Exception {
    TokenEnhancerChain tokenEnhancerChain =
    ➥ new TokenEnhancerChain();
    tokenEnhancerChain
    .setTokenEnhancers(
        Arrays.asList(
        jwtTokenEnhancer   ,
        jwtAccessTokenConverter));

     endpoints
        .tokenStore(tokenStore)             ⟵
    .accessTokenConverter(jwtAccessTokenConverter)   ⟵
    .authenticationManager(authenticationManager)
    .userDetailsService(userDetailsService);
    }

//Removed the rest of the class for conciseness
}
```

The token store you defined in listing 7.8 will be injected here.

This is the hook to tell the Spring Security OAuth2 code to use JWT.

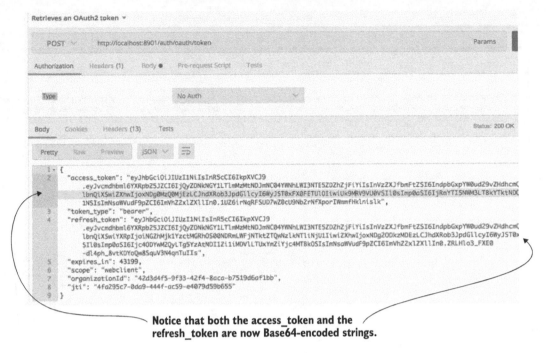

Notice that both the access_token and the refresh_token are now Base64-encoded strings.

Figure 7.9   The access and refresh tokens from your authentication call are now JWT tokens.

Now, if you rebuild your authentication service and restart it, you should see a JWT-based token returned. Figure 7.9 shows the results of your call to the authentication service now that it uses JWT.

The actual token itself isn't directly returned as JavaScript. Instead, the JavaScript body is encoded using a Base64 encoding. If you're interested in seeing the contents of a JWT token, you can use online tools to decode the token. I like to use an online tool from a company called Stormpath. Their tool, http://jsonwebtoken.io, is an online JWT decoder. Figure 7.10 shows the output from the decoded token.

NOTE   It's extremely important to understand that your JWT tokens are signed, but not encrypted. Any online JWT tool can decode the JWT token and expose its contents. I bring this up because the JWT specification does allow you extend the token and add additional information to the token. Don't expose sensitive or Personally Identifiable Information (PII) in your JWT tokens.

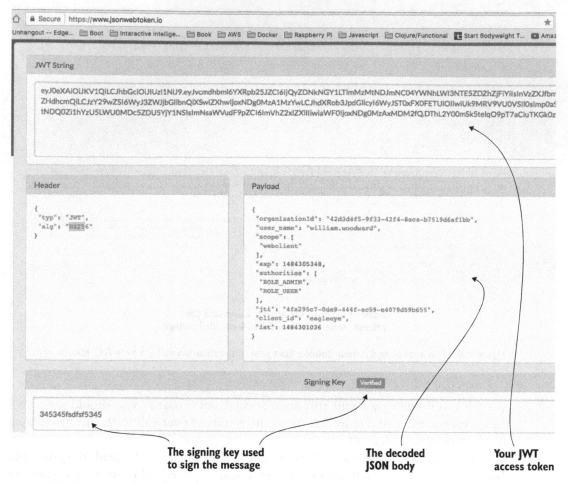

Figure 7.10   Using http://jswebtoken.io allows you to decode the contents.

7.4.2   *Consuming JavaScript Web Tokens in your microservices*

You now have your OAuth2 authentication service creating JWT tokens. The next step is to configure your licensing and organization services to use JWT. This is a trivial exercise that requires you to do two things:

1   Add the `spring-security-jwt` dependency to both the licensing service and the organization service's pom.xml file. (See the beginning of section 7.4.1, "Modifying the authentication service to issue JavaScript Web Tokens," for the exact Maven dependency that needs to be added.)

2   Set up a `JWTTokenStoreConfig` class in both the licensing and organization services. This class is almost the exact same class used the authentication service (see listing 7.8). I'm not going to go over the same material again, but you can

see examples of the `JWTTokenStoreConfig` class in both the `licensing-service/src/main/com/thoughtmechanix/licensing-service/security/JWTTokenStoreConfig.java` and `organization-service/src/main/com/thoughtmechanix/organization-service/security/JWTTokenStoreConfig.java` classes.

You need to do one final piece of work. Because the licensing service calls the organization service, you need to ensure that the OAuth2 token is propagated. This is normally done via the `OAuth2RestTemplate` class; however, the `OAuth2RestTemplate` class doesn't propagate JWT-based tokens. To make sure that your licensing service does this, you need to add a custom `RestTemplate` bean that will perform this injection for you. This custom `RestTemplate` can found in the `licensing-service/src/main/java/com/thoughtmechanix/licenses/Application.java` class. The following listing shows this custom bean definition.

Listing 7.10 Creating a custom `RestTemplate` class to inject the JWT token

```
public class Application {
   //Code removed for conciseness
   @Primary
   @Bean
   public RestTemplate getCustomRestTemplate() {
       RestTemplate template = new RestTemplate();
       List interceptors = template.getInterceptors();
       if (interceptors == null) {
         template.setInterceptors(
         ➥ Collections.singletonList(
           new UserContextInterceptor()));
       } else {
           interceptors.add(new UserContextInterceptor());     ◁
           template.setInterceptors(interceptors);
       }

       return template;
   }
}
```

The UserContextInterceptor
will inject the Authorization
header into every Rest call.

In the previous code you're defining a custom `RestTemplate` bean that will use a `ClientHttpRequestInterceptor`. Recall from chapter 6 that the `ClientHttpRequestInterceptor` is a Spring class that allows you to hook in functionality to be executed before a REST-based call is made. This interceptor class is a variation of the `UserContextInterceptor` class you defined in chapter 6. This class is in the `licensing-service/src/main/java/com/thoughtmechanix/licenses/utils/UserContextInterceptor.java`. The following listing shows this class.

Listing 7.11 The `UserContextInterceptor` will inject the JWT token into your REST calls

```
public class UserContextInterceptor
   implements ClientHttpRequestInterceptor {
```

```
@Override
public ClientHttpResponse intercept(
        HttpRequest request, byte[] body,
        ➡ ClientHttpRequestExecution execution)
        throws IOException {

    headers.add(UserContext.CORRELATION_ID,
                ➡ UserContextHolder.getContext().getCorrelationId());
        headers.add(UserContext.AUTH_TOKEN,
                ➡ UserContextHolder.getContext().getAuthToken());        ◄─┐

                                                        Adding the authorization token
                                                              to the HTTP header
        return execution.execute(request, body);
    }
}
```

The `UserContextInterceptor` is using several of the utility classes from chapter 6. Remember, every one of your service uses a custom servlet filter (called `User-ContextFilter`) to parse out the authentication token and correlation ID from the HTTP header. In listing 7.11, you're using the `UserContext.AUTH_TOKEN` value already parsed to populate the outgoing HTTP call.

That's it. With these pieces in place, you can now call the licensing service (or organization service) and place the Base64-encoded JWT encoded in your HTTP `Authorization header the value Bearer <<JWT-Token>>`, and your service will properly read and validate the JWT token.

7.4.3   *Extending the JWT Token*

If you look closely at the JWT token in figure 7.10, you'll notice the EagleEye `organizationId` field. (Figure 7.11 shows a more zoomed-in shot of the JWT Token shown

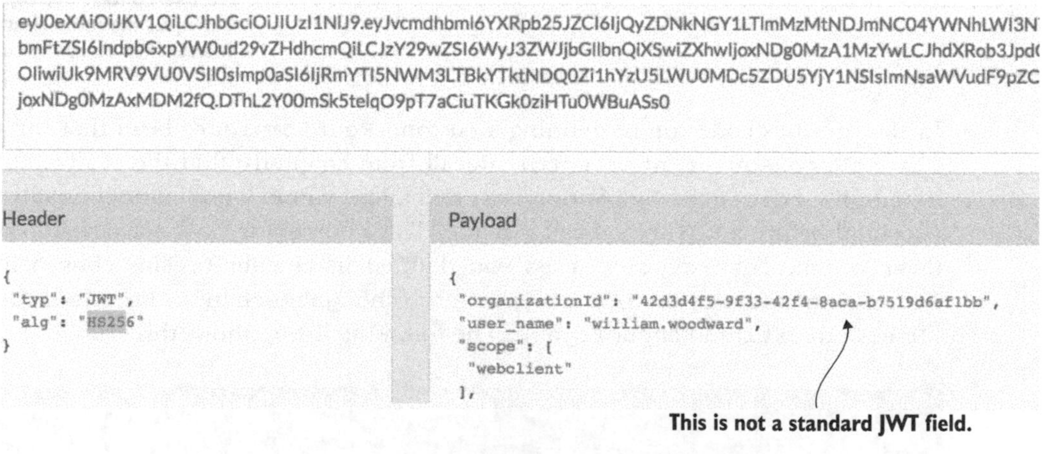

eyJ0eXAiOiJKV1QiLCJhbGciOiJIUzI1NiJ9.eyJvcmdhbml6YXRpb25JZCI6IjQyZDNkNGY1LTlmMzMtNDJmNC04YWNhLWi3N
bmFtZSI6IndpbGxpYW0ud29vZHdhcmQiLCJzY29wZSI6WyJ3ZWJjbGllbnQiXSwiZXhwIjoxNDg0MzA1MzYwLCJhdXRob3Jpd(
OliwiUk9MRV9VU0VSIl0simp0aSI6IjRmYTI5NWM3LTBkYTktNDQ0Zi1hYzU5LWU0MDc5ZDU5YjY1NSIsImNsaWVudF9pZC
joxNDg0MzAxMDM2fQ.DThL2Y00mSk5telqO9pT7aCiuTKGk0ziHTu0WBuASs0

Header	Payload

`{`
`"typ": "JWT",`
`"alg": "HS256"`
`}`
	`{`
	`"organizationId": "42d3d4f5-9f33-42f4-8aca-b7519d6af1bb",`
	`"user_name": "william.woodward",`
	`"scope": [`
	`"webclient"`
	`],`

This is not a standard JWT field.

Figure 7.11   An example of extending the JWT token with a `organizationId`

earlier in figure 7.10.) This isn't a standard JWT token field. It's one I added by inject-ing a new field into the JWT token as it was being created.

Extending a JWT token is easily done by adding a Spring OAuth2 token enhancer class to your authentication service. The source for this class can found in the authen-tication-service/src/main/java/com/thoughtmechanix/authentication /security/JWTTokenEnhancer.java class. The following listing shows this code.

Listing 7.12 Using a JWT token enhancer class to add a custom field

```java
package com.thoughtmechanix.authentication.security;

//Rest of imports removed for conciseness
import org.springframework.security.oauth2.provider.token.TokenEnhancer;

public class JWTTokenEnhancer implements TokenEnhancer {
    @Autowired
    private OrgUserRepository orgUserRepo;

    private String getOrgId(String userName){
        UserOrganization orgUser =
            orgUserRepo.findByUserName( userName );
        return orgUser.getOrganizationId();
    }

    @Override
    public OAuth2AccessToken enhance(
        OAuth2AccessToken accessToken,
        OAuth2Authentication authentication)
    {
        Map<String, Object> additionalInfo = new HashMap<>();
        String orgId =  getOrgId(authentication.getName());

        additionalInfo.put("organizationId", orgId);

        ((DefaultOAuth2AccessToken) accessToken)
            .setAdditionalInformation(additionalInfo);
        return accessToken;
    }
}
```

> You need to extend the TokenEnhancer class.

> The getOrgId() method looks up the user's org ID based on their user name.

> To do this enhancement, you need to add override the enhance() method

> All additional attributes are placed in a HashMap and set on the accessToken variable passed into the method.

The last thing you need to do is tell your OAuth2 service to use your JWTToken-Enhancer class. You first need to expose a Spring bean for your JWTTokenEnhancer class. Do this by adding a bean definition to the JWTTokenStoreConfig class that was defined in listing 7.8:

```java
package com.thoughtmechanix.authentication.security;

@Configuration
public class JWTTokenStoreConfig {
    //Rest of class removed for conciseness
    @Bean
```

```
public TokenEnhancer jwtTokenEnhancer() {
    return new JWTTokenEnhancer();
}
}
```

Once you've exposed the `JWTTokenEnhancer` as a bean, you can hook it into the `JWTOAuth2Config` class from listing 7.9. This is done in the `configure()` method of the class. The following listing shows the modification to the `configure()` method of the `JWTOAuth2Config` class.

Listing 7.13   Hooking in your `TokenEnhancer`

```
package com.thoughtmechanix.authentication.security;
@Configuration
public class JWTOAuth2Config extends AuthorizationServerConfigurerAdapter {
    //Rest of code removed for conciseness
    @Autowired                                          Auto-wire in the
    private TokenEnhancer jwtTokenEnhancer;         ◁┘  TokenEnhancer class.

    @Override
    public void configure(                              Spring OAuth allows you to
      AuthorizationServerEndpointsConfigurer endpoints)  hook in multiple token
        ➡ throws Exception {                             enhancers, so add your
     TokenEnhancerChain tokenEnhancerChain =            token enhancer to a
        new TokenEnhancerChain();               ◁────── TokenEnhancerChain class.
     tokenEnhancerChain.setTokenEnhancers(
          Arrays.asList(jwtTokenEnhancer, jwtAccessTokenConverter));

      endpoints.tokenStore(tokenStore)
              .accessTokenConverter(jwtAccessTokenConverter)
              .tokenEnhancer(tokenEnhancerChain)          ◁─────────┐
              .authenticationManager(authenticationManager)         │
              .userDetailsService(userDetailsService);              │
    }                                                               │
}                                              Hook your token enhancer chain to
                                                  the endpoints parameter passed
                                                        into the configure() call.
```

At this point you've added a custom field to your JWT tokcn. The next question you should have is, "How do I parse a custom field out of a JWT token?"

7.4.4   *Parsing a custom field out of a JavaScript token*

We're going to turn to your Zuul gateway for an example of how to parse out a custom field in the JWT token. Specifically, you're going to modify the `TrackingFilter` class we introduced in chapter 6 to decode the `organizationId` field out of the JWT token flowing through gateway.

To do this you're going to pull in a JWT parser library and add to the Zuul server's pom.xml file. Multiple token parsers are available and I chose the JJWT library (https://github.com/jwtk/jjwt) to do the parsing. The Maven dependency for the library is

```
<dependency>
  <groupId>io.jsonwebtoken</groupId>
  <artifactId>jjwt</artifactId>
  <version>0.7.0</version>
</dependency>
```

Once the JJWT library is added, you can add a new method to your `zuulsvr/src/main/java/com/thoughtmechanix/zuulsvr/filters/TrackingFilter.java` class called `getOrganizationId()`. The following listing shows this new method.

Listing 7.14 Parsing the `organizationId` out of your JWT Token

```
private String getOrganizationId(){
  String result="";
if (filterUtils.getAuthToken()!=null){
    String authToken = filterUtils
                       .getAuthToken()
                       .replace("Bearer ","");         Parse out the token out of the
                                                       Authorization HTTP header.
  try {
    Claims claims =
      Jwts.parser()                                    Use JWTS class to parse out the
                                                       token, passing in the signing key
                                                       used to sign the token.
.setSigningKey(
                    serviceConfig
                    .getJwtSigningKey()

                    .getBytes("UTF-8"))
            .parseClaimsJws(authToken)
            .getBody();
    result = (String) claims.get("organizationId");    Pull the organizationId out
  }                                                    of the JavaScript token.
  catch (Exception e){
    e.printStackTrace();
  }
}
return result;
}
```

Once the `getOrganizationId()` function is implemented, you added a `System.out.println` to the `run()` method on the `TrackingFilter` to print out the organizationId parsed from your JWT token that's flowing through the Zuul gateway, so you call any gateway-enabled REST endpoint. I used GET `http://localhost:5555/api/licensing/v1/organizations/e254f8c-c442-4ebe-a82a-e2fc1d1ff78a/licenses/f3831f8c-c338-4ebe-a82a-e2fc1d1ff78a`. Remember, when you make this call, you still need to set up all the HTTP form parameters and the HTTP authorization header to include the `Authorization` header and the JWT token.

```
zuulserver_1        | 2017-03-31 14:12:07.719  INFO 22 --- [nio-5555-exec-2] o.a.c.c.C.[Tomcat].[localhost].[/]
g FrameworkServlet 'dispatcherServlet'
zuulserver_1        | 2017-03-31 14:12:07.894  INFO 22 --- [nio-5555-exec-2] o.s.c.n.zuul.web.ZuulHandlerMapping
api/organization/**] onto handler of type [class org.springframework.cloud.netflix.zuul.web.ZuulController]
zuulserver_1        | 2017-03-31 14:12:07.895  INFO 22 --- [nio-5555-exec-2] o.s.c.n.zuul.web.ZuulHandlerMapping
api/licensing/**] onto handler of type [class org.springframework.cloud.netflix.zuul.web.ZuulController]
zuulserver_1        | 2017-03-31 14:12:07.895  INFO 22 --- [nio-5555-exec-2] o.s.c.n.zuul.web.ZuulHandlerMapping
api/auth/**] onto handler of type [class org.springframework.cloud.netflix.zuul.web.ZuulController]
zuulserver_1        | 2017-03-31 14:12:08.038 DEBUG 22 --- [nio-5555-exec-2] c.t.zuulsvr.filters.TrackingFilter
generated in tracking filter: 5984dd3e-a155-459b-aca8-e0f8be8691cd.
zuulserver_1        | The organization id from the token is : 42d3d4f5-9f33-42f4-8aca-b7519d6af1bb
zuulserver_1        | 2017-03-31 14:12:08.360 DEBUG 22 --- [nio-5555-exec-2] c.t.zuulsvr.filters.TrackingFilter
g request for /api/licensing/v1/organizations/e254f8c-c442-4ebe-a82a-e2fe1d1ff78a/licenses/f3831f8c-c338-4ebe-a82a-e2fc1d1
zuulserver_1        | 2017-03-31 14:12:08.401  INFO 22 --- [nio-5555-exec-2] s.c.a.AnnotationConfigApplicationContext
ingframework.context.annotation.AnnotationConfigApplicationContext@50ed214e: startup date [Fri Mar 31 14:12:08 GMT 2017];
mework.boot.context.embedded.AnnotationConfigEmbeddedWebApplicationContext@3c09711b
zuulserver_1        | 2017-03-31 14:12:08.460  INFO 22 --- [nio-5555-exec-2] f.a.AutowiredAnnotationBeanPostProcessor
```

Figure 7.12   The Zuul server parses out the organization ID from the JWT token as it passes through.

Figure 7.12 shows the output to the command-line console displaying your parsed `organizationId`.

7.5   *Some closing thoughts on microservice security*

While this chapter has introduced you to the OAuth2 specification and how you can use Spring Cloud security to implement an OAuth2 authentication service, OAuth2 is only one piece of the microservice security puzzle. As you build your microservices for production use, you should be building your microservices security around the following practices:

1. Use HTTPS/Secure Sockets Layer (SSL) for all service communication.
2. All service calls should go through an API gateway.
3. Zone your services into a public API and private API.
4. Limit the attack surface of your microservices by locking down unneeded network ports.

Figure 7.13 shows how these different pieces fit together. Each of the bulleted items in the list maps to the numbers in figure 7.13.

Let's examine each of the topic areas enumerated in the previous list and diagrams in more detail.

USE HTTPS/SECURE SOCKETS LAYER (SSL) FOR ALL SERVICE COMMUNICATION

In all the code examples in this book, you've been using HTTP because HTTP is a simple protocol and doesn't require setup on every service before you can start using the service.

In a production environment, your microservices should communicate only through the encrypted channels provided through HTTPS and SSL. The configuration and setup of the HTTPS can be automated through your DevOps scripts.

NOTE   If your application needs to meet Payment Card Industry (PCI) compliance for credit card payments, you'll be required to implement HTTPS for all service communication. Building all your services to use HTTPS early on is

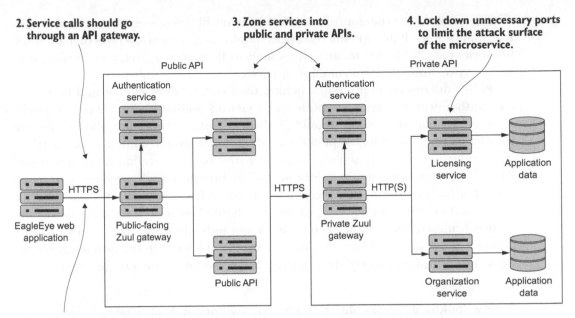

2. Service calls should go through an API gateway.

3. Zone services into public and private APIs.

4. Lock down unnecessary ports to limit the attack surface of the microservice.

I. Use HTTPS/SSL for service communications.

Figure 7.13 A microservice security architecture is more than implementing OAuth2.

much easier than doing a migration project after your application and microservices are in production.

USE A SERVICES GATEWAY TO ACCESS YOUR MICROSERVICES

The individual servers, service endpoints, and ports your services are running on should never be directly accessible to the client. Instead, use a services gateway to act as an entry point and gatekeeper for your service calls. Configure the network layer on the operating system or container your microservices are running in to only accept traffic from the services gateway.

Remember, the services gateway can act as a policy enforcement point (PEP) that can be enforced against all services. Putting service calls through a services gateway such as Zuul allows you to be consistent in how you're securing and auditing your services. A service gateway also allows you to lock down what port and endpoints you're going to expose to the outside world.

ZONE YOUR SERVICES INTO A PUBLIC API AND PRIVATE API

Security in general is all about building layers of accessing and enforcing the concept of least privilege. Least privilege is the concept that a user should have the bare minimum network access and privileges to do their day-to-day job. To this end, you should implement least-privilege by separating your services into two distinct zones: public and private.

The public zone contains the public APIs that will be consumed by clients (Eagle-Eye application). Public API microservices should carry out narrow tasks that are workflow-oriented. Public API microservices tend to be service aggregators, pulling data and carrying out tasks across multiple services.

Public microservices should be behind their own services gateway and have their own authentication service for performing OAuth2 authentication. Access to public services by client applications should go through a single route protected by the services gateway. In addition, the public zone should have its own authentication service.

The private zone acts as a wall to protect your core application functionality and data. The private zone should only be accessible through a single well-known port and should be locked down to only accept network traffic from the network subnet that the private services are running. The private zone should have its own services gateway and authentication service. Public API services should authenticate against the private zones authentication service. All application data should at least be in the private zone's network subnet and only accessible by microservices residing in the private zone.

How locked down should be the private API network zone be?

Many organizations take the approach that their security model should have a hard outer center, with a softer inner surface. What this means is that once traffic is inside the private API zone, communication between services in the private zone can be unencrypted (no HTTPS) and not require an authentication mechanism. Most of the time, this is done for convenience and developer velocity. The more security you have in place, the harder it is to debug problems, increasing the overall complexity of managing your application.

I tend to take a paranoid view of the world. (I worked in financial services for eight years, so paranoia comes with the territory.) I'd rather trade off the additional complexity (which can be mitigated through DevOps scripts) and enforce that all services running in my private API zone use SSL and are authenticated against the authentication service running in the private zone. The question that you have to ask yourself is, How willing are you to see your organization on the front page of your local newspaper because of a network breach?

LIMIT THE ATTACK SURFACE OF YOUR MICROSERVICES BY LOCKING DOWN UNNEEDED NETWORK PORTS

Many developers don't take a hard look at the absolute minimum number of ports they need to open for their services to function. Configure the operating system your service is running on to only allow the inbound and outbound access to ports needed by your service or a piece of infrastructure needed by your service (monitoring, log aggregation).

Don't focus only on inbound access ports. Many developers forget to lock down their outbound ports. Locking down your outbound ports can prevent data from being leaked off your service in the event that the service itself has been compromised by an attacker. Also, make sure you look at network port access in both your public and private API zones.

7.6 *Summary*

- OAuth2 is a token-based authentication framework to authenticate users.
- OAuth2 ensures that each microservice carrying out a user request doesn't need to be presented with user credentials with every call.
- OAuth2 offers different mechanisms for protecting web services calls. These mechanisms are called grants.
- To use OAuth2 in Spring, you need to set up an OAuth2-based authentication service.
- Each application that wants to call your services needs to be registered with your OAuth2 authentication service.
- Each application will have its own application name and secret key.
- User credentials and roles are in memory or a data store and accessed via Spring security.
- Each service must define what actions a role can take.
- Spring Cloud Security supports the JavaScript Web Token (JWT) specification.
- JWT defines a signed, JavaScript standard for generating OAuth2 tokens.
- With JWT, you can inject custom fields into the specification.
- Securing your microservices involves more than just using OAuth2. You should
- Use HTTPS to encrypt all calls between services.
- Use a services gateway to narrow the number of access points a service can be reached through.
- Limit the attack surface for a service by limiting the number of inbound and outbound ports on the operating system that the service is running on.

Event-driven architecture with Spring Cloud Stream

This chapter covers

- Understanding event-driven architecture processing and its relevance to microservices
- Using Spring Cloud Stream to simplify event processing in your microservices
- Configuring Spring Cloud Stream
- Publishing messages with Spring Cloud Stream and Kafka
- Consuming messages with Spring Cloud Stream and Kafka
- Implementing distributed caching with Spring Cloud Stream, Kafka, and Redis

When was the last time you sat down with another person and had a conversation? Think back about how you interacted with that other person. Was it a totally focused exchange of information where you said something and then did nothing else while you waited for the person to respond in full? Were you completely focused on the conversation and let nothing from the outside world distract you while you were speaking? If there were more than two people in the conversation, did you repeat something you said perfectly over and over to each conversation participant and wait in turn for their response? If you said yes to these questions, you have reached enlightenment, are a better human being than me, and should stop what you're doing because you can now answer the age-old question, "What is the sound of one object clapping?" Also, I suspect you don't have children.

The reality is that human beings are constantly in a state of motion, interacting with their environment around them, while sending out and receiving information from the things around them. In my house a typical conversation might be something like this. I'm busy washing the dishes while talking to my wife. I'm telling her about my day. She's looking at her phone and she's listening, processing what I'm saying, and occasionally responding back. As I'm washing the dishes, I hear a commotion in the next room. I stop what I'm doing, rush into the next room to find out what's wrong and see that our rather large nine-month-old puppy, Vader, has taken my three-year-old son's shoe, and is trotting around the living room carrying the shoe like a trophy. My three-year-old isn't happy about this. I run through the house, chasing the dog until I get the shoe back. I then go back to the dishes and my conversation with my wife.

My point in telling you this isn't to tell you about a typical day in my life, but rather to point out that our interaction with the world isn't synchronous, linear, and narrowly defined to a request-response model. It's message-driven, where we're constantly sending and receiving messages. As we receive messages, we react to those messages, while often interrupting the primary task that we're working on.

This chapter is about how to design and implement your Spring-based microservices to communicate with other microservices using asynchronous messages. Using asynchronous messages to communicate between applications isn't new. What's new is the concept of using messages to communicate events representing changes in state. This concept is called Event Driven Architecture (EDA). It's also known as Message Driven Architecture (MDA). What an EDA-based approach allows you to do is to build highly decoupled systems that can react to changes without being tightly coupled to specific libraries or services. When combined with microservices, EDA allows you to quickly add new functionality into your application by merely having the service listen to the stream of events (messages) being emitted by your application.

The Spring Cloud project has made it trivial to build messaging-based solutions through the Spring Cloud Stream sub-project. Spring Cloud Stream allows you to easily implement message publication and consumption, while shielding your services from the implementation details associated with the underlying messaging platform.

8.1 *The case for messaging, EDA, and microservices*

Why is messaging important in building microservice-based applications? To answer that question, let's start with an example. We're going to use the two services we've been using throughout the book: your licensing and organization services. Let's imagine that after these services are deployed to production, you find that the licensing service calls are taking an exceedingly long time when doing a lookup of organization information from the organization service. When you look at the usage patterns of the organization data, you find that the organization data rarely changes and that most of the data reads from the organization service are done by the primary key of the organization record. If you could cache the reads for the organization data without having to incur the cost of accessing a database, you could greatly improve the response time of the licensing service calls.

As you look at implementing a caching solution, you realize you have three core requirements:

1   *The cached data needs to be consistent across all instances of the licensing service*—This means that you can't cache the data locally within the licensing service because you want to guarantee that the same organization data is read regardless of the service instance hitting it.

2   *You cannot cache the organization data within the memory of the container hosting the licensing service*—The run-time container hosting your service is often restricted in size and can access data using different access patterns. A local cache can introduce complexity because you have to guarantee your local cache is synced with all of the other services in the cluster.

3   *When an organization record changes via an update or delete, you want the licensing service to recognize that there has been a state change in the organization service*—The licensing service should then invalidate any cached data it has for that specific organization and evict it from the cache.

Let's look at two approaches for implementing these requirements. The first approach will implement the above requirements using a synchronous request-response model. When the organization state changes, the licensing and organization services communicate back and forth via their REST endpoints. The second approach will have the organization service emit an asynchronous event (message) that will communicate that the organization service data has changed. With the second approach, the organization service will publish a message to a queue that an organization record has been updated or deleted. The licensing service will listen with the intermediary, see that an organization event has occurred, and clear the organization data from its cache.

8.1.1   *Using synchronous request-response approach to communicate state change*

For your organization data cache, you're going to use Redis (http://redis.io/), a distributed key-value store database. Figure 8.1 provides a high-level overview of how to build a caching solution using a traditional synchronous, request-response programming model.

In figure 8.1, when a user calls the licensing service, the licensing service will need to also look up organization data. The licensing service will first check to retrieve the desired organization by its ID from the Redis cluster. If the licensing service can't find the organization data, it will call the organization service using a REST-based endpoint

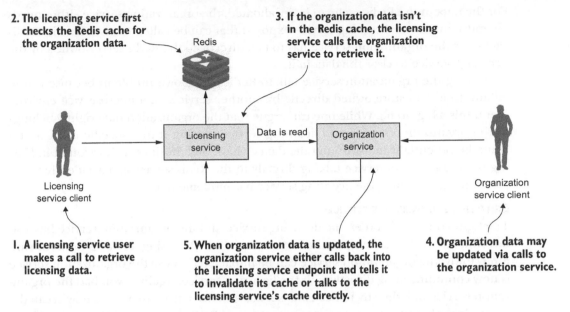

2. The licensing service first checks the Redis cache for the organization data.

Redis

3. If the organization data isn't in the Redis cache, the licensing service calls the organization service to retrieve it.

Licensing service

Data is read

Organization service

Licensing service client

Organization service client

1. A licensing service user makes a call to retrieve licensing data.

5. When organization data is updated, the organization service either calls back into the licensing service endpoint and tells it to invalidate its cache or talks to the licensing service's cache directly.

4. Organization data may be updated via calls to the organization service.

Figure 8.1 In a synchronous request-response model, tightly coupled services introduce complexity and brittleness.

and then store the data returned in Redis, before returning the organization data back to the user. Now, if someone updates or deletes the organization record using the organization service's REST endpoint, the organization service will need to call an endpoint exposed on the licensing service, telling it to invalidate the organization data in its cache. In figure 8.1, if you look at where the organization service calls back into the licensing service to tell it to invalidate the Redis cache, you can see at least three problems:

1 The organization and licensing services are tightly coupled.
2 The coupling has introduced brittleness between the services. If the licensing service endpoint for invalidating the cache changes, the organization service has to change.
3 The approach is inflexible because you can't add new consumers of the organization data even without modifying the code on the organization service to know that it has called the other service to let it know about the change.

TIGHT COUPLING BETWEEN SERVICES
In figure 8.1 you can see tight coupling between the licensing and the organization service. The licensing service always had a dependency on the organization service to retrieve data. However, by having the organization service directly communicate back to the licensing service whenever an organization record has been updated or deleted, you've introduced coupling back from the organization service to the licensing service.

For the data in the Redis cache to be invalidated, the organization service either needs an endpoint on the licensing service exposed that can be called to invalidate its Redis cache, or the organization service has to talk directly to the Redis server owned by the licensing service to clear the data in it.

Having the organization service talk to Redis has its own problems because you're talking to a data store owned directly by another service. In a microservice environment, this a big no-no. While one can argue that the organization data rightly belongs to the organization service, the licensing service is using it in a specific context and could be potentially transforming the data or have built business rules around it. Having the organization service talking directly to the Redis service can accidently break rules the team owning the licensing service has implemented.

BRITTLENESS BETWEEN THE SERVICES

The tight coupling between the licensing service and the organization service has also introduced brittleness between the two services. If the licensing service is down or running slowly, the organization service can be impacted because the organization service is now communicating directly with the licensing service. Again, if you had the organization service talk directly to licensing service's Redis data store, you've now created a dependency between the organization service and Redis. In this scenario, any problems with the shared Redis server now have the potential to take down both services.

INFLEXIBLE IN ADDING NEW CONSUMERS TO CHANGES IN THE ORGANIZATION SERVICE

The last problem with this architecture is that it's inflexible. With the model in figure 8.1, if you had another service that was interested in when the organization data changes, you'd need to add another call from the organization service to that other service. This means a code change and redeployment of the organization service. If you use the synchronous, request-response model for communicating state change, you start to see almost a web-like pattern of dependency between your core services in your application and other services. The centers of these webs become your major points of failure within your application.

Another kind of coupling

While messaging adds a layer of indirection between your services, you can still introduce tight coupling between two services using messaging. Later in the chapter you're going to send messages between the organization and licensing service. These messages are going to be serialized and de-serialized to a Java object using JSON as the transport protocol for the message. Changes to the structure of the JSON message can cause problems when converting back and forth to Java if the two services don't gracefully handle different versions of the same message type. JSON doesn't natively support versioning. However, you can use Apache Avro (https://avro.apache.org/) if you need versioning. Avro is a binary protocol that has versioning built into it. Spring Cloud Stream does support Apache Avro as a messaging protocol. However, using Avro is outside the scope of this book, but we did want to make you aware that it does help if you truly need to worry about message versioning.

8.1.2   Using messaging to communicate state changes between services

With a messaging approach, you're going to inject a queue in between the licensing and organization service. This queue won't be used to read data from the organization service, but will instead be used by the organization service to publish when any state changes within the organization data managed by the organization service occurs. Figure 8.2 demonstrates this approach.

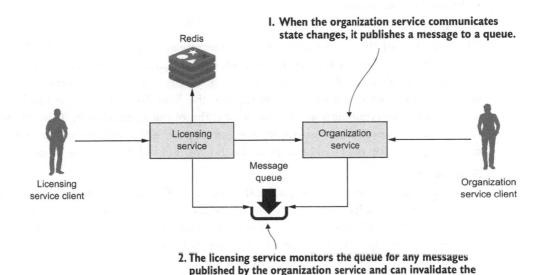

I. When the organization service communicates state changes, it publishes a message to a queue.

Redis

Licensing service

Organization service

Message queue

Licensing service client

Organization service client

2. The licensing service monitors the queue for any messages published by the organization service and can invalidate the Redis cache data as needed.

Figure 8.2   As organization state changes, messages will be written to a message queue that sits between the two services.

In the model in figure 8.2, every time organization data changes, the organization service publishes a message out to a queue. The licensing service is monitoring the queue for messages and when a message comes in, clears the appropriate organization record out of the Redis cache. When it comes to communicating state, the message queue acts as an intermediary between the licensing and organization service. This approach offers four benefits:

- Loose coupling
- Durability
- Scalability
- Flexibility

LOOSE COUPLING

A microservices application can be composed of dozens of small and distributed services that have to interact with each other and are interested in the data managed by one another. As you saw with the synchronous design proposed earlier, a synchronous HTTP response creates a hard dependency between the licensing and organization service. We can't eliminate these dependencies completely, but we can try to minimize dependencies by only exposing endpoints that directly manage the data owned by the service. A messaging approach allows you to decouple the two services because when it comes to communicating state changes, neither service knows about each other. When the organization service needs to publish a state change, it writes a message to a queue. The licensing service only knows that it gets a message; it has no idea who has published the message.

DURABILITY

The presence of the queue allows you to guarantee that a message will be delivered even if the consumer of the service is down. The organization service can keep publishing messages even if the licensing service in unavailable. The messages will be stored in the queue and will stay there until the licensing service is available. Conversely, with the combination of a cache and the queuing approach, if the organization service is down, the licensing service can degrade gracefully because at least part of the organization data will be in its cache. Sometimes old data is better than no data.

SCALABILITY

Since messages are stored in a queue, the sender of the message doesn't have to wait for a response back from the consumer of the message. They can go on their way and continue their work. Likewise, if a consumer reading a message off the queue isn't processing messages fast enough, it's a trivial task to spin up more consumers and have them process those messages off the queue. This scalability approach fits well within a microservices model because one of the things I've been emphasizing through this book is that it should be trivial to spin up new instances of a microservice and have that additional microservice become another service that can process work off the message queue holding the messages. This is an example of scaling horizontally. Traditional scaling mechanisms for reading messages off a queue involved increasing the number of threads that a message consumer could process at one time. Unfortunately, with this approach, you were ultimately limited by the number of CPUs available to the message consumer. A microservice model doesn't have this limitation because you're scaling by increasing the number of machines hosting the service consuming the messages.

FLEXIBILITY

The sender of a message has no idea who is going to consume it. This means you can easily add new message consumers (and new functionality) without impacting the original sending service. This is an extremely powerful concept because new functionality can be added to an application without having to touch existing services. Instead, the new code can listen for events being published and react to them accordingly.

8.1.3   Downsides of a messaging architecture

Like any architectural model, a messaging-based architecture has tradeoffs. A messaging-based architecture can be complex and requires the development team to pay close attention to several key things, including

- Message handling semantics
- Message visibility
- Message choreography

MESSAGE HANDLING SEMANTICS

Using messages in a microservice-based application requires more than understanding how to publish and consume messages. It requires you to understand how your application will behave based on the order messages are consumed and what happens if a message is processed out of order. For example, if you have strict requirements that all orders from a single customer must be processed in the order they are received, you're going to have to set up and structure your message handling differently than if every message can be consumed independently of one another.

It also means that if you're using messaging to enforce strict state transitions of your data, you need to think as you're designing your application about scenarios where a message throws an exception, or an error is processed out of order. If a message fails, do you retry processing the error or do you let it fail? How do you handle future messages related to that customer if one of the customer messages fails? Again, these are all topics to think through.

MESSAGE VISIBILITY

Using messages in your microservices often means a mix of synchronous service calls and processing in services asynchronously. The asynchronous nature of messages means they might not be received or processed in close proximity to when the message is published or consumed. Also, having things like a correlation ID for tracking a user's transactions across web service invocations and messages is critical to understanding and debugging what's going on in your application. As you may remember from chapter 6, a correlation ID is a unique number that's generated at the start of a user's transaction and passed along with every service call. It should also be passed with every message that's published and consumed.

MESSAGE CHOREOGRAPHY

As alluded to in the section on message visibility, messaging-based applications make it more difficult to reason through the business logic of their applications because their code is no longer being processed in a linear fashion with a simple block request-response model. Instead, debugging message-based applications can involve wading through the logs of several different services where the user transactions can be executed out of order and at different times.

Messaging can be complex but powerful

The previous sections weren't meant to scare you away from using messaging in your applications. Rather, my goal is to highlight that using messaging in your services requires forethought. I recently completed a major project where we needed to bring up and down a stateful set of AWS server instances for each one of our customers. We had to integrate a combination of microservice calls and messages using both AWS Simple Queueing Service (SQS) and Kafka. While the project was complex, I saw first-hand the power of messaging when at the end of the project we realized that we'd need to deal with having to make sure that we retrieved certain files off the server before the server could be terminated. This step had to be carried out about 75% of the way through the user workflow and the overall process couldn't continue until the process was completed. Fortunately, we had a microservice (called our file recovery service) that could do much of the work to check and see if the files were off the server being decommissioned. Because the servers communicate all of their state changes (including that they're being decommissioned) via events, we only had to plug the file recovery server into an event stream coming from the server being decommissioned and have them listen for a "decommissioning" event.

If this entire process had been synchronous, adding this file-draining step would have been extremely painful. But in the end, we needed an existing service we already had in production to listen to events coming off an existing messaging queue and react. The work was done in a couple of days and we never missed a beat in our project delivery. Messages allow you to hook together services without the services being hard-coded together in a code-based workflow.

8.2 *Introducing Spring Cloud Stream*

Spring Cloud makes it easy to integrate messaging into your Spring-based microservices. It does this through the Spring Cloud Stream project (https://cloud.spring.io/spring-cloud-stream/). The Spring Cloud Stream project is an annotation-driven framework that allows you to easily build message publishers and consumers in your Spring application.

Spring Cloud Stream also allows you to abstract away the implementation details of the messaging platform you're using. Multiple message platforms can be used with Spring Cloud Stream (including the Apache Kafka project and RabbitMQ) and the implementation-specific details of the platform are kept out of the application code. The implementation of message publication and consumption in your application is done through platform-neutral Spring interfaces.

> NOTE For this chapter, you're going to use a lightweight message bus called Kafka (https://kafka.apache.org/). Kafka is a lightweight, highly performant message bus that allows you asynchronously send streams of messages from one application to one or more other applications. Written in Java, Kafka has become the de facto message bus for many cloud-based applications because it's highly reliable and scalable. Spring Cloud Stream also supports the use of RabbitMQ as a message bus. Both Kafka and RabbitMQ are strong messaging platforms, and I chose Kafka because that's what I'm most familiar with.

To understand Spring Cloud Stream, let's begin with a discussion of the Spring Cloud Stream architecture and familiarize ourselves with the terminology of Spring Cloud Stream. If you've never worked with a messaging based platform before, the new terminology involved can be somewhat overwhelming.

8.2.1 The Spring Cloud Stream architecture

Let's begin our discussion by looking at the Spring Cloud Stream architecture through the lens of two services communicating via messaging. One service will be the message publisher and one service will be the message consumer. Figure 8.3 shows how Spring Cloud Stream is used to facilitate this message passing.

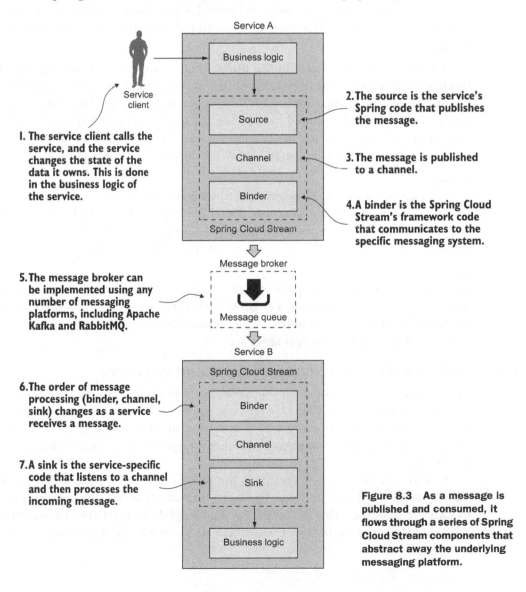

Figure 8.3 As a message is published and consumed, it flows through a series of Spring Cloud Stream components that abstract away the underlying messaging platform.

With the publication and consumption of a message in Spring Cloud, four components are involved in publishing and consuming the message:

- Source
- Channel
- Binder
- Sink

SOURCE

When a service gets ready to publish a message, it will publish the message using a source. A source is a Spring annotated interface that takes a Plain Old Java Object (POJO) that represents the message to be published. A source takes the message, serializes it (the default serialization is JSON), and publishes the message to a channel.

CHANNEL

A channel is an abstraction over the queue that's going to hold the message after it has been published by the message producer or consumed by a message consumer. A channel name is always associated with a target queue name. However, that queue name is never directly exposed to the code. Instead the channel name is used in the code, which means that you can switch the queues the channel reads or writes from by changing the application's configuration, not the application's code.

BINDER

The binder is part of the Spring Cloud Stream framework. It's the Spring code that talks to a specific message platform. The binder part of the Spring Cloud Stream framework allows you to work with messages without having to be exposed to platform-specific libraries and APIs for publishing and consuming messages.

SINK

In Spring Cloud Stream, when a service receives a message from a queue, it does it through a sink. A sink listens to a channel for incoming messages and de-serializes the message back into a plain old Java object. From there, the message can be processed by the business logic of the Spring service.

8.3   *Writing a simple message producer and consumer*

Now that we've walked through the basic components in Spring Cloud Stream, let's look at a simple Spring Cloud Stream example. For the first example, you're going to pass a message from your organization service to your licensing service. The only thing you'll do with the message in the licensing service is to print a log message to the console.

In addition, because you're only going to have one Spring Cloud Stream source (the message producer) and sink (message consumer) in this example, you're going to start the example with a few simple Spring Cloud shortcuts that will make setting up the source in the organization service and a sink in the licensing service trivial.

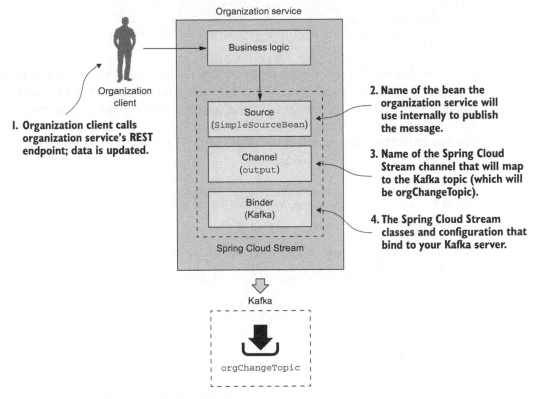

Figure 8.4 When organization service data changes it will publish a message to Kafka.

8.3.1 *Writing the message producer in the organization service*

You're going to begin by modifying the organization service so that every time organization data is added, updated, or deleted, the organization service will publish a message to a Kafka topic indicating that the organization change event has occurred. Figure 8.4 highlights the message producer and build on the general Spring Cloud Stream architecture from figure 8.3.

The published message will include the organization ID associated with the change event and will also include what action occurred (Add, Update or Delete).

The first thing you need to do is set up your Maven dependencies in the organization service's Maven pom.xml file. The pom.xml file can be found in the organization-service directory. In the pom.xml, you need to add two dependencies: one for the core Spring Cloud Stream libraries and the other to include the Spring Cloud Stream Kafka libraries:

```
<dependency>
    <groupId>org.springframework.cloud</groupId>
    <artifactId>spring-cloud-stream</artifactId>
</dependency>
```

```
<dependency>
    <groupId>org.springframework.cloud</groupId>
    <artifactId>spring-cloud-starter-stream-kafka</artifactId>
</dependency>
```

Once the Maven dependencies have been defined, you need to tell your application that it's going to bind to a Spring Cloud Stream message broker. You do this by annotating the organization service's bootstrap class organization-service/src/main/java/com/thoughtmechanix/organization/Application.java with an @EnableBinding annotation. The following listing shows the organization service's Application.java source code.

Listing 8.1   The annotated `Application.java` class

```
package com.thoughtmechanix.organization;

import com.thoughtmechanix.organization.utils.UserContextFilter;
import org.springframework.boot.SpringApplication;
import org.springframework.boot.autoconfigure.SpringBootApplication;
import org.springframework.cloud.client.circuitbreaker.EnableCircuitBreaker;
import org.springframework.cloud.netflix.eureka.EnableEurekaClient;
import org.springframework.cloud.stream.annotation.EnableBinding;
import org.springframework.cloud.stream.messaging.Source;
import org.springframework.context.annotation.Bean;
import javax.servlet.Filter;

@SpringBootApplication
@EnableEurekaClient
@EnableCircuitBreaker
@EnableBinding(Source.class)         ⟵——  The @EnableBinding annotation tells
public class Application {                  Spring Cloud Stream to bind the
    @Bean                                   application to a message broker.
    public Filter userContextFilter() {
        UserContextFilter userContextFilter = new UserContextFilter();
        return userContextFilter;
    }
    public static void main(String[] args) {
        SpringApplication.run(Application.class, args);
    }
}
```

In listing 8.1, the @EnableBinding annotation tells Spring Cloud Stream that you want to bind the service to a message broker. The use of Source.class in the @EnableBinding annotation tells Spring Cloud Stream that this service will communicate with the message broker via a set of channels defined on the Source class. Remember, channels sit above a message queue. Spring Cloud Stream has a default set of channels that can be configured to speak to a message broker.

At this point you haven't told Spring Cloud Stream what message broker you want the organization service to bind to. We'll get to that shortly. Now, you can go ahead and implement the code that will publish a message.

The message publication code can be found in the `organization-service/src/com/thoughtmechanix/organization/events/source/SimpleSource-Bean.java` class. The following listing shows the code for this class.

Listing 8.2　Publishing a message to the message broker

```
package com.thoughtmechanix.organization.events.source;

//Removed imports for conciseness

@Component
public class SimpleSourceBean {
    private Source source;

    private static final Logger logger =
     LoggerFactory.getLogger(SimpleSourceBean.class);

    @Autowired
    public SimpleSourceBean(Source source){          Spring Cloud Stream will inject a
       this.source = source;                         Source interface implementation
    }                                                for use by the service.

    public void publishOrgChange(String action,String orgId){
       logger.debug("Sending Kafka message {}
          for Organization Id: {}",
          action, orgId);
       OrganizationChangeModel change =  new OrganizationChangeModel(
             OrganizationChangeModel.class.getTypeName(),
             action,
             orgId,
             UserContext.getCorrelationId());

       source                                        When you're ready to send the
            .output()                                message, use the send() method from
            .send(                                   a channel defined on the Source class.
              MessageBuilder
                 .withPayload(change)
                 .build());
    }
}
```

The message to be published is a Java POJO.

In listing 8.2 you inject the Spring Cloud `Source` class into your code. Remember, all communication to a specific message topic occurs through a Spring Cloud Stream construct called a channel. A channel is represented by a Java interface class. In this listing you're using the `Source` interface. The `Source` interface is a Spring Cloud defined interface that exposes a single method called `output()`. The `Source` interface is a convenient interface to use when your service only needs to publish to a single channel. The `output()` method returns a class of type `MessageChannel`. The `MessageChannel` is how you'll send messages to the message broker. Later in this chapter, I'll show you how to expose multiple messaging channels using a custom interface.

The actual publication of the message occurs in the `publishOrgChange()` method. This method builds a Java POJO called `OrganizationChangeModel`. I'm not going to put the code for the `OrganizationChangeModel` in the chapter because this class is nothing more than a POJO around three data elements:

- *Action*—This is the action that triggered the event. I've included the action in the message to give the message consumer more context on how it should process an event.
- *Organization ID*—This is the organization ID associated with the event.
- *Correlation ID*—This is the correlation ID the service call that triggered the event. You should always include a correlation ID in your events as it helps greatly with tracking and debugging the flow of messages through your services.

When you're ready to publish the message, use the `send()` method on the `MessageChannel` class returned from the `source.output()` method.

```
source.output().send(MessageBuilder.withPayload(change).build());
```

The `send()` method takes a Spring `Message` class. You use a Spring helper class called `MessageBuilder` to take the contents of the `OrganizationChangeModel` class and convert it to a Spring `Message` class.

This is all the code you need to send a message. However, at this point, everything should feel a little bit like magic because you haven't seen how to bind your organization service to a specific message queue, let alone the actual message broker. This is all done through configuration. Listing 8.3 shows the configuration that does the mapping of your service's Spring Cloud Stream `Source` to a Kafka message broker and a message topic in Kafka. This configuration information can be localized in your service's application.yml file or inside a Spring Cloud Config entry for the service.

Listing 8.3   The Spring Cloud Stream configuration for publishing a message

```
spring:
  application:
    name: organizationservice
  #Remove for conciseness
    stream:
      bindings:
        output:
          destination: orgChangeTopic
          content-type: application/json
      kafka:
        binder:
          zkNodes: localhost
          brokers: localhost
```

stream.bindings is the start of the configuration needed for your service to publish to a Spring Cloud Stream message broke.

output is the name of your channel and maps to the Source.output() channel you saw in listing 8.2.

orgChangeTopic is the name of the message queue (or topic) you're going to write messages to.

The content-type gives a hint to Spring Cloud Stream of what type of message is going to be sent and received (in this case JSON).

The zknodes and brokers property tells Spring Cloud Stream the network location of your Kafka and ZooKeeper.

The stream.bindings.kafka property tells Spring you're going to use Kafka as the message bus in the service (you could have used RabbitMQ as an alternative).

The configuration in listing 8.3 looks dense, but it's straightforward. The configuration property `spring.stream.bindings.output` in the listing maps the `source.output()` channel in listing 8.2 to the `orgChangeTopic` on the message broker you're going to communicate with. It also tells Spring Cloud Stream that messages being sent to this topic should be serialized as JSON. Spring Cloud Stream can serialize messages in multiple formats, including JSON, XML, and the Apache Foundation's Avro format (https://avro.apache.org/).

The configuration property, `spring.stream.bindings.kafka` in listing 8.3, also tells Spring Cloud Stream to bind the service to Kafka. The sub-properties tell Spring Cloud Stream the network addresses of the Kafka message brokers and the Apache ZooKeeper servers that run with Kafka.

Now that you have the code written that will publish a message via Spring Cloud Stream and the configuration to tell Spring Cloud Stream that it's going to use Kafka as a message broker, let's look at where the publication of the message in your organization service actually occurs. This work will be done in the `organization-service/src/main/java/com/thoughtmechanix/organization/services/OrganizationService.java` class. The following listing shows the code for this class.

Listing 8.4 Publishing a message in your organization service

```java
package com.thoughtmechanix.organization.services;

//Imports removed for consiceness
@Service
public class OrganizationService {
    @Autowired
    private OrganizationRepository orgRepository;

    @Autowired
    SimpleSourceBean simpleSourceBean;

    //Rest of class removed for conciseness
    public void saveOrg(Organization org){
        org.setId( UUID.randomUUID().toString());

        orgRepository.save(org);
        simpleSourceBean.publishOrgChange("SAVE", org.getId());
    }
}
```

Spring autowiring is used to inject the SimpleSourceBean into your organization service.

For each method in the service that changes organization data, call simpleSourceBean.publish OrgChange().

What data should I put in the message?

One of the most common questions I get from teams when they're first embarking on their message journey is exactly how much data should go in their messages. My answer is, it depends on your application. As you may notice, in all my examples I only return the organization ID of the organization record that has changed. I never put a copy of the changes to the data in the message. In my examples (and in many

(continued)

of the problems I deal with in the telephony space), the business logic being executed is sensitive to changes in data. I used messages based on system events to tell other services that data state has changed, but I always force the other services to go back to the master (the service that owns the data) to retrieve a new copy of the data. This approach is costlier in terms of execution time, but it also guarantees I always have the latest copy of the data to work with. A chance still exists that the data you're working with could change right after you've read it from the source system, but that's much less likely than blindly consuming the information right off the queue.

Think carefully about how much data you're passing around. Sooner or later, you'll run into a situation where the data you passed is stale. It could be stale because a problem caused it to sit in a message queue too long, or a previous message containing data failed, and the data you're passing in the message now represents data that's in an inconsistent state (because your application relied on the message's state rather than the actual state in the underlying data store). If you're going to pass state in your message, also make sure to include a date-time stamp or version number in your message so that the services consuming the data can inspect the data being passed and ensure that it's not older than the copy of the data they already have. (Remember, data can be retrieved out of order.)

8.3.2   *Writing the message consumer in the licensing service*

At this point you've modified the organization service to publish a message to Kafka every time the organization service changes organization data. Anyone who's interested can react without having to be explicitly called by the organization service. It also means you can easily add new functionality that can react to the changes in the organization service by having them listen to messages coming in on the message queue. Let's now switch directions and look at how a service can consume a message using Spring Cloud Stream.

For this example, you're going to have the licensing service consume the message published by the organization service. Figure 8.5 shows where the licensing service will fit into the Spring Cloud architecture first shown in figure 8.3.

To begin, you again need to add your Spring Cloud Stream dependencies to the licensing services pom.xml file. This pom.xml file can found in licensing-service directory of the source code for the book. Similar to the organization-service pom.xml file you saw earlier, you add the following two dependency entries:

```
<dependency>
    <groupId>org.springframework.cloud</groupId>
    <artifactId>spring-cloud-stream</artifactId>
  </dependency>

<dependency>
    <groupId>org.springframework.cloud</groupId>
    <artifactId>spring-cloud-starter-stream-kafka</artifactId>
</dependency>
```

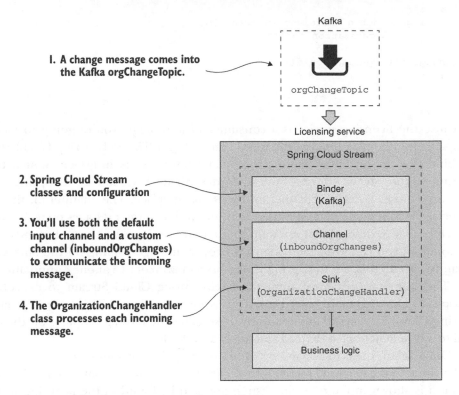

1. A change message comes into the Kafka orgChangeTopic.

2. Spring Cloud Stream classes and configuration

3. You'll use both the default input channel and a custom channel (inboundOrgChanges) to communicate the incoming message.

4. The OrganizationChangeHandler class processes each incoming message.

Figure 8.5   When a message comes into the Kafka `orgChangeTopic`**, the licensing service will respond.**

Then you need to tell the licensing service that it needs to use Spring Cloud Stream to bind to a message broker. Like the organization service, we're going to annotate the licensing services bootstrap class (`licensing-service/src/main/java/com/thoughtmechanix/licenses/Application.java`) with the `@EnableBinding` annotation. The difference between the licensing service and the organization service is the value you're going to pass to the `@EnableBinding` annotation, as shown in the following listing.

Listing 8.5   Consuming a message using Spring Cloud Stream

```
package com.thoughtmechanix.licenses;

//Imports removed for conciseness
@EnableBinding(Sink.class)
public class Application {
   //Code removed for conciseness
    @StreamListener(Sink.INPUT)
    public void loggerSink(
       OrganizationChangeModel orgChange) {
```

The @EnableBinding annotation tells the service to the use the channels defined in the Sink interface to listen for incoming messages.

Spring Cloud Stream will execute this method every time a message is received off the input channel.

```
        logger.debug("Received an event for
        ⇒ organization id {}" ,
            ⇒
orgChange.getOrganizationId());
    }

}
```

Because the licensing service is a consumer of a message, you're going to pass the @EnableBinding annotation the value Sink.class. This tells Spring Cloud Stream to bind to a message broker using the default Spring Sink interface. Similar to the Spring Cloud Steam Source interface described in section 8.3.1, Spring Cloud Stream exposes a default channel on the Sink interface. The channel on the Sink interface is called input and is used to listen for incoming messages on a channel.

Once you've defined that you want to listen for messages via the @EnableBinding annotation, you can write the code to process a message coming off the Sink input channel. To do this, use the Spring Cloud Stream @StreamListener annotation.

The @StreamListener annotation tells Spring Cloud Stream to execute the loggerSink() method every time a message is received off the input channel. Spring Cloud Stream will automatically de-serialize the message coming off the channel to a Java POJO called OrganizationChangeModel.

Once again, the actual mapping of the message broker's topic to the input channel is done in the licensing service's configuration. For the licensing service, its configuration is shown in the following listing and can be found in the licensing service's licensing-service/src/main/resources/application.yml file.

Listing 8.6   Mapping the licensing service to a message topic in Kafka

```
spring:
  application:
    name: licensingservice
    ...    #Remove for consiceness
  cloud:
    stream:                                    The spring.cloud.stream.bindings.input
      bindings:                                property maps the input channel to the
        input:                          ◄──┘   orgChangeTopic queue.
          destination: orgChangeTopic
          content-type: application/json
          group: licensingGroup       ◄───    The group property is used
        binder:                               to guarantee process-once
          zkNodes: localhost                  semantics for a service.
          brokers: localhost
```

The configuration in this listing looks like the configuration for the organization service. It has, however, two key differences. First, you now have a channel called input defined under the spring.cloud.stream.bindings property. This value maps to the Sink.INPUT channel defined in the code from listing 8.5. This property maps the input channel to the orgChangeTopic. Second, you see the introduction of a new property called `spring.cloud.stream.bindings.input.group`. The group property defines the name of the consumer group that will be consuming the message.

The concept of a consumer group is this: You might have multiple services with each service having multiple instances listening to the same message queue. You want each unique service to process a copy of a message, but you only want one service instance within a group of service instances to consume and process a message. The `group` property identifies the consumer group that the service belongs to. As long as all the service instances have the same group name, Spring Cloud Stream and the underlying message broker will guarantee that only one copy of the message will be consumed by a service instance belonging to that group. In the case of your licensing service, the `group` property value will be called `licensingGroup`.

Figure 8.6 illustrates how the consumer group is used to help enforce consume-once semantics for a message being consumed across multiple services.

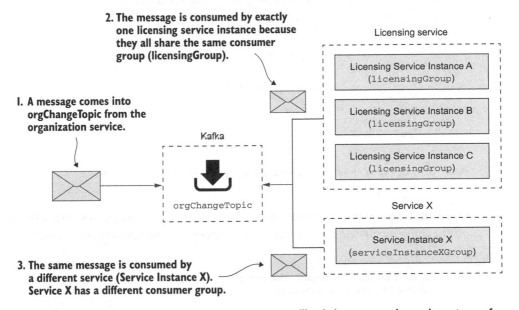

Figure 8.6   The consumer group guarantees a message will only be processed once by a group of service instances.

8.3.3   *Seeing the message service in action*

At this point you have the organization service publishing a message to the `orgChangeTopic` every time a record is added, updated, or deleted and the licensing service receiving the message of the same topic. Now you'll see this code in action by updating an organization service record and watching the console to see the corresponding log message appear from the licensing service.

To update the organization service record, you're going to issue a PUT on the organization service to update the organization's contact phone number. The endpoint you're going to update with is http://localhost:5555/api/organization/v1/organizations/e254f8c-c442-4ebe-a82a-e2fc1d1ff78a. The body you're going to send on the PUT call to the endpoint is

```
{
    "contactEmail": "mark.balster@custcrmco.com",
    "contactName": "Mark Balster",
    "contactPhone": "823-555-2222",
    "id": "e254f8c-c442-4ebe-a82a-e2fc1d1ff78a",
    "name": "customer-crm-co"
}
```

Figure 8.7 shows the returned output from this PUT call.

Figure 8.7   Updating the contact phone number using the organization service

Once the organization service call has been made, you should see the following output in the console window running the services. Figure 8.8 show this output.

Log message from the organization service indicating it sent a Kafka message

```
Sending Kafka message UPDATE for Organization Id: e254f8c-c442-4e

Adding the correlation id to the outbound headers.
Completing outgoing request for /api/organization/v1/organization

Received a message of type com.thoughtmechanix.organization.event

Received a UPDATE event from the organization service for organiz
```

Log message from the licensing service indicating that it received a message for an UPDATE event

Figure 8.8   The console shows the message from the organization service being sent and then received.

Now you have two services communicating with each other using messaging. Spring Cloud Stream is acting as the middleman for these services. From a messaging perspective, the services know nothing about each other. They're using a messaging broker to communicate as an intermediary and Spring Cloud Stream as an abstraction layer over the messaging broker.

8.4 *A Spring Cloud Stream use case: distributed caching*

At this point you have two services communicating with messaging, but you're not really doing anything with the messages. Now you'll build the distributed caching example we discussed earlier in the chapter. You'll have the licensing service always check a distributed Redis cache for the organization data associated with a particular license. If the organization data exists in the cache, you'll return the data from the cache. If it doesn't, you'll call the organization service and cache the results of the call in a Redis hash.

When data is updated in the organization service, the organization service will issue a message to Kafka. The licensing service will pick up the message and issue a delete against Redis to clear out the cache.

Cloud caching and messaging

Using Redis as a distributed cache is very relevant to microservices development in the cloud. With my current employer, we build our solution using Amazon's Web Services (AWS) and are a heavy user of Amazon's DynamoDB. We also use Amazon's ElastiCache (Redis) to

- *Improve performance for lookup of commonly held data*—By using a cache, we've significantly improved the performance of several of our key services. All the tables in the products we sell are multi-tenant (hold multiple customer records in a single table), which means they can be quite large. Because caching tends to pin "heavily" used data we've seen significant performance improvements by using Redis and caching to avoid the reads out to Dynamo.

- *Reduce the load (and cost) on the Dynamo tables holding our data*—Accessing data in Dynamo can be a costly proposition. Every read you make is a chargeable event. Using a Redis server is significantly cheaper for reads by a primary key then a Dynamo read.

- *Increase resiliency so that our services can degrade gracefully if our primary data store (Dynamo) is having performance problems*—If AWS Dynamo is having problems (it does occasionally happen), using a cache such as Redis can help your service degrade gracefully. Depending on how much data you keep in your cache, a caching solution can help reduce the number of errors you get from hitting your data store.

Redis is far more than a caching solution, but it can fill that role if you need a distributed cache.

8.4.1   *Using Redis to cache lookups*

Now you're going to begin by setting up the licensing service to use Redis. Fortunately, Spring Data already makes it simple to introduce Redis into your licensing service. To use Redis in the licensing service you need to do four things:

1. Configure the licensing service to include the Spring Data Redis dependencies
2. Construct a database connection to Redis
3. Define the Spring Data Redis Repositories that your code will use to interact with a Redis hash
4. Use Redis and the licensing service to store and read organization data

CONFIGURE THE LICENSING SERVICE WITH SPRING DATA REDIS DEPENDENCIES

The first thing you need to do is include the `spring-data-redis` dependencies, along with the `jedis` and `common-pools2` dependencies, into the licensing service's pom.xml file. The dependencies to include are shown in the following listing.

Listing 8.7   Adding the Spring Redis Dependencies

```
<dependency>
    <groupId>org.springframework.data</groupId>
    <artifactId>spring-data-redis</artifactId>
    <version>1.7.4.RELEASE</version>
</dependency>

<dependency>
    <groupId>redis.clients</groupId>
    <artifactId>jedis</artifactId>
    <version>2.9.0</version>
</dependency>

<dependency>
    <groupId>org.apache.commons</groupId>
    <artifactId>commons-pool2</artifactId>
    <version>2.0</version>
</dependency>
```

CONSTRUCTING THE DATABASE CONNECTION TO A REDIS SERVER

Now that you have the dependencies in Maven, you need to establish a connection out to your Redis server. Spring uses the open source project Jedis (`https://github.com/xetorthio/jedis`) to communicate with a Redis server. To communicate with a specific Redis instance, you're going to expose a `JedisConnection-Factory` in the `licensing-service/src/main/java/com/thoughtmechanix/licenses/Application.java` class as a Spring Bean. Once you have a connection out to Redis, you're going to use that connection to create a Spring `RedisTemplate` object. The `RedisTemplate` object will be used by the Spring Data repository classes that you'll implement shortly to execute the queries and saves of organization service data to your Redis service. The following listing shows this code.

Listing 8.8   Establishing how your licensing service will communicate with Redis

```
package com.thoughtmechanix.licenses;

//Most of th imports have been remove for conciseness
import
    org.springframework.data.redis.connection.jedis.JedisConnectionFactory;
import org.springframework.data.redis.core.RedisTemplate;

@SpringBootApplication
@EnableEurekaClient
@EnableCircuitBreaker
@EnableBinding(Sink.class)
public class Application {

    @Autowired
    private ServiceConfig serviceConfig;

    //All other methods in the class have been removed for consiceness
    @Bean
    public JedisConnectionFactory jedisConnectionFactory() {
        JedisConnectionFactory jedisConnFactory = new
 JedisConnectionFactory();
        jedisConnFactory.setHostName( serviceConfig.getRedisServer() );
        jedisConnFactory.setPort( serviceConfig.getRedisPort() );
        return jedisConnFactory;
    }

    @Bean
    public RedisTemplate<String, Object> redisTemplate() {
        RedisTemplate<String, Object> template = new RedisTemplate<String,
 Object>();
        template.setConnectionFactory(jedisConnectionFactory());
        return template;
    }
}
```

The jedisConnectionFactory() method sets up the actual database connection to the Redis server.

The redisTemplate() method creates a RedisTemplate that will be used to carry out actions against your Redis server.

The foundational work for setting up the licensing service to communicate with Redis is complete. Let's now move over to writing the logic that will get, add, update, and delete data from Redis.

DEFINING THE SPRING DATA REDIS REPOSITORIES

Redis is a key-value store data store that acts like a big, distributed, in-memory Hash-Map. In the simplest case, it stores data and looks up data by a key. It doesn't have any kind of sophisticated query language to retrieve data. Its simplicity is its strength and one of the reasons why so many projects have adopted it for use in their projects.

Because you're using Spring Data to access your Redis store, you need to define a repository class. As may you remember from early on in chapter 2, Spring Data uses user-defined repository classes to provide a simple mechanism for a Java class to access your Postgres database without having to write low-level SQL queries.

For the licensing service, you're going to define two files for your Redis repository. The first file you'll write will be a Java interface that's going to be injected into any of the licensing service classes that are going to need to access Redis. This interface (`licensing-service/src/main/java/com/thoughtmechanix/licenses/repository/OrganizationRedisRepository.java`) is shown in the following listing.

Listing 8.9 `OrganizationRedisRepository` defines methods used to call Redis

```
package com.thoughtmechanix.licenses.repository;

import com.thoughtmechanix.licenses.model.Organization;

public interface OrganizationRedisRepository {
    void saveOrganization(Organization org);
    void updateOrganization(Organization org);
    void deleteOrganization(String organizationId);
    Organization findOrganization(String organizationId);
}
```

The second file is the implementation of the `OrganizationRedisRepository` interface. The implementation of the interface, the `licensing-service/src/main/java/com/thoughtmechanix/licenses/repository/OrganizationRedisRepositoryImpl.java` class, uses the `RedisTemplate` Spring bean you declared earlier in listing 8.8 to interact with the Redis server and carry out actions against the Redis server. The next listing shows this code in use.

Listing 8.10 The `OrganizationRedisRepositoryImpl` implementation

```
package com.thoughtmechanix.licenses.repository;

//Most of the imports removed for concisenss
import org.springframework.data.redis.core.HashOperations;      The @Repository
import org.springframework.data.redis.core.RedisTemplate;       annotation tells Spring
                                                                that this class is a
@Repository                                                     Repository class used
public class OrganizationRedisRepositoryImpl implements         with Spring Data.
    OrganizationRedisRepository {
    private static final String HASH_NAME="organization";

    private RedisTemplate<String, Organization> redisTemplate;
    private HashOperations hashOperations;                       The name of the hash
                                                                in your Redis server
    public OrganizationRedisRepositoryImpl(){                    where organization
        super();                                                 data is stored
    }               The HashOperations class is a set of
                    Spring helper methods for carrying out
    @Autowired      data operations on the Redis server
    private OrganizationRedisRepositoryImpl(RedisTemplate redisTemplate) {
        this.redisTemplate = redisTemplate;
    }

    @PostConstruct
    private void init() {
```

```
        hashOperations = redisTemplate.opsForHash();
    }

    @Override
    public void saveOrganization(Organization org) {
        hashOperations.put(HASH_NAME, org.getId(), org);
    }

    @Override
    public void updateOrganization(Organization org) {
        hashOperations.put(HASH_NAME, org.getId(), org);
    }

    @Override
    public void deleteOrganization(String organizationId) {
        hashOperations.delete(HASH_NAME, organizationId);
    }

    @Override
    public Organization findOrganization(String organizationId) {
       return (Organization) hashOperations.get(HASH_NAME, organizationId);
    }
}
```

> **All interactions with Redis will be with a single Organization object stored by its key.**

The `OrganizationRedisRepositoryImpl` contains all the CRUD (Create, Read, Update, Delete) logic used for storing and retrieving data from Redis. There are two key things to note from the code in listing 8.10:

- All data in Redis is stored and retrieved by a key. Because you're storing data retrieved from the organization service, organization ID is the natural choice for the key being used to store an organization record.
- The second thing to note in is that a Redis server can contain multiple hashes and data structures within it. In every operation against the Redis server, you need to tell Redis the name of the data structure you're performing the operation against. In listing 8.10, the data structure name you're using is stored in the `HASH_NAME` constant and is called "organization."

USING REDIS AND THE LICENSING SERVICE TO STORE AND READ ORGANIZATION DATA

Now that you have the code in place to perform operations against Redis, you can modify your licensing service so that every time the licensing service needs the organization data, it will check the Redis cache before calling out to the organization service. The logic for checking Redis will occur in the `licensing-service/src/main/java/com/thoughtmechanix/licenses/clients/OrganizationRestTemplateClient.java` class. The code for this class is shown in the following listing.

Listing 8.11 `OrganizationRestTemplateClient` class will implement cache logic

```
package com.thoughtmechanix.licenses.clients;

//Imports removed for conciseness
@Component
```

```
public class OrganizationRestTemplateClient {
    @Autowired
    RestTemplate restTemplate;

    @Autowired
    OrganizationRedisRepository orgRedisRepo;    ◄─┐

    private static final Logger logger =
      LoggerFactory.getLogger(OrganizationRestTemplateClient.class);

    private Organization checkRedisCache(
        String organizationId) {                  ◄─────────
        try {
    return orgRedisRepo.findOrganization(organizationId);
    }
    catch (Exception ex){
    logger.error("Error encountered while trying to
        ➥ retrieve organization {} check Redis Cache.
        ➥ Exception {}", organizationId, ex);
            return null;
    }
}
```

The OrganizationRedisRepository class is auto-wired in the OrganizationRestTemplateClient.

Trying to retrieve an Organization class with its organization ID from Redis

```
private void cacheOrganizationObject(Organization org) {
    try {
  orgRedisRepo.saveOrganization(org);
    }catch (Exception ex){
    logger.error("Unable to cache organization {} in Redis.
        ➥ Exception {}" org.getId(), ex);
    }
}

public Organization getOrganization(String organizationId){
    logger.debug("In Licensing Service
        ➥ .getOrganization: {}",
        ➥ UserContext.getCorrelationId());

    Organization org = checkRedisCache(organizationId);

    if (org!=null){                                     ◄─────
        logger.debug("I have successfully
            ➥ retrieved an organization {}
            ➥ from the redis cache: {}", organizationId, org);
        return org;
    }

    logger.debug("Unable to locate
        ➥ organization from the
        ➥ redis cache: {}.", organizationId);

    ResponseEntity<Organization> restExchange =
        restTemplate.exchange(
            "http://zuulservice/api/organization
            ➥ /v1/organizations/{organizationId}",
            HttpMethod.GET,
            null,
```

If you can't retrieve data from Redis, you'll call out the organization service to retrieve the data from the source database.

```
        Organization.class,
        organizationId);

    /*Save the record from cache*/
    org = restExchange.getBody();

    if (org!=null) {                              Saving the retrieved
      cacheOrganizationObject(org);        ◁──    object to the cache
    }

    return org;
  }
}
```

The getOrganization() method is where the call to the organization service takes place. Before you make the actual REST call, you attempt to retrieve the Organization object associated with the call from Redis using the checkRedisCache() method. If the organization object in question is not in Redis, the code will return a null value. If a null value is returned from the checkRedisCache() method, the code will invoke the organization service's REST endpoint to retrieve the desired organization record. If the organization service returns an organization, the returned organization object will be cached using the cacheOrganizationObject() method.

> **NOTE** Pay close attention to exception handling when interacting with the cache. To increase resiliency, we never let the entire call fail if we cannot communicate with the Redis server. Instead, we log the exception and let the call go out to the organization service. In this particular use case, caching is meant to help improve performance and the absence of the caching server shouldn't impact the success of the call.

With the Redis caching code in place, you should hit the licensing service (yes, you only have two services, but you have a lot of infrastructure) and see the logging messages in listing 8.10. If you were to do two back-to-back GET requests on the following licensing service endpoint, http://localhost:5555/api/licensing/v1/organizations/e254f8c-c442-4ebe-a82a-e2fc1d1ff78a/licenses/f3831f8c-c338-4ebe-a82a-e2fc1d1ff78a, you should see the following two output statements in your logs:

```
licensingservice_1    | 2016-10-26 09:10:18.455 DEBUG 28 --- [nio-8080-exec-
    1] c.t.l.c.OrganizationRestTemplateClient    : Unable to locate
    organization from the redis cache: e254f8c-c442-4ebe-a82a-e2fc1d1ff78a.
```

```
licensingservice_1    | 2016-10-26 09:10:31.602 DEBUG 28 --- [nio-8080-exec-
    2] c.t.l.c.OrganizationRestTemplateClient    : I have successfully
    retrieved an organization e254f8c-c442-4ebe-a82a-e2fc1d1ff78a from the
    redis cache: com.thoughtmechanix.licenses.model.Organization@6d20d301
```

The first line from the console shows the first time you tried to hit the licensing service endpoint for organization e254f8c-c442-4ebe-a82a-e2fc1d1ff78a. The licensing service first checked the Redis cache and couldn't find the organization record it was looking for. The code then calls the organization service to retrieve the data. The second line that was printed from the console shows that when you hit the licensing service endpoint a second time, the organization record is now cached.

8.4.2   *Defining custom channels*

Previously you built your messaging integration between the licensing and organization services to use the default `output` and `input` channels that come packaged with the `Source` and `Sink` interfaces in the Spring Cloud Stream project. However, if you want to define more than one channel for your application or you want to customize the names of your channels, you can define your own interface and expose as many input and output channels as your application needs.

To create a custom channel, call `inboundOrgChanges` in the licensing service. You can define the channel in the `licensing-service/src/main/java/com/thoughtmechanix/licenses/events/CustomChannels.java` interface, as shown in the following listing.

Listing 8.12   Defining a custom input channel for the licensing service

```
package com.thoughtmechanix.licenses.events;

import org.springframework.cloud.stream.annotation.Input;
import org.springframework.messaging.SubscribableChannel;

public interface CustomChannels {
    @Input("inboundOrgChanges")
    SubscribableChannel orgs();
}
```

> The @Input annotation is a method-level annotation that defines the name of the channel.

> Each channel exposed through the @Input annotation must return a SubscribableChannel class.

The key takeaway from listing 8.12 is that for each custom `input` channel you want to expose, you mark a method that returns a `SubscribableChannel` class with the `@Input` annotation. If you want to define output channels for publishing messages, you'd use the `@OutputChannel` above the method that will be called. In the case of an `output` channel, the defined method will return a `MessageChannel` class instead of the `SubscribableChannel` class used with the `input` channel:

```
@OutputChannel("outboundOrg")
MessageChannel outboundOrg();
```

Now that you have a custom `input` channel defined, you need to modify two more things to use it in the licensing service. First, you need to modify the licensing service to map your custom `input` channel name to your Kafka topic. The following listing shows this.

Listing 8.13   Modifying the licensing service to use your custom input channel

```
spring:
...
  cloud:
```

```
    ...
    stream:
      bindings:
        inboundOrgChanges:                          ◄────────────  Change the name of the channel
          destination: orgChangeTopic                              from input to inboundOrgChanges.
          content-type: application/json
          group: licensingGroup
```

To use your custom input channel, you need to inject the CustomChannels inter-face you defined into a class that's going to use it to process messages. For the distrib-uted caching example, I've moved the code for handling an incoming message to the following licensing-service class: licensing-service/src/main/java/com/thoughtmechanix/licenses/events/handlers/OrganizationChange Handler.java. The following listing shows the message handling code that you'll use with the inboundOrgChanges channel you defined.

Listing 8.14 Using the new custom channel in the OrganizationChangeHandler

Move the @EnableBindings out of the Application.java class and into the OrganizationChangeHandler class. This time instead of using Sink.class, use your CustomChannels class as the parameter to pass.

```
@EnableBinding(CustomChannels.class)                     ◄──────────
public class OrganizationChangeHandler {

    @StreamListener("inboundOrgChanges")                 ◄──────────
    public void loggerSink(OrganizationChangeModel orgChange) {
        .... //We will get into the rest of the code shortly
        }
    }
}
```

With the @StreamListener annotation, you passed in the name of your channel, "inboundOrgChanges", instead of using Sink.INPUT.

8.4.3   Bringing it all together: clearing the cache when a message is received

At this point you don't need to do anything with the organization service. The service is all set up to publish a message whenever an organization is added, updated, or deleted. All you have to do is build out the OrganizationChangeHandler class from listing 8.14. The following listing shows the full implementation of this class.

Listing 8.15 Processing an organization change in the licensing service

```
@EnableBinding(CustomChannels.class)
public class OrganizationChangeHandler {

    @Autowired
    private OrganizationRedisRepository
        organizationRedisRepository;

    private static final Logger logger =
        LoggerFactory.getLogger(OrganizationChangeHandler.class);
```

The OrganizationRedisRepository class that you use to interact with Redis is injected into the OrganizationChangeHandler.

```
@StreamListener("inboundOrgChanges")
public void loggerSink(OrganizationChangeModel orgChange) {
    switch(orgChange.getAction()){
        //Removed for conciseness

case "UPDATE":
  logger.debug("Received a UPDATE event
    ➡ from the organization service for
    ➡ organization id {}",
    ➡ orgChange.getOrganizationId());
  organizationRedisRepository
    .deleteOrganization(orgChange.getOrganizationId());
  break;
case "DELETE":
  logger.debug("Received a DELETE event
    ➡ from the organization service for organization id {}",
    ➡ orgChange.getOrganizationId());
  organizationRedisRepository
    .deleteOrganization(orgChange.getOrganizationId());
  break;
default:
  logger.error("Received an UNKNOWN event
    ➡ from the organization service of type {}",
    ➡ orgChange.getType());
  break;
    }
}
```

> When you receive a message, inspect the action that was taken with the data and then react accordingly.

> If the organization data is updated or deleted, evict the organization data from Redis via the OrganizationRedisRepository class.

8.5   Summary

- Asynchronous communication with messaging is a critical part of microservices architecture.

- Using messaging within your applications allows your services to scale and become more fault tolerant.

- Spring Cloud Stream simplifies the production and consumption of messages by using simple annotations and abstracting away platform-specific details of the underlying message platform.

- A Spring Cloud Stream message source is an annotated Java method that's used to publish messages to a message broker's queue.

- A Spring Cloud Stream message sink is an annotated Java method that receives messages off a message broker's queue.

- Redis is a key-value store that can be used as both a database and cache.

Distributed tracing with Spring Cloud Sleuth and Zipkin

This chapter covers

- Using Spring Cloud Sleuth to inject tracing information into service calls
- Using log aggregation to see logs for distributed transaction
- Querying via a log aggregation tool
- Using OpenZipkin to visually understand a user's transaction as it flows across multiple microservice calls
- Customizing tracing information with Spring Cloud Sleuth and Zipkin

The microservices architecture is a powerful design paradigm for breaking down complex monolithic software systems into smaller, more manageable pieces. These manageable pieces can be built and deployed independently of each other; however, this flexibility comes at a price: complexity. Because microservices are distributed by nature, trying to debug where a problem is occurring can be maddening. The distributed nature of the services means that you have to trace one or more transactions across multiple services, physical machines, and different data stores, and try to piece together what exactly is going on.

This chapter lays out several techniques and technologies for making distributed debugging possible. In this chapter, we look at the following:

- Using correlation IDs to link together transactions across multiple services
- Aggregating log data from multiple services into a single searchable source
- Visualizing the flow of a user transaction across multiple services and understanding the performance characteristics of each part of the transaction

To accomplish the three things you're going to use three different technologies:

- *Spring Cloud Sleuth* (https://cloud.spring.io/spring-cloud-sleuth/)—Spring Cloud Sleuth is a Spring Cloud project that instruments your HTTP calls with correlation IDs and provides hooks that feed the trace data it's producing into OpenZipkin. It does this by adding the filters and interacting with other Spring components to let the correlation IDs being generated pass through to all the system calls.
- *Papertrail* (https://papertrailapp.com)—Papertrail is a cloud-based service (freemium-based) that allows you to aggregate logging data from multiple sources into single searchable database. You have options for log aggregation, including on-premise, cloud-based, open source, and commercial solutions. We'll explore several of these alternatives later in the chapter
- *Zipkin* (http://zipkin.io)—Zipkin is an open source data-visualization tool that can show the flow of a transaction across multiple services. Zipkin allows you to break a transaction down into its component pieces and visually identify where there might be performance hotspots.

To begin this chapter, we start with the simplest of tracing tools, the correlation ID.

NOTE   Parts of this chapter rely on material covered in chapter 6 (specifically the material on Zuul pre-, response, and post filters). If you haven't read chapter 6 yet, I recommend that you do so before you read this chapter.

9.1   *Spring Cloud Sleuth and the correlation ID*

We first introduced the concept of correlation IDs in chapter 5 and 6. A correlation ID is a randomly generated, unique number or string that's assigned to a transaction when a transaction is initiated. As the transaction flows across multiple services, the correlation ID is propagated from one service call to another. In the context of chapter 6, you used a Zuul filter to inspect all incoming HTTP requests and inject a correlation ID if one wasn't present.

Once the correlation ID was present, you used a custom Spring HTTP filter on every one of your services to map the incoming variable to a custom `UserContext` object. With the `UserContext` object in place, you could now manually add the correlation ID to any of your log statements by making sure you appended the correlation ID to the log statement, or, with a little work, add the correlation ID directly to Spring's Mapped Diagnostic Context (MDC). You also wrote a Spring Interceptor that would ensure that all HTTP calls from a service would propagate the correlation ID by adding the correlation ID to the HTTP headers on any outbound calls.

Oh, and you had to perform Spring and Hystrix magic to make sure the thread context of the parent thread holding the correlation ID was properly propagated to Hystrix. Wow—in the end this was a lot of infrastructure that was put in place for something that you hope will only be looked at when a problem occurs (using a correlation ID to trace what's going on with a transaction).

Fortunately, Spring Cloud Sleuth manages all this code infrastructure and complexity for you. By adding Spring Cloud Sleuth to your Spring Microservices, you can

- Transparently create and inject a correlation ID into your service calls if one doesn't exist.
- Manage the propagation of the correlation ID to outbound service calls so that the correlation ID for a transaction is automatically added to outbound calls.
- Add the correlation information to Spring's MDC logging so that the generated correlation ID is automatically logged by Spring Boots default SL4J and Logback implementation.
- Optionally, publish the tracing information in the service call to the Zipkin-distributed tracing platform.

NOTE With Spring Cloud Sleuth if you use Spring Boot's logging implementation, you'll automatically get correlation IDs added to the log statements you put in your microservices.

Let's go ahead and add Spring Cloud Sleuth to your licensing and organization services.

9.1.1 *Adding Spring Cloud sleuth to licensing and organization*

To start using Spring Cloud Sleuth in your two services (licensing and organization), you need to add a single Maven dependency to the pom.xml files in both services:

```
<dependency>
  <groupId>org.springframework.cloud</groupId>
    <artifactId>spring-cloud-starter-sleuth</artifactId>
</dependency>
```

This dependency will pull in all the core libraries needed for Spring Cloud Sleuth. That's it. Once this dependency is pulled in, your service will now

1 Inspect every incoming HTTP service and determine whether or a not Spring Cloud Sleuth tracing information exists in the incoming call. If the Spring Cloud Sleuth tracing data does exist, the tracing information passed into your microservice will be captured and made available to your service for logging and processing.
2 Add Spring Cloud Sleuth tracing information to the Spring MDC so that every log statement created by your microservice will be added to the logs.
3 Inject Spring Cloud tracing information into to every outbound HTTP call and Spring messaging channel message your service makes.

9.1.2   Anatomy of a Spring Cloud Sleuth trace

If everything is set up correctly, any log statements written within your service application code will now include Spring Cloud Sleuth trace information. For example, figure 9.1 shows what the service's output would look like if you were to do an HTTP GET http://localhost:5555/api/organization/v1/organizations/e254f8c-c442-4ebe-a82a-e2fc1d1ff78a on the organization service.

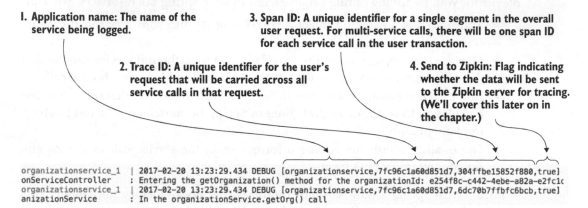

I. Application name: The name of the service being logged.

2. Trace ID: A unique identifier for the user's request that will be carried across all service calls in that request.

3. Span ID: A unique identifier for a single segment in the overall user request. For multi-service calls, there will be one span ID for each service call in the user transaction.

4. Send to Zipkin: Flag indicating whether the data will be sent to the Zipkin server for tracing. (We'll cover this later on in the chapter.)

```
organizationservice_1  | 2017-02-20 13:23:29.434 DEBUG [organizationservice,7fc96c1a60d851d7,304ffbe15852f880,true]
onServiceController    : Entering the getOrganization() method for the organizationId: e254f8c-c442-4ebe-a82a-e2fc1c
organizationservice_1  | 2017-02-20 13:23:29.434 DEBUG [organizationservice,7fc96c1a60d851d7,6dc70b7ffbfc6bcb,true]
anizationService       : In the organizationService.getOrg() call
```

Figure 9.1   Spring Cloud Sleuth adds four pieces of tracing information to each log entry written by your service. This data helps tie together service calls for a user's request.

Spring Cloud Sleuth will add four pieces of information to each log entry. These four pieces (numbered to correspond with the numbers in figure 9.1) are

1   *Application name of the service*—This is going to be the name of the application the log entry is being made in. By default, Spring Cloud Sleuth uses the name of the application (spring.application.name) as the name that gets written in the trace.

2   *Trace ID*—Trace ID is the equivalent term for correlation ID. It's a unique number that represents an entire transaction.

3   *Span ID*—A span ID is a unique ID that represents part of the overall transaction. Each service participating within the transaction will have its own span ID. Span IDs are particularly relevant when you integrate with Zipkin to visualize your transactions.

4   *Whether trace data was sent to Zipkin*—In high-volume services, the amount of trace data generated can be overwhelming and not add a significant amount of value. Spring Cloud Sleuth lets you determine when and how to send a transaction to Zipkin. The true/false indicator at the end of the Spring Cloud Sleuth tracing block tells you whether the tracing information was sent to Zipkin.

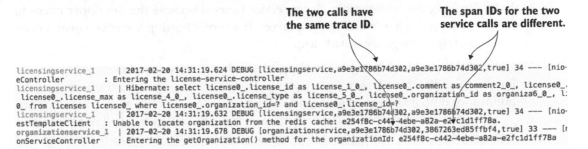

The two calls have the same trace ID.

The span IDs for the two service calls are different.

```
licensingservice_1    | 2017-02-20 14:31:19.624 DEBUG [licensingservice,a9e3e1786b74d302,a9e3e1786b74d302,true] 34 --- [nio-
eController          : Entering the license-service-controller
licensingservice_1    | Hibernate: select license0_.license_id as license_1_0_, license0_.comment as comment2_0_, license0_.
 license0_.license_max as license_4_0_, license0_.license_type as license_5_0_, license0_.organization_id as organiza6_0_, l:
0_ from licenses license0_ where license0_.organization_id=? and license0_.license_id=?
licensingservice_1    | 2017-02-20 14:31:19.632 DEBUG [licensingservice,a9e3e1786b74d302,a9e3e1786b74d302,true] 34 --- [nio-
estTemplateClient    : Unable to locate organization from the redis cache: e254f8c-c442-4ebe-a82a-e2fc1d1ff78a.
organizationservice_1 | 2017-02-20 14:31:19.678 DEBUG [organizationservice,a9e3e1786b74d302,3867263ed85ffbf4,true] 33 --- [r
onServiceController   : Entering the getOrganization() method for the organizationId: e254f8c-c442-4ebe-a82a-e2fc1d1ff78a
```

Figure 9.2   With multiple services involved in a transaction, you can see that they share the same trace ID.

Up to now, we've only looked at the logging data produced by a single service call. Let's look at what happens when you make a call to the licensing service at GET http://localhost:5555/api/licensing/v1/organizations/e254f8c-c442-4ebe-a82a-e2fc1d1ff78a/licenses/f3831f8c-c338-4ebe-a82a-e2fc1d1ff78a. Remember, the licensing service also has to call out to the organization service. Figure 9.2 shows the logging output from the two service calls.

By looking at figure 9.2, you can see that both the licensing and organization services have the same trace ID a9e3e1786b74d302. However, the licensing service has a span ID of a9e3e1786b74d302 (the same value as the transaction ID). The organization service has a span ID of 3867263ed85ffbf4.

By adding nothing more than a few POM dependencies, you've replaced all the correlation ID infrastructure that you built out in chapters 5 and 6. Personally, nothing makes me happier in this world then replacing complex, infrastructure-style code with someone else's code.

9.2   Log aggregation and Spring Cloud Sleuth

In a large-scale microservice environment (especially in the cloud), logging data is a critical tool for debugging problems. However, because the functionality for a microservice-based application is decomposed into small, granular services and you can have multiple service instances for a single service type, trying to tie to log data from multiple services to resolve a user's problem can be extremely difficult. Developers trying to debug a problem across multiple servers often have to try the following:

- Log into multiple servers to inspect the logs present on each server. This is an extremely laborious task, especially if the services in question have different transaction volumes that cause logs to rollover at different rates.
- Write home-grown query scripts that will attempt to parse the logs and identify the relevant log entries. Because every query might be different, you often end up with a large proliferation of custom scripts for querying data from your logs.

- Prolong the recovery of a down service process because the developer needs to back up the logs residing on a server. If a server hosting a service crashes completely, the logs are usually lost.

Each of the problems listed are real problems that I've run into. Debugging a problem across distributed servers is ugly work and often significantly increases the amount of time it takes to identify and resolve an issue.

A much better approach is to stream, real-time, all the logs from all of your service instances to a centralized aggregation point where the log data can be indexed and made searchable. Figure 9.3 shows at a conceptual level how this "unified" logging architecture would work.

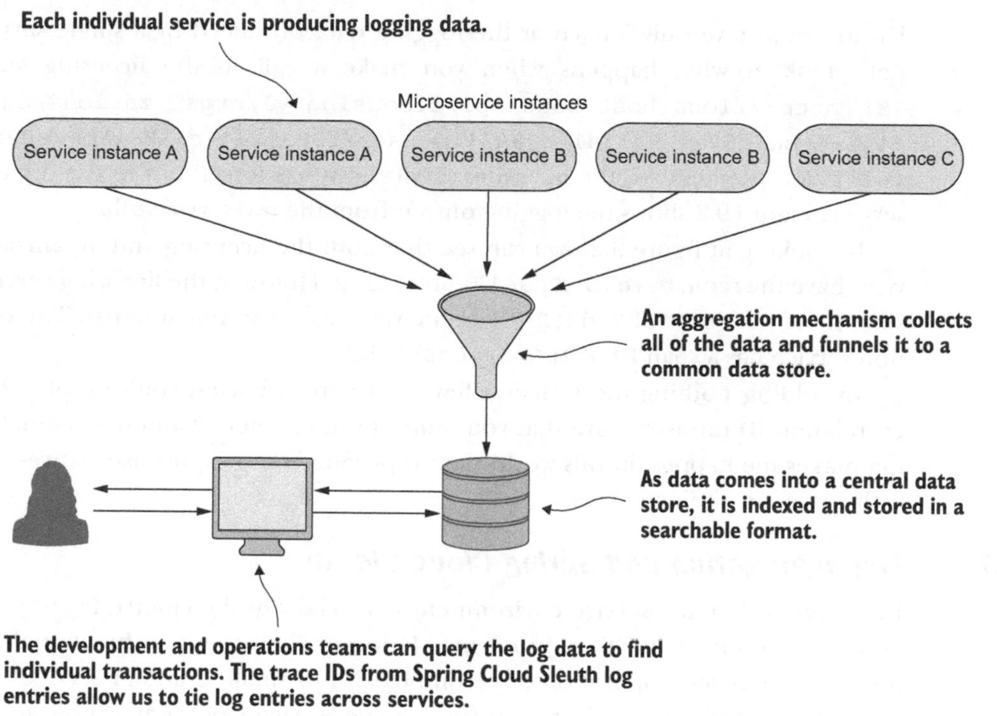

Each individual service is producing logging data.

Microservice instances

Service instance A   Service instance A   Service instance B   Service instance B   Service instance C

An aggregation mechanism collects all of the data and funnels it to a common data store.

As data comes into a central data store, it is indexed and stored in a searchable format.

The development and operations teams can query the log data to find individual transactions. The trace IDs from Spring Cloud Sleuth log entries allow us to tie log entries across services.

Figure 9.3   The combination of aggregated logs and a unique transaction ID across service log entries makes debugging distributed transactions more manageable.

Fortunately, there are multiple open source and commercial products that can help you implement the previously described logging architecture. Also, multiple implementation models exist that will allow you to choose between an on-premise, locally managed solution or a cloud-based solution. Table 9.1 summarizes several of the choices available for logging infrastructure.

Table 9.1 Options for Log Aggregation Solutions for Use with Spring Boot

Product Name	Implementation Models	Notes
Elasticsearch, Logstash, Kibana (ELK)	Open source Commercial Typically implemented on premise	http://elastic.co General purpose search engine Can do log-aggregation through the (ELK-stack) Requires the most hands-on support
Graylog	Open source Commercial On-premise	http://graylog.org Open-source platform that's designed to be installed on premise
Splunk	Commercial only On-premise and cloud-based	http://splunk.com Oldest and most comprehensive of the log management and aggregation tools Originally an on-premise solution, but have since offered a cloud offering
Sumo Logic	Freemium Commercial Cloud-based	http://sumologic.com Freemium/tiered pricing model Runs only as a cloud service Requires a corporate work account to signup (no Gmail or Yahoo accounts)
Papertrail	Freemium Commercial Cloud-based	http://papertrailapp.com Freemium/tiered pricing model Runs only as a cloud service

With all these choices, it might be difficult to choose which one is the best. Every organization is going to be different and have different needs.

For the purposes of this chapter, we're going to look at Papertrail as an example of how to integrate Spring Cloud Sleuth-backed logs into a unified logging platform. I chose Papertrail because

1 It has a freemium model that lets you sign up for a free-tiered account.
2 It's incredibly easy to set up, especially with container runtimes like Docker.
3 It's cloud-based. While I believe a good logging infrastructure is critical for a microservices application, I don't believe most organizations have the time or technical talent to properly set up and manage a logging platform.

9.2.1   *A Spring Cloud Sleuth/Papertrail implementation in action*

In figure 9.3 we saw a general unified logging architecture. Let's now see how the same architecture can be implemented with Spring Cloud Sleuth and Papertrail.

To set up Papertrail to work with your environment, we have to take the following actions:

1 Create a Papertrail account and configure a Papertrail syslog connector.
2 Define a Logspout Docker container (https://github.com/gliderlabs/logspout) to capture standard out from all the Docker containers.

3 Test the implementation by issuing queries based on the correlation ID from Spring Cloud Sleuth.

Figure 9.4 shows the end state for your implementation and how Spring Cloud Sleuth and Papertrail fit together for your solution.

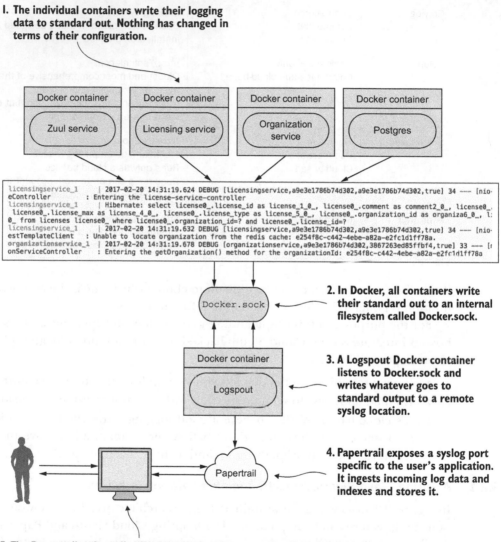

1. The individual containers write their logging data to standard out. Nothing has changed in terms of their configuration.

2. In Docker, all containers write their standard out to an internal filesystem called Docker.sock.

3. A Logspout Docker container listens to Docker.sock and writes whatever goes to standard output to a remote syslog location.

4. Papertrail exposes a syslog port specific to the user's application. It ingests incoming log data and indexes and stores it.

5. The Papertrail web application lets the user issue queries. Here you can enter a Spring Cloud Sleuth trace ID and see all of the log entries from the different services that contain that trace ID.

Figure 9.4   Using native Docker capabilities, logspot, and Papertrail allows you to quickly implement a unified logging architecture.

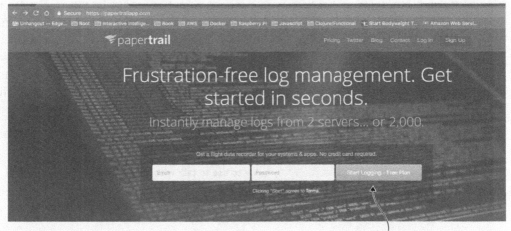

Click here to set up a
logging connection.

Figure 9.5 To begin, create an account on Papertrail.

9.2.2 Create a Papertrail account and configure a syslog connector

You'll begin by setting up a Papertrail. To get started, go to https://papertrailapp.com
and click on the green "Start Logging – Free Plan" button. Figure 9.5 shows this.

Papertrail doesn't require a significant amount of information to get started; only
a valid email address. Once you've filled out the account information, you'll be
presented with a screen to set up your first system to log data from. Figure 9.6 shows
this screen.

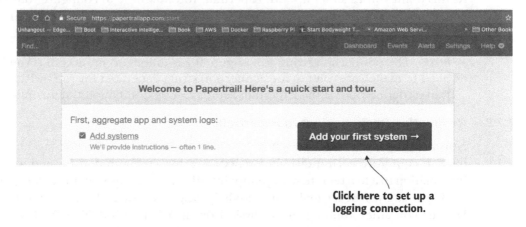

Click here to set up a
logging connection.

Figure 9.6 Next choose how you're going to send log data to Papertrail.

By default, Papertrail allows you to send log data to it via a Syslog call (https://en.wikipedia.org/wiki/Syslog). Syslog is a log messaging format that originated in UNIX. Syslog allows for the sending of log messages over both TCP and UDP. Papertrail will automatically define a Syslog port that you can use to write log messages to. For the purposes of this discussion, you'll use this default port. Figure 9.7 shows you the Syslog connect string that's automatically generated when you click on the "Add your first system" button shown in figure 9.6.

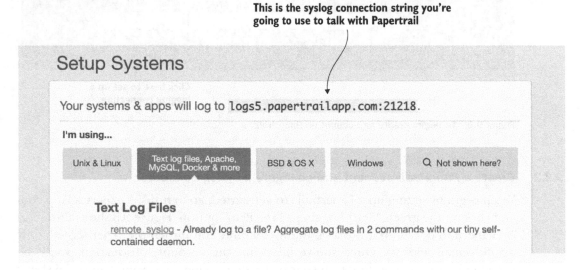

Figure 9.7   Papertrail uses Syslog as one of the mechanisms for sending data to it.

At this point you're all set up with Papertrail. You now have to configure your Docker environment to capture output from each of the containers running your services to the remote syslog endpoint defined in figure 9.7.

> **NOTE**   The connection string from figure 9.7 is unique to my account. You'll need to make sure you use the connection string generated for you by Papertrail or define one via the Papertrail Settings > Log destinations menu option.

9.2.3   *Redirecting Docker output to Papertrail*

Normally, if you're running each of your services in their own virtual machine, you'll have to configure each individual service's logging configuration to send its logging information to a to a remote syslog endpoint (like the one exposed through Papertrail).

Fortunately, Docker makes it incredibly easy to capture all the output from any Docker container running on a physical or virtual machine. The Docker daemon communicates with all of the Docker containers it's managing through a Unix socket called docker.sock. Any container running on the server where Docker is running can connect to the docker.sock and receive all the messages generated by all of the other containers running on that server. In the simplest terms, docker.sock is like a pipe that your containers can plug into and capture the overall activities going on within the Docker runtime environment on the virtual server the Docker daemon is running on.

You're going to use a "Dockerized" piece of software called Logspout (https:// github.com/gliderlabs/logspout) that will listen to the docker.sock socket and then capture any standard out messages generated in Docker runtime and redirect the output to a remote syslog (Papertrail). To set up your Logspout container, you have to add a single entry to the docker-compose.yml file you use to fire up all of the Docker containers used for the code examples in this chapter. The docker/common/docker-compose.yml file you need to modify should have the following entry added to it:

```
logspout:
    image: gliderlabs/logspout
    command: syslog://logs5.papertrailapp.com:21218
    volumes:
      - /var/run/docker.sock:/var/run/docker.sock
```

NOTE In the previous code snippet, you'll need to replace the value in the "command" attribute with the value supplied to you from Papertrail. If you use the previous Logspout snippet, your Logspout container will happily write your log entries to my Papertrail account.

Now when you fire up your Docker environment in this chapter, all data sent to a container's standard output will be sent to Papertrail. You can see this for yourself by logging into your Papertrail account after you've started chapter 9's Docker examples and clicking on the Events button in the top right part of your screen.

Figure 9.8 shows an example of what the data sent to Papertrail looks like.

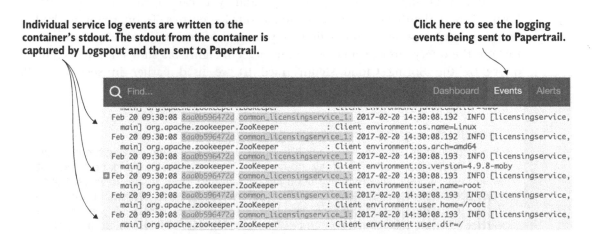

Individual service log events are written to the container's stdout. The stdout from the container is captured by Logspout and then sent to Papertrail.

Click here to see the logging events being sent to Papertrail.

Figure 9.8   With the Logspout Docker container defined, data written to each container's standard out will be sent to Papertrail.

Why not use the Docker logging driver?

Docker 1.6 and above do allow you to define alternative logging drivers to write the stdout/stderr messages written from each container. One of the logging drivers is a syslog driver that can be used to write the messages to a remote syslog listener.

Why did I choose Logspout instead of using the standard Docker log driver? The main reason is flexibility. Logspout offers features for customizing what logging data gets sent to your log aggregation platform. The features Logspout offers include

- *The ability to send log data to multiple endpoints at once.* Many companies will want to send their log data to a log aggregation platform, and will also want security monitoring tools that will monitor the produced logs for sensitive data.
- *A centralized location for filtering which containers are going to send their log data.* With the Docker driver, you need to manually set the log driver for each container in your docker-compose.yml file. Logspout lets you define filters to specific containers and even specific string patterns in a centralized configuration.
- *Custom HTTP routes that let applications write log information via specific HTTP endpoints.* This feature allows you to do things like write specific log messages to a specific downstream log aggregation platform. For example, you might have general log messages from stdout/stderr go to Papertrail, where you might want to send specific application audit information to an in-house Elasticsearch server.
- *Integration with protocols beyond syslog.* Logspout allows you to send messages via UDP and TCP protocols. Logspout also has third-party modules that can integrate the stdout/stderr from Docker into Elasticsearch.

9.2.4   *Searching for Spring Cloud Sleuth trace IDs in Papertrail*

Now that your logs are flowing to Papertrail, you can really start appreciating Spring Cloud Sleuth adding trace IDs to all your log entries. To query for all the log entries related to a single transaction, all you need to do is take a trace ID and query for it in the query box of Papertrail's event screen. Figure 9.9 shows how to execute a query by the Spring Cloud sleuth trace ID we used earlier in section 9.1.2: `a9e3e1786b74d302.`.

Consolidate logging and praise for the mundane

Don't underestimate how important it is to have a consolidated logging architecture and a service correlation strategy thought out. It seems like a mundane task, but while I was writing this chapter, I used log aggregation tools similar to Papertrail to track down a race condition between three different services for a project I was working on. It turned out that the race condition has been there for over a year, but the service with the race condition had been functioning fine until we added a bit more load and one other actor in the mix to cause the problem.

We found the issue only after spending 1.5 weeks doing log queries and walking through the trace output of dozens of unique scenarios. We wouldn't have found the problem without the aggregated logging platform that had been put in place. This experience reaffirmed several things:

1 *Make sure you define and implement your logging strategies early on in your service development*—Implementing logging infrastructure is tedious, sometimes difficult, and time-consuming once a project is well underway.

2 *Logging is a critical piece of microservice infrastructure*—Think long and hard before you implement your own logging solution or even try to implement an on-premise logging solution. Cloud-based logging platforms are worth the money that's spent on them.

3 *Learn your logging tools*—Almost every logging platform will have a query language for querying the consolidated logs. Logs are an incredible source of information and metrics. They're essentially another type of database, and the time you spend learning to query will pay huge dividends.

The logs show that the licensing service and then the organization service were called as part of this single transaction.

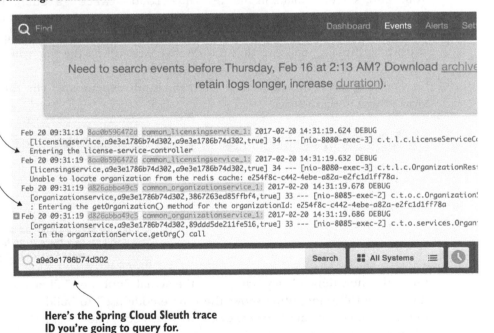

Here's the Spring Cloud Sleuth trace ID you're going to query for.

Figure 9.9   The trace ID allows you to filter all log entries related to that single transaction.

9.2.5   *Adding the correlation ID to the HTTP response with Zuul*

If you inspect the HTTP response back from any service call made with Spring Cloud Sleuth, you'll see that the trace ID used in the call is never returned in the HTTP response headers. If you inspect the documentation for Spring Cloud Sleuth, you'll see that the Spring Cloud Sleuth team believes that returning any of the tracing data can be a potential security issue (though they don't explicitly list their reasons why they believe this.)

However, I've found that the returning of a correlation or tracing ID in the HTTP response is invaluable when debugging a problem. Spring Cloud Sleuth does allow you to "decorate" the HTTP response information with its tracing and span IDs. However, the process to do this involves writing three classes and injecting two custom Spring beans. If you'd like to take this approach, you can see it in the Spring Cloud Sleuth documentation (http://cloud.spring.io/spring-cloud-static/spring-cloud-sleuth/1.0.12.RELEASE/). A much simpler solution is to write a Zuul "POST" filter that will inject the trace ID in the HTTP response.

In chapter 6 when we introduced the Zuul API gateway, we saw how to build a Zuul "POST" response filter to add the correlation ID you generated for use in your services to the HTTP response returned by the caller. You're now going to modify that filter to add the Spring Cloud Sleuth header.

To set up your Zuul response filter, you need to add a single JAR dependencies to your Zuul server's pom.xml file: `spring-cloud-starter-sleuth`. The `spring-cloud-starter-sleuth` dependency will be used to tell Spring Cloud Sleuth that you want Zuul to participate in a Spring Cloud trace. Later in the chapter, when we introduce Zipkin, you'll see that the Zuul service will be the first call in any service invocation.

For chapter 9, this file can be found in zuulsvr/pom.xml. The following listing shows these dependencies.

> **Listing 9.1   Adding Spring Cloud Sleuth to Zuul**

```
<dependency>
    <groupId>org.springframework.cloud</groupId>
    <artifactId>spring-cloud-starter-sleuth</artifactId>    ⟵
</dependency>
```

Adding spring-cloud-starter-sleuth to Zuul will cause a trace ID to be generated for every service being called in Zuul

Once this new dependency is in place, the actual Zuul "post" filter is trivial to implement. The following listing shows the source code used to build the Zuul filter. The file is located in `zuulsvr/src/main/java/com/thoughtmechanix/zuulsvr/filters/ResponseFilter.java`.

Listing 9.2 Adding the Spring Cloud Sleuth trace ID via a Zuul POST filter

```
package com.thoughtmechanix.zuulsvr.filters;

//Rest of annotations removed for conciseness
import org.springframework.cloud.sleuth.Tracer;

@Component
public class ResponseFilter extends ZuulFilter{
private static final int      FILTER_ORDER=1;
private static final boolean  SHOULD_FILTER=true;
private static final Logger logger =
    ➥ LoggerFactory.getLogger(ResponseFilter.class);

@Autowired
Tracer tracer;

@Override
public String filterType() {return "post";}

@Override
public int filterOrder() {return FILTER_ORDER;}

@Override
public boolean shouldFilter() {return SHOULD_FILTER;}

@Override
public Object run() {
  RequestContext ctx = RequestContext.getCurrentContext();
  ctx.getResponse()
    ➥ .addHeader("tmx-correlation-id",
      ➥ tracer.getCurrentSpan().traceIdString());

  return null;
}}
```

> The Tracer class is the entry point to access trace and span ID information.

> You're going to add a new HTTP Response header called tmx-correlation-ID to hold the Spring Cloud Sleuth trace ID.

Because Zuul is now Spring Cloud Sleuth-enabled, you can access tracing information from within your `ResponseFilter` by autowiring in the `Tracer` class into the `ResponseFilter`. The `Tracer` class allows you to access information about the current Spring Cloud Sleuth trace being executed. The `tracer.getCurrentSpan()` `.traceIdString()` method allows you to retrieve as a String the current trace ID for the transaction underway.

It's trivial to add the trace ID to the outgoing HTTP response passing back through Zuul. This is done by calling

```
RequestContext ctx = RequestContext.getCurrentContext();
ctx.getResponse().addHeader("tmx-correlation-id",
    ➥ tracer.getCurrentSpan().traceIdString());
```

With this code now in place, if you invoke an EagleEye microservice through your Zuul gateway, you should get a HTTP response back called `tmx-correlation-id`.

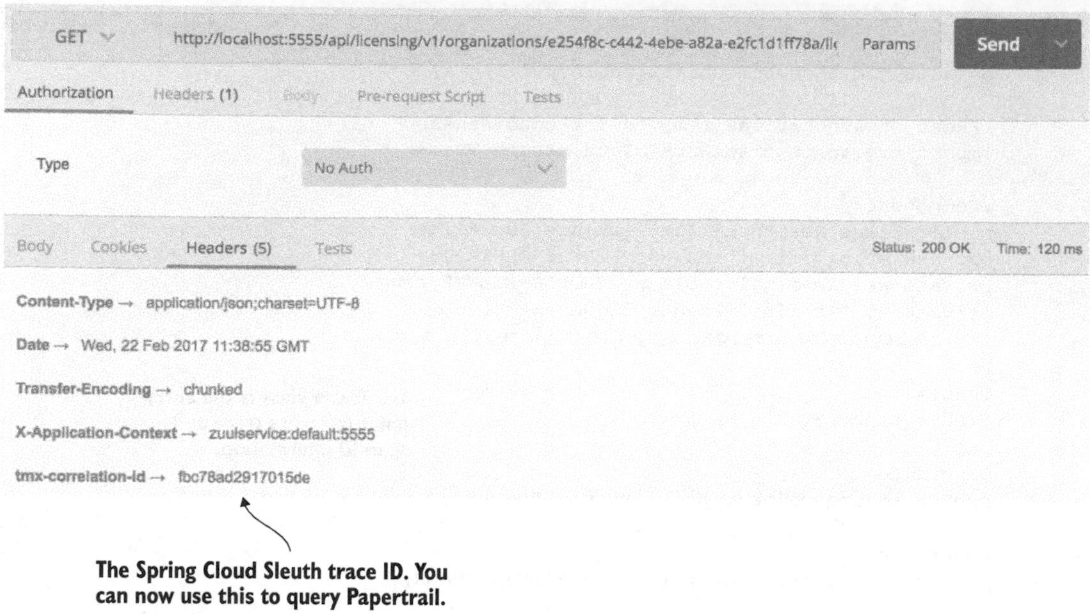

The Spring Cloud Sleuth trace ID. You can now use this to query Papertrail.

Figure 9.10   With the Spring Cloud Sleuth trace ID returned, you can easily query Papertrail for the logs.

Figure 9.10 shows the results of a call to GET `http://localhost:5555/api/licensing/v1/organizations/e254f8c-c442-4ebe-a82a-e2fc1d1ff78a/licenses/f3831f8c-c338-4ebe-a82a-e2fc1d1ff78a`.

9.3   *Distributed tracing with Open Zipkin*

Having a unified logging platform with correlation IDs is a powerful debugging tool. However, for the rest of the chapter we're going to move away from tracing log entries and instead look at how to visualize the flow of transactions as they move across different microservices. A clean, concise picture can be work more than a million log entries.

Distributed tracing involves providing a visual picture of how a transaction flows across your different microservices. Distributed tracing tools will also give a rough approximation of individual microservice response times. However, distributed tracing tools shouldn't be confused with full-blown Application Performance Management (APM) packages. These packages can provide out-of-the-box, low-level performance data on the actual code within your service and can also provider performance data beyond response time, such as memory, CPU utilization, and I/O utilization.

This is where Spring Cloud Sleuth and the OpenZipkin (also referred to as Zipkin) project shine. Zipkin (http://zipkin.io/) is a distributed tracing platform that allows you to trace transactions across multiple service invocations. Zipkin allows you to graphically see the amount of time a transaction takes and breaks down the time spent in each microservice involved in the call. Zipkin is an invaluable tool for identifying performance issues in a microservices architecture.

Setting up Spring Cloud Sleuth and Zipkin involves four activities:

- Adding Spring Cloud Sleuth and Zipkin JAR files to the services that capture trace data
- Configuring a Spring property in each service to point to the Zipkin server that will collect the trace data
- Installing and configuring a Zipkin server to collect the data
- Defining the sampling strategy each client will use to send tracing information to Zipkin

9.3.1 Setting up the Spring Cloud Sleuth and Zipkin dependencies

Up to now you've included two sets of Maven dependencies to your Zuul, licensing, and organization services. These JAR files were the `spring-cloud-starter-sleuth` and the `spring-cloud-sleuth-core` dependencies. The `spring-cloud-starter-sleuth` dependencies are used to include the basic Spring Cloud Sleuth libraries needed to enable Spring Cloud Sleuth within a service. The `spring-cloud-sleuth-core` dependencies are used whenever you have to programmatically interact with Spring Cloud Sleuth (which you'll do again later in the chapter).

To integrate with Zipkin, you need to add a second Maven dependency called `spring-cloud-sleuth-zipkin`. The following listing shows the Maven entries that should be present in the Zuul, licensing, and organization services once the `spring-cloud-sleuth-zipkin` dependency is added.

> **Listing 9.3   Client-side Spring Cloud Sleuth and Zipkin dependences**

```
<dependency>
    <groupId>org.springframework.cloud</groupId>
    <artifactId>spring-cloud-starter-sleuth</artifactId>
</dependency>
<dependency>
    <groupId>org.springframework.cloud</groupId>
    <artifactId>spring-cloud-sleuth-zipkin</artifactId>
</dependency>
```

9.3.2 Configuring the services to point to Zipkin

With the JAR files in place, you need to configure each service that wants to communicate with Zipkin. You do this by setting a Spring property that defines the URL used to communicate with Zipkin. The property that needs to be set is the `spring.zipkin.baseUrl` property. This property is set in each service's application.yml properties file.

> **NOTE** The `spring.zipkin.baseUrl` can also be externalized as a property in Spring Cloud Config.

In the application.yml file for each service, the value is set to `http://localhost:9411`. However, at runtime I override this value using the ZIPKIN_URI (http://zipkin:9411) variable passed on each services Docker configuration (docker/common/docker-compose.yml) file.

Zipkin, RabbitMQ, and Kafka

Zipkin does have the ability to send its tracing data to a Zipkin server via RabbitMQ or Kafka. From a functionality perspective, there's no difference in Zipkin behavior if you use HTTP, RabbitMQ, or Kafka. With the HTTP tracing, Zipkin uses an asynchronous thread to send performance data. The main advantage to using RabbitMQ or Kafka to collect your tracing data is that if your Zipkin server is down, any tracing messages sent to Zipkin will be "enqueued" until Zipkin can pick up the data.

The configuration of Spring Cloud Sleuth to send data to Zipkin via RabbitMQ and Kafka is covered in the Spring Cloud Sleuth documentation, so we won't cover it here in any further detail.

9.3.3   Installing and configuring a Zipkin server

To use Zipkin, you first need to set up a Spring Boot project the way you've done multiple times throughout the book. (In the code for the chapter, this is call zipkinsvr.) You then need to add two JAR dependencies to the zipkinsvr/pom.xml file. These two jar dependences are shown in the following listing.

Listing 9.4   JAR dependencies needed for Zipkin service

```
<dependency>
    <groupId>io.zipkin.java</groupId>
    <artifactId>zipkin-server</artifactId>          This dependency contains the core
</dependency>                                        classes for setting up the Zipkin server.
<dependency>
    <groupId>io.zipkin.java</groupId>               This dependency contains the
    <artifactId>zipkin-autoconfigure-ui</artifactId>   core for classes for running the
</dependency>                                        UI part of the Zipkin server.
```

@EnableZipkinServer vs. @EnableZipkinStreamServer: which annotation?

One thing to notice about the JAR dependencies above is that they're not Spring-Cloud-based dependencies. While Zipkin is a Spring-Boot-based project, the @EnableZipkinServer is not a Spring Cloud annotation. It's an annotation that's part of the Zipkin project. This often confuses people who are new to the Spring Cloud Sleuth and Zipkin, because the Spring Cloud team did write the @EnableZipkin-StreamServer annotation as part of Spring Cloud Sleuth. The @EnableZipkin-StreamServer annotation simplifies the use of Zipkin with RabbitMQ and Kafka.

I chose to use the @EnableZipkinServer because of its simplicity in setup for this chapter. With the @EnableZipkinStream server you need to set up and configure the services being traced and the Zipkin server to publish/listen to RabbitMQ or Kafka for tracing data. The advantage of the `@EnableZipkinStreamServer` annotation is that you can continue to collect trace data even if the Zipkin server is unavailable. This is because the trace messages will accumulate the trace data on a message queue until the Zipkin server is available for processing the records. If you use the `@EnableZipkinServer` annotation and the Zipkin server is unavailable, the trace data that would have been sent by the service(s) to Zipkin will be lost.

After the Jar dependencies are defined, you now need to add the `@EnableZipkin Server` annotation to your Zipkin services bootstrap class. This class is located in `zipkinsvr/src/main/java/com/thoughtmechanix/zipkinsvr/ZipkinServer Application.java`. The following listing shows the code for the bootstrap class.

Listing 9.5   Building your Zipkin servers bootstrap class

```
package com.thoughtmechanix.zipkinsvr;

import org.springframework.boot.SpringApplication;
import org.springframework.boot.autoconfigure.SpringBootApplication;
import zipkin.server.EnableZipkinServer;

@SpringBootApplication
@EnableZipkinServer
public class ZipkinServerApplication {
public static void main(String[] args) {
  SpringApplication.run(ZipkinServerApplication.class, args);
  }
}
```

The @EnableZipkinServer allows you to quickly start Zipkin as a Spring Boot project.

The key thing to note in this listing is the use of the `@EnableZipkinServer` annotation. This annotation enables you to start this Spring Boot service as a Zipkin server. At this point, you can build, compile, and start the Zipkin server as one of the Docker containers for the chapter.

Little configuration is needed to run a Zipkin server. One of the only things you're going to have to configure when you run Zipkin is the back end data store that Zipkin will use to store the tracing data from your services. Zipkin supports four different back end data stores. These data stores are

1 In-memory data
2 MySQL: http://mysql.com
3 Cassandra: http://cassandra.apache.org
4 Elasticsearch: http://elastic.co

By default, Zipkin uses an in-memory data store for storing tracing data. The Zipkin team recommends against using the in-memory database in a production system. The in-memory database can hold a limited amount of data and the data is lost when the Zipkin server is shut down or lost.

NOTE   For the purposes of this book, you'll use Zipkin with an in-memory data store. Configuring the individual data stores used in Zipkin is outside of the scope of this book, but if you're interested in the topic, you can find more information at the Zipkin GitHub repository (https://github.com/openzipkin /zipkin/tree/master/zipkin-server).

9.3.4   Setting tracing levels

At this point you have the clients configured to talk to a Zipkin server and you have the server configured and ready to be run. You need to do one more thing before you start using Zipkin. You need to define how often each service should write data to Zipkin.

By default, Zipkin will only write 10% of all transactions to the Zipkin server. The transaction sampling can be controlled by setting a Spring property on each of the services sending data to Zipkin. This property is called `spring.sleuth.sampler .percentage`. The property takes a value between 0 and 1:

- A value of 0 means Spring Cloud Sleuth won't send Zipkin any transactions.
- A value of .5 means Spring Cloud Sleuth will send 50% of all transactions.

For our purposes, you're going to send trace information for all services. To do this, you can set the value of `spring.sleuth.sampler.percentage` or you can replace the default `Sampler` class used in Spring Cloud Sleuth with the `AlwaysSampler`. The `AlwaysSampler` can be injected as a Spring Bean into an application. For example, the licensing service has the `AlwaysSampler` defined as a Spring Bean in its `licensing-service/src/main/java/com/thoughtmechanix/licenses/Application.java` class as

```
@Bean
public Sampler defaultSampler() { return new AlwaysSampler();}
```

The Zuul, licensing, and organization services all have the `AlwaysSampler` defined in them so that in this chapter all transactions will be traced with Zipkin.

9.3.5   Using Zipkin to trace transactions

Let's start this section with a scenario. Imagine you're one of the developers on the EagleEye application and you're on-call this week. You get a support ticket from a customer who's complaining that one of the screens in the EagleEye application is running slow. You have a suspicion that the licensing service being used by the screen is running slow. But why and where? The licensing service relies on the organization service and both services make calls to different databases. Which service is the poor performer? Also, you know that these services are constantly being modified, so someone might have added a new service call into the mix. Understanding all the services that participate in the user's transaction and their individual performance times is critical to supporting a distributed architecture such as a microservice architecture.

You'll begin by using Zipkin to watch two transactions from your organization service as they're traced by the Zipkin service. The organization service is a simple service that only makes a call to a single database. What you're going to do is use POSTMAN to send two calls to the organization service (`GET http://localhost:5555/api/organization/v1/organizations/e254f8c-c442-4ebe-a82a-e2fc1d1ff78a`). The organization service calls will flow through a Zuul API gateway before the calls get directed downstream to an organization service instance.

After you've made two calls to the organization service, go to http://localhost:9411 and see what Zipkin has captured for trace results. Select the "organization service" from the dropdown box on the far upper left of the screen and then press the Find traces button. Figure 9.11 shows the Zipkin query screen after you've taken these actions.

Now if you look at the screenshot in figure 9.11, you'll see that Zipkin captured two transactions. Each of the transactions is broken down into one or more spans. In Zipkin, a span represents a specific service or call in which timing information is being captured. Each of the transactions in figure 9.11 has three spans captured in it: two spans in the Zuul gateway, and then a span for the organization service. Remember, the Zuul gateway doesn't blindly forward an HTTP call. It receives the incoming HTTP call, terminates the incoming call, and then builds a new call out to the targeted service (in this case, the organization service). This termination of the original call is how Zuul can add pre-, response, and post filters to each call entering the gateway. It's also why we see two spans in the Zuul service.

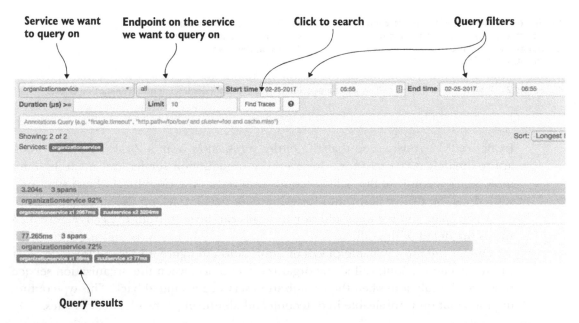

Figure 9.11   The Zipkin query screen lets you select the service you want to trace on, along with some basic query filters.

The two calls to the organization service through Zuul took 3.204 seconds and 77.2365 milliseconds respectively. Because you queried on the organization service calls (and not the Zuul gateway calls), you can see that the organization service took 92% and 72% of the total amount of time of the transaction time.

Let's dig into the details of the longest running call (3.204 seconds). You can see more detail by clicking on the transaction and drilling into the details. Figure 9.12 shows the details after you've clicked to drill down into further details.

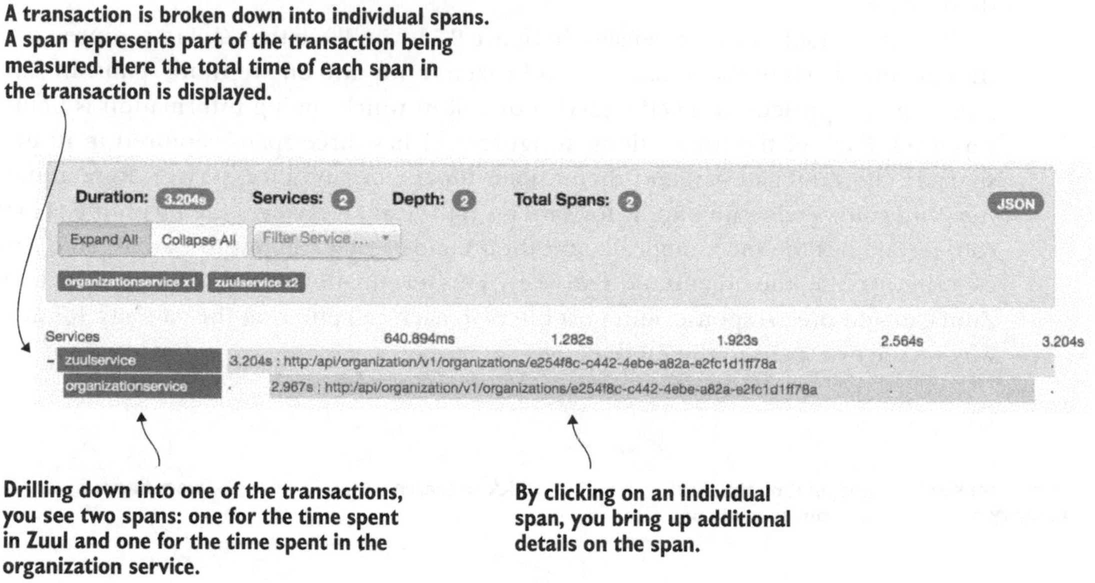

A transaction is broken down into individual spans. A span represents part of the transaction being measured. Here the total time of each span in the transaction is displayed.

Drilling down into one of the transactions, you see two spans: one for the time spent in Zuul and one for the time spent in the organization service.

By clicking on an individual span, you bring up additional details on the span.

Figure 9.12   Zipkin allows you to drill down and see the amount of time each span in a transaction takes.

In figure 9.12 you can see that the entire transaction from a Zuul perspective took approximately 3.204 seconds. However, the organization service call made by Zuul took 2.967 seconds of the 3.204 seconds involved in the overall call. Each span presented can be drilled down into for even more detail. Click on the `organization-service` span and see what additional details can be seen from the call. Figure 9.13 shows the detail of this call.

One of the most valuable pieces of information in figure 9.13 is the breakdown of when the client (Zuul) called the organization service, when the organization service received the call, and when the organization service responded back. This type of timing information is invaluable in detecting and identifying network latency issues.

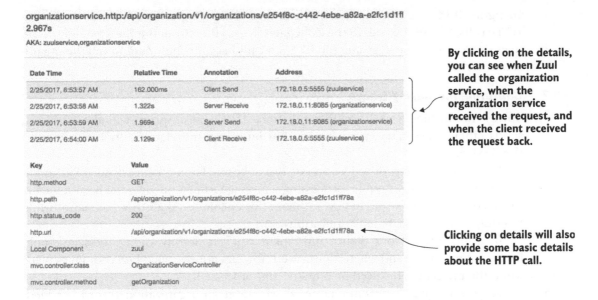

organizationservice.http:/api/organization/v1/organizations/e254f8c-c442-4ebe-a82a-e2fc1d1ff
2.967s

AKA: zuulservice,organizationservice

Date Time	Relative Time	Annotation	Address
2/25/2017, 6:53:57 AM	162.000ms	Client Send	172.18.0.5:5555 (zuulservice)
2/25/2017, 6:53:58 AM	1.322s	Server Receive	172.18.0.11:8085 (organizationservice)
2/25/2017, 6:53:59 AM	1.969s	Server Send	172.18.0.11:8085 (organizationservice)
2/25/2017, 6:54:00 AM	3.129s	Client Receive	172.18.0.5:5555 (zuulservice)

By clicking on the details, you can see when Zuul called the organization service, when the organization service received the request, and when the client received the request back.

Key	Value
http.method	GET
http.path	/api/organization/v1/organizations/e254f8c-c442-4ebe-a82a-e2fc1d1ff78a
http.status_code	200
http.url	/api/organization/v1/organizations/e254f8c-c442-4ebe-a82a-e2fc1d1ff78a
Local Component	zuul
mvc.controller.class	OrganizationServiceController
mvc.controller.method	getOrganization

Clicking on details will also provide some basic details about the HTTP call.

Figure 9.13   Clicking on an individual span gives further details on call timing and the details of the HTTP call.

9.3.6   Visualizing a more complex transaction

What if you want to understand exactly what service dependencies exist between service calls? You can call the licensing service through Zuul and then query Zipkin for licensing service traces. You can do this with a GET call to the licensing services `http://localhost:5555/api/licensing/v1/organizations/e254f8c-c442-4ebe-a82a-e2fc1d1ff78a/licenses/f3831f8c-c338-4ebe-a82a-e2fc1d1ff78a` endpoint.

Figure 9.14 shows the detailed trace of the call to the licensing service.

Figure 9.14   Viewing the details of a trace of how the licensing service call flows from Zuul to the licensing service and then through to the organization service

In figure 9.14, you can see that the call to the licensing service involves 4 discrete HTTP calls. You see the call to the Zuul gateway and then from the Zuul gateway to the licensing service. The licensing service then calls back through Zuul to call the organization service.

9.3.7   *Capturing messaging traces*

Spring Cloud Sleuth and Zipkin don't trace HTTP calls. Spring Cloud Sleuth also sends Zipkin trace data on any inbound or outbound message channel registered in the service.

Messaging can introduce its own performance and latency issues inside of an application. A service might not be processing a message from a queue quickly enough. Or there could be a network latency problem. I've encountered all these scenarios while building microservice-based applications.

By using Spring Cloud Sleuth and Zipkin, you can identify when a message is published from a queue and when it's received. You can also see what behavior takes place when the message is received on a queue and processed.

As you'll remember from chapter 8, whenever an organization record is added, updated, or deleted, a Kafka message is produced and published via Spring Cloud Stream. The licensing service receives the message and updates a Redis key-value store it's using to cache data.

Now you'll go ahead and delete an organization record and watch the transaction be traced by Spring Cloud Sleuth and Zipkin. You can issue a `DELETE http://localhost:5555/api/organization/v1/organizations/e254f8c-c442-4ebe-a82a-e2fc1d1ff78a` via POSTMAN to the organization service.

Remember, earlier in the chapter we saw how to add the trace ID as an HTTP response header. You added a new HTTP response header called `tmx-correlation-id`. In my call, I had the `tmx-correlation-id` returned on my call with a value of `5e14cae0d90dc8d4`. You can search Zipkin for this specific trace ID by entering the trace ID returned by your call via the search box in the upper-right hand corner of the Zipkin query screen. Figure 9.15 shows where you can enter the trace ID.

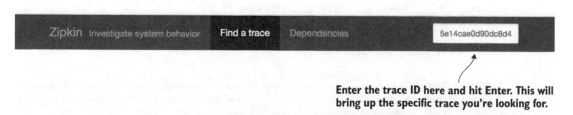

Enter the trace ID here and hit Enter. This will bring up the specific trace you're looking for.

Figure 9.15   With the trace ID returned in the HTTP Response `tmx-correlation-id` field you can easily find the transaction you're looking for.

With the trace ID in hand you can query Zipkin for the specific transaction and can see the publication of a delete message to your output message change. This message channel, `output`, is used to publish to a Kafka topic call `orgChangeTopic`. Figure 9.16 shows the `output` message channel and how it appears in the Zipkin trace.

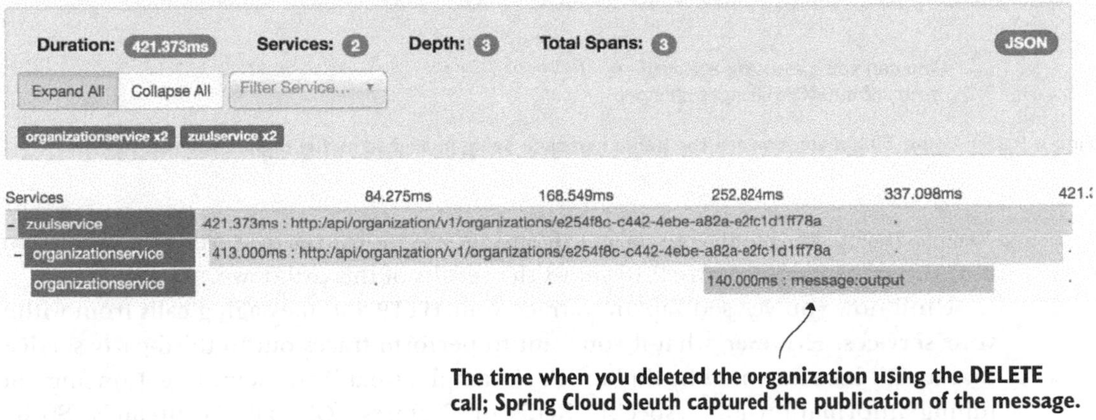

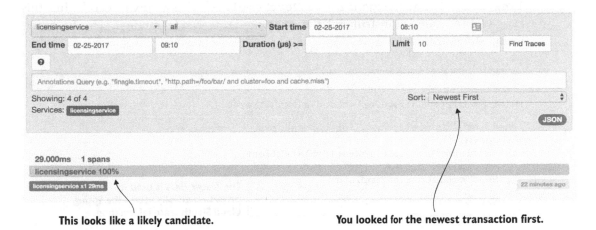

The time when you deleted the organization using the DELETE call; Spring Cloud Sleuth captured the publication of the message.

Figure 9.16   Spring Cloud Sleuth will automatically trace the publication and receipt of messages on Spring message channels.

You can see the licensing service receive the message by querying Zipkin and looking for the received message. Unfortunately, Spring Cloud Sleuth doesn't propagate the trace ID of a published message to the consumer(s) of that message. Instead, it generates a new trace ID. However, you can query Zipkin server for any license service transactions and order them by newest message. Figure 9.17 shows the results of this query.

This looks like a likely candidate.

You looked for the newest transaction first.

Figure 9.17   You're looking for the licensing service invocation where a Kafka message is received.

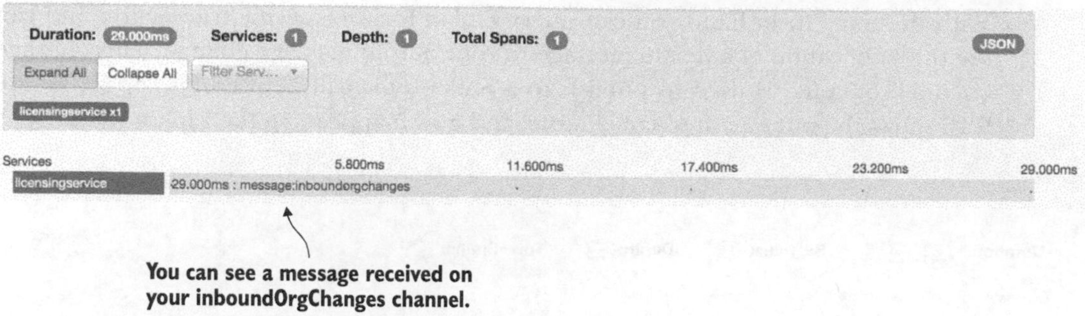

You can see a message received on
your inboundOrgChanges channel.

Figure 9.18   Using Zipkin you can see the Kafka message being published by the organization service.

Now that you've found your target licensing service transaction, you can drill down into the transaction. Figure 9.18 shows the results of this drilldown.

Until now you've used Zipkin to trace your HTTP and messaging calls from within your services. However, what if you want to perform traces out to third-party services that aren't instrumented by Zipkin? For example, what if you want to get tracing and timing information for a specific Redis or Postgres SQL call? Fortunately, Spring Cloud Sleuth and Zipkin allow you to add custom spans to your transaction so that you can trace the execution time associated with these third-party calls.

9.3.8   *Adding custom spans*

Adding a custom span is incredibly easy to do in Zipkin. You can start by adding a custom span to your licensing service so that you can trace how long it takes to pull data out of Redis. Then you're going to add a custom span to the organization service to see how long it takes to retrieve data from your organization database.

To add a custom span to the licensing service's call to Redis, you're going to instrument the `licensing-service/src/main/java/com/thoughtmechanix/licenses/clients/OrganizationRestTemplateClient.java` class. In this class you're going to instrument the `checkRedisCache()` method. The following listing shows this code.

Listing 9.6   Instrumenting the call to read licensing data from Redis

```
import org.springframework.cloud.sleuth.Tracer;

//Rest of imports removed for conciseness
@Component
public class OrganizationRestTemplateClient {
    @Autowired
    RestTemplate restTemplate;

    @Autowired
    Tracer tracer;

    @Autowired
    OrganizationRedisRepository orgRedisRepo;
```

The Tracer class is used to
programmatically access the Spring
Cloud Sleuth trace information.

```
     private static final Logger logger =
       ➡ LoggerFactory
          .getLogger(OrganizationRestTemplateClient.class);

   private Organization checkRedisCache(String organizationId) {
     Span newSpan = tracer.createSpan("readLicensingDataFromRedis");    ⟵
     try {
       return orgRedisRepo.findOrganization(organizationId);
     }                                                          For your custom span,
     catch (Exception ex){                                      create a new span called
       logger.error("Error encountered while                  "readLicensingDataFromRedis".
             ➡ trying to retrieve organization
             ➡ {} check Redis Cache.  Exception {}",
             ➡ organizationId, ex);
       return null;                                     You can add tag information to the span. In
     }                                                  this class you provide the name of the service
     finally {                                          that's going to be captured by Zipkin
       newSpan.tag("peer.service", "redis");                                        ⟵
       newSpan.logEvent(
           org.springframework.cloud.sleuth.Span.CLIENT_RECV);        ⟵
       tracer.close(newSpan);                    ⟵
     }                                                            Log an event to tell
   }                                                              Spring Cloud Sleuth
                                                                  that it should capture
      //Rest of class removed for conciseness                    the time when the
}                                                                call is complete.
```

Close the span out with a finally block.

Close out the trace. If you don't call the close() method, you'll get error messages in the logs indicating that a span has been left open

The code in listing 9.6 creates a custom span called `readLicensingDataFromRedis`. Now you'll also add a custom span, called `getOrgDbCall`, to the organization service to monitor how long it takes to retrieve organization data from the Postgres database. The trace for organization service database calls can be seen in the `organization-service/src/main/java/com/thoughtmechanix/organization/services/OrganizationService.java` class. The method containing the custom trace is the `getOrg()` method call.

The following listing shows the source code from the organization service's `getOrg()` method.

Listing 9.7 The instrumented `getOrg()` method

```
package com.thoughtmechanix.organization.services;

//Removed the imports for conciseness
@Service
public class OrganizationService {
  @Autowired
  private OrganizationRepository orgRepository;

  @Autowired
  private Tracer tracer;
```

```
   @Autowired
   SimpleSourceBean simpleSourceBean;

   private static final Logger logger =
     ➡ LoggerFactory.getLogger(OrganizationService.class);

    public Organization getOrg (String organizationId) {
   Span newSpan = tracer.createSpan("getOrgDBCall");

   logger.debug("In the organizationService.getOrg() call");
   try {
     return orgRepository.findById(organizationId);
   }finally{
     newSpan.tag("peer.service", "postgres");
     newSpan
       .logEvent(
          org.springframework.cloud.sleuth.Span.CLIENT_RECV);
     tracer.close(newSpan);
   }
   }


     //Removed the code for conciseness
   }
```

With these two custom spans in place, restart the services and then hit the GET
`http://localhost:5555/api/licensing/v1/organizations/e254f8c-c442`
`-4ebe-a82a-e2fc1d1ff78a/licenses/f3831f8c-c338-4ebe-a82a-e2fc1d1ff78a`
endpoint. If we you look at the transaction in Zipkin, you should see the addition of
the two additional spans. Figure 9.19 shows the additional custom spans added when
you call the licensing service endpoint to retrieve licensing information.

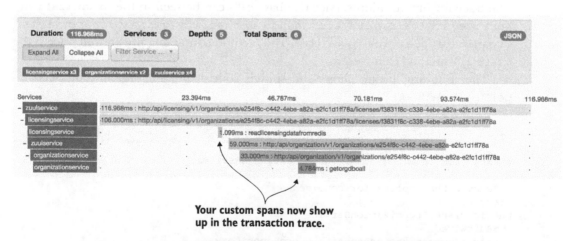

Your custom spans now show
up in the transaction trace.

Figure 9.19   With the custom spans defined, they'll now show up in the transaction trace.

From figure 9.19 you can now see additional tracing and timing information related to your Redis and database lookups. You can break out that the read call to Redis took 1.099 milliseconds. Since the call didn't find an item in the Redis cache, the SQL call to the Postgres database took 4.784 milliseconds.

9.4 Summary

- Spring Cloud Sleuth allows you to seamlessly add tracing information (correlation ID) to your microservice calls.
- Correlation IDs can be used to link log entries across multiple services. They allow you to see the behavior of a transaction across all the services involved in a single transaction.
- While correlation IDs are powerful, you need to partner this concept with a log aggregation platform that will allow you to ingest logs from multiple sources and then search and query their contents.
- While multiple on-premise log aggregation platforms exist, cloud-based services allow you to manage your logs without having to have extensive infrastructure in place. They also allow you to easily scale as your application logging volume grows.
- You can integrate Docker containers with a log aggregation platform to capture all the logging data being written to the containers stdout/stderr. In this chapter, you integrated your Docker containers with Logspout and an online cloud logging provider, Papertrail, to capture and query your logs.
- While a unified logging platform is important, the ability to visually trace a transaction through its microservices is also a valuable tool.
- Zipkin allows you to see the dependencies that exist between services when a call to a service is made.
- Spring Cloud Sleuth integrates with Zipkin. Zipkin allows you to graphically see the flow of your transactions and understand the performance characteristics of each microservice involved in a user's transaction.
- Spring Cloud Sleuth will automatically capture trace data for an HTTP call and inbound/outbound message channel used within a Spring Cloud Sleuth enabled service.
- Spring Cloud Sleuth maps each of the service call to the concept of a span. Zipkin allows you to see the performance of a span.
- Spring Cloud Sleuth and Zipkin also allow you to define your own custom spans so that you can understand the performance of non-Spring-based resources (a database server such as Postgres or Redis).

10

Deploying your microservices

This chapter covers

- Understanding why the DevOps movement is critical to microservices
- Configuring the core Amazon infrastructure used by EagleEye services
- Manually deploying EagleEye services to Amazon
- Designing a build and deployment pipeline for your services
- Moving from continuous integration to continuous deployment
- Treating your infrastructure as code
- Building the immutable server
- Testing in deployment
- Deploying your application to the cloud

We're at the end of the book, but not the end of our microservices journey. While most of this book has focused on designing, building, and operationalizing Spring-based microservices using the Spring Cloud technology, we haven't yet touched on how to build and deploy microservices. Creating a build and deployment pipeline might seem like a mundane task, but in reality it's one of the most important pieces of your microservices architecture.

Why? Remember, one of the key advantages of a microservices architecture is that microservices are small units of code that can be quickly built, modified, and deployed to production independently of one another. The small size of the service means that new features (and critical bug fixes) can be delivered with a high degree of velocity. Velocity is the key word here because velocity implies that little to no friction exists between making a new feature or fixing a bug and getting your service deployed. Lead times for deployment should be minutes, not days.

To accomplish this, the mechanism that you use to build and deploy your code needs to be

- *Automated*—When you build your code, there should be no human intervention in the build and deployment process, particularly in the lower environments. The process of building the software, provisioning a machine image, and then deploying the service should be automated and should be initiated by the act of committing code to the source repository.

- *Repeatable*—The process you use to build and deploy your software should be repeatable so that the same thing happens every time a build and deploy kicks off. Variability in your process is often the source of subtle bugs that are difficult to track down and resolve.

- *Complete*—The outcome of your deployed artifact should be a complete virtual machine or container image (Docker) that contains the "complete" run-time environment for the service. This is an important shift in the way you think about your infrastructure. The provisioning of your machine images needs to be completely automated via scripts and kept under source control with the service source code.

   In a microservice environment, this responsibility usually shifts from an operations team to the development team owning the service. Remember, one of the core tenants of microservice development is pushing complete operational responsibility for the service down to the developers.

- *Immutable*—Once the machine image containing your service is built, the run-time configuration of the image should not be touched or changed after the image has been deployed. If changes need to be made, the configuration needs to happen in the scripts kept under source control and the service and infrastructure need to go through the build process again.

   Runtime configuration changes (garbage collection settings, Spring profile being used) should be passed as environment variables to the image while application configuration should be kept separate from the container (Spring Cloud Config).

Building a robust and generalized build deployment pipeline is a significant amount of work and is often specifically designed toward the runtime environment your services are going to run. It often involves a specialized team of DevOps (developer operations) engineers whose sole job is to generalize the build process so that each team can build their microservices without having to reinvent the entire build process for themselves. Unfortunately, Spring is a development framework and doesn't offer a significant amount of capabilities for implementing a build and deployment pipeline.

For this chapter, we're going to see how to implement a build and deployment pipeline using a number of non-Spring tools. You're going to take the suite of microservices you've been building for this book and do the following:

1 Integrate the Maven build scripts you've been using into a continuous integration/deployment cloud-tool called Travis CI

2 Build immutable Docker images for each service and push those images to a centralized repository

3 Deploy the entire suite of microservices to Amazon's Cloud using Amazon's EC2 Container Service (ECS)

4 Run platform tests that will test that the service is functioning properly

I want to start our discussion with the end goal in mind: a deployed set of services to AWS Elastic Container Service (ECS). Before we get into all the details of how you're going to implement a build/deployment pipeline, let's walk through how the EagleEye services are going to look running in Amazon's cloud. Then we'll discuss how to manually deploy the EagleEye services to the AWS cloud. Once that's done, we will automate the entire process.

10.1   *EagleEye: setting up your core infrastructure in the cloud*

Throughout all the code examples in this book, you've run all of your applications inside a single virtual machine image with each individual service running as a Docker container. You're going to change that now by separating your database server (PostgreSQL) and caching server (Redis) away from Docker into Amazon's cloud. All the other services will remain running as Docker containers running inside a single-node Amazon ECS cluster. Figure 10.1 shows the deployment of the EagleEye services to the Amazon cloud.

Let's walk through figure 10.1 and dive into more detail:

1 All your EagleEye services (minus the database and the Redis cluster) are going to be deployed as Docker containers running inside of a single-node ECS cluster. ECS configures and sets up all the servers needed to run a Docker cluster. ECS also can monitor the health of containers running in Docker and restart services if the service crashes.

2 With the deployment to the Amazon cloud, you're going to move away from using your own PostgreSQL database and Redis server and instead use the Amazon RDS and Amazon ElastiCache services. You could continue to run the Postgres and Redis datastores in Docker, but I wanted to highlight how easy it is

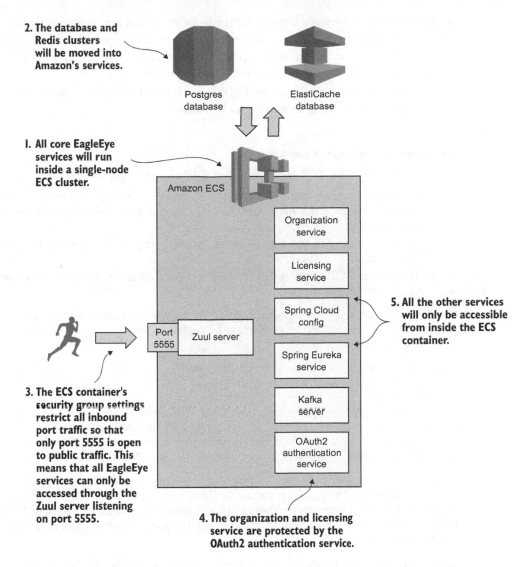

2. The database and Redis clusters will be moved into Amazon's services.

Postgres database

ElastiCache database

1. All core EagleEye services will run inside a single-node ECS cluster.

Amazon ECS

Organization service

Licensing service

Spring Cloud config

5. All the other services will only be accessible from inside the ECS container.

Port 5555 | Zuul server

Spring Eureka service

Kafka server

OAuth2 authentication service

3. The ECS container's security group settings restrict all inbound port traffic so that only port 5555 is open to public traffic. This means that all EagleEye services can only be accessed through the Zuul server listening on port 5555.

4. The organization and licensing service are protected by the OAuth2 authentication service.

Figure 10.1 By using Docker, all your services can be deployed to a cloud provider such as Amazon ECS.

to move from infrastructure that's owned and managed by you to infrastructure managed completely by the cloud provider (in this case, Amazon). In a real-world deployment you're more often than not going to deploy your database infrastructure to virtual machines before you would Docker containers.

3 Unlike your desktop deployment, you want all traffic for the server to go through your Zuul API gateway. You're going to use an Amazon security group to only allow port 5555 on the deployed ECS cluster to be accessible to the world.

4 You'll still use Spring's OAuth2 server to protect your services. Before the organization and licensing services can be accessed, the user will need to authenticate with your authentication services (see chapter 7 for details on this) and present a valid OAuth2 token on every service call.

5 All your servers, including your Kafka server, won't be publicly accessible to the outside world via their exposed Docker ports.

Some prerequisites for working

To set up your Amazon infrastructure, you're going to need the following:

1 Your own Amazon Web Services (AWS) account. You should have a basic understanding of the AWS console and the concepts behind working in the environment.

2 A web browser. For the manual setup, you're going to set up everything from the console.

3 The Amazon ECS command-line client (https://github.com/aws/amazon-ecs-cli) to do a deployment.

If you don't have any experience with using Amazon's Web Services, I'd set up an AWS account and install the tools in the list. I'd also spend time familiarizing yourself with the platform.

If you're completely new to AWS, I highly recommend you pick up a copy of Michael and Andreas Wittig's book *Amazon Web Services in Action* (Manning, 2015). The first chapter of the book (https://www.manning.com/books/amazon-web-services-in-action#downloads) is available for download and includes a well-written tutorial at the end of the chapter on how to sign up and configure your AWS account. *Amazon Web Services in Action* is a well-written and comprehensive book on AWS. Even though I've been working with the AWS environment for years, I still find it a useful resource.

Finally, in this chapter I've tried as much as possible to use the free-tier services offered by Amazon. The only place where I couldn't do this is when setting up the ECS cluster. I used a t2.large server that costs approximately .10 cents per hour to run. Make sure that you shut down your services after you're done if you don't want to incur significant costs.

NOTE: There's no guarantee that the Amazon resources (Postgres, Redis, and ECS) that I'm using in this chapter will be available if you want to run this code yourself. If you're going to run the code from this chapter, you need to set up your own GitHub repository (for your application configuration), your own Travis CI account, Docker Hub (for your Docker images), and Amazon account, and then modify your application configuration to point to your account and credentials.

10.1.1 *Creating the PostgreSQL database using Amazon RDS*

Before we begin this section, you need to set up and configure your Amazon AWS account. Once this is done, your first task is to create the PostgreSQL database that you're going to use for your EagleEye services. To do this you're going to log in into the Amazon AWS console (https://aws.amazon.com/console/) and do the following:

1 When you first log into the console you'll be presented with a list of Amazon web services. Locate the link called RDS. Click on the link and this will take you to the RDS dashboard.

2 On the dashboard, you'll find a big button that says "Launch a DB Instance." Click on it.

3 Amazon RDS supports different database engines. You should see a list of databases. Select PostgreSQL and click the "Select" button. This will launch the database creation wizard.

The first thing the Amazon database creation wizard will ask you is whether this is a production database or a dev/test database. You're going to create a dev/test database using the free tier. Figure 10.2 shows this screen.

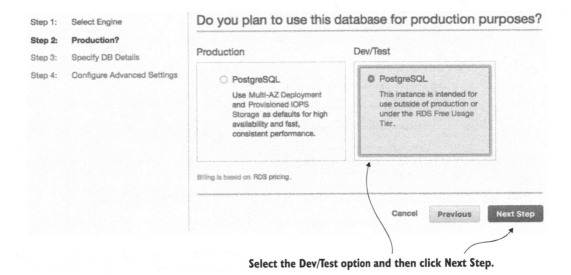

Select the Dev/Test option and then click Next Step.

Figure 10.2   Selecting whether the database is going to be a production database or a test database

Next, you're going to set up basic information about your PostgreSQL database and also set the master user ID and password you're going to use to log into the database. Figure 10.3 shows this screen.

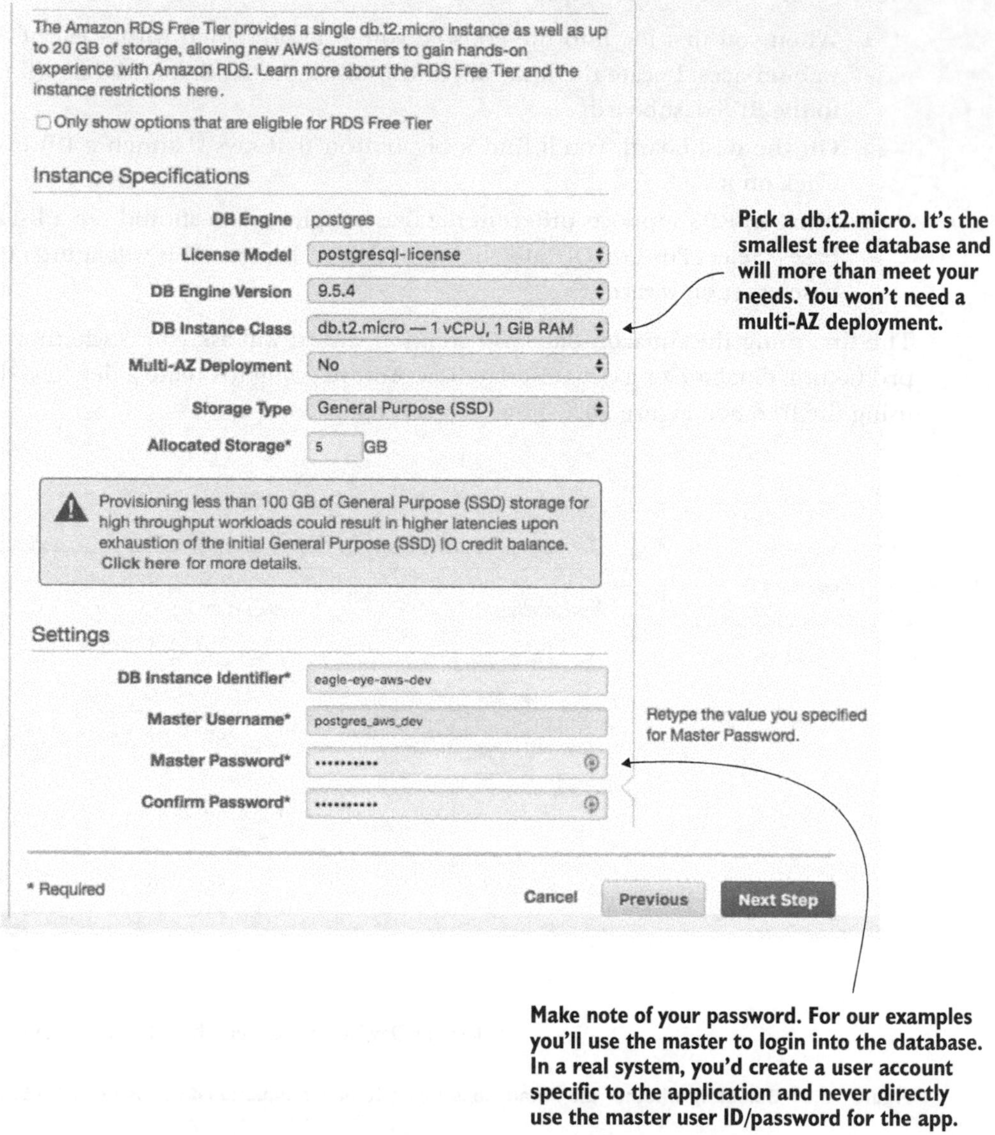

The Amazon RDS Free Tier provides a single db.t2.micro instance as well as up to 20 GB of storage, allowing new AWS customers to gain hands-on experience with Amazon RDS. Learn more about the RDS Free Tier and the instance restrictions here.

☐ Only show options that are eligible for RDS Free Tier

Instance Specifications

DB Engine   postgres
License Model   postgresql-license
DB Engine Version   9.5.4
DB Instance Class   db.t2.micro — 1 vCPU, 1 GiB RAM
Multi-AZ Deployment   No
Storage Type   General Purpose (SSD)
Allocated Storage*   5   GB

Pick a db.t2.micro. It's the smallest free database and will more than meet your needs. You won't need a multi-AZ deployment.

⚠ Provisioning less than 100 GB of General Purpose (SSD) storage for high throughput workloads could result in higher latencies upon exhaustion of the initial General Purpose (SSD) IO credit balance. Click here for more details.

Settings

DB Instance Identifier*   eagle-eye-aws-dev
Master Username*   postgres_aws_dev
Master Password*   ••••••••••
Confirm Password*   ••••••••••

Retype the value you specified for Master Password.

* Required   Cancel   Previous   Next Step

Make note of your password. For our examples you'll use the master to login into the database. In a real system, you'd create a user account specific to the application and never directly use the master user ID/password for the app.

Figure 10.3   Setting up the basic database configuration

The last and final step of the wizard is to set up the database security groups, port information, and database backup information. Figure 10.4 shows the contents of this screen.

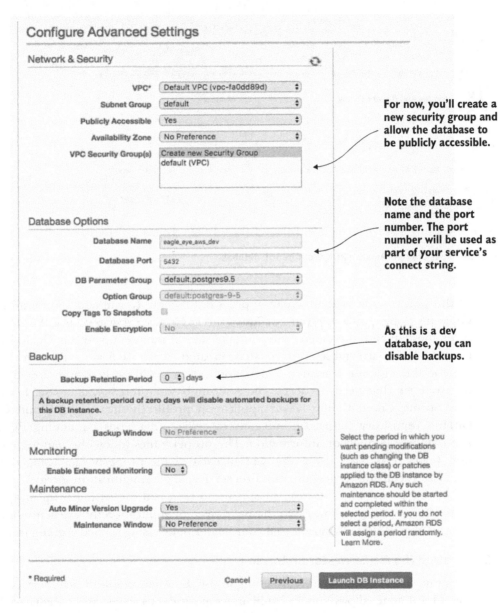

Figure 10.4 Setting up the security group, port, and backup options for the RDS database

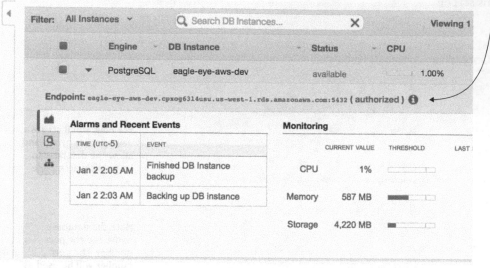

Figure 10.5   Your created Amazon RDS/PostgreSQL database

At this point, -your database creation process will begin (it can take several minutes). Once it's done, you'll need to configure the Eagle Eye services to use the database. After the database is created (this will take several minutes), you'll navigate back to the RDS dashboard and see your database created. Figure 10.5 shows this screen.

For this chapter, I created a new application profile called `aws-dev` for each microservice that needs to access the Amazon-base PostgreSQL database. I added a new Spring Cloud Config server application profile in the Spring Cloud Config GitHub repository (https://github.com/carnellj/config-repo) containing the Amazon database connection information. The property files follow the naming convention (`service-name`)`-aws-dev.yml` in each of the property files using the new database (licensing service, organization service, and authentication service).

At this point your database is ready to go (not bad for setting it up in approximately five clicks). Let's move to the next piece of application infrastructure and see how to create the Redis cluster that your EagleEye licensing service is going to use.

10.1.2 Creating the Redis cluster in Amazon

To set up the Redis cluster, you're going to use the Amazon ElastiCache service. Amazon ElastiCache allows you to build in-memory data caches using Redis or Memcached (https://memcached.org/). For the EagleEye services, you're going to move the Redis server you were running in Docker to ElastiCache.

To begin, navigate back to the AWS Console's main page (click the orange cube on the upper left-hand side of the page) and click the ElastiCache link.

From the ElastiCache console, select the Redis link (left-hand side of the screen), and then hit the blue Create button at the top of the screen. This will bring up the ElastiCache/Redis creation wizard.

Figure 10.6 shows the Redis creation screen.

Figure 10.6 With a few clicks you can set up a Redis cluster whose infrastructure is managed by Amazon.

Go ahead and hit the create button once you've filled in all your data. Amazon will begin the Redis cluster creation process (this will take several minutes). Amazon will build a single-node Redis server running on the smallest Amazon server instance available. Once you hit the button you'll see your Redis cluster being created. Once the cluster is created, you can click on the name of the cluster and it will bring you to a

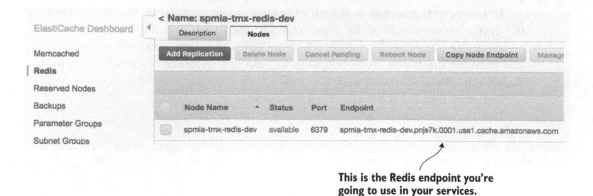

This is the Redis endpoint you're going to use in your services.

Figure 10.7   **The Redis endpoint is the key piece of information your services need to connect to Redis.**

detailed screen showing the endpoint used in the cluster. Figure 10.7 shows the details of the Redis clustered after it has been created.

The licensing service is the only one of your services to use Redis, so make sure that if you deploy the code examples in this chapter to your own Amazon instance, you modify the licensing service's Spring Cloud Config files appropriately.

10.1.3   *Creating an ECS cluster*

The last and final step before you deploy the EagleEye services is to set up an Amazon ECS cluster. Setting up an Amazon ECS cluster provisions the Amazon machines that are going to host your Docker containers. To do this you're going to again go to the Amazon AWS console. From there you're going to click on the Amazon EC2 Container Service link.

This brings you to the main EC2 Container service page, where you should see a "Getting Started" button.

Click on the "Start" button. This will bring you to the "Select options to Configure" screen shown in figure 10.8.

Uncheck the two checkboxes on the screen and click the cancel button. ECS offers a wizard for setting up an ECS container based on a set of predefined templates. You're not going to use this wizard. Once you cancel out of the ECS set-up wizard, you should see the "Clusters" tab on the ECS home page. Figure 10.9 shows this screen. Hit the "Create Cluster" button to begin the process of creating an ECS cluster.

Now you'll see a screen called "Create Cluster" that has three major sections. The first section is going to define the basic cluster information. Here you're going to enter the

1   Name of your ECS cluster.
2   Size of the Amazon EC2 virtual machine you're going to run the cluster in

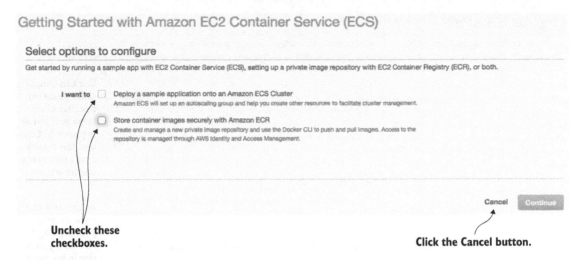

Uncheck these checkboxes.   **Click the Cancel button.**

Figure 10.8   ECS offers a wizard to bootstrap a new service container. You're not going to use it.

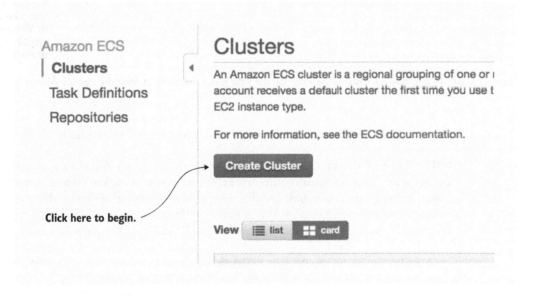

Figure 10.9   Starting the process of creating an ECS cluster

3   Number of instances you're going to run in your cluster.
4   Amount of Elastic Block Storage (EBS) disk space you're going to allocate to each node in the cluster

Create Cluster

When you run tasks using Amazon ECS, you place them on a cluster, which is a logical grouping of EC2 instances. This wizard will gu
will name your cluster, and then configure the container instances that your tasks can be placed on, the security group for your contai
your container instances so that they can make calls to the AWS APIs on your behalf.

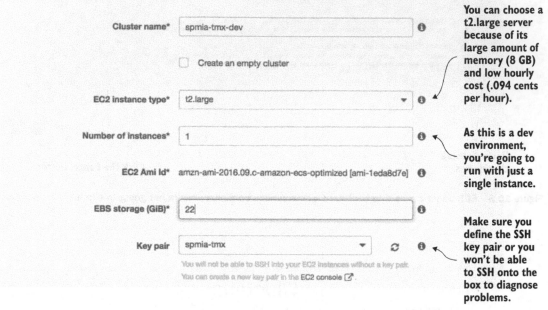

Cluster name*   spmia-tmx-dev   ⓘ

☐ Create an empty cluster

EC2 instance type*   t2.large   ▼   ⓘ ◄   **You can choose a t2.large server because of its large amount of memory (8 GB) and low hourly cost (.094 cents per hour).**

Number of instances*   1   ⓘ ◄   **As this is a dev environment, you're going to run with just a single instance.**

EC2 Ami Id*   amzn-ami-2016.09.c-amazon-ecs-optimized [ami-1eda8d7e]   ⓘ

EBS storage (GiB)*   22   ⓘ

Key pair   spmia-tmx   ▼   ⟳   ⓘ ◄   **Make sure you define the SSH key pair or you won't be able to SSH onto the box to diagnose problems.**

You will not be able to SSH into your EC2 instances without a key pair.
You can create a new key pair in the EC2 console 🗗.

Figure 10.10   In the "Create Cluster" screen size the EC2 instances used to host the Docker cluster.

Figure 10.10 shows the screen as I populated it for the test examples in this book.

> **NOTE**   One of the first tasks you do when you set up an Amazon account is
> define a key pair for SSHing into any EC2 servers you start. We're not going to
> cover setting up a key pair in this chapter, but if you've never done this
> before, I recommend you look at Amazon's directions regarding this (http://
> docs.aws.amazon.com/AWSEC2/latest/UserGuide/ec2-key-pairs.html).

Next, you're going to set up the network configuration for the ECS cluster. Figure
10.11 shows the networking screen and the values you're configuring.

The first thing to note is selecting the Amazon Virtual Private Cloud (VPC) that the
ECS cluster will run. By default, the ECS set-up wizard will offer to set up a new VPC.
I've selected to run the ECS cluster in my default VPC. The default VPC houses the
database server and Redis cluster. In Amazon's cloud, an Amazon-managed Redis
server can only be accessed by servers that are in the same VPC as the Redis server.

Next, you have to select the subnets in the VPC that you want to give access to the
ECS cluster. Because each subnet corresponds to an Amazon availability zone, I usually
select all subnets in the VPC to make the cluster available.

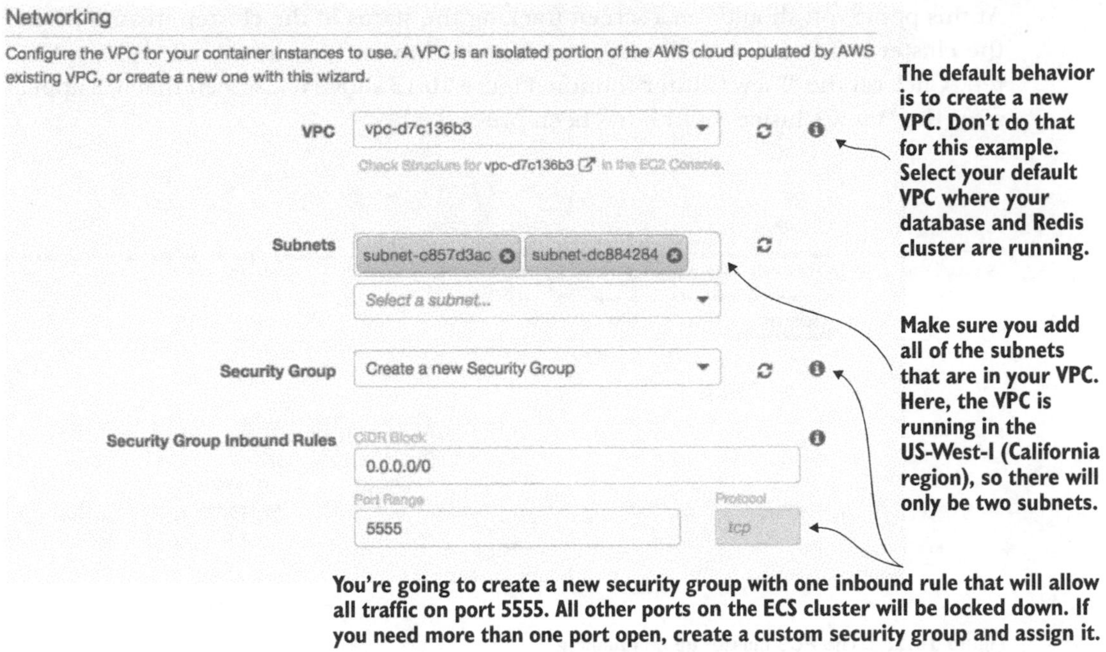

Networking

Configure the VPC for your container instances to use. A VPC is an isolated portion of the AWS cloud populated by AWS
existing VPC, or create a new one with this wizard.

VPC   vpc-d7c136b3

Check Structure for vpc-d7c136b3 in the EC2 Console.

The default behavior is to create a new VPC. Don't do that for this example. Select your default VPC where your database and Redis cluster are running.

Subnets   subnet-c857d3ac ⊗   subnet-dc884284 ⊗

Select a subnet...

Security Group   Create a new Security Group

Make sure you add all of the subnets that are in your VPC. Here, the VPC is running in the US-West-I (California region), so there will only be two subnets.

Security Group Inbound Rules   CIDR Block
0.0.0.0/0

Port Range   Protocol
5555   tcp

You're going to create a new security group with one inbound rule that will allow all traffic on port 5555. All other ports on the ECS cluster will be locked down. If you need more than one port open, create a custom security group and assign it.

Figure 10.11 Once the servers are set up, configure the network/AWS security groups used to access them.

Finally, you have to select to create a new security group or select an existing Amazon security group that you've created to apply to the new ECS cluster. Because you're running Zuul, you want all traffic to flow through a single port, port 5555. You're going to configure the new security group being created by the ECS wizard to allow all in-bound traffic from the world (0.0.0.0/0 is the network mask for the entire internet).

The last step that has to be filled out in the form is the creation of an Amazon IAM Role for the ECS container agent that runs on the server. The ECS agent is responsible for communicating with Amazon about the status of the containers running on the server. You're going to allow the ECS wizard to create a IAM role, called `ecsInstanceRole`, for you. Figure 10.12 shows this configuration step.

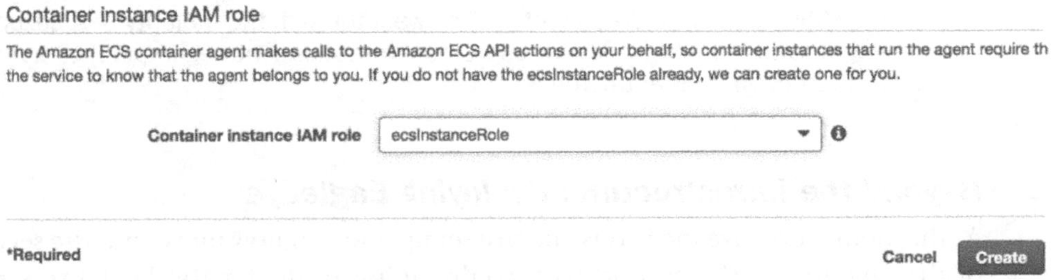

Container instance IAM role

The Amazon ECS container agent makes calls to the Amazon ECS API actions on your behalf, so container instances that run the agent require th
the service to know that the agent belongs to you. If you do not have the ecsInstanceRole already, we can create one for you.

Container instance IAM role   ecsInstanceRole

*Required   Cancel   Create

Figure 10.12 Configuring the Container IAM role

At this point you should see a screen tracking the status of the cluster creation. Once the cluster is created, you should see a blue button on the screen called "View Cluster." Click on the "View Cluster" button. Figure 10.13 shows the screen that will appear after the "View Cluster" button has been pressed.

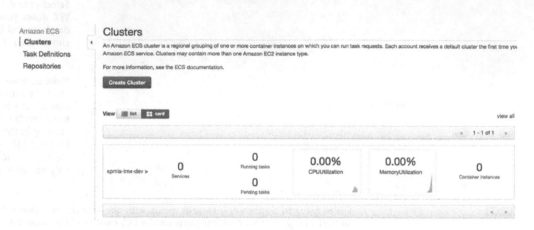

Figure 10.13   The ECS cluster up and running

At this point, you have all the infrastructure you need to successfully deploy the Eagle-Eye microservices.

On Infrastructure setup and automation

Right now, you're doing everything via the Amazon AWS console. In a real environment, you'd have scripted the creation of all this infrastructure using Amazon's Cloud-Formation scripting DSL (domain specific language) or a cloud infrastructure scripting tool like HashiCorp's Terraform (https://www.terraform.io/). However, that's an entire topic to itself and far outside the scope of this book. If you're using Amazon's cloud, you're probably already familiar with CloudFormation. If you're new to Amazon's cloud, I recommend you take the time to learn it before you get too far down the road of setting up core infrastructure via the Amazon AWS Console.

Again, I want to point the reader back to *Amazon Web Services in Action* (Manning, 2015) by Michael and Andreas Wittig. They walk through the majority of Amazon Web Services and demonstrate how to use CloudFormation (with examples) to automate the creation of your infrastructure.

10.2   *Beyond the infrastructure: deploying EagleEye*

At this point you have the infrastructure set up and can now move into the second half of the chapter. In this second part, you're going to deploy the EagleEye services to your Amazon ECS container. You're going to do this in two parts. The first part of your work is for the terminally impatient (like me) and will show how to deploy EagleEye manually to your Amazon instance. This will help you understand the mechanics of deploying the service and see the deployed services running in your container. While getting your hands dirty and manually deploying your services is fun, it isn't sustainable or recommended.

This is where the second part of this section comes into play. You're going to automate the entire build and deployment process and take the human being out of the picture. This is your targeted end state and really caps the work you've been doing in the book by demonstrating how to design, build, and deploy microservices to the cloud.

10.2.1 *Deploying the EagleEye services to ECS manually*

To manually deploy your EagleEye services, you're going to switch gears and move away from the Amazon AWS console. To deploy the EagleEye services, you're going to use the Amazon ECS command-line client (https://github.com/aws/amazon-ecs-cli). After you've installed the ECS command-line client, you need to configure the ecs-cli run-time environment to

1 Configure the ECS client with your Amazon credentials
2 Select the region the client is going to work in
3 Define the default ECS cluster the ECS client will be working against
4 This work is done by running the `ecs-cli configure` command:

```
ecs-cli configure --region us-west-1 \
                  --access-key $AWS_ACCESS_KEY \
                  --secret-key $AWS_SECRET_KEY \
                  --cluster spmia-tmx-dev
```

The `ecs-cli configure` command will set the region where your cluster is located, your Amazon access and secret key, and the name of the cluster (`spmia-tmx-dev`) you've deployed to. If you look at the previous command, I'm using environment variables (`$AWS_ACCESS_KEY` and `$AWS_SECRET_KEY`) to hold my Amazon access and secret key.

> **NOTE** I selected the us-west-1 region for purely demonstrative purposes. Depending on the country you're located in, you might choose an Amazon region more specific to your part of the world.

Next, let's see how to do a build. Unlike in other chapters, you have to set the build name because the Maven scripts in this chapter are going to be used in the build-deploy pipeline being set up later on in the chapter. You're going to set an environment variable called $BUILD_NAME. The $BUILD_NAME environment variable is used to tag the Docker image that's created by the build script. Change to the root directory of the chapter 10 code you downloaded from GitHub and issue the following two commands:

```
export BUILD_NAME=TestManualBuild
mvn clean package docker:build
```

This will execute a Maven build using a parent POM located at the root of the project directory. The parent pom.xml is set up to build all the services you'll deploy in this chapter. Once the Maven code is done executing, you can deploy the Docker images to the ECS instance you set up earlier in the section 10.1.3. To do the deployment, issue the following command:

```
ecs-cli compose --file docker/common/docker-compose.yml up
```

The ECS command line client allows you to deploy containers using a Docker-compose file. By allowing you to reuse your Docker-compose file from your desktop development environment, Amazon has significantly simplified the deployment of your services to Amazon ECS. After the ECS client has run, you can validate that the services are running and discover the IP address of the servers by issuing the following command:

```
ecs-cli ps
```

Figure 10.14 shows the output from the `ecs-cli ps` command.

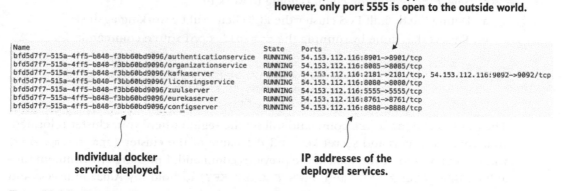

These are ports that are mapped in the Docker containers. However, only port 5555 is open to the outside world.

```
Name                                                    State    Ports
bfd5d7f7-515a-4ff5-b848-f3bb60bd9096/authenticationservice  RUNNING  54.153.112.116:8901->8901/tcp
bfd5d7f7-515a-4ff5-b848-f3bb60bd9096/organizationservice    RUNNING  54.153.112.116:8085->8085/tcp
bfd5d7f7-515a-4ff5-b848-f3bb60bd9096/kafkaserver            RUNNING  54.153.112.116:2181->2181/tcp, 54.153.112.116:9092->9092/tcp
bfd5d7f7-515a-4ff5-b848-f3bb60bd9096/licensingservice      RUNNING  54.153.112.116:8080->8080/tcp
bfd5d7f7-515a-4ff5-b848-f3bb60bd9096/zuulserver            RUNNING  54.153.112.116:5555->5555/tcp
bfd5d7f7-515a-4ff5-b848-f3bb60bd9096/eurekaserver          RUNNING  54.153.112.116:8761->8761/tcp
bfd5d7f7-515a-4ff5-b848-f3bb60bd9096/configserver          RUNNING  54.153.112.116:8888->8888/tcp
```

Individual docker services deployed.

IP addresses of the deployed services.

Figure 10.14   Checking the status of the deployed services

Note three things from the output in figure 10.14:

1   You can see that seven Docker containers have been deployed, with each Docker container running one of your services.

2   You can see the IP address of the ECS cluster (54.153.122.116).

3   It looks like you have ports other than port 5555 open. That is not the case. The port identifiers in figure 10.14 are the port mappings for the Docker container. However, the only port that's open to the outside world is port 5555. Remember that when you set up your ECS cluster, the ECS set-up wizard created an Amazon security group that only allowed traffic from port 5555.

At this point you've successfully deployed your first set of services to an Amazon ECS client. Now, let's build on this by looking at how to design a build and deployment pipeline that can automate the process of compiling, packaging, and deploying your services to Amazon.

Debugging why an ECS Container doesn't start or stay up

ECS has limited tools to debug why a container doesn't start. If you have problems with an ECS deployed service starting or staying up, you'll need to SSH onto the ECS cluster to look at the Docker logs. To do this you need to add port 22 to the security group that the ECS cluster runs with, and then SSH onto the box using the Amazon key pair you defined at the time the cluster was set (see figure 10.9) as the ec2-user. Once you're on the server, you can get a list of all the Docker containers running on the server by running the `docker ps` command. Once you've located the container image that you want to debug, you can run a `docker logs -f <<container id>>` command to tail the logs of the targeted Docker container.

This is a primitive mechanism for debugging an application, but sometimes you only need to log on to a server and see the actual console output to determine what's going on.

10.3 *The architecture of a build/deployment pipeline*

The goal of this chapter is to provide you with the working pieces of a build/deployment pipeline so that you can take these pieces and tailor them to your specific environment.

Let's start our discussion by looking at the general architecture of your build deployment pipeline and several of the general patterns and themes that it represents. To keep the examples flowing, I've done a few things that I wouldn't normally do in my own environment and I'll call those pieces out accordingly.

Our discussion on deploying microservices is going to begin with a picture you saw way back in chapter 1. Figure 10.15 is a duplicate of the diagram we saw in chapter 1 and shows the pieces and steps involved in building a microservices build and deployment pipeline.

Figure 10.15 should look somewhat familiar, because it's based on the general build-deploy pattern used for implementing Continuous Integration (CI):

1 A developer commits their code to the source code repository.
2 A build tool monitors the source control repository for changes and kicks off a build when a change is detected.
3 During the build, the application's unit and integration tests are run and if everything passes, a deployable software artifact is created (a JAR, WAR, or EAR).
4 This JAR, WAR, or EAR might then be deployed to an application server running on a server (usually a development server).

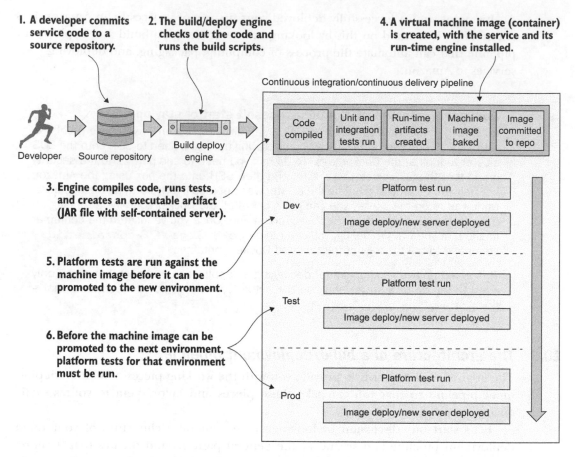

1. A developer commits service code to a source repository.

2. The build/deploy engine checks out the code and runs the build scripts.

4. A virtual machine image (container) is created, with the service and its run-time engine installed.

Continuous integration/continuous delivery pipeline

Developer   Source repository   Build deploy engine

Code compiled | Unit and integration tests run | Run-time artifacts created | Machine image baked | Image committed to repo

3. Engine compiles code, runs tests, and creates an executable artifact (JAR file with self-contained server).

Dev

Platform test run

Image deploy/new server deployed

5. Platform tests are run against the machine image before it can be promoted to the new environment.

Test

Platform test run

Image deploy/new server deployed

6. Before the machine image can be promoted to the next environment, platform tests for that environment must be run.

Prod

Platform test run

Image deploy/new server deployed

Figure 10.15   Each component in the build and deployment pipeline automates a task that would have been manually done.

With the build and deployment pipeline (shown in figure 10.15), a similar process is followed up until the code is ready to be deployed. In the build and deployment shown in figure 10.15, you're going to tack Continuous Delivery (CD) onto the process:

1 A developer commits their service code to a source repository.

2 A build/deploy engine monitors the source code repository for changes. If code is committed, the build/deploy engine will check out the code and run the code's build scripts.

3 The first step in the build/deploy process is to compile the code, run its unit and integration tests, and then compile the service to an executable artifact. Because your microservices are built using Spring Boot, your build process will create an executable JAR file that contains both the service code and self-contained Tomcat server.

4 This is where your build/deploy pipeline begins to deviate from a traditional Java CI build process. After your executable JAR is built you're going to "bake" a machine image with your microservice deployed to it. This baking process will basically create a virtual machine image or container (Docker) and install your service onto it. When the virtual machine image is started, your service will be started and will be ready to begin taking requests. Unlike a traditional CI build process where you might (and I mean might) deploy the compiled JAR or WAR to an application server that's independently (and often with a separate team) managed from the application, with the CI/CD process you're deploying the microservice, the runtime engine for the service, and the machine image all as one co-dependent unit that's managed by the development team that wrote the software.

5 Before you officially deploy to a new environment, the machine image is started and a series of platform tests are run against the running image to determine if everything is running correctly. If the platform tests pass, the machine image is promoted to the new environment and made available for use.

6 Before a service is promoted to the next environment, the platform tests for the environment must be run. The promotion of the service to the new environment involves starting up the exact machine image that was used in the lower environment to the next environment.

   This is the secret sauce of the whole process. The entire machine image is deployed. No changes are made to any installed software (including the operating system) after the server is created. By promoting and always using the same machine image, you guarantee the immutability of the server as it's promoted from one environment to the next).

Unit tests vs. integration tests vs. platform test

You'll see from figure 10.15 that I do several types of testing (unit, integration, and platform) during the build and deployment of a service. Three types of testing are typical in a build and deployment pipeline:

Unit tests—Unit tests are run immediately before the compiliation of the service code, but before it's deployed to an environment. They're designed to run in complete isolation, with each unit test being small and narrow in focus. A unit test should have no dependencies on third-party infrastructure databases, services, and so on. Usually a unit test scope will encompass the testing of a single method or function.

Integration tests—Integration tests are run immediately after packaging the service code. These tests are designed to test an entire workflow and stub or mock out major services or components that would need to be called off box. During an integration test, you might be running an in-memory database to hold data, mocking out third-party service calls, and so on. Integration tests test an entire workflow or code path. For integration tests, third-party dependencies are mocked or stubbed so that any

(continued)

calls that would invoke a remote service are mocked or stubbed so that calls never leave the build server.

Platform tests—Platform tests are run right before a service is deployed to an environment. These tests typically test an entire business flow and also call all the third-party dependencies that would normally be called in a production system. Platform tests are running live in a particular environment and don't involve any mocked-out services. Platform tests are run to determine integration problems with third-party services that would normally not be detected when a third-party service is stubbed out during an integration test.

This build/deploy process is built on four core patterns. These patterns aren't my creation but have emerged from the collective experience of development teams building microservice and cloud-based applications. These patterns include

- *Continuous Integration/Continuous Delivery (CI/CD)*—With CI/CD, your application code isn't only being built and tested when it is committed; it's also constantly being deployed. The deployment of your code should go something like this: if the code passes its unit, integration, and platform tests, it should be immediately promoted to the next environment. The only stopping point in most organizations is the push to production.
- *Infrastructure as code*—The final software artifact that will be pushed to development and beyond is a machine image. The machine image and your microservice installed on it will be provisioned time immediately after your microservice's source code is compiled and tested. The provisioning of the machine image occurs through a series of scripts that are run with each build. No human hands should ever touch the server after it's been built. The provisioning scripts are kept under source control and managed like any other piece of code.
- *Immutable servers*—Once a server image is built, the configuration of the server and microservice is never touched after the provisioning process. This guarantees that your environment won't suffer from "configuration drift" where a developer or system administrator made "one small change" that later caused an outage. If a change needs to be made, the provisioning scripts that provision the server are changed and a new build is kicked off.

On immutability and the rise of the Phoenix server

With the concept of immutable servers, we should always be guaranteed that a server's configuration matches exactly with what the machine image for the server says it does. A server should have the option to be killed and restarted from the machine image without any changes in the service or microservices behavior. This killing and resurrection of a new server was termed "Phoenix Server" by Martin Fowler (http://martinfowler.com/bliki/PhoenixServer.html) because when the old server is killed, the new server should rise from the ashes. The Phoenix server pattern has two key benefits.

First, it exposes and drives configuration drift out of your environment. If you're constantly tearing down and setting up new servers, you're more likely to expose configuration drift early. This is a tremendous help in ensuring consistency. I've has spent way too much of my time and life away from my family on "critical situation" calls because of configuration drift.

Second, the Phoenix server pattern helps to improve resiliency by helping find situations where a server or service isn't cleanly recoverable after it has been killed and restarted. Remember, in a microservice architecture your services should be stateless and the death of a server should be a minor blip. Randomly killing and restarting servers quickly exposes situations where you have state in your services or infrastructure. It's better to find these situations and dependencies early in your deployment pipeline, rather than when you're on the phone with an angry company.

The organization where I work uses Netflix's Chaos Monkey (https://github.com/Netflix/SimianArmy/wiki/Chaos-Monkey) to randomly select and kill servers. Chaos Monkey is an invaluable tool for testing the immutability and recoverability of your microservice environment. Chaos Monkey randomly selects server instances in your environment and kills them. The idea with using Chaos Monkey is that you're looking for services that can't recover from the loss of a server, and when a new server is started, it will behave in the same fashion as the server that was killed.

10.4 *Your build and deployment pipeline in action*

From the general architecture laid out in section 10.3, you can see that there are many moving pieces behind a build/deployment pipeline. Because the purpose of this book is to show you things "in action," we're going to walk through the specifics of implementing a build/deployment pipeline for the EagleEye services. Figure 10.16 lays out the different technologies you're going to use to implement your pipeline:

1. *GitHub* (http://github.com)—GitHub is our source control repository. All the application code for this book is in GitHub. There are two reasons why GitHub was chosen as the source control repository. First, I didn't want to manage and maintain my own Git source control server. Second, GitHub offers a wide variety of web-hooks and strong REST-based APIs for integrating GitHub into your build process.

2. *Travis CI* (http://travis-ci.org)—Travis CI is the continuous integration engine I used for building and deploying the EagleEye microservices and provisioning the Docker image that will be deployed. Travis CI is a cloud-based, file-based CI engine that's easy to set up and has strong integration capabilities with GitHub and Docker. While Travis CI isn't as full-featured as a CI engine like Jenkins (https://jenkins.io), it's more than adequate for our uses. I describe using GitHub and Travis CI in section 10.5 and 10.6.

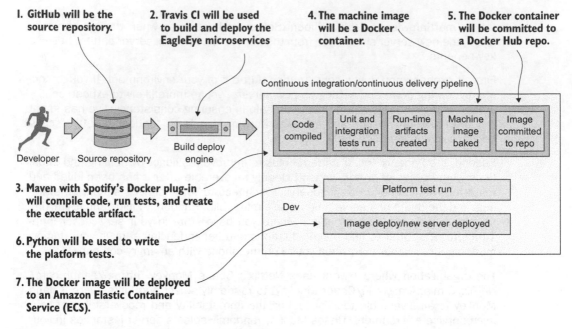

Figure 10.16   Technologies used in the EagleEye build

3   *Maven/Spotify Docker Plugin* (https://github.com/spotify/docker-maven-plugin) —While we use vanilla Maven to compile, test, and package Java code, a key Maven plug-in we use is Spotify's Docker plugin. This plugin allows us to kick off the creation of a Docker build right from within Maven.

4   *Docker* (https://www.docker.com/)—I chose Docker as our container platform for two reasons. First, Docker is portable across multiple cloud providers. I can take the same Docker container and deploy it to AWS, Azure, or Cloud Foundry with a minimal amount of work. Second, Docker is lightweight. By the end of this book, you've built and deployed approximately 10 Docker containers (including a database server, messaging platform, and a search engine). Deploying the same number of virtual machines on a local desktop would be difficult due to the sheer size and speed of each image. The setup and configuration of Docker, Maven, and Spotify won't be covered in this chapter, but is instead covered in appendix A.

5   *Docker Hub* (https://hub.docker.com)—After a service has been built and a Docker image has been created, it's tagged with a unique identifier and pushed to a central repository. For the Docker image repository, I chose to use Docker hub, Docker corporation's public image repository.

6 *Python* (https://python.org)—For writing the platform tests that are executed before a Docker image is deployed, I chose Python as my tool for writing the platform tests. I'm a firm believer in using the right tools for the job, and frankly, I think Python is a fantastic programming language, especially for writing REST-based test cases.

7 *Amazon's EC2 Container Service (ECS)*—The final destination for our microservices will be Docker instances deployed to Amazon's Docker platform. I chose Amazon as my cloud platform because it's by far the most mature of the cloud providers and makes it trivial to deploy Docker services.

Wait....did you say Python?

You might find it a little odd that I wrote the platform tests in Python rather than Java. I did this purposefully. Python (like Groovy) is a fantastic scripting language for writing REST-based test cases. I believe in using the right tool for the job. One of the biggest mind shifts I've seen for organizations adopting microservices is that the responsibility for picking the language should lie with the development teams. In too many organizations, I've seen a dogmatic embrace of standards ("our enterprise standard is Java . . . and all code must be written in Java"). As a result, I've seen development teams jump through hoops to write large amounts of Java code when a 10-line Groovy or Python script would do the job.

The second reason I chose Python is that unlike unit and integration tests, platform tests are truly "black box" tests where you're acting like an actual API consumer running in a real environment. Unit tests exercise the lowest level of code and shouldn't have any external dependencies when they run. Integration tests come up a level and test the API, but key external dependencies, like calls to other services, database calls, and so on, are mocked or stubbed out. Platform tests should be truly independent tests of the underlying infrastructure.

10.5 Beginning your build deploy/pipeline: GitHub and Travis CI

Dozens of source control engines and build deploy engines (both on-premise and cloud-based) can implement your build and deploy pipeline. For the examples in this book, I purposely chose GitHub as the source control repository and Travis CI as the build engine. The Git source control repository is an extremely popular repository and GitHub is one of the largest cloud-based source control repositories available today.

Travis CI is a build engine that integrates tightly with GitHub (it also supports Subversion and Mercurial). It's extremely easy to use and is completely driven off a single configuration file (.travis.yml) in your project's root directory. Its simplicity and opinionated nature make it easy to get a simple build pipeline off the ground

Up to now, all of the code examples in this book could be run solely from your desktop (with the exception of connectivity out to GitHub). For this chapter, if you want to completely follow the code examples, you'll need to set up your own GitHub, Travis CI, and Docker hub accounts. We're not going to walk through how to set up these accounts, but the setup of a personal Travis CI account and your GitHub account can all be done right from the Travis CI web page (http://travis-ci.org).

A quick note before we begin

For the purposes of this book (and my sanity), I set up a separate GitHub repository for each chapter in the book. All the source code for the chapter can be built and deployed as a single unit. However, outside this book, I highly recommend that you set up each microservice in your environment with its own repository with its own independent build processes. This way each service can be deployed independently of one another. With the build process, I'm deploying all of the services as a single unit only because I wanted to push the entire environment to the Amazon cloud with a single build script and not manage build scripts for each individual service.

10.6   *Enabling your service to build in Travis CI*

At the heart of every service built in this book has been a Maven pom.xml file that's used to build the Spring Boot service, package it into an executable JAR, and then build a Docker image that can be used to launch the service. Up until this chapter, the compilation and startup of the services occurred by

1   Opening a command-line window on your local machine.
2   Running the Maven script for the chapter. This builds all the services for the chapter and then packages them into a Docker image that would be pushed to a locally running Docker repository.
3   Launching the newly created Docker images from your local Docker repo, by using docker-compose and docker-machine to launch all the services for the chapter.

The question is, how do you repeat this process in Travis CI? It all begins with a single file called .travis.yml. The .travis.yml is a YAML-based file that describes the actions you want taken when Travis CI executes your build. This file is stored in the root directory of your microservice's GitHub repository. For chapter 10, this file can be found in spmia-chapter10-code/. travis.yml.

When a commit occurs on a GitHub repository Travis CI is monitoring, it will look for the .travis.yml file and then initiate the build process. Figure 10.17 shows the steps your .travis.yml file will undertake when a commit is made to the GitHub repository used to hold the code for this chapter (https://github.com/carnellj/spmia-chapter10).

1   A developer makes a change to one of the microservices in the chapter 10 GitHub repository.
2   Travis CI is notified by GitHub that a commit has occurred. This notification configuration occurs seamlessly when you register with Travis and provide your

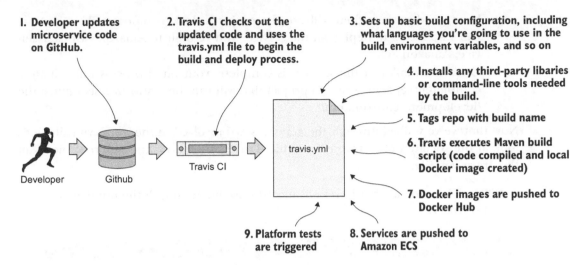

I. **Developer updates microservice code on GitHub.**

2. **Travis CI checks out the updated code and uses the travis.yml file to begin the build and deploy process.**

3. **Sets up basic build configuration, including what languages you're going to use in the build, environment variables, and so on**

4. **Installs any third-party libaries or command-line tools needed by the build.**

5. **Tags repo with build name**

6. **Travis executes Maven build script (code compiled and local Docker image created)**

7. **Docker images are pushed to Docker Hub**

Developer   Github   Travis CI   travis.yml

9. **Platform tests are triggered**

8. **Services are pushed to Amazon ECS**

Figure 10.17   **The concrete steps undertaken by the .travis.yml file to build and deploy your software**

GitHub account notification. Travis CI will start a virtual machine that will be used to execute the build. Travis CI will then check out the source code from GitHub and then use the .travis.yml file to begin the overall build and deploy process.

3   Travis CI sets up the basic configuration in the build and installs any dependencies. The basic configuration includes what language you're going to use in the build (Java), whether you're going to need Sudo to perform software installs and access to Docker (for creating and tagging Docker containers), setting any secure environment variables needed in the build, and defining how you should be notified on the success or failure of the build.

4   Before the actual build is executed, Travis CI can be instructed to install any third-party libraries or command-line tools that might be needed as part of the build process. You use two such tools, the `travis` and Amazon `ecs-cli` (EC2 Container Service client) command-line tools.

5   For your build process, always begin by tagging the code in the source repository so that at any point in the future you can pull out the complete version of the source code based on the tag for the build.

6   Your build process will then execute the Maven scripts for the services. The Maven scripts will compile your Spring microservice, run the unit and integration tests, and then build a Docker image based on the build.

7   Once the Docker image for the build is complete, the build process will push the image to the Docker hub with the same tag name you used to tag your source code repository.

8   Your build process then will use the project's docker-compose file and Amazon's `ecs-cli` to deploy all the services you've built to Amazon's Docker service, Amazon ECS.

9   Once the deploy of the services is complete, your build process will initiate a completely separate Travis CI project that will run the platform tests against the development environment.

Now that we've walked through the general steps involved in the .travis.yml file, let's look at the specifics of your .travis.yml file. Listing 10.1 shows the different pieces of the .travis.yml file.

> **NOTE**   The code annotations in listing 10.1 are lined up with the numbers in figure 10.17.

Listing 10.1   Anatomy of the .travis.yml build

```
language: java
jdk:
  - oraclejdk8
cache:
  directories:
    - "$HOME/.m2"
sudo: required
services:
  - docker
notifications:
  email:
  - youremail@gmail.com
  on_success: always
  on_failure: always
branches:
  only:
    - master
env:
  global:
  # Remove for conciseness
before_install:
  - gem install travis -v 1.8.5 --no-rdoc --no-ri
  - sudo curl -o /usr/local/bin/ecs-cli
        ⇨ https://s3.amazonaws.com/amazon-ecs-cli/
        ⇨ ecs-cli-linux-amd64-latest
  - sudo chmod +x /usr/local/bin/ecs-cli
  - export BUILD_NAME=chapter10-$TRAVIS_BRANCH-
        ⇨ $(date -u "+%Y%m%d%H%M%S")-$TRAVIS_BUILD_NUMBER
  - export CONTAINER_IP=52.53.169.60
  - export PLATFORM_TEST_NAME="chapter10-platform-tests"
script:
  - sh travis_scripts/tag_build.sh
  - sh travis_scripts/build_services.sh
  - sh travis_scripts/deploy_to_docker_hub.sh
  - sh travis_scripts/deploy_amazon_ecs.sh
  - sh travis_scripts/trigger_platform_tests.sh
```

(3) Sets up the core run-time configuration for the build

(4) Executes pre-build installations of needed command-line tools

(5) Executes a shell script that will tag the source code with the build name

(6) Builds the servers and local Docker images using Maven

(7) Pushes the Docker images to Docker Hub

(8) Starts the services in an Amazon ECS container

(9) Triggers a Travis build that execute the platform tests for the build services

We're now going to walk through each of the steps involved in the build process in more detail.

10.6.1 Core build run-time configuration

The first part of the travis.yml file deals with configuring the core runtime configuration of your Travis build. Typically this section of the .travis.yml file will contain Travis-specific functions that will do things like

1 Tell Travis what programming language you're going to be working in
2 Define whether you need Sudo access for your build process
3 Define whether you want to use Docker in your build process
4 Declare secure environment variables you are going to use

The next listing shows this specific section of the build file.

Listing 10.2 Configuring the core run-time for your build

```
language: java
jdk:
  - oraclejdk8
cache:
  directories:
    - "$HOME/.m2"
sudo: required
services:
  - docker
notifications:
  email:
  - youremail@gmail.com
  on_success: always
  on_failure: always
branches:
  only:
    - master
env:
  global:
    -secure: IAs5WrQIYjH0rpO6W37wbLAixjMB7kr7DBAeWhjeZFwOkUMJbfuHNC=z…
    #d Remove for conciseness
```

❶ Tells Travis to use Java and JDK 8 for your primary runtime environment
❷ Tells Travis to cache and re-use your Maven directory between builds
❸ Allows the build to use Sudo access on the virtual machine it's running on
❹ Configures the email address used to notify the success or failure of the build
❺ Indicates to Travis that it should only build on a commit to the master branch
❻ Sets up secure environment variables to use in your scripts

The first thing your Travis build script is doing is telling Travis what primary language is going to be used for performing the build. By specifying the language as java and jdk attributes as java and oraclejdk8, ❶ Travis will ensure that the JDK is installed and configured for your project.

The next part of your .travis.yml file, the cache.directories attribute ❷, tells Travis to cache the results of this directory when a build is executed and reuse it across multiple builds. This is extremely useful when dealing with package managers such as Maven, where it can take a significant amount of time to download fresh copies of jar dependencies every time a build is kicked off. Without the cache.directories attribute set, the build for this chapter can take up to 10 minutes to download all of the dependent jars.

The next two attributes in listing 10.2 are the sudo attribute and the service attribute. ❸ The sudo attribute is used to tell Travis that your build process will need to use sudo as part of the build. The UNIX sudo command is used to temporarily elevate a user to root privileges. Generally, you use sudo when you need to install third-party tools. You do exactly this later in the build when you need to install the Amazon ECS tools.

The services attribute is used to tell Travis whether you're going to use certain key services while executing your build. For instance, if your integration tests need a local database available for them to run, Travis allows you start a MySQL or PostgreSQL database right on your build box. In this case, you need Docker running to build your Docker images for each of your EagleEye services and push your images to the Docker hub. You've set the services attribute to start Docker when the build is kicked off.

The next attribute, notifications ❹ defines the communication channel to use whenever a build succeeds or fails. Right now, you always communicate the build results by setting the notification channel for the build to email. Travis will notify you via email on both the success and failure of the build. Travis CI can notify via multiple channels besides email, including Slack, IRC, HipChat, or a custom web hook.

The branches.only ❺ attribute tells Travis what branches Travis should build against. For the examples in this chapter, you're only going to perform a build off the master branch of Git. This prevents you from kicking off a build every time you tag a repo or commit to a branch within GitHub. This is important because GitHub does a callback into Travis every time you tag a repo or create a release. The presence of the branches.only attribute being set to master prevents Travis from going into an endless build.

The last part of the build configuration is the setting of sensitive environment variables ❻. In your build process, you might communicate with third-party vendors such as Docker, GitHub, and Amazon. Sometimes you're communicating via their command line tools and other times you're using the APIs. Regardless, you often have to present sensitive credentials. Travis CI gives you the ability to add encrypted environment variables to protect these credentials.

To add an encrypted environment variable, you must encrypt the environment variable using the travis command line tool on your desk in the project directory where you have your source code. To install the Travis command-line tool locally, review the documentation for the tool at https://github.com/travis-ci/travis.rb. For the .travis.yml used in this chapter, I created and encrypted the following environment variables:

- DOCKER_USERNAME—Docker hub user name.
- DOCKER_PASSWORD—Docker hub password.
- AWS_ACCESS_KEY—AWS access key used by the Amazon ecs-cli command line client.

- AWS_SECRET_KEY—AWS secret key used by the Amazon `ecs-cli` command-line client.
- GITHUB_TOKEN—GitHub generated token that's used to indicate the access level the calling-in application is allowed to perform against the server. This token has to be generated first with the GitHub application.

Once the `travis` tool is installed, the following command will add the encrypted environment variable DOCKER_USERNAME to the `env.global` section of you .travis.yml file:

```
travis encrypt DOCKER_USERNAME=somerandomname --add env.global
```

Once this command is run, you should now see in the `env.global` section of your .travis.yml file a `secure` attribute tag followed by a long string of text. Figure 10.18 shows what an encrypted environment variable looks like.

The Travis encryption tools don't put the name of the encrypted environment variable in the file.

```
env:
  global:
  - secure: IAs5WrQIYjH0rpO6W37wbLAixjMB7kr7DBAeWhjeZFwOk
  - secure: HRSq78OtWtfkKXZSq10ue/wV07TZIU+0mYPn1DctCnovs
  - secure: m4IkvlGXq6LBzSEHJbabS/0cfCD1IRcMjfgp8BaN+wFY+
```

Each encrypted environment variable will have a secure attribute tag.

Figure 10.18   Encrypted Travis environment variables are placed directly in the .travis.yml file.

Unfortunately, Travis doesn't label the names of your encrypted environment variables in your .travis.yml file.

NOTE Encrypted variables are only good for the single GitHub repository they're encrypted in and Travis is building against. You can't cut and paste an encrypted environment variable across multiple .travis.yml files. Your builds will fail to run because the encrypted environment variables won't decrypt properly.

Regardless of the build tool, always encrypt your credentials

Even though all our examples use Travis CI as the build tool, all modern build engines allow you to encrypt your credentials and tokens. Please, please, please make sure you encrypt your credentials. Credentials embedded in a source repository are a common security vulnerability. Don't rely on the belief that your source control repository is secure and therefore the credentials in it are secure.

10.6.2 *Pre-build tool installations*

Wow, the pre-build configuration was huge, but the next section is small. Build engines are often a source of a significant amount of "glue code" scripting to tie together different tools used in the build process. With your Travis script, you need to install two command-line tools:

- *Travis*—This command line tool is used to interact with the Travis build. You'll use it later in the chapter to retrieve a GitHub token to programmatically trigger another Travis build.
- *ecs-cli*—This is the command-line tool for interacting with the Amazon Elastic Container service.

Each item listed in the `before_install` section of the .travis.yml file is a UNIX command that will be executed before the build kicks off. The following listing shows the `before_install` attribute along with the commands that need to be run.

> **Listing 10.3   Pre-build installation steps**

```
before_install:
  - gem install travis -v 1.8.5 --no-rdoc --no-ri
  - sudo curl -o /usr/local/bin/ecs-cli
        https://s3.amazonaws.com/amazon-ecs-cli/
        ecs-cli-linux-amd64-latest
  - sudo chmod +x /usr/local/bin/ecs-cli
  - export BUILD_NAME=chapter10-$TRAVIS_BRANCH-
      $(date -u "+%Y%m%d%H%M%S")-$TRAVIS_BUILD_NUMBER

  - export CONTAINER_IP=52.53.169.60
  - export PLATFORM_TEST_NAME="chapter10-platform-tests"
```

Installs the Amazon ECS client

Installs the Travis command-line tool

Changes the permission on the Amazon ECS client to be executable

Sets the environment variables used through your process

The first thing to do in the build process is install the `travis` command-line tool on the remote build server:

```
gem install travis -v 1.8.5 --no-rdoc --no-ri
```

Later on in the build you're going to kick off another Travis job via the Travis REST API. You need the `travis` command line tool to get a token for invoking this REST call.

   After you've installed the `travis` tool, you're going to install the Amazon `ecs-cli` tool. This is a command-line tool used for deploying, starting, and stopping Docker containers running within Amazon. You install the `ecs-cli` by first downloading the binary and then changing the permission on the downloaded binary to be executable:

```
- sudo curl -o /usr/local/bin/ecs-cli https://s3.amazonaws.com/amazon-ecs-
    cli/ecs-cli-linux-amd64-latest
- sudo chmod +x /usr/local/bin/ecs-cli
```

The last thing you do in the `before_install` section of the .travis.yml is set three environment variables in your build. These three environment variables will help drive the behavior of your builds. These environment variables are

- BUILD_NAME
- CONTAINER_IP
- PLATFORM_TEST_NAME

The actual values set in these environment variables are

```
- export BUILD_NAME=chapter10-$TRAVIS_BRANCH-
  ➥ $(date -u "+%Y%m%d%H%M%S")-$TRAVIS_BUILD_NUMBER
- export CONTAINER_IP=52.53.169.60
- export PLATFORM_TEST_NAME="chapter10-platform-tests"
```

The first environment variable, BUILD_NAME, generates a unique build name that contains the name of the build, followed by the date and time (down to the seconds field) and then the build number in Travis. This BUILD_NAME will be used to tag your source code in GitHub and your Docker image when it's pushed to the Docker hub repository.

The second environment variable, CONTAINER_IP, contains the IP address of the Amazon ECS virtual machine that your Docker containers will run on. This CONTAINER_IP will be passed later to another Travis CI job that will execute your platform tests.

> NOTE I'm not assigning a static IP address to the Amazon ECS server that's spun. If I tear down the container completely, I'll be given a new IP. In a real production environment, the servers in your ECS cluster will probably have static (non-changing) IPs assigned to them, and the cluster will have an Amazon Enterprise Load Balancer (ELB) and an Amazon Route 53 DNS name so that the actual IP address of the ECS server would be transparent to the services. However, setting up this much infrastructure is outside the scope of the example I'm trying to demonstrate in this chapter.

The third environment variable, PLATFORM_TEST_NAME, contains the name of the build job being executed. We'll explore its use later in the chapter.

On auditing and traceability

A common requirement in many financial services and healthcare companies is that they have to prove traceability of the deployed software in production, all the way back through all the lower environments, back to the build job that built the software, and then back to when the code was checked into the source code repository. The immutable server pattern really shines in helping organizations meet this requirement. As you saw in our build example, you tagged the source control repository and the container image that's going to be deployed with the same build name. That build name is unique and tied into a Travis build number. Because you only promote the container image through each environment and each container image is labeled with the build name, you've established traceability of that container image back to the source code associated with it. Because the containers are never changed once they're tagged, you have a strong audit position to show that the deployed code matches the

> **(continued)**
> underlying source code repository. Now, if you wanted to play it extra safe, at the
> time you labeled the project source code, you could also label the application config-
> uration residing in the Spring Cloud Config repository with the same label generated
> for the build.

10.6.3 *Executing the build*

At this point, all the pre-build configuration and dependency installation is complete.
To execute your build, you're going to use the Travis `script` attribute. Like the
`before_install` attribute, the `script` attribute takes a list of commands that will be
executed. Because these commands are lengthy, I chose to encapsulate each major
step in the build into its own shell script and have Travis execute the shell script. The
following listing shows the major steps that are going to be undertaken in the build.

Listing 10.4 Executing the build

```
script:
  - sh travis_scripts/tag_build.sh
  - sh travis_scripts/build_services.sh
  - sh travis_scripts/deploy_to_docker_hub.sh
  - sh travis_scripts/deploy_amazon_ecs.sh
  - sh travis_scripts/trigger_platform_tests.sh
```

Let's walk through each of the major steps execute in the script step.

10.6.4 *Tagging the source control code*

The travis_scripts/tag_build.sh script takes care of tagging code in the repository with
a build name. For the example here, I'm creating a GitHub release via the GitHub
REST API. A GitHub release will not only tag the source control repository, but will also
allow you to post things like release notes to the GitHub web page along with whether
the source code is a pre-release of the code.

Because the GitHub release API is a REST-based call, you'll use curl in your shell
script to do the actual invocation. The following listing shows the code from the
travis_scripts/tag_build.sh script.

Listing 10.5 Tagging the chapter 10 code repository with the GitHub release API

```
echo "Tagging build with $BUILD_NAME"
export TARGET_URL="https://api.github.com/          Target endpoint for the
     repos/carnellj/spmia-chapter10/                GitHub release API
     releases?access_token=$GITHUB_TOKEN"

body="{                                             Body of the
  \"tag_name\": \"$BUILD_NAME\",                    REST call
  \"target_commitish\": \"master\",
  \"name\": \"$BUILD_NAME\",
```

```
    \"body\": \"Release of version $BUILD_NAME\",
    \"draft\": true,
    \"prerelease\": true
}"

curl -k -X POST \                              ◁─────  Uses curl to invoke the service
    -H "Content-Type: application/json"    \           used to kick off a build
  -d "$body" \
  $TARGET_URL
```

This script is simple. The first thing you do is build the target URL for the GitHub release API:

```
export TARGET_URL="https://api.github.com/repos/
    carnellj/spmia-chapter10/
    releases?access_token=$GITHUB_TOKEN"
```

In the TARGET_URL you're passing an HTTP query parameter called access_token. This parameter contains a GitHub personal access token set up to specifically allow your script to take action via the REST API. Your GitHub personal access token is stored in an encrypted environment variable called GITHUB_TOKEN. To generate a personal access token, log in to your GitHub account and navigate to https://github.com/settings/tokens. When you generate a token, make sure you cut and paste it right away. When you leave the GitHub screen it will be gone and you'll need to regenerate it.

The second step in your script is to set up the JSON body for the REST call:

```
body="{
    \"tag_name\": \"$BUILD_NAME\",
    \"target_commitish\": \"master\",
    \"name\": \"$BUILD_NAME\",
    \"body\": \"Release of version $BUILD_NAME\",
    \"draft\": true,
    \"prerelease\": true
}"
```

In the previous code snippet you're supplying the $BUILD_NAME for a tag_name value and the setting basic release notes using the body field.

Once the JSON body for the call is built, executing the call via the curl command is trivial:

```
curl -k -X POST \
  -H "Content-Type: application/json"    \
  -d "$body" \
  $TARGET_URL
```

10.6.5 *Building the microservices and creating the Docker images*

The next step in the Travis script attribute is to build the individual services and then create Docker container images for each service. You do this via a small script called travis_scripts/build_services.sh. This script will execute the following command:

```
mvn clean package docker:build
```

This Maven command executes the parent Maven spmia-chapter10-code/pom.xml file for all of the services in the chapter 10 code repository. The parent pom.xml executes the individual Maven pom.xml for each service. Each individual service builds the service source code, executes any unit and integration tests, and then packages the service into an executable jar.

The last thing that happens in the Maven build is the creation of a Docker container image that's pushed to the local Docker repository running on your Travis build machine. The creation of the Docker image is carried out using the Spotify Docker plugin (https://github.com/spotify/docker-maven-plugin). If you're interested in how the Spotify Docker plug-in works within the build process, please refer to appendix A, "Setting up your desktop environment". The Maven build process and the Docker configuration are explained there.

10.6.6 *Pushing the images to Docker Hub*

At this point in the build, the services have been compiled and packaged and a Docker container image has been created on the Travis build machine. You're now going to push the Docker container image to a central Docker repository via your travis_scripts/deploy_to_docker_hub.sh script. A Docker repository is like a Maven repository for your created Docker images. Docker images can be tagged and uploaded to it, and other projects can download and use the images.

For this code example, you're going to use the Docker hub (https://hub .docker.com/). The following listing shows the commands used in the travis_scripts/ deploy_to_docker_hub.sh script.

> **Listing 10.6   Pushing created Docker images to Docker Hub**

```
echo "Pushing service docker images to docker hub ...."
docker login -u $DOCKER_USERNAME -p $DOCKER_PASSWORD
docker push johncarnell/tmx-authentication-service:$BUILD_NAME
docker push johncarnell/tmx-licensing-service:$BUILD_NAME
docker push johncarnell/tmx-organization-service:$BUILD_NAME
docker push johncarnell/tmx-confsvr:$BUILD_NAME
docker push johncarnell/tmx-eurekasvr:$BUILD_NAME
docker push johncarnell/tmx-zuulsvr:$BUILD_NAME
```

The flow of this shell script is straightforward. The first thing you have to do is log in to Docker hub using the Docker command line-tools and the user credentials of the Docker Hub account the images are going to be pushed to. Remember, your credentials for Docker Hub are stored as encrypted environment variables:

```
docker login -u $DOCKER_USERNAME -p $DOCKER_PASSWORD
```

Once the script has logged in, the code will push each individual microservice's Docker image residing in the local Docker repository running on the Travis build server, to the Docker Hub repository:

```
docker push johncarnell/tmx-confsvr:$BUILD_NAME
```

In the previous command you tell the Docker command line tool to push to the Docker hub (which is the default hub that the Docker command line tools use) to the `johncarnell` account. The image being pushed will be the `tmx-confsvr` image with the tag name of the value from the `$BUILD_NAME` environment variable.

10.6.7 Starting the services in Amazon ECS

At this point, all of the code has been built and tagged and a Docker image has been created. You're now ready to deploy your services to the Amazon ECS container you created back in section 10.1.3. The work to do this deployment is found in travis_scripts/deploy_to_amazon_ecs.sh. The following listing shows the code from this script.

> **Listing 10.7 Deploying Docker Images to EC2**

```
echo "Launching $BUILD_NAME IN AMAZON ECS"
ecs-cli configure --region us-west-1 \
                  --access-key $AWS_ACCESS_KEY
                  --secret-key $AWS_SECRET_KEY
                  --cluster spmia-tmx-dev
ecs-cli compose --file docker/common/docker-compose.yml up
rm -rf ~/.ecs
```

> **NOTE** In the Amazon console, Amazon only shows the name of the state/city/country the region is in and not the actual region name (us-west-1, us-east-1, and so on). For example, if you were to look in the Amazon console and wanted to see the Northern California region, there would be no indication that the region name is us-west-1. For a list of all the Amazon regions (and endpoints for each service), please refer to http://docs.aws.amazon.com/general/latest/gr/rande.html.

Because a new build virtual machine is kicked off by Travis with every build, you need to configure your build environment's `ecs-cli` client with your AWS access and secret key. Once that's complete, you can then kick off a deploy to your ECS cluster using the `ecs-cli` compose command and a docker-compose.yml file. Your docker-compose.yml is parameterized to use the build name (contained in the environment variable `$BUILD_NAME`).

10.6.8 Kicking off the platform tests

You have one last step to your build process: kicking off a platform test. After every deployment to a new environment, you kick off a set of platform tests that check to make sure all your services are functioning properly. The goal of the platform tests is to call the microservices in the deployed build and ensure that the services are functioning properly.

I've separated the platform test job from the main build so that it can be invoked independently of the main build. To do this, I use the Travis CI REST API to programmatically invoke the platform tests. The travis_scripts/trigger_platform_tests.sh script does this work. The following listing shows the code from this script.

Listing 10.8   Kicking off the platform tests using Travis CI REST API

```
echo "Beginning platform tests for build $BUILD_NAME"
travis login --org --no-interactive \
              --github-token $GITHUB_TOKEN          ◁──── Log in with Travis CI using your
export RESULTS=`travis token --org`                        GitHub token. Store the returned
export TARGET_URL="https://api.travis-ci.org/repo/         token in the RESULTS variable.
    carnellj%2F$PLATFORM_TEST_NAME/requests"
echo "Kicking off job using target url: $TARGET_URL"

body="{
\"request\": {
  \"message\": \"Initiating platform tests for build $BUILD_NAME\",
  \"branch\":\"master\",
  \"config\": {
    \"env\": {
      \"global\": [\"BUILD_NAME=$BUILD_NAME\",        ◁──── Build the JSON body for the
                  \"CONTAINER_IP=$CONTAINER_IP\"]            call, passing in two values
    }                                                        to the downstream job.
  }
}}"

curl -s -X POST \                                    ◁──── Using Curl to invoke
  -H "Content-Type: application/json" \                     the Travis CI REST API
  -H "Accept: application/json" \
  -H "Travis-API-Version: 3" \
  -H "Authorization: token $RESULTS" \
  -d "$body" \
  $TARGET_URL
```

The first thing you do in listing 10.8 is use the Travis CI command-line tool to log in to Travis CI and get an OAuth2 token you can use to call other Travis REST APIs. You store this OAUTH2 token in the $RESULTS environment variable.

Next, you build the JSON body for the REST API call. Your downstream Travis CI job kicks off a series of Python scripts that tests your API. This downstream job expects two environment variables to be set. In the JSON body being built in listing 10.8, you're passing in two environment variables, $BUILD_NAME and $CONTAINER_IP, that will be passed to your testing job:

```
\"env\": {
 \"global\": [\"BUILD_NAME=$BUILD_NAME\",
             \"CONTAINER_IP=$CONTAINER_IP\"]
}
```

The last action in your script is to invoke the Travis CI build job that runs your platform test scripts. This is done by using the `curl` command to call the Travis CI REST endpoint for your test job:

```
curl -s -X POST \
  -H "Content-Type: application/json" \
  -H "Accept: application/json" \
  -H "Travis-API-Version: 3" \
```

```
-H "Authorization: token $RESULTS" \
-d "$body" \
$TARGET_URL
```

The platform test scripts are stored in a separate GitHub repository called chapter10-platform-tests (https://github.com/carnellj/chapter10-platform-tests). This repository has three Python scripts that test the Spring Cloud Config server, the Eureka server, and the Zuul server. The Zuul server platform tests also test the licensing and organization services. These tests aren't comprehensive in the sense that they exercise every aspect of the services, but they do exercise enough of the service to ensure they're functioning.

> **NOTE** We're not going to walk through the platform tests. The tests are straightforward and a walk-through of the tests would not add a significant amount of value to this chapter.

10.7 Closing thoughts on the build/deployment pipeline

As this chapter (and the book) closes out, I hope you've gained an appreciation for the amount of work that goes into building a build/deployment pipeline. A well-functioning build and deployment pipeline is critical to the deployment of services. The success of your microservice architecture depends on more than just the code involved in the service:

- Understand that the code in this build/deploy pipeline is simplified for the purposes of this book. A good build/deployment pipeline will be much more generalized. It will be supported by the DevOps team and broken into a series of independent steps (compile > package > deploy > test) that the development teams can use to "hook" their microservice build scripts into.
- The virtual machine imaging process used in this chapter is simplistic, with each microservice being built using a Docker file to define the software that's going to be installed on the Docker container. Many shops will use provisioning tools like Ansible (https://github.com/ansible/ansible), Puppet (https://github.com/puppetlabs/puppet), or Chef (https://github.com/chef/chef) to install and configure the operating systems onto the virtual machine or container images being built.
- The cloud deployment topology for your application has been consolidated to a single server. In the real build/deployment pipeline, each microservice would have its own build scripts and would be deployed independently of each other to a cluster ECS container.

10.8 Summary

- The build and deployment pipeline is a critical part of delivering microservices. A well-functioning build and deployment pipeline should allow new features and bug fixes to be deployed in minutes.

- The build and deployment pipeline should be automated with no direct human interaction to deliver a service. Any manual part of the process represents an opportunity for variability and failure.
- The build and deployment pipeline automation does require a great deal of scripting and configuration to get right. The amount of work needed to build it shouldn't be underestimated.
- The build and deployment pipeline should deliver an immutable virtual machine or container image. Once a server image has been created, it should never be modified.
- Environment-specific server configuration should be passed in as parameters at the time the server is set up.

appendix A
Running a cloud
on your desktop

This appendix covers

- Listing the software needed to run the code in this book
- Downloading the source code from GitHub for each chapter
- Compiling and packaging the source code using Maven
- Building and provisioning the Docker images used in each chapter
- Launching the Docker images compiled by the build using Docker Compose

I had two goals when laying out the code examples in this book and choosing the runtime technologies needed to deploy the code. The first goal was make sure that the code examples were consumable and easy to set up. Remember, a microservices application has multiple moving parts, and setting up these parts to run cleanly with minimal effort for the reader can be difficult if there is not some forethought.

The second goal was for each chapter to be completely standalone so that you could pick any chapter in the book and have a complete runtime environment available that encapsulates all the services and software needed to run the code examples in the chapter without dependencies on other chapters.

To this end, you'll see the following technology and patterns used throughout every chapter in this book:

1   All projects use Apache Maven (http://maven.apache.org) as the build tool for the chapters. Each service is built using a Maven project structure and each service structure is consistently laid chapter to chapter.

2   All services developed in the chapter compile to a Docker (http://docker.io) container image. Docker is an amazing runtime virtualization engine that runs on Windows, OS X, and Linux. Using Docker, I can build a complete runtime environment on the desktop that includes the application services and all the infrastructure needed to support the services. Also, Docker, unlike more proprietary virtualization technologies, is easily portable across multiple cloud providers.

   I'm using Spotify's Docker Maven plugin (https://github.com/spotify/docker-maven-plugin) to integrate the building of Docker container with the Maven build process.

3   To start the services after they've compiled into Docker images, I use Docker Compose to start the services as a group. I've purposely avoided more sophisticated Docker orchestration tools such as Kubernetes (https://github.com/kubernetes/kubernetes) or Mesos (http://mesos.apache.org/) to keep the chapter examples straightforward and portable.

   All provisioning of the Docker images is done with simple shell scripts.

A.1   *Required software*

To build the software for all chapters, you'll need to have the following software installed on your desktop. It's important to note that these are the versions of software I worked with for the book. The software may work with other versions, but this is what I built the code with:

1   *Apache Maven* (http://apache.maven.org)—I used version 3.3.9 of Maven. I chose Maven because while other build tools such as Gradle are extremely popular, Maven is still the predominant build tool in use in the Java ecosystem. All code examples in this book were compiled with Java version 1.8.

2   *Docker* (http://docker.com)—I built the code examples in this book using Docker V1.12. The code examples in this book will work with earlier versions of Docker, but you may have to switch to the version 1 docker-compose links format if you want to use this code with earlier versions of Docker.

3   *Git Client* (http://git-scm.com)—All the source code for this book is stored in a GitHub repository. For the book, I used version 2.8.4 of the Git client.

I'm not going to walk through how to install each of these components. Each of the software packages listed in the bulleted list has simple installation instructions and should be installable with minimal effort. Docker has a GUI client for installation.

A.2   *Downloading the projects from GitHub*

All the source code for the book is in my GitHub repository (http://github.com/carnellj). Each chapter in the book has its own source code repository. Here's a listing of all the GitHub repositories used in the book:

- Chapter 1 (Welcome to the cloud, Spring)—http://github.com/carnellj/spmia-chapter1
- Chapter 2 (Introduction to microservices)—http://github.com/carnellj/spmia-chapter2
- Chapter 3 (Spring Cloud Config)—http://github.com/carnellj/spmia-chapter3 and http://github.com/carnellj/config-repo
- Chapter 4 (Spring Cloud/Eureka)—http://github.com/carnellj/spmia-chapter4
- Chapter 5 (Spring Cloud/Hystrix)—http://github.com/carnellj/spmia-chapter5
- Chapter 6 (Spring Cloud/Zuul)—http://github.com/carnellj/spmia-chapter6
- Chapter 7 (Spring Cloud/Oauth2)—http://github.com/carnellj/spmia-chapter7
- Chapter 8 (Spring Cloud Stream)—http://github.com/carnellj/spmia-chapter8
- Chapter 9 (Spring Cloud Sleuth)—http://github.com/carnellj/spmia-chapter9
- Chapter 10 (Deployment)—http://github.com/carnellj/spmia-chapter10 and http://github.com/carnellj/chapter-10-platform-tests

With GitHub, you can download the files as a zip file using the web UI. Every GitHub repository will have a download button on it. Figure A.1 shows where the download button is in the GitHub repository for chapter 1.

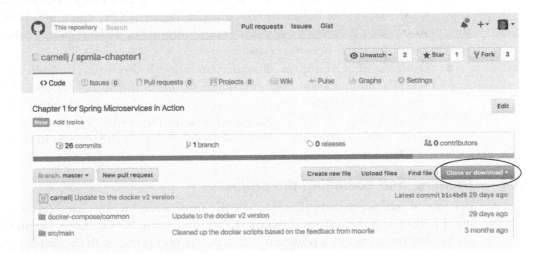

Figure A.1   The GitHub UI allows you to download a project as a zip file.

If you're a command-line user, you can install the `git` client and clone the project. For example, if you wanted to download chapter 1 from GitHub using the `git` client, you could open a command line and issue the following command:

```
git clone https://github.com/carnellj/spmia-chapter1.git
```

This will download all the chapter 1 project files into a directory called spmia-chapter1 in the directory you ran the `git` command from.

A.3   *Anatomy of each chapter*

Every chapter in the book has one or more services associated with it. Each service in a chapter has its own project directory. For instance, if you look at chapter 6 (http://github.com/carnellj/spmia-chapter6), you'll see that there are seven services in it. These services are

1 confsvr—Spring Cloud Config server
2 eurekasvr—Spring Cloud/with Eureka
3 licensing-service—Eagle Eye Licensing service
4 organization-service—Eagle Organization service
5 orgservice-new—New test version of the EagleEye service
6 specialroutes-service—A/B routing service
7 zuulsvr—EagleEye Zuul service

Every service directory in a chapter is structured as a Maven-based build project. Inside each project is a src/main directory with the following sub-directories:

1 java—This directory contains the Java source code used to build the service.
2 docker—This directory contains two files needed to build a Docker image for each service. The first file will always be called Dockerfile and contains the step-by-step instructions used by Docker to build the Docker image. The second file, run.sh, is a custom Bash script that runs inside the Docker container. This script ensures that the service doesn't start until certain key dependencies (database is up and running) become available.
3 resources—The resources directory contains all the services' application.yml files. While application configuration is stored in the Spring Cloud Config, all services have configuration that's stored locally in the application.yml. Also, the resources directory will contain a schema.sql file containing all the SQL commands used to create the tables and pre-load data for the services into the Postgres database.

A.4   *Building and compiling the projects*

Because all chapters in the book follow the same structure and use Maven as their build tool, it becomes extremely simple to build the source code. Every chapter has at the root of the directory a pom.xml that acts as parent pom for all the sub-chapters. If you want to compile the source code and build the Docker images for all the projects within a single chapter, you need to run the following at the root of the chapter:

```
mvn clean package docker:build
```

This will execute the Maven pom.xml file in each of the service directories. It will also build the Docker images locally.

If you want to build a single service within the chapter, you can change to that specific service directory and run the `mvn clean package docker:build` command.

A.5 Building the Docker image

During the build process, all the services in the book are packaged as Docker images. This process is carried out by the Spotify Maven plugin. For an example of this plugin in action, you can look at the chapter 3 licensing service's pom.xml file (chapter3/licensing-service). The following listing shows the XML fragment that configures this plugin in each service's pom.xml file.

Listing A.1   Spotify Docker Maven plugin used to create Dockerimage

```
<plugin>
  <groupId>com.spotify</groupId>
  <artifactId>docker-maven-plugin</artifactId>
  <version>0.4.10</version>
  <configuration>
        <imageName>
            ${docker.image.name}:
        [ca]${docker.image.tag}
    </imageName>
    <dockerDirectory>
        ${basedir}/target/dockerfile
    </dockerDirectory>
    <resources>
      <resource>
        <targetPath>/</targetPath>
        <directory>${project.build.directory}</directory>
        <include>${project.build.finalName}.jar</include>
      </resource>
    </resources>
  </configuration>
</plugin>
```

Every Docker image created will have a tag associated with it. The Spotify plugin will name the created image with whatever is defined in the ${docker.image.tag} tag.

All Docker images are created in this book using a Dockerfile. A Dockerfile is used to give step-by-step instructions on how the Docker image should be provisioned.

When the Spotify plugin is executed, it will copy the service's executable jar to the Docker image.

The XML fragment does three things:

1 It copies the executable jar for the service, along with the contents of the src/main/docker directory, to target/docker.

2 It executes the Dockerfile defined in the target/docker directory. The Dockerfile is a list of commands that are executed whenever a new Docker image for that service is provisioned.

3 It pushes the Docker image to the local Docker image repository that's installed when you install Docker.

The following listing shows the contents of the Dockerfile from your licensing service.

Listing A.2   Dockerfile prepares Docker image

> This is the Linux Docker image that you're going to use in your Docker run-time. This installation is optimized for Java applications.

> You install nc (netcat), a utility that you'll use to ping dependent services to see if they are up.

```
FROM openjdk:8-jdk-alpine
RUN  apk update && apk upgrade && apk add netcat-openbsd
RUN mkdir -p /usr/local/licensingservice
ADD licensing-service-0.0.1-SNAPSHOT.jar /usr/local/licensingservice/
ADD run.sh run.sh
RUN chmod +x run.sh
CMD ./run.sh
```

> You add a custom BASH shell script that will monitor for service dependencies and then launch the actual service.

> The Docker ADD command copies the executable JAR from the local filesystem to the Docker image.

In the Dockerfile from this listing you're provisioning your instance using Alpine Linux (https://alpinelinux.org/). Alpine Linux is a small Linux distribution that's often used to build Docker images. The Alpine Linux image you're using already has Java JDK installed on it.

When you're provisioning your Docker image, you're going to install a command-line utility called nc. The nc command is used to ping a server and see if a specific port is online. You're going to use it in your run.sh command script to ensure that before you launch your service, all its dependent services (for example, the database and the Spring Cloud Config service) have started. The nc command does this by watching the ports the dependent services listen on. This installation of nc is done via the RUN apk update && apk upgrade && apk add netcat-openbsd, running the services using Docker Compose.

Next, your Dockerfile will make a directory for the licensing service's executable jar file and then copy the jar file from the local file system to a directory that was created on the Docker image. This is all done via the ADD licensing-service-0.0.1-SNAPSHOT.jar /usr/local/licensingservice/.

The next step in the provisioning process is to install the run.sh script via the ADD command. The run.sh script is a custom script I wrote that launches the target service when the Docker image is started. It uses the nc command to listen for the ports of any key service dependencies that the licensing service needs and then blocks until those dependencies are started.

The following listing shows how the run.sh is used to launch the licensing service.

Listing A.3   `run.sh` script used to launch the licensing service

> The run.sh scripts waits for the port of the dependent service to be open before continuing to trying to start the service.

```
#!/bin/sh
echo "*********************************************************"
echo "Waiting for the configuration server to start on port
    $CONFIGSERVER_PORT"
echo "*********************************************************"
while ! `nc -z configserver $CONFIGSERVER_PORT `;
    [ca]do sleep 3; done
echo ">>>>>>>>>>> Configuration Server has started"

echo "*********************************************************"
echo "Waiting for the database server to start on port $DATABASESERVER_PORT"
echo "*********************************************************"
while ! `nc -z database $DATABASESERVER_PORT`; do sleep 3; done
echo ">>>>>>>>>>> Database Server has started"

echo "*********************************************************"
echo "Starting License Server with Configuration Service :
    $CONFIGSERVER_URI";
echo "*********************************************************"
java -Dspring.cloud.config.uri=$CONFIGSERVER_URI \
    -Dspring.profiles.active=$PROFILE \
    -jar /usr/local/licensingservice/licensing-service-0.0.1-SNAPSHOT.jar
```

> Launch the licensing service by using Java to call the executable jar the Dockerfile script installed. $<<VARIABLE_NAME>> represents an environment variable being passed to the Docker image.

Once the `run.sh` command is copied to your licensing service Docker image, the CMD `./run.sh` Docker command is used to tell Docker to execute the `run.sh` launch script when the actual image starts.

NOTE I'm giving you a high-level overview of how Docker provisions an image. If you want to learn more about Docker in depth, I suggest looking at Jeff Nickoloff's *Docker in Action* (Manning, 2016) or Adrian Mouat's *Using Docker* (O'Reilly, 2016). Both books are excellent Docker resources.

A.6   *Launching the services with Docker Compose*

After the Maven build has been executed, you can now launch all the services for the chapter by using Docker Compose. Docker Compose is installed as part of the Docker installation process. It's a service orchestration tool that allows you to define services as a group and then launch together as a single unit. Docker Compose includes capabilities for also defining environment variables with each service.

Docker Compose uses a YAML file for defining the services that are going to be launched. Each chapter in this book has a file called "<<chapter>>/docker/common/

docker-compose.yml". This file contains the service definitions used to launch the services in the chapter. Let's look at the docker-compose.yml file used in chapter 3. The following listing shows the contents of this file.

Each service being launched has a label applied to it. This will become the DNS entry for the Docker instance when it's started and is how other services can access it.

Docker Compose will first try to find the target image to be started in the local Docker repository. If it can't find it, it will check the central Docker hub (http://hub.docker.com).

```
version: '2'
services:
  configserver:
    image: johncarnell/tmx-confsvr:chapter3
    ports:
      - "8888:8888"
    environment:
      ENCRYPT_KEY:        "IMSYMMETRIC"
  database:
    image: postgres
    ports:
      - "5432:5432"
    environment:
      POSTGRES_USER: "postgres"
      POSTGRES_PASSWORD: "p0stgr@s"
      POSTGRES_DB:        "eagle_eye_local"
  licensingservice:
    image: johncarnell/tmx-licensing-service:chapter3
    ports:
      - "8080:8080"
    environment:
      PROFILE: "default"
      CONFIGSERVER_URI: "http://configserver:8888"
      CONFIGSERVER_PORT:  "8888"
      DATABASESERVER_PORT: "5432"
      ENCRYPT_KEY:        "IMSYMMETRIC"
```

This entry defines the port numbers on the started Docker container that will be exposed to the outside world.

The environment tag is used to pass along environment variables to the starting Docker image. In this case, the ENCRYPT_KEY environment variable will be set on the starting Docker image.

This is an example of how a service defined in one part of the Docker Compose file (configserver) is used as the DNS name in another service.

In the `docker-compose.yml` from listing A.4, we see three services being defined (configserver, database, and licensing service). Each service has a Docker image defined with it using the `image` tag. As each service starts, it will expose ports through the `port` tag and then pass environment variables to the starting Docker container via the `environment` tag.

Go ahead and start your Docker containers by executing the following command from the root of chapter directory pulled down from GitHub:

```
docker-compose -f docker/common/docker-compose.yml up
```

When this command is issued, `docker-compose` starts all the services defined in the `docker-compose.yml` file. Each service will print its standard out to the console. Figure A.2 shows the output from the docker-compose.yml file in chapter 3.

**All three services are writing
output to the console.**

```
configserver_1     | 2017-02-07 11:28:48.586  INFO 7 --- [           main] c.t.confsvr.ConfigServerApplication      : Sta
3 seconds (JVM running for 7.113)
licensingservice_1 | >>>>>>>>>>>> Configuration Server has started
licensingservice_1 | ***********************************************************
licensingservice_1 | Waiting for the database server to start on port 5432
licensingservice_1 | ***********************************************************
licensingservice_1 | >>>>>>>>>>>> Database Server has started
licensingservice_1 | ***********************************************************
licensingservice_1 | Starting License Server with Configuration Service : http://configserver:8888
licensingservice_1 | ***********************************************************
database_1         | LOG:  incomplete startup packet
licensingservice_1 | 2017-02-07 11:28:52.715  INFO 17 --- [           main] s.c.a.AnnotationConfigApplicationContext : Re
.annotation.AnnotationConfigApplicationContext@6477463f: startup date [Tue Feb 07 11:28:52 GMT 2017]; root of context hier
licensingservice_1 | 2017-02-07 11:28:53.099  INFO 17 --- [           main] trationDelegate$BeanPostProcessorChecker : Be
utoConfiguration' of type [class org.springframework.cloud.autoconfigure.ConfigurationPropertiesRebinderAutoConfiguration$
   not eligible for getting processed by all BeanPostProcessors (for example: not eligible for auto-proxying)
```

Figure A.2   All output from the started Docker containers is written to standard out.

TIP Every line written to standard out by a service started using Docker Compose will have the name of the service printed to standard out. When you're launching a Docker Compose orchestration, finding errors being printed out can be painful. If you want to look at the output for a Docker-based service, start your `docker-compose` command in detached mode with the –d option (`docker-compose -f docker/common/docker-compose.yml up -d`). Then you can look at the specific logs for that container by issuing the `docker-compose` command with the logs option (`docker-compose -f docker/common/docker-compose.yml logs -f licensingservice`).

All the Docker containers used this in this book are ephemeral—they won't retain their state when they're started and stopped. Keep this in mind if you start playing with code and you see your data disappear after your restart your containers. If you want to make your Postgres database persistent between the starting and stopping of containers, I'd point you to the Postgres Docker notes (https://hub.docker.com/_/postgres/).

appendix B
OAuth2 grant types

This appendix covers

- OAuth2 Password grant
- OAuth2 Client credentials grant
- OAuth2 Authorization code grant
- OAuth2 Implicit credentials grant
- OAuth2 Token Refreshing

From reading chapter 7, you might be thinking that OAuth2 doesn't look too complicated. After all, you have an authentication service that checks a user's credentials and issues a token back to the user. The token can, in turn, be presented every time the user wants to call a service protected by the OAuth2 server.

Unfortunately, the real world is never simple. With the interconnected nature of the web and cloud-based applications, users have come to expect that they can securely share their data and integrate functionality between different applications owned by different services. This presents a unique challenge from a security perspective because you want to integrate across different applications while not forcing users to share their credentials with each application they want to integrate with.

Fortunately, OAuth2 is a flexible authorization framework that provides multiple mechanisms for applications to authenticate and authorize users without forcing them to share credentials. Unfortunately, it's also one of the reasons why OAuth2 is considered complicated. These authentication mechanisms are called authentication grants. OAuth2 has four forms of authentication grants that client applications can use to authenticate users, receive an access token, and then validate that token. These grants are

- Password
- Client credential
- Authorization code
- Implicit

In the following sections I walk through the activities that take place during the execution of each of these OAuth2 grant flows. I also talk about when to use one grant type over another.

B.1 Password grants

An OAuth2 password grant is probably the most straightforward grant type to understand. This grant type is used when both the application and the services explicitly trust one another. For example, the EagleEye web application and the EagleEye web services (the licensing and organization) are both owned by ThoughtMechanix, so there's a natural trust relationship that exists between them.

> **NOTE** To be explicit, when I refer to a "natural trust relationship" I mean that the application and services are completely owned by the same organization. They're managed under the same policies and procedures.

When a natural trust relationship exists, there's little concern about exposing an OAuth2 access token to the calling application. For example, the EagleEye web application can use the OAuth2 password grant to capture the user's credentials and directly authenticate against the EagleEye OAuth2 service. Figure B.1 shows the password grant in action between EagleEye and the downstream services.

In figure B.1 the following actions are taking place:

1 Before the EagleEye application can use a protected resource, it needs to be uniquely identified within the OAuth2 service. Normally, the owner of the application registers with the OAuth2 application service and provides a unique name for their application. The OAuth2 service then provides a secret key back to registering the application.

   The name of the application and the secret key provided by the OAuth2 service uniquely identifies the application trying to access any protected resources.

2. User logs into EagleEye, which passes user credentials with application name and key to OAuth2 service

3. OAuth2 authenticates user and application and provides access token

I. Application owner registers application name with OAuth2 service, which provides a secret key

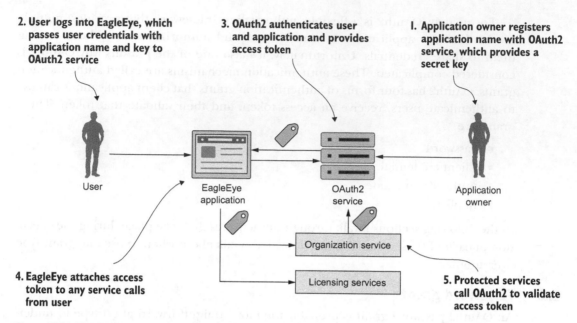

User

EagleEye application

OAuth2 service

Organization service

Licensing services

Application owner

4. EagleEye attaches access token to any service calls from user

5. Protected services call OAuth2 to validate access token

Figure B.1   The OAuth2 service determines if the user accessing the service is an authenticated user.

2 The user logs into EagleEye and provides their login credentials to the Eagle-Eye application. EagleEye passes the user credentials, along with the application name/application secret key, directly to the EagleEye OAuth2 service.

3 The EagleEye OAuth2 service authenticates the application and the user and then provides an OAuth2 access token back to the user.

4 Every time the EagleEye application calls a service on behalf of the user, it passes along the access token provided by the OAuth2 server.

5 When a protected service is called (in this case, the licensing and organization service), the service calls back into the EagleEye OAuth2 service to validate the token. If the token is good, the service being invoked allows the user to proceed. If the token is invalid, the OAuth2 service returns back an HTTP status code of 403, indicating that the token is invalid.

B.2   *Client credential grants*

The client credentials grant is typically used when an application needs to access an OAuth2 protected resource, but no human being is involved in the transaction. With the client credentials grant type, the OAuth2 server only authenticates based on application name and the secret key provided by the owner of the resource. Again, the client credential task is usually used when both applications are owned by the same company. The difference between the password grant and the client credential grant is that a client credential grant authenticates by only using the registered application name and the secret key.

For example, let's say that once an hour the EagleEye application has a data analytics job that runs. As part of its work, it makes calls out to EagleEye services. However, the EagleEye developers still want that application to authenticate and authorize itself before it can access the data in those services. This is where the client credential grant can be used. Figure B.2 shows this flow.

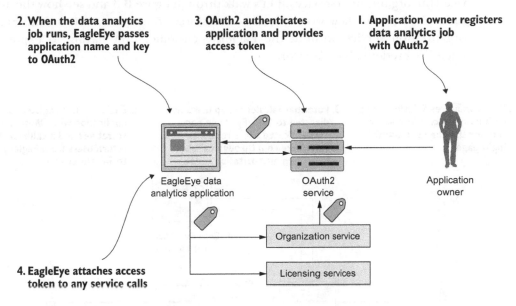

2. When the data analytics job runs, EagleEye passes application name and key to OAuth2

3. OAuth2 authenticates application and provides access token

1. Application owner registers data analytics job with OAuth2

EagleEye data analytics application

OAuth2 service

Application owner

Organization service

Licensing services

4. EagleEye attaches access token to any service calls

Figure B.2   The client credential grant is for "no-user-involved" application authentication and authorization.

1 The resource owner registers the EagleEye data analytics application with the OAuth2 service. The resource owner will provide the application name and receive back a secret key.

2 When the EagleEye data analytics job runs, it will present its application name and secret key provided by the resource owner.

3 The EagleEye OAuth2 service will authenticate the application using the application name and the secret key provided and then return back an OAuth2 access token.

4 Every time the application calls one of the EagleEye services, it will present the OAuth2 access token it received with the service call.

B.3   *Authorization code grants*

The authorization code grant is by far the most complicated of the OAuth2 grants, but it's also the most common flow used because it allows different applications from different vendors to share data and services without having to expose a user's credentials across multiple applications. It also enforces an extra layer of checking by not letting a calling application immediately get an OAuth2 access token, but rather a "pre-access" authorization code.

The easy way to understand the authorization grant is through an example. Let's say you have an EagleEye user who also uses Salesforce.com. The EagleEye customer's IT department has built a Salesforce application that needs data from an EagleEye service (the organization service). Let's walk through figure B.3 and see how the authorization code grant flow works to allow Salesforce to access data from the EagleEye organization service, without the EagleEye customer ever having to expose their EagleEye credentials to Salesforce.

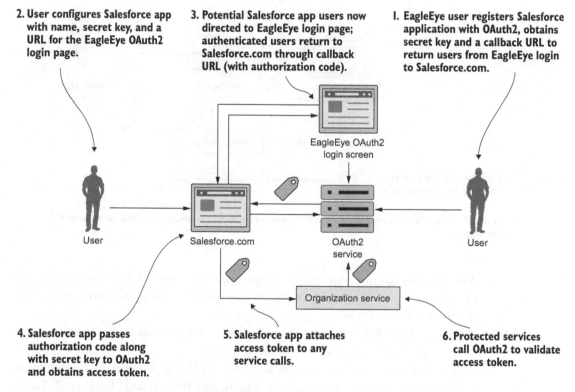

2. User configures Salesforce app with name, secret key, and a URL for the EagleEye OAuth2 login page.

3. Potential Salesforce app users now directed to EagleEye login page; authenticated users return to Salesforce.com through callback URL (with authorization code).

1. EagleEye user registers Salesforce application with OAuth2, obtains secret key and a callback URL to return users from EagleEye login to Salesforce.com.

EagleEye OAuth2 login screen

User   Salesforce.com   OAuth2 service   User

Organization service

4. Salesforce app passes authorization code along with secret key to OAuth2 and obtains access token.

5. Salesforce app attaches access token to any service calls.

6. Protected services call OAuth2 to validate access token.

Figure B.3   The authentication code grant allows applications to share data without exposing user credentials.

1   The EagleEye user logs in to EagleEye and generates an application name and application secret key for their Salesforce application. As part of the registration process, they'll also provide a callback URL back to their Salesforce-based application. This callback URL is a Salesforce URL that will be called after the EagleEye OAuth2 server has authenticated the user's EagleEye credentials.

2 The user configures their Salesforce application with the following information:
   - Their application name they created for Salesforce
   - The secret key they generated for Salesforce
   - A URL that points to the EagleEye OAuth2 login page
   - Now when the user tries to use their Salesforce application and access their EagleEye data via the organization service, they'll be redirected over to the EagleEye login page via the URL described in the previous bullet point. The user will provide their EagleEye credentials. If they've provided valid EagleEye credentials, the EagleEye OAuth2 server will generate an authorization code and redirect the user back to SalesForce via the URL provided in number 1. The authorization code will be sent as a query parameter on the callback URL.

3 The custom Salesforce application will persist this authorization code. Note: this authorization code isn't an OAuth2 access token.

4 Once the authorization code has been stored, the custom Salesforce application can present the Salesforce application the secret key they generated during the registration process and the authorization code back to EagleEye OAuth2 server. The EagleEye OAuth2 server will validate that the authorization code is valid and then return back an OAuth2 token to the custom Salesforce application. This authorization code is used every time the custom Salesforce needs to authenticate the user and get an OAuth2 access token.

5 The Salesforce application will call the EagleEye organization service, passing an OAuth2 token in the header.

6 The organization service will validate the OAuth2 access token passed in to the EagleEye service call with the EagleEye OAuth2 service. If the token is valid, the organization service will process the user's request.

Wow! I need to come up for air. Application-to-application integration is convoluted. The key to note from this entire process is that even though the user is logged into Salesforce and they're accessing EagleEye data, at no time were the user's EagleEye credentials directly exposed to Salesforce. After the initial authorization code was generated and provided by the EagleEye OAuth2 service, the user never had to provide their credentials back to the EagleEye service.

B.4   *Implicit grant*

The authorization grant is used when you're running a web application through a traditional server-side web programming environment like Java or .NET. What happens if your client application is a pure JavaScript application or a mobile application that runs completely in a web browser and doesn't rely on server-side calls to invoke third-party services?

This is where the last grant type, the implicit grant, comes into play. Figure B.4 shows the general flow of what occurs in the implicit grant.

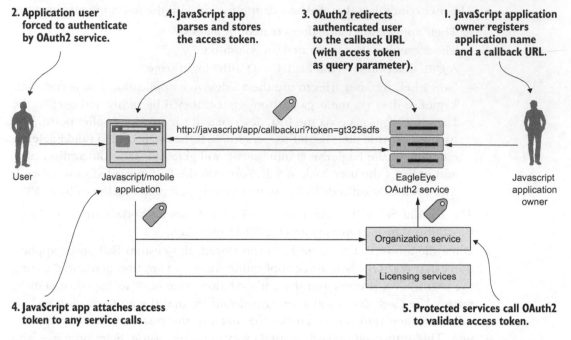

2. Application user forced to authenticate by OAuth2 service.

4. JavaScript app parses and stores the access token.

3. OAuth2 redirects authenticated user to the callback URL (with access token as query parameter).

I. JavaScript application owner registers application name and a callback URL.

http://javascript/app/callbackuri?token=gt325sdfs

User

Javascript/mobile application

EagleEye OAuth2 service

Javascript application owner

Organization service

Licensing services

4. JavaScript app attaches access token to any service calls.

5. Protected services call OAuth2 to validate access token.

Figure B.4   The implicit grant is used in a browser-based Single-Page Application (SPA) JavaScript application.

With an implicit grant, you're usually working with a pure JavaScript application running completely inside of the browser. In the other flows, the client is communicating with an application server that's carrying out the user's requests and the application server is interacting with any downstream services. With an implicit grant type, all the service interaction happens directly from the user's client (usually a web browser). In figure B.4, the following activities are taking place:

1 The owner of the JavaScript application has registered the application with the EagleEye OAuth2 server. They've provided an application name and also a callback URL that will be redirected with the OAuth2 access token for the user.

2 The JavaScript application will call to the OAuth2 service. The JavaScript application must present a pre-registered application name. The OAuth2 server will force the user to authenticate.

3 If the user successfully authenticates, the EagleEye OAuth2 service won't return a token, but instead redirect the user back to a page the owner of the JavaScript application registered in step one. In the URL being redirected back to, the OAuth2 access token will be passed as a query parameter by the OAuth2 authentication service.

4 The application will take the incoming request and run a JavaScript script that will parse the OAuth2 access token and store it (usually as a cookie).

5   Every time a protected resource is called, the OAuth2 access token is presented to the calling service.

6   The calling service will validate the OAuth2 token and check that the user is authorized to do the activity they're attempting to do.

Keep several things in mind regarding the OAuth2 implicit grant:

- The implicit grant is the only grant type where the OAuth2 access token is directly exposed to a public client (web browser). In the authorization grant, the client application gets an authorization code returned back to the application server hosting the application. With an authorization code grant, the user is granted an OAuth2 access by presenting the authorization code. The returned OAuth2 token is never directly exposed to the user's browser.

  In the client credentials grant, the grant occurs between two server-based applications. In the password grant, both the application making the request for a service and the services are trusted and are owned by the same organization.

- OAuth2 tokens generated by the implicit grant are more vulnerable to attack and misuse because the tokens are made available to the browser. Any malicious JavaScript running in the browser can get access to the OAuth2 access token and call the services you retrieved the OAuth2 token for on your behalf and essentially impersonate you.

- The implicit grant type OAuth2 tokens should be short-lived (1-2 hours). Because the OAuth2 access token is stored in the browser, the OAuth2 spec (and Spring Cloud security) doesn't support the concept of a refresh token in which a token can be automatically renewed.

B.5   *How tokens are refreshed*

When an OAuth2 access token is issued, it has a limited amount of time that it's valid and will eventually expire. When the token expires, the calling application (and user) will need to re-authenticate with the OAuth2 service. However, in most of the Oauth2 grant flows, the OAuth2 server will issue both an access token and a refresh token. A client can present the refresh token to the OAuth2 authentication service and the service will validate the refresh token and then issue a new OAuth2 access token. Let's look at figure B.5 and walk through the refresh token flow:

1   The user has logged into EagleEye and is already authenticated with the Eagle-Eye OAuth2 service. The user is happily working, but unfortunately their token has expired.

2   The next time the user tries to call a service (say the organization service), the EagleEye application will pass the expired token to the organization service.

3   The organization service will try to validate the token with the OAuth2 service, which return an HTTP status code 401 (unauthorized) and a JSON payload

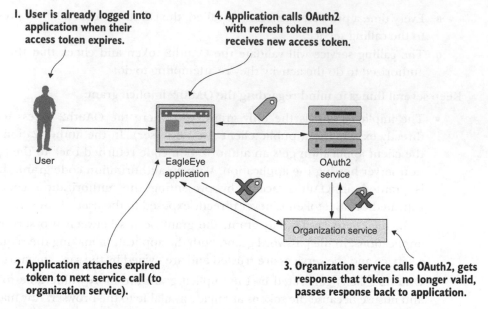

I. User is already logged into application when their access token expires.

4. Application calls OAuth2 with refresh token and receives new access token.

User

EagleEye application

OAuth2 service

Organization service

2. Application attaches expired token to next service call (to organization service).

3. Organization service calls OAuth2, gets response that token is no longer valid, passes response back to application.

Figure B.5   The refresh token flow allows an application to get a new access token without forcing the user to re-authenticate.

indicating that the token is no longer valid. The organization service will return an HTTP 401 status code back to the calling service.

4   The EagleEye application gets the 401 HTTP status code and the JSON payload indicating the reason the call failed back from the organization service. The EagleEye application will then call the OAuth2 authentication service with the refresh token. The OAuth2 authentication service will validate the refresh token and then send back a new access token.

index